Asylum Law in the European Union

This book examines the rules governing the right to asylum in the European Union. Drawing on the 1951 United Nations Convention relating to the Status of Refugees (and the 1967 Protocol) and the case law of the European Court of Human Rights, Francesco Cherubini asks how asylum obligations under international law have been implemented in the European Union.

The book draws from international law, EU law and the case law of the European Court of Human Rights, and focuses on the prohibition of *refoulement*, the main obligation that EU law must confront. Cherubini explores the dual nature of this principle, examining both the obligation to provide a fair procedure that determines the conditions of risk in the country of origin or destination, and the obligation to respond to a possible removal.

Through this study the book sheds light on EU competence in asylum (also when regarding the different positions of Member States). The book will be of great use and interest to researchers and students of asylum and immigration law, EU law and public international law.

Francesco Cherubini is Assistant Professor of EU Law at LUISS Guido Carli, Italy.

Routledge Research in Asylum, Migration and Refugee Law

Asylum Law in the European Union

Francesco Cherubini

Routledge
Taylor & Francis Group

LONDON AND NEW YORK

First published 2015
by Routledge
2 Park Square, Milton Park, Abingdon, Oxon, OX14 4RN

and by Routledge
711 Third Avenue, New York, NY 10017

Routledge is an imprint of the Taylor & Francis Group, an informa business

British Library Cataloguing in Publication Data
A catalogue record for this book is available from the British Library

Library of Congress Cataloging-in-Publication Data
Cherubini, Francesco, 1975– author.
  Asylum law in the European Union : from the Geneva Convention
  to the law of the EU / Francesco Cherubini.
    pages cm—(Routledge research in asylum, migration and
    refugee law)
  ISBN 978-0-415-74109-5 (hardback)—ISBN 978-1-315-81442-1
  (ebk) 1. Asylum, Right of—European Union countries.
  2. International and municipal law—European Union countries.
  I. Title.
  KJE5202.C476 2015
  342.2408'3—dc23   2014023224

ISBN: 978-0-415-74109-5 (hbk)
ISBN: 978-1-315-81442-1 (ebk)

Typeset in Baskerville
by RefineCatch Limited, Bungay, Suffolk

To Carlo and Claudio Pojer,
in memoriam

Contents

Acknowledgements

First of all, I would like to thank Christine Stone for all the hard work she undertook on the English version: without her contribution, it would be almost impossible to have a final version of this book. I have also a great debt to the LSE Centre for the Study of Human Rights, where I have carried out most of my research: a sincere thank you to the Director, Professor Chetan Bhatt, and to the Centre Manager, Dr Zoe Gillard, for the opportunity they gave me and for their helpfulness. Finally, and not least, my profound gratitude goes to the person who has had the patience, the ability and the fortitude to undertake my scientific training, and also the time to read this work: Professor Ugo Villani. Obviously, the responsibility for its contents is only mine.

Translation of the Italian revised version by Christine Stone.

Introduction

According to an early but still well-regarded authority, while it is true that 'current international law is largely built upon the events that transformed Europe's political structure during the transition from the medieval to the modern world', equally,

> numerous principles, institutions and theories of international relations developed before that time or were passed down from the Greco-Roman world and continued without interruption even throughout the period concerned, although sooner or later they came under the influence, to a greater or lesser degree, of the new state of affairs.[1]

These include the practice of asylum, which has roots stretching far back in human history. The etymology of the word is the Ancient Greek particle *a-*, denoting absence, and the word *sŷlon*, from *sŷlán*, the verb used to indicate seizure by pirates.[2] An 'asylum' was thus a place secure from danger. The right of asylum subsequently developed chiefly as a concept of international law almost certainly because of the principles that governed its exercise. Indeed, only a body of rules that binds entities effectively exercising control over a given territory, as does international law, can contemplate an institution of this kind. This much is evident from even the briefest review of the history of asylum over the centuries.

According to one stream of legal theory,

> asylum was the word used in centuries past to denote certain places which were thought to possess the privilege of protecting from persecution anyone who took refuge there; right of asylum was the term given to the immunity or privilege enjoyed by those specific places or buildings.[3]

---

1 D. Anzilotti (1923: 2, trans. added).
2 M. Giriodi (1896: 778) and A. Quintano Ripollés (1951: 50).
3 M. Giriodi (1896: 777, trans. added). On this point see also C. Perris (1937: 767) and U. E. Paoli (1968: 1035). The latter mentions the temples of Athena Alea at Tegea, Poseidon on the island of Calauria, Athena Chalkioikos in Sparta, and Asclepius at Pergamum.

From the very outset, therefore, the right of asylum was determined *ratione loci* ('on account of the place'),[4] distinguishing itself in this way from other types of immunity, such as the '*asilía personale*' (personal asylum), also based on Greek law.[5] But this principle alone does not explain the inviolability of the places deputed to provide asylum: in the beginning, at least, the concept of asylum was

> tied to a religious or sacred quality, whereby the person or thing coming into contact with a sacred site somehow also enjoyed the protection that the deity bestowed on that place by taking up residence there.[6]

In other words, the right of asylum rested on the protection that divine authority afforded specific places and, conversely, on the fact that divine authority was itself outside human control. This is substantiated by the fact, according to authoritative sources, that these refuges offered sanctuary not only to individuals but also to their chattels.[7] Evidently, the institution of asylum owed much of its early fortune to the superstitions and taboos associated with violating places of refuge. This is amply illustrated in Greek literature, from which it would appear that violation of a place of asylum was regarded as an act of sacrilege against the deity residing there.[8] And indeed the gods had no hesitation in reacting

4 See M. Giriodi (1896: 778), E. Reale (1938: 481) and L. Bolesta-Koziebrodzki (1962: 32).
5 The term was coined, according to G. Crifò (1958: 191), by F. Woess to denote the immunity granted to individuals for a wide variety of reasons. Crifò further explains that this privilege was given to 'individuals belonging to categories that were highly respected by society: hence, athletes travelling from their homeland to the places where ritual games were held ... ambassadors; foreigners who had rendered special service to the city, such as *proxeni*; heralds; workers engaged in projects of public usefulness' (trans. added).
6 G. Crifò (1958: 191, trans. added).
7 According to U. E. Paoli (1968: 1035), 'it was customary for people to leave valuables in sacred places and for cities to leave their riches there, and any man who took refuge in a temple or beside an altar or who had embraced the statue of a god became inviolable' (trans. added). The places of asylum apparently retained this privilege of 'extended' protection throughout the Middle Ages for, according to G. Vismara (1958: 199), 'the right of asylum fostered the development of markets, and even of villages and towns, in the areas around churches and monasteries' (trans. added).
8 A. Quintano Ripollés (1951: 50) and U. E. Paoli (1968: 1035). A. Bahramy (1938: 13) writes that 'à la suite de la profanation de l'autel des Euménides, par Mégaclès, qui immola Cylon et ses compagnons, une peste désola Athènes. Une peste qui ne disparut qu'après que le peuple, sur le conseil de l'oracle de Delphes, eut fait une solennelle expiation du sacrilège de son Archonte. C'était pour la même raison qu'on égorgea Neoptalème, pour avoir égorgé Priam sur les autels d'Apollon. On raconte aussi qu'à la suite du massacre des Ilates, dans le temple de Ténare, il y eut un tremblement de terre qui désola Sparte. D'autre part on attribuait la terrible maladie de Sylla au fait d'avoir violé l'autel de Minerve pour mettre à mort Aristion'.

violently to such affronts.[9] The religious roots of asylum ran so deep that 'reflected' protection was extended without distinction to all human beings. It was only later, when the religious and sacred aspect lost some of its importance, that limits may have been imposed, so that convicted criminals could no longer be accorded asylum.[10]

The right of asylum also existed in Ancient Rome, although it was invoked with far greater circumspection than in Greece, mainly as a result of the Romans' very narrow concept of law and citizenship.[11] Places of refuge were fewer in number, and Tiberius is believed to have reduced them further.[12] This may be why a similar institution, at least as far as concerns its outcome, enjoyed greater fortune in the Rome of that time, namely *exilium* (exile), which gave any citizen who had received a capital sentence the option to avoid execution by choosing exile.[13] As in Rome, the right of asylum recognised by Hebrew law was also

9 When Ajax the Lesser dragged Cassandra from Athena's altar, the latter sought the help of the gods to exact revenge. Unfortunately, she struck not only Ajax, but all the Greeks returning from Troy. She then called on Poseidon: 'When they are sailing off home from Troy. And Zeus will send rain and vast hailstones and dark gusting blasts of wind. He says that he will give me the fire of his thunderbolt to strike the Achaeans and burn their ships with its flames. And you for your part must make the Aegean sea roar with huge waves and whirlpools and fill the hollow bay of Euboea with corpses so that for the future the Achaeans may learn to revere my sanctuaries and respect the other gods' (Euripides, *The Trojan Women and Other Plays*, Oxford, 2001, 78–84).

10 G. Crifò (1958: 193). This theory is disputed, however. According to U. E. Paoli (1968: 1035–6) 'it would appear, from the writings of the orator Lycurgus, that there was no requirement to recognise the right of asylum in the case of criminals convicted by a court. In all likelihood, though, this exception to the immunity of the refugee did not apply in temples that constituted an asylum in the full sense of the word' (trans. added).

11 E. Reale (1938: 482) notes that 'La conception que Rome avait de la loi et du citoyen ne pouvait pas se concilier avec le respect du droit d'asile'. See also A. Bahramy (1938: 17), L. Bolesta-Koziebrodzki (1962: 32) and U. E. Paoli (1968: 1036).

12 See M. Giriodi (1896: 778) and C. Perris (1937: 767).

13 According to G. Crifò (1958: 196), 'the prohibition – which a magistrate places on a citizen who chooses exile before being convicted – against the exercise of a faculty conferred and guaranteed by the law constitutes an *improbe factum* [wicked act]: this circumstance, and the possible intervention of the censorship, as a vehicle of public opinion, are sufficient to ensure that the individual's right to decide is respected, for by choosing exile that individual exercises a right, founded on the recognition of a socially and legally impelling interest in evading a capital sentence' (trans. added). G. Crifò (ibid.: 195–6) interpreted as a form of right of asylum the principle of the inviolability of the home. It should be noted that the concept of exile also existed in the Greek world. And not only in ancient times: in the Middle Ages – bearing out the text cited above – exile and asylum became almost interchangeable, so that if asylum were not granted – for example, because the bishop did not intercede successfully or because the asylum-seeker was accused of offences for which the privilege did not apply – the only option was to resort to exile. G. Vismara (1958: 198) confirms that 'if intercession was unsuccessful, the refugee could only avoid the feared conviction or violence by choosing voluntary exile' (trans. added). Furthermore (ibid.: 201), 'the institution was thus voided of content [the Author alludes to the practice of prior removal, whereby a

invoked less often than in Greece;[14] a person who had committed manslaughter was allowed to seek refuge in certain cities, although it would appear that this privilege was granted principally in order to prevent an unfair trial.[15] Perpetrators were not given shelter permanently, only as a precautionary measure. The trial would take place in the city of refuge, presided over by a group of elders. Defendants who were found innocent would be allowed to return to their home city; those found guilty would be driven from the sheltering city to suffer the vengeance of their victim's family.[16]

The right of asylum only enjoyed something of a revival with the establishment of Christianity, which restored the Greek practice, albeit with important variations. As in Ancient Greece, the principle of asylum according to the Christian Church was based on the existence of places which for religious reasons were outside the control of the community; thus, the respect owed to the person taking refuge in that place essentially flowed from the deference due to the authority that had taken up residence there. The Greek concept of asylum, however, lacked certain elements that were only introduced with Christianity; these included the principles of charity and penitence, which underpinned the right of asylum.[17]

person seeking refuge was first removed from the altars, only to be allowed to return if not convicted of offences barred from asylum]; . . . Hence, criminals avoided seeking refuge in sacred places, preferring exile and banditry to the danger of falling into the hands of justice' (trans. added). On the broader subject of exile see G. Crifò (1966: 712 ff.).

14 A. Bahramy (1938: 15) notes that 'Les juifs, peuple religieux par excellence, restaient complètement étrangers à cette loi [asylum], c'est seulement lorsqu'ils s'établirent en terre promise, qu'ils ont admis à titre exceptionnel le droit d'asile dans certaines villes, pour les auteurs d'homicide involontaire'. For a contrasting view, see E. Reale (1938: 478), who maintains that the principle of asylum was 'largement pratiqué' among the Jews. According to the Book of Exodus (21, 12–14), 'whoever strikes a man so that he dies shall be put to death. But if he did not lie in wait for him, but God let him fall into his hand, then I will appoint for you a place to which he may flee. But if a man wilfully attacks another to kill him by cunning, you shall take him from my altar, that he may die'.

15 M. Giriodi (1896: 778) and L. Bolesta-Koziebrodzki (1962: 31). The six cities were, according to A. Bahramy (1938: 15), 'Kedès, Sichem, Hébron, Golan, Ramoth et Béser'. This opinion is shared by E. Reale (1938: 479).

16 C. H. Toy (1902: 256) notes that persons who avenged manslaughter in any of the cities of refuge would themselves become guilty of murder.

17 G. Vismara (1958: 198). A famous episode in the life of John Chrysostom provides an example: one Eutropius, chamberlain and chief minister of the fourth-century emperor Arcadius, attempted to persuade the latter to abolish the right to seek asylum in churches but fell into disgrace for undeservedly insulting the empress Eudoxia and was consigned to the vengeance of the people, who hated him because of his cruelty. A. Butler, *The Lives of the Fathers, Martyrs and Other Principal Saints*, vol. I, London, 1857, p. 126, narrates that 'Eutropius found himself in a moment forsaken by all the herds of his admirers and flatterers, without one single friend, and fled for protection to the church, and to those very altars whose immunities he had infringed and violated. The whole city was in an uproar against him; the army called aloud for his death, and a troop of soldiers surrounded the church with naked swords in their hands, and fire in

Moreover, the Christian form of asylum emphasised an aspect given little consideration by the Greeks: the belief that there existed an authority able to afford real protection to specific places. The events surrounding the development of the Christian concept of asylum, and the systematic clashes between Church and State on the extension of this right, are emblematic.[18] Eventually, the Christian practice of asylum fell into disuse as the Church's temporal power waned and nation states began to form.[19] Even before then, in the anonymous treatise *Dei delitti e delle pene*, published in 1764 by the Leghorn printer Coltellini, it had been remarked that

> Impunity and asylum differ only in degree, and since the certainty of punishment makes more of an impression than its harshness, asylums invite men to commit crimes more than punishments deter them from them.[20]

The practice of asylum was abolished under the Savoy kings by the Siccardi laws of 1850, and may well have been eliminated before then in other parts of the Italian peninsula.[21]

Once the religious right of asylum no longer existed,[22] the practice was reinstated by many nation states,[23] which stripped it of its roots and replaced them

their eyes'. John Chrysostom interceded in favour of Eutropius with one of the speeches that earned him the name Golden Mouth, asking them 'how they could beg of God the pardon of their own sins if they did not pardon a man who then, by repentance, was perhaps a saint in the eyes of God' (ibid.: 127).

18 According to G. Vismara (1958: 201), 'it was thus that conflict arose between the Church, which ordinarily claimed jurisdiction in matters of asylum, particularly for passing judgment on excepted cases, and secular doctrine, which instead claimed sole right to determine whether the requirements of the canonical definition of the right of asylum had been met, and by this means sought to impose a restrictive interpretation on the canonical rule in order increasingly to circumscribe the right of asylum' (trans. added).

19 G. Vismara (1958: 200) wrote: 'in the meantime experts in civil law sought to establish a broad interpretation of excepted cases and, starting from the same canonical rule that had allowed some of these cases in order to overcome serious difficulties, now excluded from the right of asylum all persons accused of the worst crimes, wrongdoers who had eluded justice, blasphemers, those guilty of sacrilege, non-Christians. The exception was greater than the rule; the principle of canon law whereby no one should be excluded from the sanctuary of asylum was being replaced by the opposite principle, that asylum could only be granted in specific cases' (trans. added). See also E. Reale (1938: 490), L. Bolesta-Koziebrodzki (1962: 34) and P. G. Caron (1966: 1038).

20 C. Beccaria, '*On Crimes and Punishments' and Other Writings*, Cambridge, 1995, p. 92.

21 In 1827 A. Manzoni, *The Betrothed*, vol. I, New York, 1845, p. 67, wrote: 'The scene had taken place near a Capuchin convent, an asylum *in those days*, as every one knows, impenetrable to bailiffs, and all that complication of persons and things which went by the name of justice' (emphasis added).

22 It is still invoked today in very rare circumstances: see F. Lenzerini (2009: 21).

23 In reality, some forms of non-religious asylum vaguely resembling the modern institution existed before the birth of nation states. See F. Lenzerini (2009: 21 ff.).

with an ideological framework. The French Constitution of 1793 (Article 120) states that the French nation 'donne asile aux étrangers bannis de leur patrie pour la cause de la liberté. Il le refuse aux tyrans'. This pronouncement was echoed in the constitutions of the States founded on liberal principles.[24] Conversely, in the ideology that inspired the Socialist countries asylum was interpreted as a form of workers' protection.[25] This is clearly set out in Article 129 of the 1936 Soviet Constitution: 'The USSR affords the right of asylum to foreign citizens persecuted for defending the interests of the working people, or for their scientific activities, or for their struggle for the national liberation'.

Legal theory introduced a number of distinctions within the new concept of asylum, differentiating between asylum granted in the territory of the host country (territorial asylum) and asylum granted outside it (extraterritorial asylum) and, within the latter category, according to whether this was in an embassy (diplomatic asylum) or on a ship, or at the seat of an international organisation and so on. These distinctions aside, the granting of asylum remained nonetheless firmly linked to political considerations, to the point where it depended entirely on the discretion of the host country. According to an authoritative text of 1968,

> the expression 'right of asylum' denotes two entirely separate things in international law. On the one hand, it indicates the right of nations to give hospitality in their territory – or in equivalent locations – to individuals persecuted by other nations and to offer them protection; on the other hand, it indicates the right of nations to give hospitality in their legations or embassies in other countries to persons persecuted or wanted in the territory of the States in which that embassy or legation is located.[26]

A few years earlier the history of asylum had taken a completely new direction when human rights were codified in international law, principally as a result of the

24 As E. Reale (1938: 542–3) rightly points out, 'avant que la Révolution française proclame le droit à l'insurrection en donnant une base morale et juridique aux actes dirigés contre le gouvernement, celui qui est banni de sa patrie ou a été obligé de la quitter pour des raisons politiques, commence à être considéré comme inviolable'.

25 On this point see, among the preparatory papers for the Twelfth Meeting of the International Association of Penal Law (AIDP) in Freiburg, 1–3 September 1977, the articles by G. Antoniu (1978: 577–8), V. P. Choupilov (1978: 616–7), M. Cieslak and W. Michalski (1978: 569 ff.) and D. Mikhaïlov (1978: 458–9).

26 A. Migliazza (1968: 1039, trans. added). See also G. Balladore Pallieri (1938: 523 ff.). H. Cabral de Moncada (1945: 57) also notes that 'Em direito internacional, direito de asilo significa portanto, em sentido subjetivo, o direito de qualquer Estado, em relação a outro Estado, de conceder a qualquer indivíduo perseguido pelas autoridades dêste último qualquer espécie de asilo de direito internacional'. The only distinction recognised by legal theory related to the internal or external nature of the asylum, that is, whether it was granted in the territory of the State (political asylum) or in one of its missions abroad (diplomatic asylum). Other authors, such as L. Alcindor (1929: 33), added the further category of asylum 'à bord des navires'.

work of the United Nations (UN) and several regional organisations such as the Council of Europe. It is to these that we owe two instruments which more than any other have shaped the development of the institution of asylum; they are the 1951 Geneva Convention Relating to the Status of Refugees (and its Protocol of 1967) and the European Convention on Human Rights of 1950, Article 3 (and others) of which was used by the European Court of Human Rights to extend the application of the principle of *non-refoulement* beyond the limits of the Geneva Convention. Before this last development, the right of asylum was inseparable from the authority that ruled over the places of refuge (deities, Church or State), so that it was merely a consequence of the 'sovereignty' exercised over them and the respect owed to it. A very different and much more revolutionary concept of asylum has gained currency since then, as an institution mainly destined for the protection of individual human rights. Unsurprisingly, the idea (still debated by legal theorists) has taken root that alongside the traditional concept of right of asylum – still vested in States but largely fallen into disuse – an *individual right of asylum* has developed, linked to the protection of fundamental rights.

This book discusses this individual right of asylum, particularly as it relates to the European Union (EU). From the signing of the Treaty of Maastricht the EU has been heedful of an issue that has gained increasing importance in international law, even though as an organisation it is not concerned with all the forms of asylum described so far, only the narrower version based on considerations of a humanitarian nature. In other words, the body of laws governing the EU deals only with the 'new' types of asylum and is in no way concerned with the traditional concept of political asylum in its various strands of territorial, diplomatic and other. As to terminology, therefore, this first meaning of asylum is the one I use here. However, within the *genus* it may be useful to distinguish two *species* that differ according to whether the conditions of access to protection are laid down in the Geneva Convention (in which case the term is 'refuge') or in the case law of the European Court of Human Rights (in which case the term, adopted only recently, is 'subsidiary protection'). In practice, as many official documents of the EU use the term 'asylum' as a synonym of 'refuge', the distinction will be made only where necessary.

1 The Geneva Convention of 1951 and its Protocol of 1967

1.1 Definition of refugee

The first international treaty regulating the right of asylum is the 1951 Geneva Convention Relating to the Status of Refugees (the Refugee Convention), together with its Protocol of 1967.[1] The articles of the treaty, which have been given an authoritative, though not binding, interpretation by the Office of the United Nations High Commissioner for Refugees (UNHCR), were drawn up essentially in order to supply a definition of persons in need of protection and to provide them with a system of support ranging from the prohibition on *refoulement* to the right to work.[2] The beneficiaries of the Refugee Convention are listed in Article 1A(2), which defines as refugee someone who

> As a result of events occurring before 1 January 1951 and owing to well-founded fear of being persecuted for reasons of race, religion, nationality, membership of a particular social group or political opinion, is outside the

1 Convention Relating to the Status of Refugees (adopted Geneva 28 July 1951 and entered into force 22 April 1954), 189 UNTS 147 ff. To date there are 145 parties to the Convention, including the United Kingdom, which ratified it on 11 March 1954. Protocol Relating to the Status of Refugees (adopted New York 31 January 1967 and entered into force 4 October 1967), 606 UNTS 267 ff.; 146 states signed, including the United Kingdom, which ratified it on 4 September 1968. Only very few of the States parties to the Convention failed to ratify the Protocol, and vice versa; respectively, they were Madagascar and Saint Kitts and Nevis, and Cape Verde, the United States and Venezuela. As will be explained later, this has major consequences only where the States are parties to the Convention alone.

2 The Office of the High Commissioner was founded as a subsidiary organ of the United Nations General Assembly (UNGA) under Article 22 of the Charter, UNGA Resolution 319 (IV), December 1949, A/RES/319(IV)[A–B]. Broadly speaking, it took over the functions of the former International Refugee Organization (IRO), the Constitution of which was adopted by UNGA Resolution 62, 15 December 1946, A/RES/62(I)[I–II]. The organisation was originally intended to operate only until 31 December 1953; however, its mandate was renewed every five years (see UNGA Resolution 727, 3 October 1953, A/RES/727(VIII); Resolution 1165, 26 November 1957, A/RES/1165(XII); Resolution 1783, 7 December 1962, A/RES/1783(XVII);

country of his nationality and is unable or, owing to such fear, is unwilling to avail himself of the protection of that country; or who, not having a nationality and being outside the country of his former habitual residence as a result of such events, is unable or, owing to such fear, is unwilling to return to it.[3]

It should be clarified that this definition relates to refugees *ipso iure*. In other words, it is universally acknowledged that recognition of a person's status as a refugee does not make them such, it merely ascertains that status:[4] a person becomes a refugee as soon as (and only because) he or she meets the requirements set out in Article 1A of the Refugee Convention. This raises two points: first, while in theory the (positive) determination of refugee status would appear irrelevant, in practice without it the protection which the Convention affords the refugee becomes meaningless. Thus, while States have considerable freedom as to the method of determining refugee status[5] – and while UNHCR, unlike the contracting States, has no duty to uphold the provisions of the Convention that would eliminate, or at least reduce, the broad scope for their interpretation – they have nonetheless several obligations, procedural and of substance, designed to safeguard people

Resolution 2294, 11 December 1967, A/RES/2294(XXII); Resolution 2957, 12 December 1972, A/RES/2957(XXVII); Resolution 32/68, 8 December 1977, A/RES/32/68; Resolution 37/196, 18 December 1982, A/RES/37/196; Resolution 42/108, 7 December 1987, A/RES/42/108; Resolution 47/104, 16 December 1992, A/RES/47/104; Resolution 52/104, 12 December 1997, A/RES/52/104; and Resolution 57/186, 18 December 2002, A/RES/57/186) until the General Assembly eventually decided, Resolution 58/153, 22 December 2003, A/RES/58/153, para. 9, 'to remove the temporal limitation on the continuation of the Office of the High Commissioner contained in its Resolution 57/186 and to continue the Office until the refugee problem is solved'. UNHCR has limited means at its disposal, having no judicial or even quasi-judicial authority, nor any general power of enforcement, similarly to the bodies responsible for other international instruments for the protection of human rights, such as the European Court of Human Rights (ECtHR), or the Human Rights Committee, or the Committee of Ministers of the Council of Europe. On this point see V. Türk (2003: 4–5) and C. W. Wouters (2009: 39 ff.). More generally, on UNHCR's control functions see W. Kälin (2003: 613 ff.).

3 Article 1A also contains a clause (1) giving a definition of 'history' or 'statutory' refugees: see A. Grahl-Madsen (1966–1972, II: 108 ff.) and, more recently, S. Schmahl (2011a: 247 ff.).

4 See C. W. Wouters (2009: 47). This is developed further in UNHCR (1992a: para. 28), which states that 'A person is a refugee within the meaning of the 1951 Convention as soon as he fulfils the criteria contained in the definition. This would necessarily occur prior to the time at which his refugee status is formally determined. Recognition of his refugee status does not therefore make him a refugee but declares him to be one. He does not become a refugee because of recognition, but is recognized because he is a refugee'. Similar opinions are found in the case law: see the decision of the High Court of Ireland of 17 December 2010, *Artur Abramov* v. *Minister of Justice, Equality and Law Reform* (*Abramov*), para. 20. Where not specified, mentioned case law is available online at www.refworld.org.

5 UNHCR (1992a: para. 189).

who are already refugees even before their status is recognised. These obligations derive mainly, though not only, from Article 33 of the Refugee Convention enshrining a rule rightly deemed to be one of the cornerstones of international law: the prohibition on *refoulement*.[6]

The provisions of the Refugee Convention, moreover, do not always employ the same terms, and this is the second point. While there is only one concept of refugee (though not unambiguous), in the articles of the Convention the term acquires different nuances case by case. There would appear to be three categories of refugee: refugee *tout court*, refugee lawfully present in the country, and refugee lawfully staying in the country.[7] The first two have an important feature in common: in both categories the refugees have not had their status officially (and positively) determined; the only difference is that refugees lawfully present in the host country are there in compliance with the laws on foreign nationals – that is, they have entry documents (valid ID, travel papers and so on) and a temporary permit to stay (usually a three-month visa). On the other hand, refugees lawfully staying in the country generally have a recognised status or, if not, hold a long-term permit to stay, though not necessarily a permanent one (again, three months is the term usually fixed in the legislation on foreign nationals). The differences between these categories of refugee are reflected in the degree of protection provided by the Convention: the stronger the link with the host country, the broader the rights of the refugee.[8] Consequently, all categories enjoy the protection associated with the prohibition on *refoulement*, but only some are allowed to move freely about the territory of the host country and even fewer have the right of association, the right to housing, and so on.[9]

This brings us back to the concept of refugee. Some elements of the definition have changed over the years, at times quite considerably. The Refugee Convention, for instance, still talks of two limitations, one temporal, the other geographical. Article 1A(2) establishes a *dies ad quem* (date at which) – 1 January 1951 – the events that led the person to be outside his or her country, and unable or unwilling to

6 A. Grahl-Madsen (1983: 14).
7 Some authors, such as J. C. Hathaway (2005: 156 ff.), make a further distinction between refugees under the jurisdiction of States and refugees physically present in their territory, although there is no actual basis for this in the Refugee Convention. The Convention, however, does envisage a further category, that of refugees with habitual residence (see Articles 14 and 16(2)), which is more or less equivalent to the category of refugees lawfully staying in the country, although the argument has been made (ibid.: 907–8) that an additional element is required: recognition of refugee status.
8 V. M. Teichmann (2011: 922).
9 According to Article 15, only resident refugees have the right of association; see references in footnote 423. Henceforth, the three categories will be referred to as 'refugee', 'refugee lawfully present' and 'refugee lawfully staying'. Instead, the Refugee Convention contains no reference to the category of asylum-seekers, although it is found frequently in both legal writings and practice. Henceforth, the term will be used to denote people who leave their country of origin to seek some form of international protection, regardless of whether or not they have made an official application.

return there, ceases to have any bearing on the application of the Convention. This limitation is evidently based on the same rationale that led the States to draft such a treaty, that is, to remedy the effects of the Second World War on population movements. However, when other events occurred potentially entailing similar consequences for population movements but falling outside the field of application of the Refugee Convention because of the limitation,[10] it was eliminated by the 1967 Protocol, which was ratified by all the States parties to the Convention except two (Madagascar and Saint Kitts and Nevis[11]).

The other limitation, of a geographical nature, is based on a similar rationale: the events of the Second World War led to population movements that took place mostly within Europe.[12] However, unlike the first limitation, Article 1B allows the contracting States to decide whether to sign the treaty without the geographical limitation, which all of them did with the exception of Congo, Monaco, Madagascar and Turkey. Subsequently, the 1967 Protocol did not eliminate the geographical limitation as Article 1(3) allows States parties to the Convention that opted for the limitation to retain it unless they reconsider.[13] And in fact, when three of the four countries mentioned ratified the Protocol, one of them (Turkey) declared, in an accompanying statement, that the 'provisions of the declaration made under section B of Article 1 of the Convention Relating to the Status of Refugees' would be retained.[14]

While, as some scholarly writers have pointed out,[15] Article 1A(2) of the Refugee Convention gives an overarching definition of refugee, this can clearly be broken down into a number of elements: well-founded fear, being persecuted (the thing feared), the reasons for the persecution, being outside the country of nationality (or residence) and 'unable or, owing to such fear . . . unwilling to return to it'. As to the 'well-founded fear', the main question relates to its nature: should that fear, as the letter of the clause would suggest, be assessed *also* in terms of the refugee's state of mind or only on the basis of objective elements whatever

10 According to S. Schmahl (2011c: 614), the provisions of Article 1A(2) were extended to include some subsequent events, such as the Hungarian uprising of 1956, because, to stretch the meaning slightly, they 'were considered to be a result of the communist takeover shortly after the Second World War. While they fled in 1956, it was the "effect" of an "event" which occurred prior to 1 January 1951 (so called "after-effect")'. This stratagem could not be used again for later events, such as those occurring in Asia and Africa.

11 The Protocol was also ratified by three States not parties to the Refugee Convention but subject to its rules without the temporal limitation: Cape Verde, United States and Venezuela. See footnote 1.

12 See S. Schmahl (2011b: 469).

13 Article 1B(2) states that 'Any Contracting State which has adopted alternative (a) [the geographical limitation] may at any time extend its obligations by adopting alternative (b) [no geographical restriction] by means of a notification addressed to the Secretary-General of the United Nations'.

14 The other two were Congo and Monaco; Madagascar did not ratify the Protocol.

15 F. Lenzerini (2009: 221).

the applicant's perception of the situation.[16] The *travaux préparatoires* for the treaty do not provide any useful indications. Some small contribution comes from the work of the Ad Hoc Committee on Statelessness and Related Problems, which the United Nations Economic and Social Council (ECOSOC) in its Resolution 248B of 8 August 1949 charged with preparing a draft convention on the status of refugees.[17] The draft was examined by ECOSOC itself and by the UN General Assembly before being adopted as the basis for the work of the Conference of Plenipotentiaries. At the Ad Hoc Committee's eighteenth meeting Mr Robinson (for Israel) insisted on the need for a 'subjective clause' and proposed an amendment to the definition of refugee that would include 'emotional and sentimental reasons' among the motives why a person might be unwilling to return to his or her home country.[18] Robinson sought to extend the concept of refugee to include Jews who did not want to return to Germany because of their 'horrifying memories', not because of fears of undergoing 'future' persecution. It was rejected, but the Committee's position on the point remained ambiguous, leading the British representative Sir Leslie Brass to complain that 'if an individual did not have good reasons for not wishing to return to his own country, he would cease to be considered as a refugee'. The Committee's own final comments on the draft convention were by no means unequivocal:

> The expression 'well-founded fear of being the victim of persecution for reasons of race, religion, nationality or political opinion' means that a person has either been actually a victim of persecution or can show good reasons why he fears persecution.[19]

The words of the Committee have been interpreted in some quarters as suggesting a willingness to consider subjective elements when determining what constitutes well-founded fear according to Article 1A(2).[20] The position of UNHCR on this point is clear: 'since fear is subjective, the definition involves

---

16 As A. Grahl-Madsen (1966–1972, I: 173) points out, '"fear" is, generally speaking, a subjective condition, a state of mind'.

17 ECOSOC Resolution 248 (IX) B, 8 August 1949, in *ECOSOC, Official Records: 4th Year, 9th Sess.*, pp. 60–61.

18 Ad Hoc Committee on Statelessness and Related Problems, First Session: Summary Record of the Eighteenth Meeting held at Lake Success, New York, on Tuesday, 31 January 1950, available online at www.refworld.org.

19 Report of the Ad Hoc Committee on Statelessness and Related Problems, 17 February 1950, E/1618, E/AC.32/5, available online at www.refworld.org, p. 39.

20 A. Zimmermann and C. Mahler (2011: 336). Instead, it is my opinion that the expression 'good reasons' emphasises the objective nature of the evaluation; the ambiguous nature of the Committee's position is apparent in every discussion concerning this aspect of Article 1 of the Refugee Convention, which has been the subject of much reconsideration.

a subjective element in the person applying for recognition as a refugee';[21] national case law tends to follow the same line.[22]

Much of the legal theory, however, is strongly critical of this approach, for the fairly obvious reason that the state of mind of applicants for refugee status may not be a good indicator of the real risk they run in their home country: they may show little fear of returning, for reasons of either disposition or lack of news, when instead they objectively are 'at risk'. In other words, the addition of a subjective element, which does not emerge clearly from the *travaux préparatoires*, in reality narrows the definition of refugee by ruling out, for highly debatable reasons, persons nonetheless objectively at risk of the type of persecution envisaged by the clause.[23] Previous studies had noted that

> the adjective 'well-founded' suggests that it is not the frame of mind of the person concerned which is decisive for his claim to refugeehood, but that his claim should be measured with a more objective yardstick.[24]

Removing the subjective element from the authorities' decisions does not mean that the applicant's personal situation is disregarded. Some people may be at risk, even though the objective elements are less impelling, because they occupy a public position, or because of their personality or the context in which they live.[25] The objective nature of the risk in no way rules out the possibility that the authorities examining the application may 'be satisfied' with less forcible proof where the applicant is the leader of a movement opposing an anti-democratic regime rather than just a sympathiser, or is a minor not an adult, and so on.

Some national judges continue nonetheless to place a limit on the role of such factors and hesitate to acknowledge the existence of a risk of persecution when it is the result of personal choices that could have been avoided by exercising what is known as 'reasonable tolerability'. They therefore refuse to grant the status

---

21 UNHCR (1992a: para. 37).
22 For some examples among many see High Court of Ireland, decision of 12 March 2009, *S. H. M. v. Refugee Appeals Tribunal & Anor*; US Court of Appeals, Eleventh Circuit, decision of 20 April 2010, *Villarreal v. U.S. Attorney General*; US Court of Appeals, Third Circuit, decision of 8 September 2010, *Huang v. Attorney General*; and Australian Federal Court, decision of 12 February 2011, *Fonnoll v. Canada (Minister of Citizenship and Immigration)*, respectively, *passim*, especially p. 8, especially p. 18 ff., and para. 55. For the most important cases, see A. Zimmermann (2011: 338).
23 See also J. C. Hathaway (1991: 66).
24 A. Grahl-Madsen (1966–1972, I: 173). The prevailing approach in legal literature is the one that excludes any subjective element when assessing whether a fear is well-founded: see E. Adjin-Tettey (1997–1998: 127 ff.), R. Haines (2003: 319 ff.) and J. C. Hathaway and W. S. Hicks (2004–2005: 505 ff.). The approach is adopted only in some case law: see A. Zimmermann and C. Mahler (2011: 340). More recently, see Australian Refugee Review Tribunal, decision of 18 January 2013, *RRT Case No. 1209185 (1209185)*, para. 13.
25 A. Grahl-Madsen (1966–1972, I: 175). On this point see also UNHCR (1992a: para. 43).

of refugee to individuals who could have avoided persecution in their home country by behaving more 'discreetly', a practice that is widespread with regard to religious motives or to homosexuality in the sense of membership of a particular social group. Belgium's Conseil du Contentieux des Etrangers decreed that because homosexuality is tolerated in Iran on condition that it is practised privately, there could be no well-founded fear as the decision to employ 'self-restraint' is reasonably tolerable.[26] This, again, is a minority position, and one that leaves itself open to criticism according to the New Zealand Refugee Status Appeals Authority:

> By requiring the refugee applicant to abandon a core right the refugee decision-maker is requiring of the refugee claimant the same submissive and compliant behaviour, the same denial of a fundamental human right, which the agent of persecution in the country of origin seeks to achieve by persecutory conduct.[27]

Several objective elements need to be examined to determine whether there exists a well-founded fear (in the sense described above). The UNHCR *Handbook on Procedures and Criteria* mentions several, such as the applicant's personal experience, including past experience,[28] and also 'what . . . happened to his friends and relatives and other members of the same racial or social group', the laws in force in the country of origin and how they are applied in practice, and so on.[29]

---

26 According to the judge, 'In de Iraanse maatschappij bestaat er een groot verschil tussen de publieke ruimte en de privé-sfeer. In de praktijk is homoseksualiteit onder mannen uitgebreid en wordt ze in veel islamitische samenlevingen aanvaard zolang de relatie privé gehouden wordt en men er niet over praat. De algemene "de facto-tolerantie" houdt echter in dat, zolang de homoseksuelen hun seksualiteit als een privé-aangelegenheid beleven, het weinig waarschijnlijk is dat de Iraanse overheden belangstelling voor de betrokken persoon zullen tonen. De maatschappij kent geslachtelijke segregatie en homoseksuele mannen kunnen, indien zij de spelregels volgen, sociaal met elkaar blijven omgaan, samenwonen, reizen en een hotelkamer delen zonder de aandacht te trekken. Het is voor homoseksuelen ook gemakkelijker een lokaal te huren en grote feesten te organiseren dan voor heteroseksuelen, omdat gemengde gezelschappen in Iran verboden zijn. Over het algemeen hebben homoseksuelen geen problemen om gelijkgezinden te vinden in parken en sportcentra, die bekend staan als ontmoetingsplaatsen voor homoseksuelen' (decision of the Conseil du Contentieux des Etrangers, 31 March 2010, *X tegen de Commissaris-generaal voor de vluchtelingen en de staatlozen*, available online at www.rvv-cce.be, para. 2).

27 Refugee Status Appeals Authority of New Zealand, decision of 7 July 2004, *Refugee Appeal No. 74665*, para. 114. On the relative legal literature see A. Zimmermann and C. Mahler (2011: 343 ff.) and also UNHCR (2008d: para. 25).

28 For instance, persecution previously suffered by the applicant. See Court of Appeal (Civil Division) of England and Wales, decision of 23 July 1999, *Haci Demirkaya* v. *Secretary of State for the Home Department*, and, more recently, Court of Session of Scotland, decision of 10 November 2010, *MD* v. *Secretary of State for the Home Department*, the latter at para. 5 ff.

29 See UNHCR (1992a: para. 43).

In sum, a prediction must be made based on objective elements pointing to a strong likelihood (well-founded reasons) that if the applicant is rejected he or she will suffer persecution according to Article 1A(2).

The object of well-founded fear is a persecutory act or acts; thus, the prediction must be able to infer from those objective elements a specific consequence, although on this point the Refugee Convention is largely silent. According to some theorists,[30] this gap was left on purpose, considering the *travaux préparatoires*, to allow States the utmost flexibility to define what constitutes a persecutory act; as a result, practices differ widely among national judges. One thing remains certain, though: taken jointly, Articles 1A(2) and 33(1) of the Refugee Convention point to the existence of a threshold beyond which there is always persecution. As we will see later (section 1.3), Article 33 prohibits States from expelling or returning a refugee to a country 'where his life or freedom would be threatened'. Accordingly, as the concepts of refugee adopted in the two articles are clearly identical, regardless of any literal differences, a threat to a person's life or liberty is persecution also under the terms of Article 1A even though it is not mentioned there.[31] The question is whether, as a minority of authoritative writers would have it,[32] the concept of persecution does not go beyond what can be deduced from the few indications found in Article 33(1), or whether the threshold is in fact lower and encompasses violations of human rights *tout court*. Standard practice would appear to lean in this second direction, as would the prevailing theory.[33] Thus, violation of any of the human rights recognised in the relevant treaties for their protection may, if the other conditions are also met, constitute persecution for the purposes of the Refugee Convention.[34]

30 P. Weis (1960: 928 ff., especially 970).
31 See the commentary, beginning with an analysis of Article 31, of P. Weis (1995: 303) and that of A. Grahl-Madsen (1997: 102). See also J. C. Hathaway (2005: 304–5). For the case law see, among many, Seoul District Court, 13th Administration, decision of 15 January 2004, *Adjudication in the Seoul District Court on an Appeal from a Dismissal of Refugee Recognition (Seoul District Court)*, para. 3A.
32 K. F. Zink (1962: 74 ff.).
33 Regarding the case law, see the decision in *Seoul District Court*, para. 3B; New Zealand Refugee Status Appeals Authority, decision of 19 October 2010, *Refugee Appeal Nos. 76508 & 76509*, especially para. 72; and Australian Refugee Review Tribunal, decision of 6 April 2011, *RRT Case No. 1011616*, para. 14 (this decision in fact applies Article 91R of the Migration Act, which already makes provision for some situations of persecution, including 'denial of access to basic services, where the denial threatens the person's capacity to subsist'). Among the legal literature, see A. Grahl-Madsen (1966–1972, I: 193 ff.), J. C. Hathaway (1991: 108), G. S. Goodwin-Gill and J. McAdam (2007: 90 ff.), F. Lenzerini (2009: 236 ff.) and A. Zimmermann and C. Mahler (2011: 345 ff., especially 353).
34 For a brief list of human rights see G. S. Goodwin-Gill and J. McAdam (2007: 93). As A. Zimmermann and C. Mahler (2011: 354 ff.) point out, in practice, continuous additions are made to the set of human rights violation of which may constitute persecution. Thus, as well as the right to physical integrity and personal freedom, in some instances the right to education, the right to work and other 'second generation' rights have also been taken into consideration.

This does not mean that every violation of the human rights listed will constitute persecution because, as the New Zealand Refugee Status Appeals Authority has explained, 'the breach . . . must be of sufficient severity to amount to persecution'.[35] Presumably, the threshold that must be overstepped in order to be able to talk of persecution varies according to the human right concerned. A classification has been attempted that takes account of the 'weight' of a specific human right and establishes a threshold beyond which there may be persecution. Thus, in the case of rights from which there can be no derogation (such as the prohibition on torture) any violation will suffice; in the case of other rights (those which are derogable), it must be proved that the State did not act in a situation of emergency; for 'second generation' rights, there can only be persecution if the State acts in a discriminatory manner even where the resources are available; and, finally, violations of rights not yet recognised by treaty are disregarded.[36] This approach has rightly been criticised because it links the presence of persecution to the extent to which each human right is derogable, regardless of the reason why such derogations were incorporated in the treaties.[37] A broader derogation does not always correspond to a 'lesser' human right, and vice versa. A better approach would be to allow greater flexibility in assessing the situation, bearing in mind that some violations of human rights (torture, for example) are so serious that there is no need for systematic repetition in order to constitute persecution.[38] Greater flexibility would also allow, as explained below, a clearer separation to be operated between human rights on the one side (violation of which may amount to persecution depending on the case) and the reasons for the persecution on the other.

While a possible, feared and grave infringement of human rights is not sufficient to constitute persecution, in principle the alleged conduct must be attributable to the country of origin. This is not a problem where there is no doubt as to the State's responsibility, for instance if the violation is perpetrated by bodies (*de jure* or *de facto*) of the State, by bodies controlled by the State,[39] or by the State itself, or can be ascribed to entities answering to an authority that is a nascent subject of international law by virtue of its power over a given territory.[40] Uncertainties arise, instead, if the violation is committed by one or more individuals (or non-State actors), in which case a distinction should be made between those acting inside the sovereign territory of a State and those acting in a context where there is no longer any State authority (such as Somalia). In the first instance, there is now no question as to the State's responsibility: for some years it has been recognised, in both practice and theory, that States have an obligation to protect individuals within their

---

35 Refugee Status Appeals Authority, decision of 30 June 1998, *Refugee Appeal No. 70618.* For a broader treatment, see F. Lenzerini (2009: 247 ff.).
36 See J. C. Hathaway (1991: 109).
37 A. Zimmermann and C. Mahler (2011: 351–2).
38 Ibid.
39 See footnote 260.
40 On a general level see J. Crawford (2010: *passim*).

jurisdiction (wherever they come from) against potential infringements of their human rights.[41] If the State fails in its duty of protection by not exercising due diligence, it is clearly responsible under international law. It follows, as the Spanish Supreme Court declared, that refugee status can be accorded

> no sólo cuando tal persecución provenga de las autoridades del país de origen, sino también cuando proceda de sectores de la población cuya conducta sea deliberadamente tolerada por las autoridades o *éstas se muestren incapaces* de proporcionar una protección eficaz.[42]

The situation may be less clear if no State authority exists (failed States) as there is no way to attribute the persecution to a State, a condition apparently required by Article 1A(2) of the Refugee Convention. However, part of the literature cites the general purpose of the Convention and the fact that 'failed States remain subjects of international law even if they no longer have any functioning authorities', and concludes that the concept of persecution remains valid even in such cases.[43] National judges, with some

41 Other examples found in the relevant case law, apart from those mentioned by A. Zimmermann and C. Mahler (2011: 364 ff.), include the judgment of the ECtHR, 8 July 2004, Application No. 48787/99, *Ilaşcu and others* v. *Moldova and Russia*, available online at www.echr.coe.int, especially para. 333, in which the Court goes even further in defining the obligations of a contracting State: 'where a Contracting State is prevented from exercising its authority over the whole of its territory by a constraining *de facto* situation, such as obtains when a separatist regime is set up, whether or not this is accompanied by military occupation by another State, it does not thereby cease to have jurisdiction within the meaning of Article 1 of the Convention over that part of its territory temporarily subject to a local authority sustained by rebel forces or by another State'. Previously, French and German judges had issued decisions based on the opposite view, since 'blocked' by the entry into force of Council Directive 2004/83/EC of 29 April 2004 on minimum standards for the qualification and status of third country nationals or stateless persons as refugees or as persons who otherwise need international protection and the content of the protection granted, OJ L 304, 30/09/2004, p. 12 ff.: see the French Conseil d'Etat, decision of 27 May 1983, *No. 42074*, and the more recent decision of the same judge, 25 October 2004, *No. 242145*, both available online at www.conseil-etat.fr. In the literature, see D. Wilsher (2003: 68 ff.), G. S. Goodwin-Gill and J. McAdam (2007: 99–100), F. Lenzerini (2009: 254 ff., especially 258) and A. Zimmermann and C. Mahler (2011: 366–7). UNHCR takes the same line: see UNHCR (1992a: para. 65).

42 Tribunal Supremo, decision of 6 October 2005, *Recurso No. 2098/2002*. See also, more recently, US Court of Appeals, Seventh Circuit, decision of 26 September 2011, *Rasa Jonaitiene and Marius Bubenas* v. *Attorney General*, available online at www.refugeecaselaw. org, and of the Australian Refugee Review Tribunal *1209185*, para. 10.

43 The general purpose of the Refugee Convention is cited by A. Zimmermann and C. Mahler (2011: 368). Instead, the passage quoted is from W. Kälin (2000–2001: 430), who bases the assertion on the fact that 'Failed States . . . usually do not terminate their membership in international organizations; their territory cannot be annexed by another state as stateless land, and an invasion of this territory still constitutes, according to the UN Charter, a violation of the prohibition of the use

exceptions,[44] have adopted this approach. Thus, as the Australian Refugee Review Tribunal ruled in the case of Somalia,

> The persecution must have an official quality, in the sense that it is official, or officially tolerated or uncontrollable by the authorities of the country of nationality. However, the threat of harm need not be the product of government policy; it may be enough that the government *has failed* or is unable to protect the applicant from persecution.[45]

Not every persecution that individuals might undergo in their country of origin will turn them into refugees, even if the other requirements are met. Article 1A(2) of the Refugee Convention limits qualifying behaviour on the basis of the reasons that led to it: race, religion, nationality, membership of a given social group, and political opinions. Only if the persecution stems from one of these five reasons does it fall within the scope of the article. Before examining them individually, it should be noted that in practice there is not always a clear causal link between persecution and the reasons for it.[16] Several approaches are possible, and in many cases result in a negative decision.[47] The literature lists three main ones:[48] the first, very narrow, approach holds that persecution can only occur for one of the reasons enumerated in the Refugee Convention;[49] the second, known as the 'but for' test, holds that one of the Convention reasons must be decisive in causing

of force'. Nevertheless, some questions do arise in the case of Somalia, which has had its membership of the United Nations 'suspended' pending progress that will warrant its return to full international subjectivity: on this point see D. Shraga (1999: 653–4).

44 All of which relate to the decisions of judges in European States issued before the creation of a European Community (and later EU) asylum system: see B. Vermeulen, T. Spijkerboer, K. Zwann and R. Fernhout (1998: 23 ff.).

45 Decision of 27 December 2011, *RRT Case No. 1107868*, para. 13 (emphasis added). See also New Zealand Refugee Status Appeals Authority, decision of 29 September 2009, *Refugee Appeal Nos. 76335 and 76364*, para. 58, and Immigration and Refugee Board of Canada, decision of 23 January 2013, *X* v. *Canada*, VB0-04912.

46 The UNHCR comments only summarily on these approaches: see UNHCR (1992a: para. 66–7). K. Musalo (2002: 37) points out that nothing on the subject is to be found in the *travaux préparatoires* and this fact, together with the 'economy' of the *Handbook*, has prompted national judges to borrow 'standards of causation existing in other jurisprudential areas'.

47 K. Musalo (2002: vii).

48 M. Foster (2001–2002: 265 ff.). In addition to the three approaches, Foster includes cases in which the judges have left the matter of causation open or even viewed it merely as a problem of the persecutor's intention.

49 This is a minority view, adopted mainly in some US cases. According to M. Foster (2001–2002: 270 and references), 'Notwithstanding the very important rejection of a sole cause test in principle, an analysis of the application of abstract principle to individual determinations reveals that in practice courts frequently apply an *effective* sole cause test'.

the persecution (even though it may not be the only motive);[50] and the third, probably the prevailing approach requires that one of the reasons listed at least contribute to the persecution.[51] In drawing up the classification, Foster rightly points out that it does not necessarily provide a precise framework, particularly as the problem of causal link often compounds that of the role of 'intentions' in the act of persecution.[52] Thus, not only do judges have to identify an element linking the reasons of the Refugee Convention to the act of persecution, but in doing so they often tend to ascribe such reasons to the persecutor, assuming it to be a necessary condition. The Australian court, adopting the prevailing approach – that one of the Convention reasons must at least contribute to the persecution – ruled that 'one person may be *motivated* to persecute another for more than one reason', thereby combining causal link and persecutor's intentions.[53]

Scholarly writers are unanimous in maintaining that the persecutor's intentions are not the only condition that must be satisfied in order for the Refugee Convention to apply. Although the opposite approach has prevailed on occasion, the correct view is that causation is by no means tied to rigid, pre-set parameters but can be deduced

> from the intention of the persecutor, *or* from the unwillingness or inability, not necessarily intention, of the country of origin to provide protection, *or* . . . from the fear or the predicament of the individual concerned.[54]

50 This approach originated in the literature, which borrowed it from the law of tort: see J. C. Hathaway (1991: 140). It was adopted by the Australian courts and by a few British judges but with a significant variation: not only did the Convention reason have to play a decisive role, but common sense also had to be applied. This is explained by Justice Sedley in the decision of 5 April 2000, *Queen v. Secretary of State for the Home Department ex parte Velasco*, using the example of 'an individual who, on the way to church, witnesses a crime and is then threatened with serious retribution by the criminals if he or she exposes them. But for that person's religion . . . they would not have been put in fear of persecution': quoted in J. C. Hathaway and M. Foster (2003: 472). For the opinion of the Australian judges see High Court, decision of 13 April 2000, *Chen Shi Hai v. The Minister for Immigration and Multicultural Affairs*, especially para. 68, and, for more recent cases, Refugee Review Tribunal, decision of 25 July 2011, *RRT Case No. 1011563*, especially para. 111 ff., and the already mentioned decision of the Australian Refugee Review Tribunal *1209185*, para. 12.

51 This is the principle applied by US judges: see US Court of Appeals, Ninth Circuit, decision of 19 May 2000, *Maini v. INV*, available online at www.ca9.uscourts.gov. A. Zimmermann and C. Mahler (2011: 373) point out that some US judges tend to depart significantly from this line, veering very close to the 'but for' test on the ground that the Convention reason should play a central or paramount role.

52 M. Foster (2001–2002: 269).

53 Australian Federal Court, decision of 17 February 1999, *Minister for Immigration and Multicultural Affairs v. Sarrazola*, 'Australian Law Reports', 1999, p. 645.

54 C. W. Wouters (2009: 80, emphasis added). Arguments against the practice of attributing importance to the persecutor's intentions for the purposes of Article 1A(2) of the Refugee Convention are found in G. S. Goodwin-Gill and J. McAdam (2007: 102 ff.) and A. Zimmermann and C. Mahler (2011: 373–4).

Moreover, the reasons for the persecution must not be set above the human rights that are violated, otherwise the derogations of those rights may spill over onto the reasons. In other words, in order to establish whether the limitation of a right is lawful and hence does not constitute persecution it is necessary to consider the possible derogations of that right: religious motives can never justify torture, even though religious freedom may be subject to exceptions. A greater degree of flexibility, as discussed earlier, makes it easier to operate the distinction, especially where it is necessary to decide when violation of a right becomes persecution because of its systematic nature. If racial motives are behind just one act of torture this may be enough to constitute persecution but, even though the prohibition on racial discrimination is virtually absolute, there must be racial *motives* why a State has *systematically* violated the right to education for this conduct also to qualify as persecution.

The first motive for persecution, race, is very rarely encountered in practice as in most cases in which racial or ethnic reasons are at play they overlap with other reasons linked to membership of a given social group or to nationality.[55] Anyway, the notion of race is now largely regarded as obsolete,[56] and indeed non-legal disciplines have for some time seriously questioned its validity.[57] UNHCR offers no indications,[58] and therefore to find a juridical concept of race we need to look at the rulings of the European Court of Human Rights (ECtHR), specifically the decision in *Timishev* v. *Russia*, which makes a distinction between race and ethnicity:

> Ethnicity and race are related and overlapping concepts. Whereas the notion of race is rooted in the idea of biological classification of human beings into subspecies according to morphological features such as skin colour or facial characteristics, ethnicity has its origin in the idea of societal

55 For one example, see Court of Appeal (Civil Division) of England and Wales, decision of 31 July 2007, *EB* v. *Secretary of State for the Home Department*. See also F. Lenzerini (2009: 267) and A. Zimmermann and C. Mahler (2011: 375–6).

56 A. Zimmermann and C. Mahler (2011: 375–6, especially footnote 652).

57 See the reconstruction by A. Morning (2008: S106 ff.).

58 See UNHCR (1992a: para. 68), which simply states that 'Race, in the present connexion, has to be understood in its widest sense to include all kinds of ethnic groups that are referred to as "races" in common usage. Frequently it will also entail membership of a specific social group of common descent forming a minority within a larger population'. The International Convention on the Elimination of All Forms of Racial Discrimination (ICERD) (adopted New York 7 March 1966, 660 UNTS 195 ff.) fails to give a precise definition. The Committee of the same name (set up under the Convention to monitor its implementation by the States parties to it) adopted, by General Recommendation 8, 22 August 1990, 'Membership of racial or ethnic groups based on self-identification' (Articles 1.1 and 1.4), A/45/18, the criterion of self-identification by the individual concerned, which is generally used for the related problem of indigenous populations. For a summary of the discussions held during the *travaux préparatoires* for the above Convention see N. Lerner (1980: 25 ff.).

groups marked by common nationality, tribal affiliation, religious faith, shared language, or cultural and traditional origins and backgrounds.[59]

As has been pointed out in connection with other motives such as religion, 'Regardless of whether race is a scientific category with biological or genetic markers, there is no doubt that racism exists and that people are persecuted because of their *perceived racial characteristics*'.[60] It is therefore not so much the concept itself of race that is at issue as the problem of understanding 'whether an asylum applicant has suffered because of the persecutors' belief that the applicant belongs to a disfavored race'.[61]

Unlike racial motives, religious ones occur very frequently in practice, particularly, in the view of authoritative writers,[62] as a consequence of the proliferation of fundamentalist, and even theocratic, States within the international community. This raises a twofold problem: of definition and of conduct. As to the still unsolved problem of definition, the same considerations apply as for racial motives;[63] cases of uncertainty – where no clear criteria exist for including a phenomenon such as, say, Scientology,[64] to name but one, under the term 'religion' – are truly very rare.[65]

59   ECtHR, judgment of 13 December 2005, App. Nos. 55762/00 and 55974/00, *Timishev* v. *Russia*, available online at www.echr.coe.int, para. 55.
60   T. J. Gunn (2003: 198).
61   Ibid.
62   F. Lenzerini (2009: 269).
63   UNHCR (2004a: para 6 ff.) has come up with a concept of religion based on three elements: religion as belief ('"Belief", in this context, should be interpreted so as to include theistic, non theistic and atheistic beliefs. Beliefs may take the form of convictions or values about the divine or ultimate reality or the spiritual destiny of humankind. Claimants may also be considered heretics, apostates, schismatic, pagans or superstitious, even by other adherents of their religious tradition and be persecuted for that reason'); religion as identity ('"Identity" is less a matter of theological beliefs, rituals, traditions, ethnicity, nationality, or ancestry. A claimant may identify with, or have a sense of belonging to, or be identified by others as belonging to, a particular group or community. In many cases, persecutors are likely to target religious groups that are different from their own because they see that religious identity as part of a threat to their own identity or legitimacy'); and religion as a way of life ('For some individuals, "religion" is a vital aspect of their "way of life" and how they relate, either completely or partially, to the world. Their religion may manifest itself in such activities as the wearing of distinctive clothing or observance of particular religious practices, including observing religious holidays or dietary requirements. Such practices may seem trivial to non-adherents, but may be at the core of the religion for the adherent concerned').
64   The status of Scientology is hesitantly recognised in national case law in an *obiter dictum* of the Australian High Court, decision of 21 April 2004, *Minister for Immigration and Multicultural Affairs* v. *Respondents S152/2003*, available online at www.refugeecaselaw. org, para. 9. On the question see also A. C. Helton and J. Münker (1999: 310 ff.).
65   The case usually cited is that of the Falun Gong 'movement' in Canada: see Federal Court of Canada, decision of 26 September 2001, *Hui Qing Yang* v. *The Minister of Citizenship and Immigration*, available online at www.fct-cf.gc.ca, especially para. 19, in which the Court solved the problem by ruling that 'If Falun Gong is considered by

Instead, it is easier and more meaningful to identify types of conduct inspired by religious motives: according to UNHCR, religious persecution may occur where there is

> prohibition of membership of a religious community, of worship in community with others in public or in private, or religious instruction, or serious measures of discrimination imposed on individuals because they practice religion, belong to or are identified with a particular religious community, or have changed their faith.[66]

Depending on the human right affected, it will therefore be necessary to establish whether the restrictions imposed are among the derogations normally envisaged. Thus, religious freedom in particular – which is often the target of religion-based conduct[67] – cannot be invoked in order to claim that restrictions designed to prevent proselytising (when done wrongfully[68]), incitement to violence, ritual killings and, more generally, the commission of crimes, constitute persecution.[69]

Nationality, as a motive for persecution, is an ambiguous concept:[70] its inclusion among the reasons listed in Article 1A(2) is based on an assumption that the State of origin is the persecutor, because otherwise a refugee would be able to claim the protection of his or her 'own' State and would cease to be a refugee. While other provisions of the Refugee Convention give the term the meaning

the Government of China to be a religion, then it must be so for the purposes of the instant claim'. Also on this question see the same judge's more recent decision of 22 March 2012, *Zhang Sheng Wang* v. *The Minister of Citizenship and Immigration*, available online at www.fct-cf.gc.ca.

66 UNHCR (2004a: para. 12). UNHCR adds that 'in communities in which a dominant religion exists or where there is a close correlation between the State and religious institutions, discrimination on account of one's failure to adopt the dominant religion or to adhere to its practices could amount to persecution in a particular case. Persecution may be inter-religious (directed against adherents or communities of different faiths), intra-religious (within the same religion, but between different sects, or among members of the same sect), or a combination of both. The claimant may belong to a religious minority or majority. Religion-based claims may also be made by individuals in marriages of mixed religions'.

67 UNHCR (2004a: para. 11) in fact begins its list of such forms of conduct with a consideration of what constitutes religious freedom; as explained earlier, however, while it is likely that religious reasons are at the root of a violation of that freedom, the two concepts should not be confused. Religious freedom may be violated for racial, national or other reasons (for example, prohibiting women from professing their religious belief), just as religious reasons may lead to violations of personal or other freedoms (as where degrading treatment is inflicted on Hindu prisoners).

68 On this point see A. Zimmermann and C. Mahler (2011: 385).

69 UNHCR (2004a: para. 15 ff.).

70 A. Zimmermann and C. Mahler (2011: 388). See also G. S. Goodwin-Gill and J. McAdam (2007: 72) and F. Lenzerini (2009: 277), according to whom 'the inclusion of nationality . . . may seem a little bizarre at first' (trans. added).

of citizenship in the narrow sense, UNHCR adopts a broader approach:[71] 'the term "nationality" in this context is not to be understood only as "citizenship". It refers also to membership of an ethnic or linguistic group and may occasionally overlap with the term "race"'.[72] Situations in which persecution is solely nationality-based are nevertheless extremely rare, being confined to cases in which the term is considered synonymous with ethnicity or minority. This is illustrated by the ruling of the US Court of Appeals (Ninth Circuit) in the case of a Guatemalan citizen of the K'iche' minority who was subjected to repeated persecution while he was a member of the army:

> we use 'race' to designate the ground on account of which Guinac was persecuted. More precisely, he was persecuted on account of his 'ethnicity', a category which falls somewhere between and within the protected grounds of 'race' and 'nationality'.[73]

Other cases are documented in which nationality-based motives are invoked where the matter is one of ethnicity.[74] In reality, a situation that comes closer to persecution based almost exclusively on nationality is that of 'mixed' families, where the nationality of one of the parents or another family member is grounds for the type of conduct referred to in the Refugee Convention. Thus, the US Court of Appeals agreed that the requirements for recognising refugee status had been met in the case of an Israeli citizen, the son of an Arab, who was subjected to repeated threats, discrimination and more by Israeli marines during the ten years he worked as a fisherman.[75]

The concept of persecution owing to membership of a specific social group has evolved in probably the least expected manner. According to authoritative sources[76] it was originally incorporated to cover the case of people belonging to the 'ruling' class fleeing from States that had adopted Soviet-style socialism and had consequently nationalised all means of production,[77] before eventually

---

71 See in Article 1A(2) the provision that 'In the case of a person who has more than one nationality, the term "the country of his nationality" shall mean each of the countries of which he is a national, and a person shall not be deemed to be lacking the protection of the country of his nationality if, without any valid reason based on well-founded fear, he has not availed himself of the protection of one of the countries of which he is a national.'

72 UNHCR (1992a: para. 74).

73 US Court of Appeals, Ninth Circuit, decision of 8 June 1999, *Mildred Yesenia Duarte de Guinac and Mauro José Guinac Quiej* v. *Immigration and Naturalization Service*, available online at www.ca9.uscourts.gov, para. II.

74 This is the case of Ethiopian citizens of Eritrean origin, a discussion of which, including references to the case law, can be found in F. Lenzerini (2009: 277–8).

75 See US Court of Appeals, Ninth Circuit, decision of 11 July 2003, *Abrahim Baballah, Ula Baballah and Ahmad Baballah* v. *Attorney General*, available online at www.ca9.uscourts.gov.

76 G. S. Goodwin-Gill and J. McAdam (2007: 74).

77 The socialist countries did not contribute to the drafting of the Refugee Convention and did not participate until the first meeting of the Ad Hoc Committee on Statelessness

becoming the form of persecution most often 'singled out' in accepted practice. Being so 'broad' it acts as a residual catch-all category, to be used whenever it is unclear which of the other Convention grounds applies.[78] Yet, however broad the concept of specific social group may be, some boundaries do exist, although they vary case by case. Case law in the United States follows the approach that the elements identifying a group are internal to it, meaning that members must share one or more immutable, as it were innate, or at least inescapable characteristics.[79] The Australian courts, on the other hand, focus on external elements of identification, insofar as the common characteristic of the group is not necessarily inherent in its members but externally perceived to be so.[80]

We can be virtually certain that in standard practice other factors, such as the size of the group, the cohesion of its members, or, as a rule, the fact that they are persecuted, have no bearing. Some judges are of the opinion, however, that the last element does serve to identify a group. Accordingly, a group that would not, in theory, fall within the field of application of the Refugee Convention (left-handers, to quote the example given by Justice McHugh[81]) could be forcibly included by the fact that its members are subject to persecution, which thus becomes the group's qualifying characteristic. What appears to be a tautological definition of a specific social group is in fact a variation of the theory whereby

and Related Problems. It is interesting, from a historical viewpoint, to understand the reasons for this: at the opening of the Committee's first session, the Soviet delegate Klimov questioned whether it was right that the seat of China should be occupied by a member of the Kuomintang and not by a representative of the government of the People's Republic of China, which he thought would be more correct, adding that he would not take part 'in the work of the Committee until that exclusion [of the representative of the Kuomintang] took place'. Regardless of the objections raised by the US delegate, and obviously also the delegate for China, the USSR forced the Committee's hand by putting a resolution to exclude the delegate from the vote. The majority voted against and the USSR and Poland withdrew from the Committee. See Ad Hoc Committee on Statelessness and Related Problems, First Session: Summary Record of the First Meeting Held at Lake Success, New York, Monday, 16 January 1950, available online at www.refworld.org, especially para. 6 ff.

78 See S. C. Helton (1983–1984: 41) and F. Lenzerini (2009: 279).

79 See US Board of Immigration Appeals, decision of 1 March 1985, *Matter of Acosta*, and, more recently, Court of Appeals, Eleventh Circuit, decision of 20 September 2012, available online at www.refugeecaselaw.org. However, for the last ten years the US authorities, followed by the country's courts, have adjusted this approach to take account of external factors as well, the 'social visibility' element already mentioned in US Court of Appeals, Eleventh Circuit, decision of 20 April 2006, *Diego F. Castillo-Arias and Others* v. *U.S. Attorney General*, 04-14662, and, more recently, in US Court of Appeals, Ninth Circuit, decision of 13 February 2013, *Henriquez-Rivas* v. *Attorney General*, No. 09-71571.

80 See Australian High Court, decision of 24 February 1997, *Applicant A and another* v. *Minister for Immigration and Ethnic Affairs and another*, 'Australian Law Reports', 1997, p. 331 ff.

81 Ibid., para. 101.

the group is identified *also* by the way in which it is perceived externally:[82] to clarify, the stage of 'determining the persons whose rights are to be violated' precedes the stage in which that violation takes place, so that 'persecution serves only to make evident the existence of discriminatory treatment based on the specific characteristic identifying the group ... – it does not *constitute* such treatment'.[83]

An approach that takes account of both internal and external elements is supported by legal literature and UNHCR.[84] In point of fact, neither approach produces a very different outcome as internal and external perceptions usually coincide.[85] Thus, national judges, applying different theories, have granted the status of particular social group to transport workers who had decided not to support the Colombian FARC,[86] to military personnel responsible for the massacre of civilians,[87] to persons who are HIV positive,[88] to relatives of prosecution witnesses in trials of gang members in El Salvador,[89] to homosexuals,[90] and above all to women.[91]

The last reason for persecution mentioned in Article 1A(2) of the Refugee Convention is political opinion. It is defined very broadly to include 'any opinion

---

82 A. Zimmermann and C. Mahler (2011: 395).

83 F. Lenzerini (2009: 295, 297).

84 See, respectively, G. S. Goodwin-Gill and J. McAdam (2007: 74) and UNHCR (2002b: para. 11), which states that '*a particular social group is a group of persons who share a common characteristic other than their risk of being persecuted, or who are perceived as a group by society. The characteristic will often be one which is innate, unchangeable, or which is otherwise fundamental to identity, conscience or the exercise of one's human rights*' (the italics appear in the original text).

85 A. Zimmermann and C. Mahler (2011: 393).

86 US Court of Appeals, Seventh Circuit, decision of 31 May 2011, *Sergio Escobar* v. *Attorney General*, available online on www.ca7.uscourts.gov.

87 US Court of Appeals, First Circuit, decision of 21 March 2011, *David Eduardo Castañeda* v. *Attorney General*, available online at www.ca1.uscourts.gov.

88 See Federal Court of Canada, decision of 5 February 2010, *A.B. and Others* v. *Minister of Citizenship and Immigration (F.C.)*, and US Court of Appeals, Seventh Circuit, decision of 4 August 2010, *Aguilar-Mejia* v. *Attorney General*.

89 US Court of Appeals, Fourth Circuit, decision of 8 December 2010, *Orlando Crespin-Valladares, Sandra Yanira Melgar-Melgar, S.E.C.M. and S.O.C.M.* v. *Attorney General*, available online at www.ca4.uscourts.gov.

90 Among many examples, see US Court of Appeals, Ninth Circuit, decision of 7 March 2005, *Nasser Mustapha Karouni* v. *Alberto Gonzales, Attorney General*, especially para. 3, and Australian Refugee Review Tribunal, decision of 18 August 2009, *RRT Case No. 903707*, especially para. 113. For UNHCR's position on this issue, see footnote 91 and, more recently, UNHCR (2012: para. 44 ff.).

91 On this point see F. Lenzerini (2009: 288 ff.) for an extensive bibliography and many references to the case law. UNHCR (2002a: para. 30) has taken a firm stance on this point, that 'sex can properly be within the ambit of the social group category, with women being a clear example of a social subset defined by innate and immutable characteristics, and who are frequently treated differently than men. Their characteristics also identify them as a group in society, subjecting them to different treatment and standards in some countries. Equally, this definition would encompass homosexuals, transsexuals, or transvestites'. See also UNHCR (2012: para. 44 ff.).

on any matter in which the machinery of State, government, and policy may be engaged'.[92] As a result, this reason has been attributed to the fear of persecution for exposing a paramilitary group to which the person previously belonged,[93] for making a complaint about alleged corruption in general government,[94] and for the failure of a marriage in a society where the marginalisation of women has political connotations.[95] It is important to emphasise – although this is generally true for all of the reasons – that even the perception that a person holds a certain political opinion can politically motivate an act of persecution. This much is clear not only from the practice of the courts,[96] but also from that of UNHCR, which states that to provide grounds for a well-founded fear of persecution it must be demonstrated that 'such [political] opinions have come to the notice of the authorities or are attributed by them to the applicant'.[97] This brings us full circle, as people who have never expressed any political opinion (contrary to the government, that is) may do so once (or if) they return to their country of origin. The UNHCR *Handbook on Procedures and Criteria* clearly envisages this possibility:

> Due to the strength of his convictions, however, it may be reasonable to assume that his opinions will sooner or later find expression and that the applicant will, as a result, come into conflict with the authorities.[98]

In this case, alleged refugees must be able to set the strength of their convictions against the fact that they expressed their political opinions timidly or not at all. This conclusion is not always supported in the case law: in a decision of 1998 the Federal Court of Canada refused to allow a Congolese national belonging to Lumumba's party to obtain refugee status 'by merely stating that he will fight the AFDL [Alliance of Democratic Forces for the Liberation of Congo-Zaire]'.[99]

This motive for persecution raises the separate problem of the suppression of political crimes. While it can be taken for granted that a political opinion has been expressed in such cases, *res ipsa loquitor*, the line between persecution, on the one hand, and lawful exercise of penal sanctions and punitive powers, on the other, should be drawn on the basis of the general categories discussed above. Thus, even where a political crime has been committed and entails a reaction that could qualify, in abstract, as politically motivated conduct, there will be persecution if

---

92 G. S. Goodwin-Gill and J. McAdam (2007: 87).
93 See Supreme Court of Canada, decision of 30 June 1993, *Attorney General* v. *Ward*.
94 Federal Court of Appeal of Canada, decision of 22 February 2000, *Klinko* v. *Minister of Citizenship and Immigration*.
95 New Zealand Refugee Status Appeals Authority, decision of 11 September 2008, *Refugee Appeal No. 76044*.
96 See Federal Court of Canada, decision of 26 September 2001, *Yang* v. *Minister of Citizenship and Immigration*, especially para. 19.
97 UNHCR (1992a: para. 80).
98 Ibid.: para. 82.
99 Federal Court of Canada, decision of 17 July 1998, *Makala* v. *Minister of Citizenship and Immigration*, para. 32.

the State's conduct is such as to violate the prohibition on torture.[100] Instead, other elements, such as the discriminatory nature of the conduct or the observance of the cases and procedures prescribed by law – to quote Article 5 of the Convention for the Protection of Human Rights and Fundamental Freedoms (ECHR) – will have to be assessed where it is the right to personal liberty that is violated. Of course, this approach must take account of the existence of any exclusion clauses, a condition that applies in all cases, though more so in respect of political motives because more likely (see section 1.2): if a political crime falls within the scope of Article 1F of the Refugee Convention the problem will never arise as the applicant cannot be recognised as a refugee.[101]

The last of the elements that contribute to the definition of refugee is the fact of being outside the country of origin (i.e. the country of citizenship[102]) and being unable or, owing to well-founded fear, unwilling to return there.[103] This requirement is expanded at the end of Article 1A(2) of the Refugee Convention. This clause states that an applicant who has multiple citizenship must demonstrate his or her inability or unwillingness to enjoy the protection of *all* the States of which he or she is citizen; at the same time, it broadens the category of refugee to include stateless persons, identifying their State of citizenship as their 'former

---

100 According to Article 1 of the UN Convention against Torture (adopted New York 10 December 1984 and entered into force 26 June 1987, 1465 UNTS 85 ff.) this 'does not include pain or suffering arising only from, inherent in or incidental to lawful sanctions'.

101 The cases are only those enumerated at (a) and (c) (crimes against peace, war crimes, crimes against humanity, or acts contrary to the purposes and principles of the United Nations); (b) only applies in the case of a 'serious non-political crime'. The question of the political or non-political nature of the crime (and hence the possibility of applying the last clause) remains open, but this is another matter.

102 See A. Zimmermann and C. Mahler (2011: 442–3).

103 Despite the wording of Article 1A(2), an applicant's presence outside his/her country of origin is completely unrelated to events 'occurring before 1 January 1951'. In other words, for an applicant to be granted refugee status he/she does not need to be outside his/her country of origin *because of* those events. In any case, the problem no longer arises as the reference to such 'events' was eliminated in the 1967 Protocol. Instead, there needs to be a link between the fact of the applicant being outside his/her country of origin and the well-founded fear, although this should not be interpreted too narrowly: the fear of persecution could arise when the applicant is no longer in the country of origin. These refugees are termed *sur place*, and they become such after leaving their country of origin. An example would be where the government of the home country is unexpectedly overturned, or an applicant begins to voice political opinions that are critical of the government after moving abroad. The fear has a dual significance (only) where an applicant *does not want* to return to his/her country of origin. The wording of the article differs on this point, as the expression 'owing to such fear' reappears only in respect of the applicant's unwillingness to return, and not in connection with the inability to do so. According to legal theorists – see A. Zimmermann and C. Mahler (2011: 443) – the rule is intended to apply to cases in which fear is not the reason for the applicant's failure to return to the country of origin, for instance where he/she has been stripped of citizenship or when the State of origin refuses protection, such as by confiscating or refusing to issue identity documents.

habitual residence'. The requirement that applicants be outside their 'own' State has an important consequence: where an applicant has been forced to flee his or her home region to avoid the risk of persecution but remains inside the State of origin (in an area where the risk does not exist), he or she will not qualify for refugee status. This is the situation of 'internally displaced persons' (IDPs). In its conclusion on this question, UNHCR Executive Committee (EXCOM),[104] after reaffirming that insofar as these persons are inside their State of origin 'the primary responsibility for their welfare and protection lies with the State concerned', merely expresses the hope that the international community will provide 'timely and speedy humanitarian assistance and support to countries affected by internal displacement'.[105] Naturally, the reverse also applies, so that a person outside his or her State of origin, which can nonetheless offer protection in a part of its territory other than the person's habitual residence, cannot enjoy refugee status. This is not a case of IDPs (although in principle the concept is the same) but of 'internal flight alternative', which is no more nor less than the repatriation of IDPs in an area of their State of origin where they need not fear persecution. UNHCR has drawn up a list of situations in which this concept will rule out refugee status: the zone must be 'secure', a condition that does not apply where the original persecution was by agents of the State (on the assumption that the State has control over the *whole* of its territory) or by non-State agents against which the State cannot protect the applicant, *in that zone*, or where the zone is inaccessible.[106]

To conclude, all the situations briefly examined above acquire different nuances for different categories of applicants, so that 'adaptations' are necessary,[107] as UNHCR itself points out.[108] These transversal categories do not always fit into the particular social group according to Article 1A(2) of the Refugee Convention. The first example is that of children: because they are not fully mature either physically or intellectually, it would be appropriate to assume that even less serious acts qualify as persecution, or to give less weight to the child's subjective state (where relevant) and perception of being persecuted, or to rule out, at least in

104 The Executive Committee was set up by ECOSOC, Resolution No. 672 (30 April 1958) E/3123, at the request of UNGA, Resolution 1166 (26 November 1957) A/RES/1166(XII). Initially, the Executive Committee consisted of representatives of some (24) contracting States (which now number 87), appointed by ECOSOC. Its functions include 'To advise the High Commissioner, at his request, in the exercise of his functions under the Statute of his Office', but in practice it constitutes, alongside UNHCR, an authoritative, though not binding, source of interpretation of the rules of the Refugee Convention. Its positions are decided by consensus and are usually expressed in the form of 'conclusions'. On the importance of the role of the Committee in the evolution of refugee law, see A. Corkery (2006: 97 ff.).
105 UNHCR EXCOM Conclusion on Internally Displaced Persons No. 75 (XLV) (1993) available online at www.refworld.org, para. d) ff. On this question see T. G. Weiss and D. A. Korn (2006: *passim*).
106 UNHCR (2003c: para. 7).
107 On this point in general see A. Zimmermann and C. Mahler (2011: 404 ff.).
108 Among many others see UNHCR (1994), UNHCR (1997a) and UNHCR (2002a).

principle, that certain reasons (such as those based on political opinion) may be relevant for the purposes of alleged persecution. Naturally, the same also applies to women. However, some acts that are not persecutory but nonetheless brutal, intense and profoundly offensive may 'avoid' the clause because of the absence of a reason according to the Refugee Convention; this may be due to the difficulty, in some contexts, of assigning the women to a particular social group, or to an inability to link persecution by private individuals to the State of origin. Case law has developed a somewhat depressing list of reasons that should fall within the scope of the Refugee Convention, which includes rape and other forms of sexual violence, female genital mutilation, forcible termination of pregnancy and sterilisation, forced marriage, domestic violence and in some cases even the infliction of punishment for failure to observe rules of conduct such as those regulating matters of dress.[109] A last group for which some adaptations are necessary is the one based on sexual orientation: the main difficulty in this case, according to UNHCR, is that 'freedom of sexual orientation is not explicitly recognized as an international human right'.[110]

1.2 Cessation of refugee status and exclusion clauses

The Refugee Convention also makes provision for situations in which the status of refugee no longer exists or where it cannot, and should not, be granted. Minor cases aside,[111] the most important situations are set out in Articles 1C and 1F. Article 1C spells out a series of circumstances, all involving the (re-)establishment of links between the refugee and his or her country of nationality (or residence), in which the Convention 'shall cease to apply'. Article 1F, on the other hand, provides that where there are serious reasons for believing that a person has committed crimes of some gravity, the Convention 'shall not apply'.[112] This use

---

109 A. Zimmermann and C. Mahler (2011: 409 ff.).
110 UNHCR (2008d: para. 9).
111 Minor cases are listed in Article 1D, which provides that 'This Convention shall not apply to persons who are at present receiving from organs or agencies of the United Nations other than the United Nations High Commissioner for Refugees protection or assistance. When such protection or assistance has ceased for any reason, without the position of such persons being definitively settled in accordance with the relevant resolutions adopted by the General Assembly of the United Nations, these person shall ipso facto be entitled to the benefits of this Convention', and in Article 1E, which provides that 'This Convention shall not apply to a person who is recognized by the competent authorities of the country in which he has taken residence as having the rights and obligations which are attached to the possession of the nationality of that country'. See A. Grahl-Madsen (1966–1972, I: 263 ff.), G. S. Goodwin-Gill and J. McAdam (2007: 151 ff.), R. Marx (2011: 571 ff.) and M. M. Qafisheh and V. Azarov (2011: 537 ff.).
112 These are situations in which '(a) he has committed a crime against peace, a war crime, or a crime against humanity, as defined in the international instruments drawn up to make provision in respect of such crimes; (b) he has committed a serious non-political crime outside the country of refuge prior to his admission to that country

of different expressions suggests that refugee status can only be revoked where one of the conditions listed in Article 1C is met, although according to well-established practice the conditions set out in Article 1F also warrant revocation of refugee status.[113] Yet, the opposite is also true, in the sense that Article 1C can be used to 'cancel' the refugee status of people to whom it should never have been granted in the first place. This occurs most often where recognition of refugee status was obtained by fraud.[114] Instead, the rationale underlying the application of these clauses differs significantly: the purpose of Article 1C is to place responsibility for protecting the refugee – where the reasons why he or she had sought protection elsewhere no longer apply – firmly back with the country on which it falls in the first instance, that is the country of nationality or residence.[115] The purpose of Article 1F, on the other hand, is to exclude from refugee status persons who, having allegedly committed serious crimes, do not deserve the protection offered by the Convention.[116] Some authoritative writers maintain that Article 1F also aims 'to ensure that those who had committed grave crimes in the Second World War or other serious non-political crimes, or who were guilty of acts contrary to the purposes and principles of the United Nations, did not escape prosecution'.[117] The *travaux préparatoires*, which Gilbert cites in support of his contention, do not appear to offer a clear indication in this regard.[118] Indeed, the author acknowledges[119] that any connection made there between asylum and extradition (theoretically, extradition would serve the intended purpose of Article 1F) is either ambiguous or entirely absent.[120]

Article 1C enumerates six situations in which refugee status ceases to apply. These can be divided into three categories: the first covers the case in which the refugee no longer intends to refuse the protection of the country of origin, in other words where 'he has voluntarily re-availed himself of the protection of the country of his nationality'. The article assumes that the refugee possesses a nationality and, according to UNHCR, imposes certain requirements: the decision must express

as a refugee; (c) he has been guilty of acts contrary to the purposes and principles of the United Nations'.

113 See UK Special Immigration Appeal Commission, decision of 29 October 2003, *C. v. Secretary of State for the Home Department (C.)*, paras 28–9, and Court of Appeal (Civil Division) of England and Wales, decision of 30 July 2007, *MT, RBand U v. Secretary of State for the Home Department*, in *International Journal of Refugee Law*, 2007, p. 536 ff., especially para. 79 ff. For a more recent case see Asylum and Immigration Tribunal of England and Wales, decision of 9 March 2009, *IH v. The Secretary of State for the Home Department (IH)*, ibid., 2009, p. 308 ff., especially para. 68.
114 See UNHCR (1992a: para. 117).
115 On this point see F. Lenzerini (2009: 504 ff.).
116 See A. Zimmermann and P. Wennholz (2011a: 583).
117 G. Gilbert (2003: 428).
118 See Conference of Plenipotentiaries on the Status of Refugees and Stateless Persons: Summary Record of the 24th Meeting, 27 November 1951, A/CONF.2/SR.24.
119 G. Gilbert (2003: 428, especially footnote 6).
120 See also footnote 209 to this chapter.

an intention, it must be taken voluntarily by the refugee, and it must result in obtaining the protection of the country of nationality.[121] The first of these requirements once again raises the question of subjectivity discussed earlier. Here, it is not a matter of understanding whether the refugee was aware, when deciding to benefit again from the protection of the country of nationality, that objectively there was no longer any risk of persecution, but of determining whether the refugee is still 'unwilling to avail himself of the protection of that country'. In other words, the article does not require an assessment of whether the risk is objectively still present but of whether the refugee, by acting in a certain way (for instance, by applying for a passport from the country of origin or by returning there for a brief period), has manifested an intention to benefit once again from protection.[122] The refugee's fate will be determined by his or her behaviour; standard practice ranges from very cautious assessment, as advocated in the legal literature,[123] to decisions based on far less 'conclusive' conduct on the part of the refugee.[124] Paradoxically, UNHCR itself has encouraged this practice by explaining, in relation to the situation that arises most frequently (application for a passport), that 'If a refugee applies for and obtains a national passport or its renewal, it will, in the absence of proof to the contrary, be *presumed* that he intends to avail himself of the protection of the country of his nationality'.[125] Any considerations concerning the situation that the refugee will find in his or her country of origin when returning there arise out of the other factor, that is, whether the protection he or she chooses to re-acquire is actually obtained. In reality, it is a matter of determining whether the refugee has resumed a normal relationship with his or her home country, but not of going so far as to verify if the risk of persecution still exists as this is dealt with in Article 1C(5) and (6) (see below).

A refugee's intention to benefit from the protection of his or her former home country may be deduced from more specific actions. According to Article 1C(2) this happens when a refugee, 'having lost his nationality . . . has voluntarily re-acquired it'. The purpose of the two articles is the same: to identify a specific

121 UNHCR (1992a: para. 118 ff.).
122 A. Grahl-Madsen (1966–1972, I: 390–1) makes the point that the host country must still envisage the possibility that in deciding to re-avail himself/herself of the protection of the country of his/her nationality the refugee has assessed the situation there incorrectly and may therefore change his/her mind later and require refugee status to be restored (by the host country).
123 J. Fitzpatrick and R. Bonoan (2003: 524–5).
124 For example, the Swiss Federal Administrative Court found that a woman's two-month stay in Kosovo, her country of origin, did meet the requirements for cessation of refugee status despite her explanation that she made the trip because of her brother's deteriorating health. See the decision of 22 February 2011, *A., B. and C. v. Swiss Federal Office for Migration*, available online at www.refugeecaselaw.org. See also footnote 131.
125 UNHCR (1992a: para. 121, emphasis added). See Immigration and Refugee Board of Canada, decision of 15 September 2011, *Minister of Public Safety and Emergency Preparedness v. X*, MA9-09969. On more practice of States see S. Kneebone and M. O'Sullivan (2011: 509 ff.).

action indicating the refugee's willingness to re-acquire the protection of his or her home country, that is, the voluntary re-acquisition of a former nationality. Again, it is important to discover the refugee's intention, as this may be unclear if, for instance, nationality is re-acquired automatically by marriage,[126] or where the law of the home country offers an option to reject nationality that the refugee does not exercise.[127] Article 1C(4) provides that cessation of refugee status may also ensue if the refugee has 'voluntarily re-established himself in the country which he left or outside which he remained owing to fear of persecution'.[128] Again, it must be ascertained that the refugee's re-establishment in his or her home country was voluntary – which would exclude forcible repatriation[129] – and it must be reasonable to deduce from his or her actions an intention to go back to the country of origin.[130] Consequently, short visits, especially in order to care for sick relatives, are not a certain indication of a desire to return to the home country and therefore cannot lead to cessation of refugee status.[131]

The second category of Article 1C(3) is that of a refugee who has acquired a new nationality and can claim the protection of his or her new country, which may well be the one which originally offered refuge.[132] This is most often the case where

126 See J. C. Hathaway (1991: 197).
127 UNHCR (1992a: para. 128).
128 According to UNHCR this clause completes the first two, being intended to regulate cases in which, for whatever reason, a refugee returns to his/her home country without having previously lost refugee status under the first two clauses: 'This fourth cessation clause . . . relates to refugees who, having returned to their country of origin or previous residence, have not previously ceased to be refugees under the first or second cessation clauses while still in their country of refuge' (1992a: para. 133). I rather think that the residual clause is the one provided for in Article 1C(1): when refugee status has not ceased as a consequence of specific actions, as in Article 1C(2) and (4), it must be established whether there are other actions, as in Article 1C(1), indicating the refugee's willingness to return to the protection of his or her home country.
129 See, including regarding the other clauses, J. Fitzpatrick and R. Bonoan (2003: 529).
130 This was the deduction of the Immigration and Refugee Board of Canada in the decision of 18 October 2004, *VA301194* v. *Canada*, available online at www.refugeecaselaw.org, based on the fact that a Russian refugee, claiming his mother was seriously ill (although this was not proven), had returned to his home country and remained there for five years.
131 Of course, short visits may also point to a refugee's intention to re-acquire the home country's protection and entail cessation of refugee status under Article 1C(1). An example is the case of a Kosovar refugee living in Switzerland who returned to his home country several times for short spells (Swiss Asylum Appeal Commission, decision of 5 July 2002, *B. T.* v. *Swiss Federal Office of Refugees*, available online at www.refugeecaselaw.org). The Swiss judges pronounced that the numerous elements produced showed that even not entirely 'conclusive' conduct was sufficient for the application of Article 1C(1): see Asylum Appeal Commission, decision of 19 January 1996, *V. T. N.* v. *Swiss Federal Office for Refugees*, ibid., and the decision of 26 August 2002, *N. M.* v. *Swiss Federal Office of Refugees*, ibid. This is further indication of the residual character of the clause (1), as pointed out in footnote 128.
132 Article 1C(3) states that a refugee loses that status if he/she acquires 'a new nationality, and enjoys the protection of the country of his new nationality'.

the refugee is treated on a par with the citizens of the host country as a result of naturalisation, marriage or the provisions of the law.[133] Unlike the situations discussed previously, this circumstance does not require an intention on the part of the refugee to obtain the protection of the State whose nationality he or she acquires, but the cessation of refugee status explicitly ensues from the fact that the refugee enjoys the protection of that State. Although the state of mind of the refugee is not entirely disregarded in practice – as it would otherwise create a clear separation between this situation and the others[134] – legal theory holds that because no reference is made to a voluntary decision on the part of the refugee an objective element such as the protection of the third State must be explicitly included.[135] Assuming that the refugee acquires a new nationality against his or her will, the explicit inclusion of that objective element will act as a safeguard against the cessation of refugee status should protection (objectively) not be provided in the State of new nationality. An example, cited in the literature, is 'where the third State is a successor State to the refugee's State of origin, and the refugee involuntarily acquires its nationality through passage of a general law'.[136]

The third and last category contemplated by Article 1C covers the situation in which the risk of persecution in the country of origin no longer exists. Article 1C(5) states that refugee status ceases to exist where the refugee

> can no longer, because the circumstances in connexion with which he has been recognized as a refugee have ceased to exist, continue to refuse to avail himself of the protection of the country of his nationality.

This clause, together with Article 1C(6),[137] which concerns stateless persons, was used at one time almost exclusively for groups of refugees affected by changes

---

133 See S. Kneebone and M. O'Sullivan (2011: 499).
134 S. Kneebone and M. O'Sullivan (2011: 512). According to J. Fitzpatrick and R. Bonoan (2003: 527), 'A traditional example concerns women who automatically acquire their husband's nationality upon marriage, even though they do not wish it and have taken no steps to acquire it other than through the marriage itself. Cessation in such cases is questionable under modern human rights norms, including prohibitions on gender-based discrimination'.
135 A. Grahl-Madsen (1966–1972, I: 396).
136 J. Fitzpatrick and R. Bonoan (2003: 527).
137 Article 1C(6) refers to stateless persons: 'Being a person who has no nationality he is, because the circumstances in connexion with which he has been recognized as a refugee have ceased to exist, able to return to the country of his former habitual residence'. The wording differs from that used in 1C(5); the reference to 'ability to return' has been included as stateless persons often encounter practical difficulties in returning to their country of residence because (as explained further on; see footnote 315) only a State of nationality is obliged to re-admit its citizens – which is why 'ability to return' is not mentioned in 1C(5): the State whose protection the refugee cannot continue to refuse is that of nationality, which is obliged to allow him/her to return. On this point see also S. Kneebone and M. O'Sullivan (2011: 503).

of circumstances in their country of origin;[138] such would be the case of the overthrow or debellation of a government guilty of persecution, or the end of a civil war. Only lately, and in a limited number of cases, has it become the practice of States to extend the application of these clauses to individuals. The focal point of the clauses is the same as that of Article 1A(2): assessing the likelihood that the refugee does not risk persecution in his or her country of origin. Any change of circumstances must be 'fundamental, durable, and effective' and UNHCR enumerates several elements that may indicate a return to normality – at least as far as human rights safeguards are concerned – in the country of origin.[139] For instance, a radical change may be apparent from 'significant reforms altering the basic legal or social structure of the State', or from 'democratic elections, declarations of amnesties, repeal of oppressive laws and dismantling of former security services'.[140] As to whether the change is lasting, the Executive Committee has ruled that 'a minimum period of 12 to 18 months (always depending on the circumstances) should normally elapse before a judgment on ceased circumstances can be considered reliable'.[141] When assessing whether the changed circumstances have effectively made the country a safe place,

> States must carefully assess the fundamental character of the changes in the country of nationality or origin, including the general human rights situation as well as the particular cause of fear of persecution, in order to make sure in an objective and verifiable way that the situation which justified the granting of refugee status has ceased to exist.[142]

In the few instances where such a situation has arisen the procedure has not followed the recommendations of UNHCR. The Australian courts in particular tend to assess whether the cessation clauses apply by placing the burden of proving continuation of the circumstances that led to the granting of refugee status on the refugee, with the result that in one well-known case the High Court confirmed the cessation of status of an Afghan refugee on the grounds that the risk of persecution no longer existed after the fall of the Taliban regime.[143] Elsewhere, the

---

Both clauses make a special exception in the case of 'history' or 'statutory' refugees, on which see A. Grahl-Madsen (1966–1972, I: 410–1).

138 See S. Kneebone and M. O'Sullivan (2011: 489). There are many examples in the recent practice of UNHCR: see UNHCR (2002d, 2008b and 2014).

139 UNHCR (1997b: para. 19).

140 Ibid.: para. 20

141 UNHCR EXCOM, Discussion Note on the Application of the 'Ceased Circumstances' Cessation Clauses in the 1951 Convention, 20 December 1991, available online at www.refworld.org, para. 12.

142 UNHCR EXCOM, Conclusion on Cessation of Status No. 69 (XLIII), (1992), available online at www.refworld.org, para. a).

143 Australian High Court, decision of 15 November 2006, *Minister for Immigration and Multicultural and Indigenous Affairs* v. *QAAH of 2004*, a critical commentary on which can be found in M. O'Sullivan (2008: 586 ff.).

scope of the clause has been broadened by considering elements 'outside' the situation in the country of origin when evaluating changes in circumstances. The Norwegian Supreme Court, ruling on the cessation of status of an Iranian woman who had been recognised as a refugee because of her homosexuality and had subsequently married a man of her same nationality, declared that 'if refugees, following changes in their personal circumstances, no longer risk persecution in their country of origin, it is difficult to see why they should have a claim to asylum in Norway'.[144] This is easily countered by the argument that a woman who has suffered persecution in the past because of her homosexuality will not receive better treatment on her return to her country of origin even if she has apparently changed sexual orientation. In reality, the question is another: did she commit fraud when she made her original application for asylum, never having had homosexual tendencies, as her subsequent behaviour would appear to indicate? In other cases, national case law seems to follow the line recommended by UNHCR. In 2009 the US Court of Appeals ruled that a Liberian refugee had not ceased to fear persecution merely because the former President Taylor was no longer head of government.[145]

The grounds for excluding persons from refugee status are set out in Article 1F. The application of these clauses raises a number of problems, particularly since 11 September 2001, which heralded a widespread return to a state of emergency in the West and elsewhere.[146] The Article recites:

> The provisions of this Convention shall not apply to any person with respect to whom there are serious reasons for considering that: (a) he has committed a crime against peace, a war crime, or a crime against humanity, as defined in the international instruments drawn up to make provision in respect of such crimes; (b) he has committed a serious non-political crime outside the country of refuge prior to his admission to that country as a refugee; (c) he has been guilty of acts contrary to the purposes and principles of the United Nations.

There are therefore three situations in which the Refugee Convention 'shall not apply'. Before examining them more closely, it should be noted that Article 1F is closely related to Article 33(2) of the Convention, which enumerates the exceptions to the prohibition on *refoulement*. I will discuss the relationship between the

---

144 Norwegian Supreme Court, decision of 29 June 2010, *A. v. Appeals Board,* available online at www.refugeecaselaw.org, para. 49.
145 According to the Court, 'general evidence of improved country conditions will not suffice to rebut credible testimony and other evidence establishing past persecution; evidence of changed country conditions can successfully rebut the presumption *only* if it addresses the specific basis for the alien's fear of persecution' (US Court of Appeals, Third Circuit, decision of 24 November 2009, *Martina Sheriff* v. *Attorney General,* available online at www.refugeecaselaw.org).
146 See M. Zard (2002: 32 ff.).

two clauses in section 1.5 and focus here on Article 1F only. As explained, the purpose of Article 1F is to exclude individuals who are not considered to merit the benefits of refugee status.[147] This is illustrated by the position of the French delegate Mr Rain during the work of the Ad Hoc Committee on Statelessness. He objected to the definition of refugee proposed by the United States – designed to exclude from the benefits of refugee status 'persons of "German ethnic origin residing in Germany"' – because of its implicit racial discrimination, but quickly added that in any case 'war criminals would naturally be excluded from the protection of the Convention'.[148]

One element that the three cases envisaged by Article 1F have in common is 'serious reasons for considering' that the situation exists. Plainly, proof of conviction is not required for the clause to apply. Generally speaking, the standard is lower, requiring only the existence of sufficient proof to bring a criminal prosecution in a national court.[149] Where terrorist acts are concerned, UNHCR, having affirmed that suspicion alone does not meet the standard established in Article 1F, has ruled that the clause will apply automatically, without need to examine the case on its individual merits, where the applicant for refugee status has been brought to trial before an international tribunal.[150] Such acts, however, make the application of Article 1F problematical, partly because of the standard to be met regarding the person's connection with the crimes listed at 1F(a), (b) and (c). The question has been raised whether mere membership of a terrorist organisation can be regarded as 'serious reasons for considering' or whether other elements must

147 See footnote 116.
148 Ad Hoc Committee on Statelessness and Related Problems, First Session: Summary Record of the Fourth Meeting Held at Lake Success, New York, on Wednesday, 18 January 1950, available online at www.refworld.org, para. 25. There was a very lively debate about the exclusion clauses, particularly as the various bodies involved in drafting the Refugee Convention, from the Ad Hoc Committee to the Conference of Plenipotentiaries, were doing so in the wake of the Second World War and all its horrors. The climate is well illustrated by the 'discussion' that took place between the German delegate and the delegate for Israel concerning the need for the definition of crimes against peace, war crimes and crimes against humanity to include a reference to the Charter of London of 8 August 1945, which instituted the Nuremberg Tribunal. The argument put forward by the German delegate in support of the amendment removing the reference to the Charter (see Conference of Plenipotentiaries on the Status of Refugees and Stateless Persons: Summary Record of the 19th Meeting, 13 July 1951, A/CONF.2/SR.19, pp. 27–8) was rejected by the delegate for Israel Mr Robinson, who opened his speech by stating clearly that the amendment 'seemed to have been inspired by a fear of calling things by their right name' (see Conference of Plenipotentiaries on the Status of Refugees and Stateless Persons: Summary Record of the 24th Meeting, p. 14).
149 G. Gilbert (2003: 470). See, for a recent case, Upper Tribunal, Immigration and Asylum Chamber, decision of 5 August 2013, *AH* v. *Secretary of State for the Home Department*, available online at www.refugeecaselaw.org, para. 8.
150 UNHCR (2001d: para. 17).

be present.[151] Both procedure and theory would seem to lean towards the latter interpretation,[152] while UNHCR tends to be less flexible, taking a clear stance on membership of 'an extremist international terrorist group, such as those involved in the 11 September attacks'.[153] In any event, account must be taken of the organisation's purposes when deciding whether the exclusion clauses apply in such situations, because the less doubt there is about the organisation's criminal objectives, the smaller the degree of participation required for Article 1F to apply.

The first set of reasons for considering a person to be not deserving of international protection is the commission of crimes against peace, war crimes and crimes against humanity. Article 1F(a) makes no mention of genocide, however. According to several authoritative writers,[154] this is surprising as the UN had adopted an *ad hoc* convention only shortly beforehand.[155] In reality, the omission is not a flaw, for although genocide does not fit easily among the reasons listed in Article 1F(b) – it may be described as having a political nature, where 1F(b) talks of non-political crimes – it is certainly contrary to the principles and purposes of the UN enumerated at (c) and may also qualify as a crime against humanity.

The definition of the crimes contemplated by this clause should be viewed as dynamic. There is no need to stress that the international treaties alluded to in 1F(a) are not limited to the Charter of the International Military Tribunal (the London Charter) and the Geneva Conventions[156] – even though during the *travaux préparatoires* some delegates called for them to be mentioned.[157] Naturally, they comprise other instruments, mainly the statutes of the two *ad hoc* criminal tribunals, for the former Yugoslavia and for Rwanda, and that of the International

151 This mirrors the current debate in criminal law theory concerning criminal conspiracy and participation in a criminal enterprise.

152 See G. Gilbert (2003: 471) for national case law as well. Also see A. Zimmermann and P. Wennholz (2011a: 593–4). The problem does not just arise in connection with affiliation to or membership of terrorist organisations, but in relation to any type of crime among those listed in Article 1F(a), (b) and (c) that falls within the notion of criminal enterprise in the broad sense. In other words, it includes belonging to a government that has committed crimes again humanity or against peace. See Federal Court of Appeal of Canada, decision of 15 July 2011, *Minister of Citizenship and Immigration* v. *Rachidi Ekanza Ezokola*, available online at www.refugeecaselaw.org, especially para. 40 ff., which contains an extensive reconstruction of Canadian case law in regard. More generally, see J. Rikhof (2009: 459 ff.).

153 UNHCR (2001d: para. 18).

154 A. Zimmermann and P. Wennholz (2011a: 594).

155 This is the Convention on the Prevention and Punishment of the Crime of Genocide (adopted Paris 9 December 1948, 78 UNTS 278 ff.).

156 These are the four treaties that make up the Geneva Conventions, signed on 12 August 1949, respectively for the Amelioration of the Condition of the Wounded and Sick in Armed Forces in the Field; for the Amelioration of the Condition of Wounded, Sick and Shipwrecked Members of Armed Forces at Sea; on the Treatment of Prisoners of War; and on the Protection of Civilian Persons in Time of War, 75 UNTS 31 ff.

157 See footnote 148.

Criminal Court (ICC).[158] A discussion of this complex matter is beyond the scope of the present work, which merely wishes to highlight some of the specific problems of application of Article 1F.

Crimes against peace – a situation not theoretically impossible but rarely invoked within the context of the Refugee Convention – are more or less equivalent to aggression.[159] According to legal theory, Article 1F(a) is intended to apply only to persons who, being part of a government organisation, or as part of groups, gangs and similar whose conduct is attributable to the State, occupy a high position of authority.[160] Although virtually no international instruments provide a definition of aggression,[161] one can now be found in the new Article 8 *bis* of the Statute of the ICC.[162] Although the amendment introduced by the 2010

158 G. S. Goodwin-Gill and J. McAdam (2007: 166) and A. Zimmermann and P. Wennholz (2011a: 595), on war crimes, which are probably more likely to require a dynamic interpretation. This would help to overcome the problem of defining the crimes listed at 1F(a) by allowing the case law of the two tribunals and the ICC to be invoked; see J. C. Simeon (2009: 202). The International Criminal Tribunal for the former Yugoslavia and the International Criminal Tribunal for Rwanda were set up by resolution of the UN Security Council, UNSC Resolution (25 May 1993) S/RES/827 (1993) and UNSC Resolution (8 November 1994) S/RES/955 (1994), respectively. The ICC was created by the Rome Statute of 17 July 1998, 2187 UNTS I-38544 ff.

159 According to A. Zimmermann and P. Wennholz (2011a: 595). The question was considered incidentally by the Federal Court of Canada, decision of 31 May 2006, *Jeremy Dean Hinzman et al.* v. *Minister of Citizenship and Immigration*, available online at www.refugeecaselaw.org, on which see J. Rikhof (2009: 459).

160 G. S. Goodwin-Gill and J. McAdam (2007: 166). The same interpretation is found in UNHCR (2003d: para. 11).

161 The only one that does is UNGA Resolution (14 December 1974) A/RES/3314 (XXIX) containing the note 'Definition of Aggression'.

162 See the Resolution of the Review Conference of the Rome Statute (11 June 2010) RC/res.6: '1. For the purpose of this Statute, "crime of aggression" means the planning, preparation, initiation or execution, by a person in a position effectively to exercise control over or to direct the political or military action of a State, of an act of aggression which, by its character, gravity and scale, constitutes a manifest violation of the Charter of the United Nations. 2. For the purpose of paragraph 1, "act of aggression" means the use of armed force by a State against the sovereignty, territorial integrity or political independence of another State, or in any other manner inconsistent with the Charter of the United Nations. Any of the following acts, regardless of a declaration of war, shall, in accordance with United Nations General Assembly resolution 3314 (XXIX) of 14 December 1974, qualify as an act of aggression: (a) The invasion or attack by the armed forces of a State of the territory of another State, or any military occupation, however temporary, resulting from such invasion or attack, or any annexation by the use of force of the territory of another State or part thereof; (b) Bombardment by the armed forces of a State against the territory of another State or the use of any weapons by a State against the territory of another State; (c) The blockade of the ports or coasts of a State by the armed forces of another State; (d) An attack by the armed forces of a State on the land, sea or air forces, or marine and air fleets of another State; (e) The use of armed forces of one State which are within the territory of another State with the agreement of the receiving State, in contravention

Kampala Review Conference will enter into force by means of the simpler mechanism of Article 121(5) of the Statute,[163] the crime of aggression will not come under the ICC's jurisdiction until 1 January 2017, and only on condition that two-thirds of the States parties to the Review Conference approve the amendment (incorporating Article 8 *bis* in the Statute) and that the thirtieth ratification has taken place at least one year beforehand.[164]

Article 1F(a) lists in second place war crimes, on which there is more case law than on crimes against peace.[165] It has become increasingly well-established practice, since the case of *Tadic*,[166] for war crimes to include the situations now covered by Article 8(c) of the ICC Statute,[167] so that a person may be excluded from refugee status for committing war crimes in the course of a non-international armed conflict.[168] Of course, not all violations of *ius in bello* (the law of armed conflict) exclude the person committing them from the benefits of refugee status; referring again to the ICC Statute, they must be 'grave' violations. According to

of the conditions provided for in the agreement or any extension of their presence in such territory beyond the termination of the agreement; (f) The action of a State in allowing its territory, which it has placed at the disposal of another State, to be used by that other State for perpetrating an act of aggression against a third State; (g) The sending by or on behalf of a State of armed bands, groups, irregulars or mercenaries, which carry out acts of armed force against another State of such gravity as to amount to the acts listed above, or its substantial involvement therein'. See C. McDougall (2013).

163 'Any amendment to articles 5, 6, 7 and 8 of this Statute shall enter into force for those States Parties which have accepted the amendment one year after the deposit of their instruments of ratification or acceptance. In respect of a State Party which has not accepted the amendment, the Court shall not exercise its jurisdiction regarding a crime covered by the amendment when committed by that State Party's nationals or on its territory'. Note that the Resolution of the Review Conference was adopted by consensus.

164 See Article 15 *bis* contained in the Resolution of the Review Conference cited above. On this point see J. Trahan (2011: 49 ff., especially 82).

165 Decisions based only on the (alleged) commission of war crimes are very few as the latter tend to be confused in the case law with crimes against humanity.

166 Appeals Chamber, decision of 2 October 1995, *Prosecutor* v. *Disko Tadic*, available online at www.icty.org, para. 72 ff. See also on this point UNHCR (2003d: para. 12).

167 These are crimes taking place in the course of non-international conflicts such as hostage taking, 'violence to life and person, in particular murder of all kinds, mutilation, cruel treatment and torture', and so on. Article 8(d) clarifies that the situations listed at 8(c) – that is relating to non-international conflicts – do not apply 'to situations of internal disturbance and tensions, such as riots, isolated and sporadic acts of violence or other acts of a similar nature'.

168 Article 8 of the Statute of the ICC enumerates several categories in addition to the one mentioned in footnote 167: '(a) Grave breaches of the Geneva Conventions of 12 August 1949 . . . (b) Other serious violations of the laws and customs applicable in international armed conflict, within the established framework of international law . . . (e) Other serious violations of the laws and customs applicable in armed conflicts not of an international character, within the established framework of international law . . .'.

UNHCR, 'minor' crimes should be evaluated in proportion to the consequences of exclusion, although according to authoritative writers[169] it is unclear what is meant by 'less serious war crimes'.[170]

As noted earlier, the courts have on many occasions found the commission of war crimes to be grounds for exclusion. They generally follow the practice of international criminal judges as regards the definition of war crimes, as well as UNHCR, especially in relation to the standard that should be applied to determine whether a war crime has been committed.[171] Thus, the Federal Court of Canada found that the exclusion clause did not apply in the case of an officer in the Peruvian army whose subordinates had committed war crimes against members of the *Partido comunista del Perù* (otherwise known as *Sendero luminoso*) and the *Movimiento Revolucionario Tupac Amaru* because he was unaware of the atrocities committed.[172] The Immigration and Refugee Board of Canada reached the same conclusion regarding a Croatian member of the Yugoslav national army, sentenced *in absentia* by the Croatian judges for alleged war crimes committed in 1991 on the basis of unreliable testimony, which the Canadian authorities then used to exclude him from refugee status.[173]

Article 7 of the ICC Statute defines crimes against humanity – the last category mentioned in Article 1F(a) – as serious acts against persons (including murder, rape, enforced disappearance, torture, and others) determined by a specific context, that is, 'when committed as part of a widespread or systematic attack directed against any civilian population, with knowledge of the attack'. While terrorist attacks may be included in the definition of war crimes – though

---

169 A. Zimmermann and P. Wennholz (2011a: 595).
170 UNHCR (2003d: para. 24).
171 According to the findings of a study of case law in Australia, Canada, New Zealand, the United Kingdom and United States conducted by J. Rikhof (2009: 453 ff.), the US judges were more likely to disregard the decisions of international criminal judges, possibly because there is no rule replicating Article 1F of the Refugee Convention.
172 Federal Court of Canada, decision of 31 May 2007, *Alex Yale Ventocilla et al.* v. *Ministre de la citoyenneté et de l'immigration*. The Court also found that the defendant could not have committed war crimes within the context of an internal conflict as the Statute of the ICC was not yet in force in the period in which the crimes were alleged to have occurred (1985–92), ruling that it could not apply retroactively. This decision is debatable, however, not so much as regards the principle that penal laws cannot apply retroactively, but concerning the assumption that since the Statute of the ICC did not exist at the time, war crimes committed during internal conflicts were *in any case* not subject to criminal prosecution. The 'international instruments drawn up to make provision in respect of such crimes' mentioned in Article 1F(a) might well include the additional Protocol to the Geneva Conventions relating to the Protection of the Victims of Non-International Armed Conflicts (adopted Geneva 8 June 1977) 1125 UNTS 609 ff., of which Peru was a contracting party as of 14 January 1990.
173 Immigration and Refugee Board, decision of 19 November 2008, *Josip Budimic* v. *Counsel for the Minister*.

the matter is still under debate[174] – and, of course, of acts contrary to the principles and purposes of the UN, they will naturally qualify as crimes against humanity when they become sufficiently serious.[175] Again, the main problem arising in practice is to determine whether the applicant has *committed* such crimes according to the terms of Article 1F. To cite just a few examples, the UK High Court ruled that membership of the anti-government group known as the Tamil Tigers was not of itself, regardless of the applicant's senior position, reason to deduce that he, along with others, had committed crimes against humanity.[176] The Australian Administrative Appeals Tribunal ruled that a member of the armed forces of Sri Lanka had committed crimes against humanity for having, between 1997 and 2000, among other acts systematically tortured some prisoners in order to obtain information on the activities of the Tamil Tigers.[177]

Article 1F(b) concerns the commission of a 'serious non-political crime' and imposes two limitations not present in 1F(a) and 1F(c): the crime must be committed *outside* the country of refuge and it must be committed *before* admission to that country. The Australian Federal Court's position in this regard is unique, having ruled that it is sufficient to meet the 'geographical' condition that the crime be committed only partly outside Australia. The judge in the case did not cite the continuous nature of the crime, which itself would have justified applying the exclusion clause, but the alleged aim of the clause, which is to protect the

174 According to A. Gioia (2004: 38 ff.), not all terrorist attacks committed in the context of an international armed conflict are war crimes. Consider Article 33(1) of the Fourth Geneva Convention Relating to the Protection of Civilian Persons in Time of War ('No protected person may be punished for an offence he or she has not personally committed. Collective penalties and likewise all measures of intimidation or of terrorism are prohibited') and Article 51(2) of the Additional Protocol (I) of 8 June 1977 Relating to the Protection of Victims of International Armed Conflicts, 1125 UNTS 33 ff. ('The civilian population as such, as well as individual civilians, shall not be the object of attack. Acts or threats of violence the primary purpose of which is to spread terror among the civilian population are prohibited'). The case law tends in the opposite direction: see First Chamber of the International Criminal Tribunal for the former Yugoslavia, judgment of 5 December 2003, v., available online at www.icty.org, para. 113 ff., which comes to the opposite conclusion regarding the same Article 51(2). Authoritative legal writers have taken the same line: see A. Cassese (2006: 945).
175 See A. Zimmermann and P. Wennholz (2011a: 596).
176 Decision of the High Court of 17 March 2010, *R (on the application of JS)* v. *Secretary of State for the Home Department*. Interestingly, according to the court 'It could not be said of the LTTE [Liberation Tigers of Tamil Eelam] – nor even, on the available evidence, of its Intelligence Division – that as an organisation it was ... "predominantly terrorist in character" ... or "an extremist international terrorist group"' (ibid., para. 27). However, see the French Conseil d'Etat, decision of 28 February 2001, No. 195356, which found that Article 1F(a) should apply to a person belonging to the same organisation, who was proved to have taken part in the commission of 'crimes graves de droit commun'.
177 Administrative Appeals Tribunal, decision of 5 April 2006, *SRYYY* v. *Minister for Immigration and Multicultural Affairs*.

interests of the receiving country.[178] Scholarly writers have criticised this position, asserting that the purpose of Article 1F is to prevent the place of refuge being used to escape punishment, and as the applicant was subsequently found guilty in Australia there was no reason to deny him refugee status.[179] However, the purpose of Article 1F relates not so much to the potential 'immunity' that asylum offers as to the need to deprive of this benefit anyone who has committed an act of persecution, in other words the act that 'created' the refugee and qualifies him or her as such.[180] While the position of the Federal Court can be criticised for not invoking the continuous nature of the crime, I do not think that conviction in the receiving country rules out the application of Article 1F(b).

The concept of crime should be understood in a non-technical sense, and therefore without undue emphasis on the definitions contained in national legislation (such as the distinction in Italian law between *delitto* and *contravvenzione*). There being no category of *international* common-law crime, it should be enough that the offence exist at least in the legislation of the host country. The reasons why the applicant is considered to be not deserving of protection must relate to their negative social value in the State offering protection.[181] This is because a distinction should be made between persecution and lawful exercise of the authority to punish in cases where a derogation of human rights is possible. Thus, a person applying for asylum who is wanted for apostasy – assuming this is not regarded as a political crime – cannot come within the scope of the exclusion clause.[182] The same holds for the crime of insolvency.[183] More debatable is the case in which the applicant is guilty of selling obscene material as, assuming the offence is considered 'serious', it does not appear to unlawfully affect any human right. In reality, the question does not usually arise as the 'serious' nature of the offence means that it is punished in virtually all States. And although States have a margin of discretion in determining the gravity of the crime, this is greatly limited by the restrictions of international law.[184]

---

178 Federal Court of Australia, decision of 25 October 1995, *Tenzin Dhayakpa v. The Minister for Immigration and Ethnic Affairs*.

179 J. C. Hathaway and C. J. Harvey (2001: 300–1).

180 See *supra*, at the beginning of § 1.2.

181 See, for example, Article 4(1)(b) of the Refugees Act No. 130 of 1998 passed by the South African Parliament.

182 See Human Rights Committee, General Comment No. 22, *The Right to Freedom of Thought, Conscience and Religion*, 30 July 1993, CCPR/C/21/Rev.1/Add.4, available online at www.un.org.

183 See Article 11 of the International Covenant on Civil and Political Rights (adopted New York 16 December 1966 and entered into force 23 March 1976, 999 UNTS 171 ff.): 'No one shall be imprisoned merely on the ground of inability to fulfil a contractual obligation'.

184 See A. Zimmermann and P. Wennholz (2011a: 600–1). Recently, the South African High Court recognised the refugee status of a Libyan national belonging to a clandestine organisation linked to Al-Qaeda that opposed the regime of the deceased Colonel Gaddafi on the grounds that the acts ascribed to him (the theft of gold) were unrelated to his membership of that organisation (and therefore non-political)

According to UNHCR, States must take a number of factors into account, such as 'the nature of the act, the actual harm inflicted, the form of procedure used to prosecute the crime, the nature of the penalty, and whether most jurisdictions would consider it a serious crime'.[185]

Lastly, it must be a common-law crime, that is, it must not be of a political nature. This limitation creates, first, a problem of coordination: while it is not difficult, following the recommendation of UNHCR, to operate a theoretical distinction,[186] there exist a large number of treaties, not only relating to extradition,[187] that seek to repress a certain crime by requiring States not to ascribe to it a political motive.[188] In the majority of such treaties the problem does not arise because they contain an escape clause. The most important example is that of Article 3(2) of the European Convention on Extradition, which states that extradition will not be granted

> if the requested Party has substantial grounds for believing that a request for extradition for an ordinary criminal offence has been made for the purpose of prosecuting or punishing a person on account of his race, religion, nationality or political opinion, or that that person's position may be prejudiced for any of these reasons.[189]

and in all likelihood fabricated by the Libyan government and therefore not considered 'serious'; see the decision of 14 August 2007, *Ibrahim Ali Abubaker Tantoush v. The Refugee Appeal Board et al.* For an analysis of the gravity of crimes relating to drug trafficking see M. Gottwald (2006: 81 ff.).

185 UNHCR (2003d: para. 14).

186 'A serious crime should be considered non-political when other motives (such as personal reasons or gain) are the predominant feature of the specific crime committed. Where no clear link exists between the crime and its alleged political objective or when the act in question is disproportionate to the alleged political objective, non-political motives are predominant. The motivation, context, methods and proportionality of a crime to its objectives are important factors in evaluating its political nature' (UNHCR (2003d: para. 15)).

187 See Article 11 of the Inter-American Convention against Terrorism (adopted Bridgetown 3 June 2002) in *International Instruments Related to the Prevention and Suppression of International Terrorism*, New York, 2008, p. 241 ff. See also Article 7 of the UN Convention on the Prevention and Punishment of the Crime of Genocide.

188 This is a revised edition of what is known as the Belgian clause. It was included for the first time in the Belgian Law of 22 March 1856 when, after the failed attempt to assassinate Napoleon III in September 1854, Belgium refused to extradite two of the alleged authors of the crime (Célestin and Jules Jacquin), citing the prohibition on extradition for political crimes enshrined in the Belgian Law of 1 October 1833. On this point see also A. F. Panzera (1978: 9–10).

189 Convention adopted in Paris 13 December 1957, 359 UNTS 273 ff. Article 3(1) allows the same exception in the case of political offences. However, it should be read, at least as far as terrorism is concerned, in conjunction with the 'Belgian clause' of the European Convention on the Suppression of Terrorism (adopted Strasbourg 27 January 1977), 1137 UNTS 93 ff.

Those treaties that establish the principle of *aut dedere aut iudicare* (extradite or prosecute) contain similar clauses.[190] It follows, therefore, that the rule according to which the offences listed in these treaties cannot have a political motive does not override the clauses of the Refugee Convention, although they can provide States with useful indications in that regard.[191] Applying the *predominance test* recommended by UNHCR – according to which the act is not political if that is not its main feature (or of the means employed) – it was decided to include within the field of application of Article 1F(b), because they are common-law offences, 'egregious acts of violence, such as acts those [*sic*] commonly considered to be of a "terrorist" nature'.[192] In other words, terrorist acts such as those of 11 September 2001 against the United States fall within the category of non-political acts because the means used are disproportionate to the political objectives pursued.[193] The same rationale should apply where these acts are committed as part of a fight for self-determination. In point of fact, the question of the political nature of either the one or the other is unimportant as it may be easier to bring both within the scope of Article 1F(c), which refers to acts contrary to the purposes of the UN, avoiding any allusion to their political or non-political nature.

Even where such acts are included under Article 1F(c), however, the problem, though different, is equally complex: it is not a matter of deciding whether or not the act is political, but of drawing a clear line between terrorists and freedom fighters. In the first case, the exclusion clause could come into effect, and in the second case not. Clearly, it is a matter of defining international terrorism, an issue widely debated by legal theorists and within the competent organisations.[194] At this point it is worth noting that in national case law there is a tendency to pursue different approaches depending on whether the notion of terrorist act is that of general international law or of *ius in bello*. Lord Pill expressed the opinion that

> serious violence against members of the government forces would normally be designed to influence the government and be used for the purpose of

---

190   See Article 12 of the International Convention for the Suppression of Terrorist Bombings (adopted New York 15 December 1997), 2149 UNTS 256 ff. In reality, the clauses are less necessary in this case because States have an alternative to extradition: criminal action (*iudicare*).

191   UNHCR (2003d: para. 15): 'The fact that a particular crime is designated as non-political in an extradition treaty is of significance, but not conclusive in itself'.

192   UNHCR (2003d: para. 15).

193   The practice is to include terrorist acts within the crimes considered in Article 1F(b). On this point see W. Kälin and J. Künzli (2000: 47 ff.).

194   Mainly the UN following the institution by the General Assembly (UNGA Resolution, 17 December 1996, A/RES/51/210) of an *ad hoc* committee charged with drafting 'an international convention for the suppression of terrorist bombings and, subsequently, an international convention for the suppression of acts of nuclear terrorism'. The committee's mandate was later extended by a series of resolutions, the last of which on 9 December 1999, A/RES/54/110, assigned it the task of drafting a global treaty on terrorism. See F. Cherubini (2011: 1213 ff.).

advancing a political, religious or ideological cause. . . . On the other hand, it is difficult to hold that every act of violence in a civil war, the aim of which will usually be to overthrow a legitimate government, is an act of terrorism.[195]

More generally, legal theory has identified other categories, apart from acts of terrorism, that fall within the scope of Article 1F(c). These are acts committed by members of a government with the intention of enacting policies contrary to the respect of human rights, the maintenance of peace and the other purposes and principles of the UN Charter, that do not fall within the other categories of crime.[196] As UNHCR itself has acknowledged,[197] this is confirmation of the residual nature of the 1F(c) exclusion clause, although that is also why it often results in a 'generous' bias in favour of the exception, well beyond what the narrow interpretation required in such cases would allow.[198]

To conclude, something should be said about the procedural aspects of both the cessation and the exclusion clauses. Cessation clauses are applied very

195 Court of Appeal (Civil Division) of England and Wales, decision of 10 December 2010, *Secretary of State for the Home Department* v. *DD*, para. 55. Where the assessment required by the exclusion clause is undertaken *after* refugee status has been determined (see below) the problem may be solved at its root because the applicant would have no reason to fear persecution in his/her country of origin: see High Court of Ireland, decision of 10 November 2012, *A.B.* v. *Refugee Appeals Tribunal and the Minister for Justice, Equality and Law Reform*, in *International Journal of Refugee Law*, 2012, p. 111 ff., upholding the opinion of the Tribunal that an Afghan 'terrorist' who had fought against Karzai's Government and the NATO forces could not fear persecution in his country of origin (Afghanistan) because, citing the words of the Tribunal, 'no evidence was placed before the Tribunal member to suggest that the authorities [of Afghanistan] intended to behave unreasonably towards the applicant in the context of these activities [of prosecution]. . . . the applicant is in fact fleeing prosecution as a result of those activities which he volunteered to the Tribunal that he had participated in and the same cannot be said to amount to persecution for the purposes of the Convention'. The High Court criticised the Tribunal because, in hazarding an assessment of the exclusion clause for which there was no need, it had used an inadequate yardstick to establish a link between the applicant and the acts mentioned in Article 1F(b) and (c), taking it for granted that they had been committed because of the applicant's membership of an organisation opposing the Karzai Government, among other by military means.
196 G. S. Goodwin-Gill and J. McAdam (2007: 184 ff.). See also A. Zimmermann and P. Wennholz (2011a: 603). An example can be drawn from the recent judgment of the Federal Court of Canada, decision of 29 January 2009, *The Minister of Citizenship and Immigration* v. *Contreras Garcia*, concerning an applicant who had been refused refugee status because of his links to the Peruvian *Servicio de Inteligenzia Nacional* of Fujimori's Government, which was attributed with acts contrary to the principles and purposes of the UN. The Court rejected his application on procedural grounds.
197 UNHCR (2003d: para. 17).
198 See E. Kwakwa (2000: 79 ff.). The author correctly points out that in 1F(c) the use of the words 'he has been guilty' in place of the wording of 1F(a) and (b) ('he has committed') would suggest an even narrower interpretation (ibid.: 84).

infrequently[199] and the procedural rules should be the same as for the determination of refugee status (see section 1.4): chiefly, assessment is on an individual basis, the burden of proof of grounds for cessation is on the State, and there is the option to appeal in the event of a negative decision.[200] The standard practice of States in respect of exclusion clauses, however, contains a variation, which although probably abused, is nonetheless approved by UNHCR: given that exclusion must be assessed according to the same standards as applied in the 'inclusion' procedure,[201] according to UNHCR there are situations in which the terms may be reversed, so that 'exclusion' is determined first. Such situations include instances in which the applicant is being prosecuted before an international tribunal, or where there is extremely compelling evidence that a crime has been committed, particularly a crime contrary to the principles and purposes of the UN.[202] One factor that weighs strongly in favour of the absolutely exceptional nature of prior exclusion is the proportionality test. This test would require that throughout the whole of the Refugee Convention – the test is also discussed in relation to exceptions to the prohibition on *refoulement* – any elements excluding (or limiting) the protection afforded by the Convention be weighed against the seriousness of the risk of suffering persecution. Evidently, were States required to carry out such a test, it would automatically follow that the application of the exclusion clauses could only be considered after assessment of the risk; in other words, it is impossible to balance the two terms when the content of one of them (the seriousness of the risk) is unknown. It is extremely unlikely, however, that the Refugee Convention requires a proportionality test, as we will see later (section 1.5).[203]

---

199 J. Fitzpatrick and R. Bonoan (2003: 512).

200 J. Fitzpatrick and R. Bonoan (ibid.: especially 515) list the minimum requirements as 'notice to appear, provided in a language understandable by the refugee; a neutral decision maker; a hearing or interview at which the refugee may present evidence of continued eligibility for refugee status and rebut or explain evidence that one of the cessation grounds applies; interpretation during the interview, if necessary; an opportunity to seek either a continuation of refugee status or alternative relief where compelling reasons exist to avoid repatriation or where the refugee qualifies for another lawful status; and the possibility of appeal'.

201 On this point, and particularly regarding the matter of evidence, see G. Gilbert (2005: 161 ff.). The purpose of the 'inclusion' procedure is to evaluate the elements that bring a person under the protection of the Refugee Convention by recognising him or her as a refugee.

202 UNHCR (2003d: para. 31). Another situation is that in which the decision of the court of first instance regarding the interpretation of Article 1F is called into question on appeal.

203 For an analysis of standard practice regarding the proportionality test specifically in regard to the exclusion clauses, see G. Gilbert (2003: 450 ff.) and A. Zimmermann and P. Wennholz (2011a: 607 ff.). In reality, the problem does not arise in relation to the exclusion clauses provided for at 1F(a) and 1F(c) because the acts enumerated are so serious that there can be no weighing one term against the other. Regarding Article 1F(b), despite UNHCR's recommendations to the contrary – see UNHCR (2003d: para. 24) – almost all the case law takes the opposite line, as noted in the literature. For Australian case law, see also A. Duxbury (2008: 208 ff.).

1.3 The principle of *non-refoulement*, cornerstone of the Refugee Convention: A) Entry and temporary stay

As several authoritative writers have pointed out, the Refugee Convention does not effectively grant the right to obtain refugee status.[204] In other words, a refugee's enjoyment of the rights accorded by the Convention depends, as explained earlier, on the assessment of the State, which has a fairly wide scope for manoeuvre, and the contracting States have no obligation to grant a person refugee status.[205] This notwithstanding, the Convention does contain a fairly incisive provision on an aspect related to the recognition of refugee status but distinct from it.[206] This is Article 33(1), which recites:

> No Contracting State shall expel or return ('refouler') a refugee in any manner whatsoever to the frontiers of the territories where his life or freedom would be threatened on account of his race, religion, nationality, membership of a particular social group or political opinion.

The provision is designed to prevent a contracting State from returning a refugee to the country where his or her life or freedom would be in danger for the reasons listed. Despite differences of language, Article 33(1) does appear to protect refugees in the same manner as Article 1:[207] 'the frontiers of the territories' in Article 33(1) are the same as those of the country in which, according to Article 1A(2), a refugee has a 'well-founded fear of being persecuted for reasons of race, religion, nationality, membership of a particular social group or political opinion'. Therefore, while it is true that the Refugee Convention does not compel States to grant certain individuals (those answering the definition of Article 1A(2)) the status of refugee and entitle them to the rights associated with that status, it does prohibit them from removing such persons from their territory to a country where they would be 'at risk' of persecution. This provision has several implications, but the crucially important one is the position of States regarding the admission of asylum-seekers.[208]

---

204 Including, among others, E. Lauterpacht and D. Bethlehem (2003: 113) and C. W. Wouters (2009: 147). On this point see also P. Weis (1995: 342): 'The State admitting the refugee is not obliged to grant him asylum, and may even expel him to another country willing to admit him'. This is explicitly affirmed by UNHCR (2007a: para. 8).
205 See G. S. Gilbert (1983: 633 ff., especially 650).
206 The importance of Article 33 is borne out by Article 42 of the Convention, which includes it among the provisions to which the States may not add any reservations.
207 See footnote 31.
208 See footnote 7. The close connection between the problem of removal in general and that of admission had already been highlighted in the literature: see, in particular, A. M. Calamia (1980: 40 ff.), who argues very effectively that 'based on the assumption that a State has an obligation to allow a foreigner entry into its territory, it implicitly follows that an expulsion order can only be issued on specific conditions. Instead, if

One of the main problems raised by Article 33(1) is how to identify clearly what State actions are included or, in other words, what removal orders fall within the field of application of the prohibition on *refoulement*. In the early years of the Refugee Convention the article was understood to exclude removal orders issued against persons who had not yet entered the territory of the contracting State. Thus, it applied to any conduct on the part of the State that entailed the refugee's removal from its territory (starting with expulsion[209]), while rejection at the frontier continued to be allowed. During the *travaux préparatoires* the Swiss delegate Mr Zutter, commenting on the article, was eager to stress that the term *refoulement* 'could not . . . be applied to a refugee who had not yet entered the territory of a country'.[210] In the many years that have passed since the intergovernmental conferences that resulted in the Refugee Convention and the principal commentaries of authoritative writers in regard,[211] a broader concept of the prohibition on *refoulement* has taken shape, one that is probably more in line with the rationale of the Convention and especially of Article 33(1). It would appear that this broader concept embraces even rejection at the frontier, with extremely important consequences for the admission of asylum-seekers and possibly also, more generally, of

the State is recognised as having complete freedom to decide whether to admit foreigners to its territory, as a rule the removal order will be lawful . . .' (trans. added).

209 The matter of extradition raised several questions: according to some statements made during the *travaux préparatoires*, the principle of *non-refoulement* did not apply to extradition proceedings. The British delegate Mr Hoare commented that 'The matter of extradition treaties between countries of refuge and countries of persecution was outside the purview of the Convention' (Conference of Plenipotentiaries on the Status of Refugees and Stateless Persons: Summary Record of the Sixteenth Meeting, 11 July 1951, A/CONF.2/SR.16, p. 13), while the French delegate Mr Rochefort asked 'that the summary record of the meeting should state that article 33 was without prejudice to the right of extradition' (Conference of Plenipotentiaries on the Status of Refugees and Stateless Persons: Summary Record of the Thirty-Fifth Meeting, 3 December 1951, A/CONF.2/SR.35, p. 21). Subsequent practice went in the opposite direction, however: see G. S. Goodwin-Gill and J. McAdam (2007: 258 ff.). Legal theory on this point is clear: see P. Weis (1995: 342) and E. Lauterpacht and D. Bethlehem (2003: 112 ff.). UNHCR has also pronounced positively on the matter: see UNHCR (1997c: para. D).

210 Conference of Plenipotentiaries on the Status of Refugees and Stateless Persons: Summary Record of the Sixteenth Meeting, p. 6. However, as J. C. Hathaway (2005: 355) rightly points out, Mr Zutter probably (see also footnote 405) wished to exclude mass inflows of displaced persons from the scope of Article 33. On this point see also A. Grahl-Madsen (1997: 136–7) and G. S. Goodwin-Gill and J. McAdam (2007: 206–7). The US continued to hold the same position as the Swiss delegate even at the end of the 1980s: see the statements made by Mr Kelly to UNHCR EXCOM during the discussion of a document on international protection, A/AC.96/SR.442, para. 80 ff.

211 See A. Grahl-Madsen (1966–1972, II: 94), according to whom 'Article 33 only prohibits the expulsion or return (*refoulement*) of refugees to territories where they are likely to suffer persecution; it does not obligate the Contracting States to admit any person who has not already set foot on their respective territories'. See also A. M. Calamia (1980: 124 ff.) and, with some signs of a more open approach, P. Weis (1966: 183 ff.).

any alien without entry papers.[212] In fact, as the alternative to temporary admission is the removal of the asylum-seeker, a contracting State can only take such action after having ascertained that the measure does not fall within the scope of the prohibition on *refoulement*. In other words, because the State does not know whether failure to admit an asylum-seeker, which is normally followed by removal, violates the prohibition on *refoulement*, it must, if it wishes to remove that person, first determine by appropriate means that the territory of destination is not one where he or she will be at risk of persecution. It also follows – and this is the important point – that for the purpose and duration of the determination process the State must temporarily admit the asylum-seeker until it can assess whether he or she is deserving of the protection afforded by the Convention or whether, as a result of one or more impediments, he or she can be removed without the State violating any of its obligations.

There is ample support for this interpretation of Article 33(1).[213] As noted in the literature, the joint reading of this article with Article 31(1) of the Refugee Convention already implies that asylum-seekers enjoy a right of entry and temporary residence.[214] Article 31(1) obligates States not to impose any penalties on refugees who enter the host country *illegally* provided they come directly from a territory in which they risk persecution.[215] Not acknowledging that refugees arriving at the frontier – and who therefore have not yet entered the territory of the host country – have the right to cross it and to remain in the country would in fact create an unjustified and indeed unusual discrimination: persons who had entered the host country illegally would enjoy the protection afforded by Article 33(1),

212 Note that the obligation on States to admit a person arriving at their frontier and to initiate proceedings to determine whether he or she fulfils the conditions for recognition of refugee status should not, in all logic, depend on the presentation of an official application. In other words, the host country should begin steps to verify the lawfulness of any removal order and in the meantime admit the person to its territory (assuming he or she does not have other entry documents) even though no application has been made for recognition of refugee status. While there may still be some doubts in this regard as far as the Refugee Convention is concerned, the situation is clear in respect of the Rome Convention; the ECtHR has ruled clearly on the point: judgment of 23 February 2012, Application No. 27765/09, *Hirsi Jamaa et al.* v. *Italy* (*Hirsi Jamaa*), available online at www.echr.coe.int, para. 133: 'Having regard to the circumstances of the case, the fact that the parties concerned had failed to explicitly request asylum did not exempt Italy from fulfilling its obligations under Article 3'. See also below, § 4.7.

213 It is the prevailing interpretation in legal theory. See J. C. Hathaway (2005: 301), according to whom 'Art. 33 amounts to a de facto duty to admit refugees, since admission is normally the only means of avoiding the alternative, impermissible consequence of exposure to risk'. The same position is taken by N. Coleman (2003: 40 ff.), E. Lauterpacht and D. Bethlehem (2003: 113), G. S. Goodwin-Gill and J. McAdam (2007: 206 ff.), A. Hurwitz (2009: 176) and C. W. Wouters (2009: 148 ff.). For the opposite opinion see the references in footnote 211.

214 I. Castrogiovanni (1994: 476).

215 However, Article 31 also requires such persons to report immediately to the authorities and to show good reason why they entered the territory of the host country illegally. On this point see § 1.8.

being already in the territory, while persons *attempting* to enter without the necessary papers could be turned back at the frontier and so forgo, probably for ever, any chance of applying for refugee status.[216]

The right of entry and temporary residence of asylum-seekers is also sanctioned in several documents of UNHCR and the UN General Assembly.[217] In its 2007 opinion regarding extraterritorial application of the *non-refoulement* principle, UNHCR explicitly states:

> As a general rule, in order to give effect to their obligations under the 1951 Convention and/or 1967 Protocol, States will be required to grant individuals seeking international protection *access to the territory.* . . .[218]

The Executive Committee of UNHCR has intervened on many occasions to defend and clarify the principle of *non-refoulement*. In 1993 it issued a note stating that

> Respect for the principle of non-refoulement requires that asylum-seekers, that is, persons who claim to be refugees, be protected against return to a place where their life or freedom might be threatened until their status as refugees has been reliably ascertained.[219]

In its Conclusion No. 82 of 1997 the Executive Committee, calling on States to respect the institution of asylum, emphasised even more strongly 'the need to *admit* refugees into the territories of States, which includes no rejection at frontiers'.[220]

216 Moreover, according to E. Lauterpacht and D. Bethlehem (2003: 117), the principle of *non-refoulement* is applied also to refusal of entry as a result of its juxtaposition to Article 31(1): 'To the extent that Article 31 applies regardless of whether a person who meets the criteria of a refugee has been formally recognized as such, it follows, a fortiori, that the same appreciation must apply to the operation of Article 33(1) of the Convention. The refoulement of a refugee would put him or her at much greater risk than would the imposition of penalties for illegal entry. It is inconceivable, therefore, that the Convention should be read as affording greater protection in the latter situation than in the former'. This argument assumes that the penalties mentioned in Article 31(1) may involve some form of *refoulement*, which has to be ruled out (see § 1.8).
217 For a more general overview of the practice of the UN and UNHCR regarding this concept of *non-refoulement* see G. S. Goodwin-Gill and J. McAdam (2007: 211 ff.).
218 UNHCR (2007a: para. 8, emphasis added).
219 Note on International Protection (submitted by the High Commissioner), UNHCR EXCOM, 31 August 1993, A/AC.96/815, para. 11.
220 UNHCR EXCOM Conclusion on Safeguarding Asylum No. 82 (XLVIII), 1997, available online at www.refworld.org, para. d) (emphasis added). See also UNHCR EXCOM General Conclusion No. 55 (XL), 1989, para. c); UNHCR EXCOM Conclusions on international protection No. 85 (XLIX), 1998, para. q); and UNHCR EXCOM General Conclusion No. 90 (LV), 2004, para. l), all available online at www. refworld.org. Regarding the obligation on States to admit asylum-seekers to their territory, see also the UNHCR Report, 1 September 1989, A/44/12, which, although

The UN General Assembly pronounced on the same lines as UNHCR and the Executive Committee, although less systematically: in Resolution 52/103 of 12 December 1997, after affirming 'that everyone is entitled to the right to seek and enjoy in other countries asylum from persecution', it called on States

> to refrain from taking measures that jeopardize the institution of asylum, in particular by returning or expelling refugees or asylum-seekers contrary to international human rights and to humanitarian and refugee law.[221]

The well-known Declaration on Territorial Asylum, unanimously adopted in 1997 by the General Assembly, attests to an obligation, albeit not absolute, of States to guarantee admission to persons who seek 'asylum from persecution', in accordance with Article 14 of the Universal Declaration of Human Rights.[222]

Moving away from the interpretation of Article 33(1) of the Refugee Convention, other international instruments give an equally broad meaning to the term *refoulement*. Article 2(3) of the Organization of African Unity (OUA) Convention Governing Refugee Problems makes clear reference, in setting out the prohibition on *refoulement*, to the case of 'rejection at the frontier'.[223] The Asian-African Legal Consultative Organization (AALCO) recently expressed the same opinion, reaffirming the principles laid down by the Committee of that name which

admitting that there is no formal legal obligation for States to admit asylum-seekers, asserts that responsibility to admit 'derives from broader obligations towards refugees, which depend, for their fulfilment, on the person being admitted and having his or her status determined'.

221 UNGA Resolution 52/103 (12 December 1997) A/RES/52/103, para. 5. On this point see also UNGA Resolution 50/152 (21 December 1995) A/RES/50/152; Resolution 53/125 (12 February 1999) A/RES/53/125; Resolution 54/146 (17 December 1999) A/RES/54/146; and Resolution 55/74 (4 December 2000) A/RES/55/74. A similar statement can be found in the Vienna Declaration and Programme of Action adopted by the World Conference on Human Rights, held in Vienna from 14 to 25 June 1993, A/CONF.157/24, para. 23.

222 According to Article 3 of the Declaration on Territorial Asylum adopted by UNGA Resolution 2312 (14 December 1967) A/RES/2312 (XXII), no asylum-seeker, in the sense specified by Article 14 of the Universal Declaration of Human Rights, 'shall be subjected to measures such as rejection at the frontier or, if he has already entered the territory in which he seeks asylum, expulsion or compulsory return to any State where he may be subjected to persecution'. The Declaration on Territorial Asylum allows some exceptions, in particular, 'for overriding reasons of national security or in order to safeguard the population, as in the case of a mass influx of persons'. The exceptions to the prohibition on *refoulement* are discussed in the following pages (§ 1.5 ff.). For other comments on the Declaration see M. Udina (1968: 293 ff.).

223 Organization of African Unity Convention Governing the Specific Aspects of Refugee Problems in Africa (adopted Addis Ababa 10 September 1969 and entered into force 20 June 1974) 1001 UNTS 45 ff. Forty-five members of the African Union (AU), which replaced the OAU, among the 53 States party to the AU, are members of the Convention.

preceded it.[224] There are also numerous documents attributable to the Council of Europe and, particularly, to the European Convention on Human Rights (ECHR). The various approaches to the prohibition on *refoulement* embodied in these instruments are examined later (see Chapter 2), but it is worth recalling here that the same position as the OAU Convention and the Principles drawn up by the AALCO ('rejection at the frontier') had already been adopted by the Committee of Ministers of the Council of Europe in 1967 when it called on States to

> ensure that no one shall be subjected to refusal of admission at the frontier, rejection, expulsion or any other measure which would have the result of compelling him to return to, or remain in, a territory where he would be in danger of persecution for reasons of race, religion, nationality, membership of a particular social group or political opinion;[225]

and was again expressed a few years later by the Parliamentary Assembly of the Council of Europe.[226] Concepts not too dissimilar to these have been expressed in Latin America: in 2004 a number of States approved a Declaration and a Plan of Action to strengthen the international protection of refugees,[227] followed in 2010 by a Declaration on Protection in the Americas.[228] The preambles to both

---

224 See Article III(1) of the Asian-African Legal Consultative Organization Final Text of the 1966 Bangkok Principles on Status and Treatment of Refugees as adopted 24 June 2001 at AALCO's Fortieth Session, New Delhi, available online at www.aalco.int. The AALCO was formed as a result of the Conference held in Bandung, Indonesia, 18 to 24 April, which led, among other things, to the creation in November 1956 of an international organisation known as the Asian Legal Consultative Committee (ALCC), of which Burma (Myanmar), Ceylon (Sri Lanka), India, Indonesia, Iran, Japan and the United Arab Republic (which split back into Egypt and Syria) were part. In order to allow some of the African States to join, in April 1958 the ALCC changed its name to the Asian-African Legal Consultative Committee (AALCC), which it kept until 2001 when it became the AALCO. At present it has 47 member States from the two continents of Asia and Africa.

225 Committee of Ministers Resolution, 29 June 1967, (67) 14, 'Asylum to Persons in Danger of Persecution', available online at www.coe.int, para. 2.

226 'No alien shall be subjected to measures such as rejection at the frontier, return, expulsion or extradition, which would result in compelling him to return to or to remain in either a territory in which he has well-founded fear of being persecuted for reasons of his race, religion, nationality, membership of a particular social group or political opinion, or a territory where he is in danger of being sent to such a territory': Recommendation 769 (1975) 3 October 1975, 'Legal Status of Aliens', available online at www.coe.int. The Parliamentary Assembly only acquired its name in September 1974, following a decision by the Committee of Ministers, but no change was made to the Statute of the Council of Europe which continues to refer to it as the Consultative Assembly; its present name will be used from now on.

227 Mexico Declaration and Plan of Action to Strengthen the International Protection of Refugees in Latin American, Mexico City, 16 November 2004, available online at www.refworld.org.

228 Brasilia Declaration on the Protection of Refugees and Stateless Persons in the Americas, Brasilia, 11 November 2010, available online at www.refworld.org.

treaties explicitly include within the prohibition on *refoulement* a right of asylum-seekers to not be rejected at the frontier, which is reinforced by the references to the treaties found in recent resolutions of the General Assembly of the Organization of American States (OAS).[229]

Alongside this trend, however, it has been the practice among a few States to deny asylum-seekers entry into their territory by a number of means.[230] In recent decades, and especially since the beginning of the present century, there have been several episodes of this type.[231] However, such instances have provoked fairly strong reactions among the international community, prompting the States concerned to attempt a justification of their actions by citing the alleged exceptions to the prohibition on *refoulement*, while not denying that it covers rejection at the frontier. For example, during the Second Gulf War and consequent fall of Saddam Hussein, Jordan and Syria were faced with a massive influx of fleeing Iraqis and justified closing their frontiers on the grounds that they were economically and materially unable to cope with such a major event without the help of the international community, not because they alleged there was no prohibition on such rejection.[232] The same argument was used by Pakistan when large numbers of Afghans arrived at the border after the Taliban gained power and especially after 11 September and the ensuing war.[233] Just a few months before closing the frontier with Colombia and ordering military intervention to stem the influx of people, the Venezuelan president Hugo Chavez, responding to the first signs of an exodus that would swell dramatically in the following months, issued a statement to the press in which he promised not to send anyone fleeing Colombia back to certain death.[234] Moreover, during the affair of the Norwegian ship *Tampa*,[235] Australia – making a decisive contribution to the introduction of the so-called Pacific Solution – did not deny that the prohibition on *refoulement* also applied to asylum-seekers who had not yet entered the territory of the State, but ruled that there could be no violation where non-admission of such persons was followed by their return to a 'safe' country in which they would not be at risk of persecution per Article 33(1) of the Refugee Convention.[236]

229 See Resolution 2597 (8 June 2010) 'Protection of Asylum Seekers and Refugees in the Americas', AG/RES.2597 (XL-O/10), OASGA, Fortieth Regular Session, Lima, Peru, June 6–8, 2010, *Proceedings*, vol. I, p. 379 ff.; and Resolution 2678 (7 June 2011) 'Protection of Asylum Seekers and Refugees in the Americas', AG/RES.2678 (XLI-O/11), OASGA, Forty-first Regular Session, San Salvador, El Salvador, June 5–7, 2011, ibid., vol. I, p. 248 ff.
230 For an authoritative account see G. S. Goodwin-Gill and J. McAdam (2007: 208).
231 Broadly, on this point see J. C. Hathaway (2005: 279 ff.).
232 On this point see R. Bettis (2010: 264).
233 See J. C. Hathaway (2005: 281–2).
234 'Venezuela set to repatriate Colombians who fled violence', 5 June 1999, available online at www.cnn.com.
235 See C. M.-J. Bostock (2002: 279 ff.), M. Fornari (2002: 61 ff.), C. M. Bailliet (2003: 741 ff.) and also A. Edwards (2003: 192 ff.), E. Willheim (2003: 160 ff.), T. Magner (2004: 53 ff.) and S. Kneebone (2006: 696 ff.).
236 On the Pacific Solution see below in this section.

A last example is the conduct of Italy in applying cooperation agreements with Libya against irregular immigration (recently confirmed by the Monti Government with the new Libyan government).[237] These are the Accordo di Roma of 13 December 2000,[238] which consists mainly of a programme of action against terrorism, organised crime, drug trafficking and illegal immigration,[239] and its two protocols, signed in Tripoli on 29 December 2007,[240] and the treaty of friendship of 30 August 2008, Article 19 of which reiterates and reaffirms the contents of the previous agreements.[241] A delegation from the European Committee for the Prevention of Torture (CPT), the controlling body set up under the Convention of the same name,[242] visited Italy from 27 to 31 July 2009 to examine 'the new policy . . . of the Italian authorities to intercept, at sea, migrants approaching Italy's Southern Mediterranean maritime border and to send them back to Libya or other non-European States'.[243] After recalling

237 See M. Castellaneta (2012), which contains the minutes of the meeting in Tripoli on 3 April 2012 between the Italian Minister of the Interior Annamaria Cancellieri and her opposite number in Libya H. E. Fawzi El-Taher Abdulali, published in the Italian daily newspaper *La Stampa*. According to the article, 'in a prevailing climate of mutual understanding, harmony and reciprocal respect, the two parties agreed the following: . . . The urgent need for Libya to assess the requirements associated with control of its borders, immediately informing the Italian authorities thereof, without prejudice to Libya's continued commitment to reinforce its sea and land frontiers with a view to impeding departures of migrants from its territory' (trans. added). See also U. Villani (2012: 9 ff.).
238 Accordo tra il governo della Repubblica italiana e la Grande Giamahiria Araba Libica Popolare Socialista per la collaborazione nella lotta al terrorismo, alla criminalità organizzata, al traffico illegale di stupefacenti e di sostanze psicotrope ed all'immigrazione clandestina, *GURI*, Supplemento ordinario, Serie Generale n. 111, 15 May 2003, p. 55 ff.
239 According to N. Ronzitti (2009a: 3).
240 These are the Protocollo tra la Repubblica italiana e la Grande Giamahiria Araba Libica Popolare Socialista and the Protocollo aggiuntivo tecnico-operativo (on technical cooperation). The signing of the agreements was announced by the Ministry of the Interior (see *Immigrazione clandestina: il ministro dell'Interno Amato firma a Tripoli un accordo per il pattugliamento congiunto della costa libica*, 29 December 2007, available online at www.interno.it) but the text was not published: it can be found at www.ilvelino.it. The two protocols were implemented with some delay, mainly because of resistance on the part of Libya, by a Protocollo di attuazione of 4 February 2009. See, particularly on Italian–Libyan cooperation, C. Fioravanti (2009: 539 ff.), R. Andrijasevic (2010: 148 ff.), A. Di Pascale (2010: 281 ff.), S. Klepp (2010b: 77 ff.) and E. Paoletti (2010: 54 ff.).
241 Trattato di amicizia, partenariato e cooperazione tra il governo della Repubblica italiana e la Grande Giamahiria Araba Libica Popolare Socialista, signed at Bengasi on 30 August 2008, ratified by Law No. 7 of 6 February 2009, *GURI*, Serie Generale n. 40, 18 February 2009, p. 1 ff. On the treaty in general see N. Ronzitti (2009b: 125 ff.) and V. Delicato (2011: 279 ff.).
242 European Convention for the Prevention of Torture and Inhuman or Degrading Treatment or Punishment (adopted Strasbourg 26 November 11987) 1561 UNTS 363 ff., on which see, in general, M. Fornari (2006: 571 ff.).
243 Report of the European Committee for the Prevention of Torture, 28 April 2010, CPT/Inf (2010) 14, available online at www.cpt.coe.int, para. 3.

the nature of the obligation associated with the prohibition on *refoulement*,[244] the Committee criticised fairly explicitly Italy's policy regarding the implementation of its cooperation agreements with Libya and called on the authorities 'to substantially review forthwith the current practice of intercepting migrants at sea'.[245] In response the Italian government did not deny that the principle of *non-refoulement* also covered the non-admission of asylum-seekers, but put forward the argument – in reality, fairly paradoxical – that none of the people 'rescued' on the high seas and then handed over to the Libyan authorities 'expressed his/her intention to apply for asylum'.[246] The Committee had no difficulty countering this by pointing out, as affirmed above,[247] that 'the absence of an explicit request for asylum does not necessarily absolve the Italian authorities of their *non-refoulement* obligations'.[248] The Italian government attempted to defend its agreements with Libya, including before national bodies, by reiterating the argument put forward to the CPT. Thus, during a debate in the Senate on 2 March 2010, the then Minister for the Interior Roberto Maroni explained that the operations to return 'illegal immigrants' to Libya were conducted 'in compliance with the principle of *non-refoulement* because none of the illegal immigrants intercepted were refused the opportunity to ask for asylum'.[249]

244 'As a result of the principle of *non-refoulement*, States are obliged to screen intercepted migrants with a view to identifying persons in need of protection, assessing those needs and taking appropriate action' (ibid., para. 30).
245 Ibid., para. 51.
246 Response of Italy of 26 February 2010 on the Report of the CPT following the latter's *ad hoc* mission to Italy, CPT/Inf (2010) 15, available online at www.cpt.coe.int, para. 3.
247 See footnote 212.
248 Report of the CPT of 28 April 2010, para. 32.
249 Speech by the Minister for the Interior Roberto Maroni at the joint session of the Chamber of Deputies and Senate during the debate on the Resolution (Doc. XVIII, n. 16) of the Third Standing Committee on the Communication of the Commission to the European Parliament, the Council, the European Economic and Social Committee and the Committee of Regions, *Strengthening the global approach to migration: increasing coordination, coherence and synergies*, (COM/2008/611final) and motions 1-00190, 1-00245, 1-00246, 1-00247 and 1-00250 presented at the Senate sitting No. 343 of 2 March 2010, available online in Italian at www.senato.it (trans. added). The government had already used the same argument, expressed by the Undersecretary of the Interior Nitto Francesco Palma, during the debate on the motions proposed by Soro and others (1-00260), Di Pietro and others (1-00230), Pezzotta and others (1-00266) and Cicchitto, Cota, Lo Monte and others (1-00275), concerning measures to counter illegal immigration and ensure compliance with constitutional and international rules, with special reference to rejection measures, which took place at the Chamber of Deputies sitting No. 251 of 24 November 2009, available online in Italian at www.camera.it. Curiously, in a previous disclosure to the Senate at sitting No. 214 of 25 May 2009, available online in Italian at www.senato.it, Roberto Maroni had stated that 'the joint patrols carried out so far do not, therefore, involve either rejection at the Italian frontier nor failure to rescue at sea', before adding shortly after that 'the permissive policy and merely apparent solidarity of previous years has generated insecurity and hostility, while a policy of rigorous return and rejection at the

The principle that the prohibition on *refoulement* applies to measures taken by States at the frontier is further confirmed, and indeed reinforced, by the standard practice relating to its extraterritorial application. Several States have asserted, and continue to assert, that the prohibition does not apply outside their territory. In reality, this alleged territorial limitation arises out of some States' need to ensure that operations carried out beyond their territorial waters do not fall within the scope of the prohibition. Perhaps the best-known example is that of the policy followed by the United States to prevent illegal immigration following its agreement with Haiti, which was first set out in Executive Order 12.324 of 29 September 1981, then confirmed (and tightened) by Executive Order 12.807 of 24 May 1992, both authorising the Coast Guard to reject asylum-seekers, particularly from Haiti, on their way to the US coast.[250] Other examples include the creation of a zone, called according to the case 'international zone' or 'migration zone', in which, based on a theory upheld precisely by the United States,[251] the rule of law (including the prohibition on *refoulement*) is somehow 'suspended' because, again, the said zones are outside the territory of the State concerned.[252]

While this may be a minority practice – and regardless of its implications, however significant, for the law of the sea[253] – it is clearly disputed by a number of elements confirming that the prohibition on *refoulement* does not cease to apply outside the territory of the State. The first of these is a general argument easily deduced from the practice of the courts regarding human rights treaties and the structure of State responsibility that arises from it. Violation of the rules embodied in such treaties has long been associated with the overall control exercised by the State, the territory in which the State's action takes place merely constituting

frontier, *as part of Italian–Libyan cooperation*, is in line with the European Pact on Immigration' (trans. and emphasis added).

250 Executive Order 12.807 eliminated even the summary screening that took place on vessels of the US Coast Guard following the massive increase in the influx of people from Haiti when Jean-Bertrand Aristide took power. For the text of the agreement see M. N. Leich (1982: 374 ff.). On US policy regarding immigrants from the Caribbean see, more generally, S. H. Legomsky (2006: 607 ff.).

251 I refer here to the well-known position of the US concerning the 'extraterritoriality' of its base at Guantanamo.

252 It was at one time the policy of France and other European States to create 'international zones' where they could conduct very summary screenings of asylum applications that inevitably resulted in mass rejections: on this point see J. C. Hathaway (2005: 298). Of far greater impact is Australia's Pacific Solution, which consists in diverting asylum-seekers arriving by sea either towards 'safe' third countries (see below § 1.6) or towards one of a number of islands which form part of the territory of Australia (such as Milingimbi Island, less than two miles from the mainland coast) but have been designated 'migration zones' by the government. Screening procedures are conducted there in flagrant violation of the standards required by the Refugee Convention. See A. Edwards (2003: 192 ff.), T. Magner (2004: 53 ff.) and S. Kneebone (2006: 696 ff.).

253 On the implications for the law of the sea see S. Trevisanut (2008b: 205 ff.; 2011: 241 ff.). See also R. Barnes (2004: 47 ff.) and B. Miltner (2006–2007: 75 ff.).

evidence. Thus, one the ECtHR – from the judgment in the case of *Loizidou*[254] to the more recent one in *Hirsi Jamaa*, which specifically involves a case of *refoulement at sea*[255] – has rejected arguments put forward by the defendant States based on the extraterritoriality of the place where the conduct of which they are accused took place, and has clearly ruled that the decisive criterion is that of overall control or, to use the wording of Article 1 ECHR, of State 'jurisdiction'.[256] This concept has been reiterated by other bodies supervising international human rights protection. For example, the Human Rights Committee set up under the International Covenant on Civil and Political Rights (ICCPR) has expressed the same view.[257] More importantly, the Inter-American Commission on Human Rights (IACHR) itself took the very same position in respect of US policy on Haitian asylum-seekers.[258] Lastly, the Committee of the UN Convention against

254 ECtHR, judgment of 18 December 1996, Application No. 15318/89, *Loizidou* v. *Turkey (Loizidou)*, available online at www.echr.coe.int.

255 *Hirsi Jamaa*. For initial comments see F. Lenzerini (2012: 721 ff.), A. Liguori (2012: 415 ff.), V. Moreno-Lax (2012: 574 ff.), N. Napoletano (2012: 436 ff.), U. Villani (2012: 491 ff.) and M. den Heijer (2013: 265 ff.).

256 The judgment in the case of *Hirsi Jamaa*, para. 74, reads: 'Whenever the State through its agents operating outside its territory exercises control and authority over an individual, and thus jurisdiction, the State is under an obligation under Article 1 to secure to that individual the rights and freedoms under Section 1 of the Convention that are relevant to the situation of that individual'.

257 See the Consideration by the Human Rights Committee, 29 July 1981, Communication No. R.12/52, *Sergio Euben Lopez Burgos* v. *Uruguay*, available online at www.umn.edu, especially para. 12(3), and on the same date Communication No. R.56/1979, *Lilian Celiberti de Casariego* v. *Uruguay*, ibid., especially para. 10(3). Article 2(1) ICCPR affirms that States parties are required 'to respect and to ensure to all individuals within its territory and *subject to its jurisdiction* the rights recognized in the present Covenant' (emphasis added). The Human Rights Committee has provided a general clarification of the meaning of this article: 'This means that a State Party must respect and ensure the rights laid down in the Covenant to anyone within the power or effective control of that State Party, even if not situated within the territory of the State Party'; and moreover 'This principle also applies to those within the power or effective control of the forces of a State Party acting outside its territory, regardless of the circumstances in which such power or effective control was obtained, such as forces constituting a national contingent of a State Party assigned to an international peace-keeping or peace-enforcement operation' (Human Rights Committee, General Comment No. 31, *The Nature of the General Legal Obligation Imposed on States Parties to the Covenant*, 29 March 2004, CCPR/C/21/Rev.1/Add. 13, available online as www.un.org, para. 10).

258 IACHR, decision of 13 March 1997, Case 10.675, *The Haitian Centre for Human Rights et al.* v. *United States*, available online at www.cidh.org, especially para. 156 ff. The Commission has reiterated the concept in a more recent ruling, also against the US: see the decision of 29 September 1999, Case 10.951, *Coard et al.* v. *United States*, ibid., especially para. 37, which reads: 'the Commission finds it pertinent to note that, under certain circumstances, the exercise of its jurisdiction over acts with an extraterritorial locus will not only be consistent with but required by the norms which pertain'. The IACHR's authority extends, by virtue of the joint provisions of Article 106 of the Charter of the OAS (Bogotà, 30 April 1948, 119 UNTS 48 ff.), Article 20 of the

Torture has voiced exactly the same opinion.[259] The International Court of Justice (ICJ), in its famous opinion on the *Legal Consequences of the Construction of a Wall in the Occupied Palestinian Territory*, stated, referring to Article 2(1) of the ICCPR, that 'while the jurisdiction of States is primarily territorial, it may sometimes be exercised outside the national territory'.[260]

Other arguments more closely based on Article 33(1) of the Refugee Convention weigh in favour of the extraterritorial application of the prohibition on *refoulement*. As UNHCR underlines, the article contains no restrictions of a territorial nature:

> The obligation set out in Article 33(1) of the 1951 Convention is subject to a geographic restriction only with regard to the country where a refugee may not be sent to, not the place where he or she is sent from.[261]

Therefore, according to UNHCR, as well as virtually all scholarly writers,[262] Article 33(1) only considers the asylum-seeker's destination, not the place from which he or she was rejected, and the only question becomes whether that rejection is attributable to the State in accordance with the rules of international law.[263] Moreover, again according to UNHCR, if the prohibition on *refoulement* applies

Statute of the IACHR and Articles 51 and 52 of its Procedural Rules, even to States members of the organisation which, like the US, have not ratified the American Convention on Human Rights (San José, 22 November 1969, 1144 UNTS 144 ff.). For such States, the Commission's critique is based on several provisions of the American Declaration of the Rights and Duties of Man of 1948.

259 See Conclusions and recommendations of the Committee against Torture, United States, CAT/C/USA/CO/2, 25 July 2006, available online at www.un.org, para. 20 (note that the concerns expressed by the Committee related, among other things, to the US policy mentioned in footnote 251).

260 ICJ, opinion of 9 July 2004, 'Legal Consequences of the Construction of a Wall in the Occupied Palestinian Territory', *I.C.J. Reports*, 2004, p. 136 ff., para. 109. However, the criterion applied by the ICJ to attribute responsibility to a State for alleged violations of international law, and especially of the provisions safeguarding human rights, is very different from the criterion applied by other international judges, first and foremost the ECtHR. Indeed, the ICJ deviates from the principle of overall control adopted by the ECtHR (see, for example, ICJ, judgment of 27 June 1986, 'Military and Paramilitary Activities in and against Nicaragua', and more recently its judgment of 26 February 2007, 'Application of the Convention on the Prevention and Punishment of the Crime of Genocide', *I.C.J. Reports*, respectively 1986, p. 14 ff., especially para. 115 ff., and 2007, p. 43 ff. especially para. 402 ff.).

261 UNHCR (2007a: para. 26).

262 Among the many champions of an interpretation of the principle of *non-refoulement* in favour of its extraterritorial nature see C. M. Bailliet (2003: 751), E. Lauterpacht and D. Bethlehem (2003: 68 ff.), A. Roberts (2004: 745 ff.), J. C. Hathaway (2005: 335 ff.), G. S. Goodwin-Gill and J. McAdam (2007: 244 ff.) and A. Fischer-Lescano, T. Löhr and T. Tohidipur (2009: 256 ff.).

263 However, see footnote 260. On this point see also M. Arcari (2007: 565 ff.) and M. Frulli (2007: 579 ff.).

to refugees (or asylum-seekers) who have not yet entered the host country, then equally it must be possible for any action by a State that has a bearing on compliance to be performed outside its territory.[264] Accordingly, UNHCR calls attention to the use of the term '*refouler*' in Article 33(1), which was included specifically to extend the scope of the article to the case of refugees (or asylum-seekers) who are merely about to cross the frontier of a State.[265]

There are other, more systematic arguments in favour of such an interpretation: not following it would betray the very rationale of the Refugee Convention which, being of a humanitarian nature, would lose all useful purpose.[266] A State would only need to move controls beyond its frontiers to evade the prohibition on *refoulement*, a practice that is anyway forbidden by the general rule, enshrined in Article 26 of the Vienna Convention on the Law of Treaties, that every treaty must be performed in good faith.[267]

The US Supreme Court found in favour of the government in the case of Haitian asylum-seekers, sanctioning the political strategy set out in Executive Order 12.807. The decision upholds the territorial nature of the prohibition on *refoulement* set out in the Refugee Convention, at Article 33(2), which in establishing some exceptions to the rule makes explicit reference to the country which the refugee is in.[268] In the Court's opinion,

> If Article 33.1 applied extraterritorially, therefore, Article 33.2 would create an absurd anomaly: Dangerous aliens on the high seas would be entitled to the benefits of 33.1 while those residing in the country that sought to expel them would not. It is more reasonable to assume that the coverage of 33.2 was limited to those already in the country because it was understood that 33.1 obligated the signatory state only with respect to aliens within its territory.[269]

264 UNHCR (2007a: paras 27–8).
265 'The ordinary meaning of "return" includes "to send back" or "to bring, send, or put back to a former or proper place". . . . It is difficult to conceive that these words are limited to refugees who have already entered the territory of a Contracting State. The ordinary meaning of the terms "return" and "refouler" does not support an interpretation which would restrict its scope to conduct within the territory of the State concerned, nor is there any indication that these terms were understood by the drafters of the 1951 Convention to be limited in this way' (UNHCR (2007a: para. 27)).
266 UNHCR (2007a: para. 29).
267 See A. Fischer-Lescano, T. Löhr and T. Tohidipur (2009: 270).
268 'The benefit of the present provision may not, however, be claimed by a refugee whom there are reasonable grounds for regarding as a danger to the security of the country *in which he is* . . .' (emphasis added).
269 US Supreme Court, decision of 21 June 1993, *Sale* v. *Haitian Centers Council (Sale)*, in *United States Reports*, vol. 509, 1997, pp. 179–80. For a criticism of the decision see I. Castrogiovanni (1994: 474) and H. H. Koh (1994: 1–2), as well as the references at footnote 262.

However, when reading rule and exception together, which the Court rightly appears to advocate, there is a crucial circumstance that should also be taken into account: although the rule was formulated in very narrow terms – at least according to the statements issued during the *travaux préparatoires*, to which the Court makes reference and which I have mentioned earlier – it has undergone considerable changes in the course of its practical application. Citing the *travaux préparatoires*, which cannot carry decisive weight,[270] in order to confirm the literal meaning of an exception without considering how the rule has evolved in practice is indeed an 'absurd anomaly'.[271]

Although the same line as the US Supreme Court has been followed in some cases, the standard practice tends in the opposite direction.[272] It is sufficient to consider the many statements of UNHCR Executive Committee reaffirming 'the fundamental importance of the observance of the principle of *non-refoulement* both at the border and within the territory of a State'.[273] And then there is national case law, which includes, to give just one example, the decision of the Court of Appeal of England and Wales in the case of the *European Roma Rights Centre*. Lord Brown, referring specifically to the decision of the US Supreme Court in *Sale*, declared it offended 'one's sense of fairness' and deemed it to be 'wrongly decided'.[274] It is

270 According to Article 32 of the Vienna Convention on the Law of Treaties (1155 UNTS 331 ff.) the *travaux préparatoires* are 'only' an aid to interpretation, designed to confirm the interpretation based on the general principles set out in its Article 31.
271 For this reason, I repute some of the arguments put forward, albeit by authoritative writers – see A. Fischer-Lescano, T. Löhr and T. Tohidipur (2009: 270) and also UNHCR (2007a: para. 28) – against the decision of the Supreme Court to be danger-ously misleading. To assume that there can only be danger to the security of the State when the refugee is inside its territory, or that the rule and the exception are based on different rationales as a means of diminishing the 'territorial' element of Article 33(2) also diminishes the value of the practice that has overturned the territorial nature of *non-refoulement* which in fact existed at the outset.
272 See, for all, Australian High Court, decision of 11 April 2002, *Minister for Immigration and Multicultral Affairs* v. *Khawar*, para. 42.
273 UNHCR EXCOM Conclusion on non-refoulement No. 6 (XXVIII), 1977, para. c). More explicit in relation to rejection at sea is the statement that 'It is the humanitarian obligation of all coastal States to allow vessels in distress to seek haven in their waters and to grant asylum, or at least temporary refuge, to persons on board wishing to seek asylum' (UNHCR EXCOM Conclusion on Refugees without an Asylum Country No. 15 (XXX), 1979, para. c)). See also UNHCR EXCOM Conclusion on Stowaway Asylum Seekers No. 53 (XXXIX), 1988, para. 2.
274 Court of Appeal (Civil Division) of England and Wales, decision of 20 May 2003, *European Roma Rights Centre and Others* v. *the Immigration Officer at Prague Airport and the Secretary of State for the Home Department (European Roma Rights Centre)*, para. 34. The decision was upheld by the House of Lords, which expressed, more hesitantly, the same position regarding the issue discussed here: see the opinion of Lord Bingham of Cornhill (House of Lords, decision of 9 December 2004, *Regina* v. *Immigration Officer at Prague Airport and Another, Ex parte European Roma Rights Centre and Others (Regina* v. *Immigration Officer at Prague Airport)*, para. 21). Lord Hope of Craighead, on the other hand, took the opposite view, agreeing fully with the *ratio decidendi* in *Sale* (ibid., para. 68 ff.).

highly significant that the opinion in the *Sale* decision was not shared by the whole bench: Justice Blackmun's dissenting opinion was extremely critical and amounted in places almost to a reprimand of the majority.[275] At one point it runs,

> Article 33.1 is clear not only in what it says, but also in what it does not say: It does not include any geographical limitation. It limits only where a refugee may be sent 'to', not where he may be sent from. This is not surprising, given that the aim of the provision is to protect refugees against persecution.[276]

As far as the other cases relating to the application of the principle of *non-refoulement* go, a distinction must be made. There can be no doubt that where the 'free zone' is within the territory of the State, as in Australia's Pacific Solution, the prohibition on *refoulement* and the obligations that derive from it (temporary entry and appropriate screening process) apply in full.[277] In fact, were it not for the 'quasi extraterritoriality' fiction created by Australia, the problem would not even arise, in that the islands where the prohibition becomes less binding are certainly inside the territory of the country, albeit at the very edge. Instead, where part of the State's alleged violation takes place in the territory of another State – as when officials from the UK conducted a very summary screening in a dedicated area inside Prague Airport and therefore outside the territory of the State – this is unlikely to constitute a violation of the prohibition on *refoulement* because the migrants are obviously not outside their own State of origin and therefore are not refugees.[278] At most, apart from the potential violation of other rules, including

---

275 According to Justice Blackmun, 'What is extraordinary in this case is that the Executive, in disregard of the law, would take to the seas to intercept fleeing refugees and force them back to their persecutors – and that the Court would strain to sanction that conduct' (dissenting opinion of Justice Blackmun in *Sale*, in *United States Reports*, vol. 509, 1997, p. 179); moreover, 'The ordinary meaning of "return" is "to bring, send, or put (a person or thing) back to or in a former position". . . . That describes precisely what petitioners are doing to the Haitians. By dispensing with ordinary meaning at the outset, and by taking instead as its starting point the assumption that "return", as used in the treaty, "has a legal meaning narrower than its common meaning", . . . the majority leads itself astray' (ibid., p. 191); and lastly, 'That the clarity of the text and the implausibility of its theories do not give the majority more pause is due, I think, to the majority's heavy reliance on the presumption against extraterritoriality. The presumption runs throughout the majority's opinion, and it stacks the deck by requiring the Haitians to produce "affirmative evidence" that, when Congress prohibited the return of "any" alien, it indeed meant to prohibit the interception and return of aliens at sea' (ibid., p. 205).

276 Ibid., p. 193.

277 See A. Edwards (2003: 192 ff.), T. Magner (2004: 53 ff.) and S. Kneebone (2006: 696 ff.).

278 Although the decision in the case of *European Roma Rights Centre* upheld the extraterritoriality of the prohibition on *refoulement*, the appeal was rejected, among other reasons because the applicants were not, as Article 1(A) of the Refugee Convention requires, 'outside the country of [their] nationality'. This view was upheld by the House of Lords in the decision in *Regina v. Immigration Officer at Prague Airport*. According to G. S. Goodwin-Gill and J. McAdam (2007: 250–1), this is why it is also unlikely that *refoulement* can be said to occur when the State's action takes place within

international treaties,[279] the State of origin may have infringed the right of its citizens to leave its territory, an offence to which the destination State (here the UK) would be party.[280]

1.4 B) Right to fair procedure

The obligations of States are influenced by a further factor. The duty to grant asylum-seekers temporary entry to their territory is not an end in itself, but it is clearly instrumental for determining refugee status. Because a contracting State may not reject asylum-seekers – and probably also, as we have seen, illegal migrants[281] – until it can be sure that they would not be at risk of persecution in the countries to which they are sent, it has only two options: to forgo any action to turn the asylum-seekers away if they have some other form of entitlement to be allowed into the country on a permanent basis, or to take steps to determine whether they have refugee status. If the outcome of the screening is negative, the State may authorise and carry out measures to remove the person (assuming this does not violate other international rules). If the outcome is positive, an obligation of protection arises that will endure as long as the conditions established by the Refugee Convention are met. In other words, when Article 33(1) prohibits the *refoulement* of 'refugees' it implies that they must be identified as such, thereby 'fixing' their presence in the territory of the State. It follows – although, as UNHCR notes,[282] this is not mentioned in the Refugee Convention[283] – that the process of determination is central to refugee status, which is the primary means of achieving

a diplomatic mission abroad, even though there may be other factors preventing the return of the person taking refuge there. On this point see also G. Noll (2005d: 542 ff.).

279 Note that the House of Lords granted the appeal on the grounds of violation of the principle of non-discrimination in the case *Regina* v. *Immigration Officer at Prague Airport*, para. 34.

280 For the sake of completeness it should be added that according to Article 40(1) of the Refugee Convention 'Any State may, at the time of signature, ratification or accession, declare that this Convention shall extend to all or any of the territories for the international relations of which it is responsible. Such a declaration shall take effect when the Convention enters into force for the State concerned'. This is known as the 'colonial clause', and it was meant to allow 'territories' without the required international subjectivity to participate. It is currently used by some States (Georgia and Moldova) to issue declarations designed to remove from the scope of the Convention those areas within their territory over which they do not have effective control. In general, on this article see M.-T. Gil-Bazo (2011: 1567 ff.).

281 See footnote 212.

282 UNHCR (1997a: para. 189).

283 The Refugee Convention does, however, contain a provision that may provide some information about procedure. This is Article 16(1), which states that 'A refugee shall have free access to the courts of law on the territory of all Contracting States'. Despite the enormous potential of this provision, it is unlikely that it can be applied in relation to the process of determining refugee status. On this point see B. Elberling (2011: 944 ff.).

the main purpose of the whole Convention, i.e. observance of the prohibition on *refoulement*.

There can be little doubt about the nature of this process, either in standard practice or, more importantly, in legal theory. Determination of refugee status must come about as a result of a procedure that follows due process of law, in that the State must acquire all the information needed to comply with the prohibition on *refoulement* and, consequently, to justify a possible removal of the applicant. UNHCR Executive Committee has issued a clear statement to this effect. In Conclusion No. 82 of 1997 it calls the attention of the contracting States to the need to guarantee 'access, consistent with the 1951 Convention and the 1967 Protocol, of asylum-seekers to *fair and effective procedures* for determining status and protection needs'.[284] The Committee describes in greater detail in Conclusion No. 8 of 1977 the rules governing the procedure for determining status, including the requirement that

> (vi) If the applicant is not recognized, he should be given a reasonable time to appeal for a formal reconsideration of the decision, either to the same or to a different authority, whether administrative or judicial, according to the prevailing system.[285]

This Conclusion is repeated verbatim in the *Handbook on Procedures and Criteria for Determining Refugee Status*[286] and has been reiterated by the Executive Committee on numerous subsequent occasions.[287]

While the procedure is under way the State must ensure that it serves a 'useful purpose', which would not happen if the applicant did not have the right to remain in the territory of the State. Since its inception the Executive Committee has firmly maintained that the asylum-seeker must be allowed to stay in the territory of the State where he or she has made the application for the whole duration of the procedure to determine status. Conclusion No. 8 of 1977 states that the applicant's residence in the territory of the State 'should be permitted . . . unless it has been established . . . that his request is clearly abusive'.[288] Indeed, as

---

284 Conclusion on Safeguarding Asylum No. 82, para. d) (emphasis added).
285 Conclusion on the Determination of Refugee Status No. 8 (XXVIII), 1977, available at www.refworld.org, para. e).
286 UNHCR (1997a: para. 189 ff., especially para. 192). See also UNHCR (2007a: para. 8), which states that 'As a general rule, in order to give effect to their obligations under the 1951 Convention and/or 1967 Protocol, States will be required to grant individuals seeking international protection access to the territory and to *fair and efficient asylum procedures*' (emphasis added).
287 See UNHCR EXCOM General Conclusion No. 55, para. f); General Conclusion No. 65 (XLII), 1991, para. o); General Conclusion No. 71 (XLIV), 1993, para. i); General Conclusion No. 81 (XLVIII), para. h); Conclusion on International Protection No. 85, para. q); and Conclusion on Reception of Asylum-Seekers in the Context of Individual Asylum Systems No. 93 (LIII), 2002, para. a), all available online at www.refworld.org.
288 Conclusion on the Determination of Refugee Status No. 8, para. E).

underlined in Conclusion No. 30 of 1983 dealing specifically with the problem of clearly unfounded or abusive requests, States must provide certain guarantees even in such cases, although they may conduct more summary procedures. One of these guarantees is to allow the applicant 'to have a negative decision reviewed before rejection at the frontier or forcible removal from the territory'.[289]

Authoritative writers have also stressed the importance of the procedural aspect of the prohibition on *refoulement*:

> the principle of *non-refoulement* ties in with the individual's right to enter and stay in the territory of the State for as long as necessary to complete the procedure with the necessary jurisdictional guarantees.[290]

It is the usual practice of States to ensure that the procedure to determine whether asylum-seekers are entitled to stay in the territory of the host country respects the parameters stipulated by UNHCR. Examples are to be found in the legislation of Brazil,[291] Canada,[292] Japan,[293] and

---

289 UNHCR EXCOM Conclusion on the Problem of Manifestly Unfounded or Abusive Applications for Refugee Status or Asylum No. 30 (**XXXIV**), 1983, available online at www.refworld.org, para. e).

290 F. Salerno (2011: 9, trans. added). The importance of the procedural aspect is emphasised by G. S. Goodwin-Gill and J. McAdam (2007: 529 ff.). The case law offers further confirmation: see, for example, US Court of Appeals, Ninth Circuit, decision of 14 December 2010, *Su Haw She* v. *Attorney General*, available online at www.ca9.uscourts.gov, especially para. 3.

291 Article 21 of Lei n. 9474 of 22 July 1997 provides for the assignment of a 'residência provisória' (temporary residence) to the asylum-seeker and family members during the procedure to determine status, while Article 30 recognises that 'Durante a avaliação do recurso, será permitido ao solicitante de refúgio e aos seus familiares permanecer no território nacional, sendo observado o disposto nos §§ 1° e 2° do artigo 21 desta Lei'. The application is made to the Ministry of Justice as Lei 9474/97 does not make provision for a role of the judicial authorities. However, as L. L. Jubilut (2006: 36) notes, 'a specific provision for access to the judicial system need not be mentioned in the law as it is implicit, on the basis that the 1988 Federal Constitution stipulates that laws cannot exclude from the appreciation of the judiciary any violation or possibility of violation of rights (Article 5, **XXXV**)'. The author adds that 'as refugees are for-eigners and are not familiar with the Brazilian legal system, the assurance of being able to take their cases to the judiciary seems relevant and a major aspect of the right to an effective remedy for violations of human rights'.

292 In Canada the matter is regulated by the Immigration and Refugee Protection Act, which divides the determination procedure into two stages, one before the Immigration and Refugee Board, the other before the Department of Citizenship and Immigration of the Ministry for Citizenship, Immigration and Multiculturalism (originally, a Refugee Appeal Division was also intended to have jurisdiction but it has not yet come into operation). The procedure is administrative and is subject to the review of the Federal Court. See G. P. Heckman (2008: 79 ff.).

293 The Immigration Control and Refugee Recognition Act (Cabinet Order No. 319 of 1951), which regulates the matter in Japan, makes provision for a 'permission for pro-visional stay' designed to officialise the asylum-seeker's position during determination

New Zealand.[294] Compliance is less uniform regarding the right to appeal an adverse decision: some States do not envisage such a right; others limit appeal to points of law only.[295] In the EU the rules are enshrined in the Asylum Procedures Directive.[296] One of the major guarantees that EU Member States must observe is set out in Article 7 of the Directive, which allows asylum-seekers 'to remain in the Member State, for the sole purpose of the procedure, until the determining authority has made a decision . . .'. Article 39 recognises the applicant's right to an effective remedy and, if the expulsion order is not suspended pending the outcome, stipulates that States must provide for 'the possibility of legal remedy or protective measures'.[297]

As mentioned earlier, UNHCR has published a guide to assist States in developing procedures for the determination of status, the *Handbook on Procedures and Criteria*. It is an extremely useful tool because the Refugee Convention contains no mention of required procedures. This shortcoming is understandable given the detail involved – drawing up rules of universal validity would have been further complicated by the diversity of national legal systems – but it might very well have undermined the whole structure of the Convention without the authoritative guidance of UNHCR. It is patently clear that it is on the State's determination procedure that recognition of refugee status effectively depends, and hence also enjoyment of the rights accorded by the Convention.[298]

The procedures adopted in the contracting States are not always designed simply to determine status, as UNHCR would wish.[299] In some cases determination of status is part of more general procedures for the admission of foreigners,

of status (Article 61–2(4)). This may be extended for the duration of the appeal procedure, which takes place before a section of the Ministry of Justice. As in many other countries, the decision of the Ministry of Justice is administrative and can be appealed before the competent authority. See S. Yamagami (1995: 60 ff.). The latest update of the Japanese regulations is explained in a leaflet published by the Immigration Bureau of the Ministry of Justice and titled *A Guide to the Procedure for Recognition of Refugee Status*, 2006, available online at www.immi-moj.go.jp.

294 See Immigration Act 2009, especially Sections 129 ff. and 193 ff.

295 See G. S. Goodwin-Gill and J. McAdam (2007: 535 ff.).

296 Council Directive 2005/85/EC of 1 December 2005 on minimum standards on procedures in Member States for granting and withdrawing refugee status, OJ L 326 of 13 December 2005, p. 13 ff., on which see § 4.7 below.

297 Similar rules are laid down in the new Procedures Directive, although the deadline for implementation has not yet passed: see Article 9 of Directive 2013/32/EU of the European Parliament and of the Council of 26 June 2013, on common procedures for granting and withdrawing international protection, OJ L 180 of 29 June 2013, p. 60 ff.

298 See footnote 205.

299 UNHCR (1997a: para. 190), according to which a request for asylum 'should . . . be examined within the framework of specially established procedures by qualified personnel having the necessary knowledge and experience, and an understanding of an applicant's particular difficulties and needs'.

in others of informal procedures.[300] As well as the minimum standards already mentioned (the right to stay in the territory of the host State during the process of determination and to appeal a negative decision), UNHCR has stipulated other requirements: the application for asylum must be examined by qualified personnel, preferably as part of an *ad hoc* procedure; the applicant must receive 'the necessary guidance as to the procedure to be followed'; the competent authority, preferably a single centralised body, must be clearly identified; and, lastly, the applicant has the right to the assistance of an interpreter and to contact UNHCR.[301]

A key part of the determination procedure is the evaluation of evidence. For obvious reasons asylum-seekers are unlikely to be able to provide more than their own testimony. Thus, although the burden to prove the facts on which the application is based naturally still lies with the applicant (the prospective refugee), UNHCR believes that the examiner has an independent duty to ascertain the facts, and cannot reject the version provided by the applicant merely because he or she is unable to provide documentary evidence.[302] A useful means of assessing the facts in cases like this, where evidence is almost totally lacking, is to make a credibility assessment. This involves assessing the reliability of the information provided by the applicant on the basis of such elements as the intrinsic consistency of his or her account of events (though not proven), contradictions with the account given in previous asylum applications, including in other countries, and so on. All this should emerge during the course of one or more interviews at which the applicant provides the most detailed account possible. A very important aspect in this regard is stressed by UNHCR, one which is not always taken into account in practice even though it is often decisive:[303]

> It will be necessary for the examiner to gain the confidence of the applicant in order to assist the latter in putting forward his case and in fully explaining his opinions and feelings.[304]

This is particularly important given that the applicant's experiences (i.e. of persecution) will normally lead him or her to be fearful of strangers, and that this is unlikely to help in obtaining a full account of the facts.

---

300 UNHCR (1997a: para. 191).
301 Ibid.: para 192. On this point, for the legal theory see G. S. Goodwin-Gill and J. McAdam (2007: 528 ff.).
302 UNHCR (1997a: para. 196).
303 See R. Rycroft (2005: 223 ff.).
304 UNHCR (1997a: para. 200). Special care should be taken with applicants belonging to 'vulnerable' categories. Thus, in the case of mentally disturbed people a doctor should normally be present, and in the case of unaccompanied minors there should be 'experts conversant with child mentality' (ibid.: para. 214).

1.5 Some controversial applications of the prohibition on *refoulement*: A) Exceptions per Article 33(2)

While it is clear that States must put in place a mechanism to provide specific guarantees before removing an asylum-seeker, equally the general practice appears to contemplate ostensible exceptions to the prohibition on *refoulement* to which States often appeal. Therefore, before looking at the other obligations, in addition to *non-refoulement*, which the Refugee Convention imposes on States, some observations should be made concerning these alleged exceptions. First, the Refugee Convention itself introduces an explicit exception to the principle of *non-refoulement*. Article 33(1) is not conclusive; the following clause (2) stipulates that the provisions of (1)

> may not, however, be claimed by a refugee whom there are reasonable grounds for regarding as a danger to the security of the country in which he is, or who having been convicted by a final judgment of a particularly serious crime, constitutes a danger to the community of that country.

The provision envisages two separate cases.[305] A refugee can be sent back to a country where he or she risks persecution if (a) there are reasonable grounds for considering that the person constitutes a security threat in the host country, and if (b) he or she has been convicted of a very serious offence and therefore may be a threat to the public. The provision clearly allows the removal of *refugees*, that is of people with the characteristics listed in Article 1A.[306] Its purpose is to protect the host country so that the principle of *non-refoulement* does not become a loophole through which its stability can be threatened. This point is illustrated by the words of the British delegate to the Conference of Plenipotentiaries that drafted the text of the Refugee Convention (when the exception was added by request of the British and French delegates): according to Mr Hoare, 'Among the great mass of refugees it was inevitable that some persons should be tempted to engage in activities on behalf of a foreign Power against the country of their asylum'.[307]

For a clearer understanding of how this exception to Article 33(1) works it is worth noting that its rationale is very close to, and often barely distinguishable from, that of similar but separate provisions. Indeed, elsewhere in the Refugee Convention we find clauses excluding specific categories of individuals from the concept of refugee (Article 1C–F)[308] and clauses that allow, on certain conditions, the expulsion of a refugee lawfully present in the territory of the host country (Article 32). The latter provision, as we know, prohibits the contracting States

---

305 See A. Grahl-Madsen (1997: 319).
306 According to J. C. Hathaway (2005: 344).
307 Conference of Plenipotentiaries on the Status of Refugees and Stateless Persons: Summary Record of the Sixteenth Meeting, p. 8.
308 See § 1.2 for an analysis of these provisions.

from expelling 'a refugee lawfully in their territory save on grounds of national security or public order' (Article 32(1)) and obligates them to ensure the procedure follows due process of law in accordance with Article 32(2). Article 32 is discussed more in detail below (see § 1.8), but a brief comparison with Article 33 highlights some evident differences of language. Article 32 mentions only refugees 'lawfully in' the territory of the host country, while Article 33 refers, more generally, to refugees; Article 32 does not use all the verb forms of Article 33 ('expel or return ("refouler")'), only the first ('expel'); furthermore, Article 33 makes no reference to due process of law; lastly, Article 32 does not mention expulsion to countries where the refugee would be at risk of persecution, while this is explicitly stated in Article 33.

The most important difference between the two articles, for the present purposes, lies in the way each relates to the prohibition on *refoulement*. Unlike Article 33(2), Article 32 does not specify that the conditions stipulated apply to the contracting States in respect of expulsion *to a country where the refugee is at risk of persecution*. What is the effect of this omission? It may be to exclude, in which case a refugee can only be expelled to a country where he or she is at risk of persecution under the general exception provided for in Article 33(2).[309] Or it may be to include, so that the expulsion of a refugee (lawfully present), *even* to a country where he or she is at risk, must comply with the provisions of Article 32.[310] Authoritative writers[311] have pointed out that although the substantive conditions stipulated in the two articles partly overlap, Article 32 adds a procedural element by obligating States to observe due process of law.[312] It is perfectly logical,

---

309 According to J. C. Hathaway (2005: 659 ff., especially 694): 'To summarize, Art. 32 is a supplement to the protection against *refoulement* set by Art. 33. It is intended to limit the right of states to expel refugees to even non-persecutory states on both procedural and substantive grounds'. G. S. Goodwin-Gill and J. McAdam (2007: 263) are of the same opinion. This interpretation is explicitly followed in the case law: see the decision in the case of *Abramov*, para. 22, according to which 'If a Contracting State considers that . . . the presence of the refugee in its territory has become intolerable because of the conduct of the refugee, the appropriate course of action lies under Article 32, namely, expulsion. Where the effect of the decision to expel is to return the refugee to the country of nationality, expulsion is only permissible in accordance with Article 33(2) of the Convention, namely upon the ground that the refugee has been convicted by a final judgment of a particularly serious crime and thus constitutes a danger to the community of the country of refuge'. See also Supreme Court of New Zealand, decision of 21 June 2005, *Attorney-General* v. *Ahmed Zaoui (Zaoui)*.
310 See A. Grahl-Madsen (1997: 117).
311 'To be sure, if any of the provisions of Article 33 (2) may be applied to an individual refugee, grounds of national security or public order may be said to exist, and Article 32 (1) does not, therefore, constitute any additional safeguard for the refugee concerned. On the other hand, the procedural provisions in Article 32 (2) and (3) do constitute such safeguards' (ibid.: 117).
312 Reasons of national security and public order may well consist in the fact that the refugee is a threat to the host country or to its population, but the opposite is also true. Other substantive differences are similarly nuanced: although only the words 'to expel' are used, it is clear, as A. Grahl-Madsen (ibid.: 115 ff.) notes, that Article 32 covers all

therefore, that a refugee with closer ties to the host country should enjoy greater safeguards than a refugee who, say, arrives at the frontier or is on the way there. The alternative, 'excluding' interpretation would create an apparently insuperable contradiction: the expulsion of a refugee lawfully in the territory to a country where he or she is at risk of persecution would be subject to less limiting conditions (under Article 33(2)) than expulsion to a country where there is no risk.

The arguments are perfectly valid, but they are based on an incorrect premise: the requirements stipulated in Article 33(2) are not necessarily less restrictive than those of Article 32, and in fact the opposite theory has prevailed of late.[313] Moreover, procedural differences have been overturned in actual practice: even an expulsion order permitted, under certain conditions, by Article 33(2) must follow a procedure that observes certain safeguards for the rights of the person about to be expelled. What, if anything, is lacking from Article 33(2) is the condition, not binding, stipulated in Article 32(3), that 'The Contracting States shall allow such a refugee a reasonable period within which to seek legal admission into another country . . .'.[314] In fact, the obligation on States to allow a refugee, who is about to be expelled for reasons of national security or public order, a reasonable period of time to obtain admission to another country assumes that the refugee cannot be sent to the only country obliged to accept him or her, the country of nationality, which is probably precisely the one in which there is a risk of persecution.[315] In other words, the provision implicitly rules out the use of Article 32 to expel a refugee lawfully in the territory to a country where there is a risk of persecution. If these premises hold, it must follow that Article 32 does not constitute an exception to the prohibition on *refoulement* because it is designed to offer refugees lawfully in the territory (and only them) an additional safeguard with respect to Article 33 by subjecting the contracting States to substantive and procedural requirements *even* for the expulsion of refugees to countries where they are not at risk. Instead, the provisions

cases of the refugee's involuntary departure from the territory, except perhaps extradition. Instead, there is much uncertainty about the concept of a refugee lawfully in the territory, as opposed to that of a refugee *tout court* (on this point see § 1.8 below).

313 On all points see G. S. Goodwin-Gill and J. McAdam (2007: 263), according to whom 'The permitted power of expulsion, however, does not include the power to return the individual to the country in which his or her life or freedom may be threatened, unless *the further exacting provisions* which regulate exceptions to the principle of *non-refoulement* are also met' (emphasis added). See also G. Gilbert (2003: 458).

314 However, according to UNHCR, even when Article 33(2) is applied, the State expelling the refugee should make every effort, where possible, to find him or her a 'safe' destination: 'Read in conjunction with Articles 31 and 32 of the 1951 Convention, a State should allow a refugee a reasonable period of time and all necessary facilities to obtain admission into another country, and initiate *refoulement* only when all efforts to obtain admission into another country have failed' (UNHCR (1997c: para. F)). See also E. Lauterpacht and D. Bethlehem (2003: 134).

315 On the obligation of States to re-admit their nationals see G. S. Goodwin-Gill (1978: 136 ff.) and more recently K. Hailbronner (1997b: 1–2).

of Article 33(2) apply to the *refoulement*, which includes expulsion, of refugees *tout court* to a 'persecutory State'.[316]

A different connection exists between Article 33(2) and the provisions excluding some categories of persons from refugeehood – provisions contained in Articles 1C and 1F of the Refugee Convention. The main difference is that while Articles 1C and 1F exclude such categories from the application of the whole of the Convention, Article 33(2) excludes them only from the application of a rule, albeit an essential one, stipulated therein, which is the prohibition on *refoulement*.[317] This has an important consequence: the application of Articles 1C and 1F results in the cessation of refugee status or precludes its acquisition, while the application of Article 33(2), which creates an exception only to the prohibition on *refoulement*, does not change refugee status in any way and allows the refugee to obtain the same protection elsewhere if possible.[318] This is perfectly logical: the reasons for cessation and exclusion have nothing to do with the host country, in the sense that the decision does not depend on 'national' factors, whereas the exception to the prohibition on *refoulement* refers specifically to the security of the host country or the safety of its community. In other words, a person who has committed a war crime will in all likelihood be refused refugee status regardless of the country in which he or she seeks protection, while another person might represent a threat to the security of one State and therefore be removed from it, but not to another State and so find refuge there (assuming, of course, that all the other conditions are met).[319] The High Court of Ireland took the same view, though only in relation to the link between Article 1C and Article 33(2), affirming that the two procedures of revocation of refugee status and application of the exception to *non-refoulement* should remain separate. According to the Irish judges,

> A refugee may have his or her status revoked without necessarily being expelled from the territory of the Contracting State in question. Alternatively,

---

316 The UK Special Immigration Appeal Commission took the same view in the decision on the case of *C.*, para. 27.
317 See Supreme Court of Canada, decision of 4 June 1998, *Veluppillai Pushpanathan* v. *The Minister of Citizenship and Immigration*, para. 58, according to which 'The purpose of Article 1 is to define who is a refugee. Article 1F then establishes categories of persons who are specifically excluded from that definition. The purpose of Article 33 of the Convention, by contrast, is not to define who is and who is not a refugee, but rather to allow for the refoulement of a bona fide refugee to his or her native country where he or she poses a danger to the security of the country of refuge, or to the safety of the community. . . . Thus, the general purpose of Article 1F is not the protection of the society of refuge from dangerous refugees, whether because of acts committed before or after the presentation of a refugee claim; that purpose is served by Article 33 of the Convention'. Consider the very peremptory wording in UK Immigration Appeal Tribunal, decision of 2 February 2004, *Secretary of State for the Home Department* v. *JN*, para. 17.
318 See J. C. Hathaway (2005: 344 ff.).
319 There are similar examples for the cessation clauses as well, but only in the sense that there are no situations in which refugee status can cease only in respect of some States and not others.

a refugee may be expelled from that territory while remaining a refugee, that status not having been lost or revoked.[320]

It goes without saying that once refugee status has been denied *ab initio* or revoked, there is nothing, at least in the Refugee Convention,[321] to prevent the host country from removing the person from its own territory to a country where he or she is at risk of persecution. If Article 1C is applied, there is absolutely no chance of the person being sent to such a country because refugee status can only cease with the (re-)emergence of a source of protection, or with the disappearance of the risk of persecution.[322] This is not so if Article 1F is applied as the risk of persecution may, and indeed probably does, exist. These considerations, along with the many other points of contact between Article 1F and Article 33(2), particularly those relating to the conditions for substantive application, are why the two provisions and related procedures are often confused in practice.[323]

It is clear where the provisions potentially overlap: commission of one of the crimes listed under Article 1F may also come under Article 33(2). For example, committing a war crime or an act contrary to the purposes and principles of the UN might easily make the person responsible a danger to the security of the host country. In abstract, though, the rationale underlying the two provisions is not the same: as explained earlier, Article 1F has a 'punitive' purpose, in the sense that it does not deem certain individuals to be deserving of refugee status, while Article 33(2) aims to safeguard the interests of the host country. This is borne out by the fact that in the latter case – unlike Article 1F – the central element is the threat posed by the refugee, be it to the security of the host country or to that of its community, and the alleged commission of a serious crime is not sufficient to warrant *refoulement*. Moreover, in the second alternative put forward in Article 33(2) ('conviction by a final judgment of a particularly serious crime' creating 'a danger to the community' of the host country) the differences are even greater: there must be a final judgment, where Article 1F requires only 'serious reasons for considering'; and the crime must be of a 'particularly serious' nature, as opposed to

---

320 *Abramov*, para. 18.

321 But see below, Chapter 2.

322 As noted in S. Kneebone and M. O'Sullivan (2011: 486), in line with the decision in the case of *Abramov*, cessation of refugee status does not necessarily entail the refugee's expulsion from the territory of the host State.

323 On this point see G. Gilbert (2003: 457 ff., especially 458). Significantly, in the decision in *C.*, para. 31, the judge affirms that 'There can be little doubt that a person who fosters or supports terrorism is a danger to the security of the country in which he is. There can also be little doubt that fostering or supporting international terrorism are acts contrary to the purposes and principles of the United Nations. . . . If therefore there are serious reasons or reasonable grounds for considering that a person has taken part in fostering or supporting international terrorism, therefore, it may not matter very much whether his case is considered under Article 1(F) or 33: the outcome is that he is not entitled to protection from refoulement'.

just 'serious' in Article 1F(b),[324] which further restricts application of the clause to non-political crimes.[325]

That said, here, as in the rest of the Refugee Convention, it is up to States to draw the line between the two provisions. However much the provisions may be based, in theory, on different rationales, it is quite possible that the commission of a crime can be used simultaneously to exclude a person from refugee status and to rule out the application of just the prohibition on *refoulement*, it being left to the discretion of each State to make the truly subtle distinction between the two. The similarity of the provisions has major consequences: the substantive standards imposed by Article 1F give States more scope than Article 33(2), with the result that their proximity allows States a margin for manoeuvre that can be used against the asylum-seeker, particularly in connection with alleged membership of a terrorist organisation. Article 1F, especially at (b), could offer a loophole to remove an asylum-seeker from the

---

324 This aspect is highlighted by F. Lauterpacht and D. Bethlehem (2003: 136), who observe that 'As the threshold of prospective danger in Article 33(2) is higher than in Article 1F, it would hardly be consistent with the scheme of the Convention more generally to read the term "danger" in Article 33(2) as referring to anything less than very serious danger'. This theory has been explicitly disputed in the case law: see Court of Appeal (Civil Division) of England and Wales, decision of 26 June 2009, *EN* v. *The Secretary of State for the Home Department* and *The Secretary of State for the Home Department* v. *KC (South Africa) (EN and KC)*, para. 43. The opposite view is taken in US Court of Appeals, Ninth Circuit, decision of 19 August 2011, *Hernan Ismael Delgado* v. *Attorney General (Delgado)*, available online at www.ca9.uscourts.gov, p. 11084.

325 Furthermore, according to E. Lauterpacht and D. Bethlehem (2003: 136), Article 33(2) refers only to crimes committed after entry into (and within) the territory of the host country: 'A common sense reading of Article 33(2) in the light of Article 1F(b) requires that it be construed so as to address circumstances not covered by Article 1F(b). Any other approach would amount to treating the scope of the two provisions as being very largely the same and would raise the question of why Article 33(2) was required at all. In our view, therefore, construed in the context of the 1951 Convention as a whole, Article 33(2) must be read as applying to a conviction for a particularly serious crime committed in the country of refuge, or elsewhere, subsequent to admission as a refugee, which leads to the conclusion that the refugee in question is a danger to the community of the country concerned'. In fact, the correct way to interpret the two provisions is to circumscribe the scope of each so that they do not overlap; however, I do not think that to do so requires an affirmation that Article 33(2) applies only to crimes committed after recognition of refugee status. There are, as I have said, differences between the two provisions, at least in theory. In practice, where a particularly serious crime has been committed in the territory of the host State, the easiest (and possibly only) route open to that State is the second alternative envisaged in Article 33(2). The options offered by Article 1F are unlikely to be applicable, either because they are very specific (crimes against peace, war crimes or crimes against humanity, acts contrary to the purposes and principles of the United Nations), or because they relate to the commission of crimes at an earlier time, as explicitly provided for in the rule (this is Article 1F(b), the only clause that contains a clear and explicit restriction *ratione temporis* and *ratione loci*). See also G. Gilbert (2003: 459). The mention of the country of refuge in Article 33(2) was removed from the text of the Convention, although for other reasons: see A. Grahl-Madsen (1997: 141).

territory of the State to a country where he or she would be at risk of persecution in situations that do not allow the application of Article 33(2). Thus, unlike the alternatives envisaged in Article 32 of the Convention, the provisions of Article 1F, although not based on the same rationale and mechanism as an exception to the prohibition on *refoulement*, in the end also function as such.

Given these considerations concerning the line separating Article 33(2) from other provisions of the Refugee Convention that may be interpreted as exceptions to the principle of *non-refoulement*, it is worth taking a closer look at its content. Two different alternatives are provided for in Article 33(2): in the first, the refugee constitutes a danger for the security of the State in which he or she is and there are reasonable grounds for believing this to be so. The expression 'reasonable grounds' implies a lower standard than full proof,[326] although, as the reference to reasonableness implies, it nonetheless prevents States from making an unreasonable, 'capricious' or arbitrary assessment.[327] The purpose of including this expression was to allow States some discretion in assessing the threat to their security. During the *travaux préparatoires*, in answer to the questions raised by the delegate from the Holy See, the British delegate (who, together with the French delegate, had proposed the existing formulation of Article 33(2)) believed that States should be allowed to determine 'whether there were sufficient grounds for regarding any refugee as a danger to the security of the country'.[328]

Evaluating the other element in Article 33(2) – that is, the danger to the security of the country – is a more complex matter. First, the danger must be present or prospective, although it cannot be ruled out that a refugee may be removed to a country where he or she is at risk of persecution as a result of some earlier conduct: according to legal theory,

> While past conduct may be relevant to an assessment of whether there are reasonable grounds for regarding the refugee to be a danger to the country in the future, the material consideration is whether there is a prospective danger to the security of the country.[329]

The threshold at which such danger will trigger the exception to the provision is a matter of considerable uncertainty. While it is clear that the danger must be

---

326 See A. Grahl-Madsen (1997: 139).

327 See E. Lauterpacht and D. Bethlehem (2003: 135). See also Supreme Court of Canada, decision of 11 January 2002, *Manickavasagam Suresh v. The Minister of Citizenship and Immigration and the Attorney General of Canada (Suresh)*, especially para. 90, according to which 'The threat must be "serious", in the sense that it must be grounded on objectively reasonable suspicion based on evidence and in the sense that the threatened harm must be substantial rather than negligible'.

328 Conference of Plenipotentiaries on the Status of Refugees and Stateless Persons: Summary Record of the Sixteenth Meeting, p. 8. See also G. S. Goodwin-Gill and J. McAdam (2007: 235).

329 E. Lauterpacht and D. Bethlehem (2003: 135). See also A. Grahl-Madsen (1997: 139).

serious, some writers maintain that Article 33(2) requires a particularly high level of threat.[330] This is because of the humanitarian nature of the provision to which the exception may apply, and it follows on from a comparison with Article 1F, which sets strict requirements but of a lower standard than Article 33(2).[331]

The tendency in general practice is not only to overlap this provision with Article 1F, but above all to broaden its scope, particularly since 11 September 2001.[332] The decision of the Supreme Court of Canada in the case of *Suresh* is a good example because it introduces, in connection with the crime of terrorism, the notion of 'indirect danger': where the terrorist activities in which the refugee has participated – even simply by helping to finance them – take place abroad, there may still be a danger for the host country, thus opening the way for the application of Article 33(2).[333] However, as can be deduced from the decision in question, if the refugee constitutes a danger only for third countries, the exception cannot be applied,[334] and the host State cannot justify removing the refugee on the grounds that failure to deliver him or her to the other State (to which he or she is a danger) will in turn create a threat to the host State by causing a political and diplomatic crisis between the two countries.[335] The danger must be not to the State but to its security, which according to legal theory narrows the scope to threats such as the defeat of the host country (for example, through spying or sabotage) or the overturning of its government.[336] In other words, the threat must be capable of bringing down the State or its government, naturally by unlawful means.

The other alternative hypothesised in Article 33(2) is set out in greater detail and requires more elements to be present: danger to the community of the host

---

330 E. Lauterpacht and D. Bethlehem (2003: 136). A fairly neutral position is taken by G. S. Goodwin-Gill and J. McAdam (2007: 237).

331 See footnote 313.

332 See footnote 323.

333 See the decision in the case of *Suresh*, para. 88, according to which 'to insist on direct proof of a specific threat to Canada as the test for "danger to the security of Canada" is to set the bar too high. There must be a real and serious possibility of adverse effect to Canada. But the threat need not be direct; rather it may be grounded in distant events that indirectly have a real possibility of harming Canadian security'.

334 E. Lauterpacht and D. Bethlehem (2003: 135).

335 See J. C. Hathaway (2005: 346 ff.). Moreover, A. Grahl-Madsen (1997: 140) notes how the British delegate – responding to the objection of his Danish counterpart who was concerned about the possibility of using a political crisis as an 'expedient' to apply Article 33(2) by confirming that it did not fall within the scope of the provision (see Conference of Plenipotentiaries on the Status of Refugees and Stateless Persons: Summary Record of the Sixteenth Meeting, p. 10 ff.) – mildly observed that 'He might have added that it is generally recognized in international law that the granting of asylum is not an unfriendly act and has to be respected by other States including the country of origin'.

336 See A. Grahl-Madsen (1997: 140), who includes activities 'directed against a foreign Government, which as a result threatens the Government of the country of residence with repercussions of a serious nature'. However, this is very close to a 'political crisis', indeed almost indistinguishable from it (see footnote 335), which the author had ruled out as grounds justifying the application of the exception.

country and conviction by final judgment for a 'particularly serious crime'. The first point to be made is that the link between the two elements is not always interpreted in the same way. There is a tendency, in US practice, to not separate the two, as the mere fact of having been convicted of a particularly serious crime itself makes the refugee a danger for the community.[337] Following another line, the practice in Australia and the UK is that although according to case law the two elements should be evaluated separately, domestic legislation makes certain presumptions.[338] In Australia's Migration Act the presumption concerns the particularly serious nature of the crime, in the sense that while Section 91U regards certain crimes themselves as 'particularly serious', the danger to the community is nonetheless assessed independently.[339] By contrast, in standard UK practice the presumption extends to the danger to the community, as is evident from Section

---

337 See US Court of Appeals, Tenth Circuit, decision of 8 February 1995, *Nader Ghloum Al-Salehi* v. *Immigration and Naturalization Service*, discussed in G. Van De Mark (1995–1996: 212 ff.). For a more recent case, see US Court of Appeals, Tenth Circuit, decision of 20 November 2009, *N-A-M* v. *Attorney General*, available online at www.ca10.uscourts.gov, especially para. 2. The presiding judge, Justice Henry, in his concurring opinion, clearly criticised the established practice because '*Stare decisis* binds us to the language of *Al-Salehi* . . . which affirmed the BIA's determination that § 1231 does not require a separate inquiry into whether an alien constitutes a danger to the community. I find, however, N-A-M and amici's arguments persuasive that the interpretation from *Al-Salehi* is at odds with the language of § 1231, with some basic principles of statutory construction, the purpose and intent behind the Refugee Act, and the international legal principles embodied in the Refugee Act'. He was referring to the consideration made, as *amicus curiae*, by UNHCR, *Brief for the United Nations High Commissioner for Refugees as Amicus Curiae in Support of Petitioner*, available online at www.refworld.org, especially p. 3 ff. See also for other cases and considerations, J. C. Hathaway (2005: 351, especially footnote 324).

338 See Federal Court of Australia, decision of 16 March 1999, *A.* v. *Minister for Immigration and Multicultural Affairs*, available online at www.fedcourt.gov.au, para. 3, which reads: '. . . we should state that we would not, as at present advised, construe this article as intending to make the conviction of *any* particularly serious crime the sole determinant of a deportation decision. The logic of the syntax of the provision moves in the opposite direction. The principal statement of exclusion is "who constitutes a danger to the community". The phrase "having been convicted . . . of a particularly serious crime" adds an additional element, but it is not expressed as if that additional element swallowed up the principal statement. This aspect of the drafting is perhaps made clearer when attention is directed to the first alternative contained in the provision, that "there are reasonable grounds for regarding [the person] as a danger to the security of the country in which he is". The whole provision is concerned with perils represented by the refugee, either because of a threat to the security of the country, or because of a danger to its community'. The ruling, which seems to ascribe greater importance to the danger posed by the refugee to the community, of which the conviction is merely evidence, is reiterated in the decision of the Asylum and Immigration Tribunal in the case of *IH*, para. 75.

339 See the considerations of the Department of Immigration and Multicultural and Indigenous Affairs in the volume *Interpreting the Refugees Convention – An Australian Contribution*, Canberra, 2002, p. 55.

72 of the 2002 Nationality, Immigration and Asylum Act.[340] Moreover, in the Act the presumption has different implications: the presumption that the commission of a particularly serious crime makes the refugee a danger to the community can be rebutted; while the presumption that a sentence to imprisonment of at least two years – to cite the example of Section 72(2) – makes the crime particularly serious allows for no rebuttal.[341] According to the British judges, only a conclusive presumption, such as the latter, is contrary to Article 33(2) of the Refugee Convention, while the presumption that the commission of a particularly serious crime makes the refugee a danger to the community is not, being relative and therefore allowing for rebuttal.[342]

This approach is not entirely acceptable, as any type of presumption, whether relative or conclusive, raises a problem of procedural compliance with Article 33(2). According to the theory, all the circumstances of the case must be taken into account, for a conviction by final judgment is insufficient basis for a series of questionable presumptions.[343] Any exception, which should be narrowly interpreted,[344] must take account of several factors, including not only

340 Subsections 2–4 read: '(2) A person shall be presumed to have been convicted by a final judgment of a particularly serious crime *and to constitute a danger* to the community of the United Kingdom if he is – (a) convicted in the United Kingdom of an offence, and (b) sentenced to a period of imprisonment of at least two years. (3) A person shall be presumed to have been convicted by a final judgment of a particularly serious crime *and to constitute a danger* to the community of the United Kingdom if – (a) he is convicted outside the United Kingdom of an offence, (b) he is sentenced to a period of imprisonment of at least two years, and (c) he could have been sentenced to a period of imprisonment of at least two years had his conviction been a conviction in the United Kingdom of a similar offence. (4) A person shall be presumed to have been convicted by a final judgment of a particularly serious crime *and to constitute a danger* to the community of the United Kingdom if – (a) he is convicted of an offence specified by order of the Secretary of State, or (b) he is convicted outside the United Kingdom of an offence and the Secretary of State certifies that in his opinion the offence is similar to an offence specified by order under paragraph (a)' (emphasis added).

341 See Section 72(6): 'A presumption under subsection (2), (3) or (4) *that a person constitutes a danger* to the community is rebuttable by that person' (emphasis added).

342 *IH*, para. 78. More recently, see *EN and KC*, para. 66 ff.

343 See J. C. Hathaway (2005: 349 ff.). According to G. S. Goodwin-Gill and J. McAdam (2007: 240), '*a priori* determinations of seriousness by way of legislative labeling or other measures substituting executive determinations for judicial (and judicious) assessments are inconsistent with the *international* standard which is required to be applied, and with the humanitarian intent of the Convention. After all, what is at issue here is action by the State in manifest disregard of what is recognized as serious danger (persecution) to the life or liberty of a refugee. It is the nature of presumptions that they disregard context and circumstances, and therefore also the principle of individual assessment'. Along the same lines see also UNHCR (2004b: 4 ff.). Also in favour of individual assessment is C. W. Wouters (2009: 117).

344 See F. Lenzerini (2009: 392). A. Grahl-Madsen (1997: 144) is explicit on this point: 'it is quite clear that the provisions . . . contained in Article 33 (2) of the 1951 Convention were only meant to be applied in extremely rare occasions'.

the seriousness of the crime in abstract,[345] but also the circumstances in which it was committed,[346] the chance of repeat offending,[347] and evidently the thing to which the refugee constitutes a danger.[348]

Standard practice and legal theory offer few indications concerning an aspect of the application of Article 33(2) that is by no means negligible: the need to check whether the conviction conforms to certain substantive procedural standards. While the conduct that constitutes a particularly serious crime may have taken place in a third country, and hence the conviction by a final judgment will have been issued by a foreign judge, it does not go without saying that such conduct constitutes a criminal offence in the host State, or that the conviction conforms with the procedural standards required there. It would seem, on the basis of the little case law there is, that a judge who has to assess the grounds for applying Article 33(2) cannot take the conviction as a given, but must evaluate whether it conforms in substance and procedure with domestic legislation.[349] While

345 See footnote 324.
346 See Australian Federal Court, decision of 29 July 1998, *Betkhoshabeh v. Minister for Immigration and Multicultural Affairs*, available online at www.fedcourt.gov.au, para. 102.
347 It is important to stress that the possibility of repeat offending cannot be deduced automatically from the number of offences committed in the past, or from testimony that the refugee is a habitual offender. As A. Grahl-Madsen (1997: 143) recalls, the Conference did not accept Italy's proposal to include such a reference in the text of Article 33(2) so that the final text would have read 'or who, having been convicted by a final judgment of a particularly serious crime *or having been declared by the Court a habitual offender* constitutes a danger to the community of that country' (emphasis added). The case law seems to lean in this direction: see the decision in the case of *Delgado*, p. 11088, which reads, 'The bar to relief applies if the Attorney General determines that "the alien, having been convicted by a final judgment of *a* particularly serious crime, constitutes *a* danger to the community of the United States." . . . The statutes do not mention "a particularly long rap sheet," "a particularly egregious repeat offender," or "a particularly serious series of offenses." The singular article "a" could not make any clearer the singular nature of "a particularly serious crime": the agency must identify *one* offense of conviction that constitutes "a particularly serious crime" in order to relieve the Attorney General of the opportunity to exercise his discretion and to bar the alien's application for relief'.
348 According to A. Grahl-Madsen (1997: 143), 'a "danger to the community" means a danger to the peaceful life of the population in its many facets. In this sense a man will be a danger to the community if he sabotages means of communication, blows up or sets fire to houses and other constructions, assaults or batters peaceful citizens, commits burglaries, holdups or kidnapping etc., in short if he disrupts or upsets civil life, and particularly if this is done on a large scale, so that the person concerned actually becomes a public menace'.
349 See *EN and KC*, para. 40, which reads: 'The criminal laws of member states vary. What are crimes under the laws of one member state are not crimes under the laws of another. To take a subject of topical interest, to assist a person to commit suicide is a crime under the laws of some member states (including the United Kingdom) but not under the laws of others. Abortion is a crime under the laws of some member states, but is permitted under our law. Even more obviously, acts that were criminal when the Convention was entered into are so no longer. Until the Abortion Act 1967 abortion was always a crime in this country; the Act regulated the medical termination of

substantive incongruities may be remedied when assessing the other requirement (danger to the community), greater care must be taken regarding the possibility of procedural shortcomings:[350] otherwise, the (unjust) conviction could, at least in theory, have been passed down by a judge in the State to which the refugee is being sent, so that the refugee would be handed to his or her persecutors as a result of a decision they themselves made.[351]

Some brief observations complete the overview of these exceptions. There can be no doubt that they open a breach in the principal (and fundamental) rule that is the prohibition on *refoulement*. It is clear that under Article 33(2), and on the grounds set out therein, a person who fulfils the definition of refugee under Article 1A (even without formal recognition) can be sent to a persecutory State. This does not mean that the exception eliminates all the safeguards implicit in the principle of *non-refoulement*: logically, all the elements described must be verified before a removal order can be issued, and therefore all the procedural safeguards relating to the prohibition on *refoulement* apply, *a fortiori*, to any exceptions to it, including the exception uniquely provided for in Article 1F. Articles 1F and 33(2) introduce exceptions to *non-refoulement* only because they allow removal to a State where the refugee is at risk of persecution; they do not also allow the contracting States to apply such exceptions without first following a fair procedure. Thus, a contracting State may not reject a person at the border because he or she is a danger to its security or because there are reasonable grounds to believe he or she is a war criminal unless those grounds have been determined by means of a procedure that meets specific standards. Articles 1F and 33(2) do not provide for any renunciation of the 'core' principle of *non-refoulement* as interpreted here, that is, as a right to remain in the territory of the contracting State until a procedure such as that described has been completed. Legal theory is firm on this point:

> 'Seriousness', 'security', and 'danger' are not self-applying concepts and their application in a particular case requires, as a matter of due process, that an

> pregnancy; homosexual acts between consenting adults were criminal until the passing of the Sexual Offences Act 1967. Similar considerations apply to assessing the seriousness of crimes. We now regard some crimes, such as causing death by dangerous driving, rape and sexual offences involving children, more seriously than was the case 50 years ago. So I do not think that the crimes that are particularly serious are a constant, not varying from member state and not varying in time. Rather, the expression "particularly serious crime" must be applied to what is a crime under the domestic law of the member state when the question of refoulement arises'.

350 There can be no difficulty maintaining that a refugee convicted in a third country for conduct that does not constitute an offence under the law of the host State cannot represent a danger to the community.

351 *Mutatis mutandis*, see House of Lords, decision of 8 December 2005, *A (FC) and others (FC) (Appellants) v. Secretary of State for the Home Department (Respondent) (2004)* and *A and others (Appellants) (FC) and others v. Secretary of State for the Home Department (Respondent) (Conjoined Appeals)*, available online at www.bailii.org. For a short summary see A. T. H. Smith (2006: 251 ff.) and for a longer comment see N. Rasiah (2006: 995 ff.).

individual should know and be able to meet the case against him or her, and have the opportunity to show why, in the circumstances, applying the exception would be disproportionate.[352]

Other writers underline that this conclusion follows from a comparison of Article 33(2) and Article 32:

> Compliance with due process is expressly required by Article 32(2) of the 1951 Convention in respect of expulsion. To the extent that *refoulement* would pose a potentially greater threat to a refugee or asylum-seeker than expulsion, we are of the view that, at the very least, the due process safeguards applicable to expulsion must be read into the application of the exceptions to *refoulement*. The strict observance of due process safeguards would also be required by general principles of human rights law.[353]

Because standard practice tends, for the reasons described above, to confuse exclusion clauses with the exceptions under Article 33(2), it almost always subsumes the verification of whether they apply into what might be called the 'principal' process, that is, the determination of refugee status. It is generally the practice of States to not separate, as they should, the process of determining status – including, of course, the exclusion clauses of Article 1F of the Refugee Convention – from the process of evaluating whether exceptions to the principle of *non-refoulement* apply. The tendency for the former procedure to absorb the latter has the effect of extending the safeguards attached to the determination of status to the exceptions to *non-refoulement* as well. This is well illustrated by the situation in the EU: under Article 23 of Directive 2005/85 (discussed in section 4.7 ff.), the procedures for determining refugee status are subject to the detailed rules of Chapter II of the Directive, which establishes important safeguards for asylum-seekers, including the guarantee contained in Article 7 of the Asylum Procedures Directive.[354] At the same time, Directive 2011/95[355] (the Qualification Directive, discussed in section 4.3 ff.) lists the exceptions under Article 33(2) of the Refugee Convention among the reasons why 'Member States *may* decide not to grant status to a refugee, where such a decision has not yet been taken'

---

352 G. S. Goodwin-Gill and J. McAdam (2007: 241) (see also footnote 343). See also F. Lenzerini (2009: 404).

353 E. Lauterpacht and D. Bethlehem (2003: 134).

354 That is, the right of the applicant to stay in the Member State while the application is being processed. See also, respectively, Articles 31 and 9 of the new Procedures Directive 2013/32/EU.

355 Directive 2011/95/EU of the European Parliament and of the Council of 13 December 2011 on standards for the qualification of third-country nationals or stateless persons as beneficiaries of international protection, for a uniform status for refugees or for persons eligible for subsidiary protection, and for the content of the protection granted, OJ L 337 of 20 December 2011, p. 9 ff.

(Article 14(5), emphasis added),[356] so that the exceptions may be evaluated according to the procedural standards of Article 23 of Directive 2005/85, designed to regulate the determination of status.

There is another possible reason why a very close analysis of the two exceptions is necessary: according to much of the theory,[357] the danger that the refugee represents for the security of the State or its community must be compared with the risk the refugee would run in the persecutory State.[358] In other words, States must assess the danger in proportion to the risk, which according to UNHCR means that

> There must be a rational connection between the removal of the refugee and the elimination of the danger; *refoulement* must be the last possible resort to eliminate or alleviate the danger; and, the danger to the country of refuge must outweigh the risk to the refugee upon *refoulement*.[359]

Thus, it is clear that no removal order can be issued without a thorough investigation into a series of elements, exactly as happens during the procedure to determine refugee status.

Standard practice does not entirely follow this approach, although it is the one that prevails in legal theory: while UNHCR leans firmly in the direction of the theory,[360] national case law diverges significantly. Sometimes the predominant theory is followed,[361] at others the danger represented by the refugee is assessed entirely separately from the degree of persecution he or she risks in the country of destination: in the case of *Zaoui*, mentioned earlier, the Supreme Court of New Zealand ruled that

> the judgment or assessment to be made under article 33.2 is to be made in its own terms, by reference to danger to the security, in this case, of New Zealand,

---

356 However, adding at Article 21(2) that, for the same reasons, 'Member States may *refoule* a refugee, whether formally recognised or not'.

357 See P. Weis (1995: 342) and also E. Lauterpacht and D. Bethlehem (2003: 137). For the opposite view see J. C. Hathaway (2005: 353 ff.), F. Lenzerini (2009: 392) and also J. C. Hathaway and C. J. Harvey (2001: 294 ff.). More recently, along the latter line, see C. W. Wouters (2009: 114). A different, and somewhat unique, reconstruction of the link between Article 33(2) and Article 1F specifically as regards the proportionality test can be found in G. Carella (2005: 191 ff.).

358 The same applies to balancing the risk of persecution and the seriousness of the crime of which the applicant is suspected (see § 1.2).

359 UNHCR (2006: para. D).

360 See UNHCR (1997c: para. F). The concept is reiterated in UNHCR (2004b: 4).

361 See Court of Appeal (Civil Division) of England and Wales, decision of 22 October 1993, *Chahal v. Secretary of State for the Home Department*, in which the Court reversed its earlier position as stated by Justice Neill in the decision of 23 March 1988, *'NSH' v. Secretary of State for the Home Department ('NSH')*.

and without any balancing or weighing or proportional reference to the matter dealt with in article 33.1.[362]

As rightly pointed out in that decision, echoed by authoritative writers, the argument usually put forward in favour of the need to balance danger, on the one hand, and risk, on the other, rests on ambiguous elements.[363] It should be recalled that a proportionality test does not necessarily favour the refugee, but, according to the literature, may work against him or her:

> This is because, in practice, the suggestion that there are some individuated forms of harm that could be more compelling than national security or danger to the community of reception has trivialized the significance of the latter two concepts and justified an unacceptably broad reading of the scope of Art. 33(2).[364]

Where the risk concerns particularly 'significant' crimes, such as torture, the refugee is in any case safeguarded, in Europe, by other international rules, which

---

362 *Zaoui*, para. 42. Along the same lines, see the decision in the case of *'NSH'* and, for a more recent case, the decision in *IH*, p. 308 ff., especially p. 326, para. 47. The existence of a causal link between the crime of which the refugee has been convicted and the danger he or she represents is rejected by the decision in the case of *EN and KC*, para. 46, implicitly discrediting the theory that a proportionality test is required.

363 *Zaoui*, para. 38. This is the passage in which the British delegate states that 'It must be left to States to decide whether the danger entailed to refugees by expulsion *outweighed* the menace to public security that would arise if they were permitted to stay' (Conference of Plenipotentiaries on the Status of Refugees and Stateless Persons: Summary Record of the Sixteenth Meeting, p. 8, emphasis added). As J. C. Hathaway (2005: 353) points out, 'the British reference to the importance of letting states weigh relative risks was actually an answer to a proposal to restrict states' margin of appreciation, not an argument for a super-added proportionality test'. The proposal had been put forward by the delegate for the Holy See because 'With regard to the joint amendment, it was admittedly very difficult to avoid exceptions to any rule. What was meant for example by the words "reasonable grounds"? . . . The wording: "may not, however, be claimed by a refugee *who constitutes* a danger to the security of the country" would be preferable' (Conference of Plenipotentiaries on the Status of Refugees and Stateless Persons: Summary Record of the Sixteenth Meeting, p. 7; note that emphasis is in the original).

364 J. C. Hathaway (2005: 354). Another decision appears to lean in the same direction, adding to those mentioned in footnote 362: UK Immigration Appeal Tribunal, decision of 7 February 2005, *SB Haiti* v. *Secretary of State for the Home Department*, according to which 'The effect of there being no balance in Article 33(2), as we conclude, is to emphasise that the tests for "a particularly serious crime" and "danger" must be higher than they would be if there were a balance to be undertaken. We have allowed for this in our conclusions on those issues. It is in particular the "danger" threshold which would be affected by the risk on return to the refugee, if a balance were to exist and which we see as quite a high threshold in its absence' (para. 84).

certainly do not envisage any balancing against other interests because they are of an absolute nature, as we will see below (Chapter 2).[365]

1.6 B) The notion of 'safe' country

One of the stratagems used often and for many years by States to get round the main obligation implied and imposed by the prohibition on *refoulement* (i.e. access to a fair procedure during which the applicant is entitled to stay in the territory of the State) is to remove the applicant summarily to a country with which he or she has 'links' of a sort and which will guarantee his or her safety.[366] There are several theories as to what such 'links' might be: they range from the more obvious, such as citizenship or residence, to others related to the protection of minors or the need to keep the family together, and finally to more tenuous connections based on even temporary transit. Different elements determine whether the country of destination is safe, including, among others, observance of the principle of *non-refoulement*, without which what is termed indirect *refoulement* occurs, also prohibited by Article 33(1) of the Refugee Convention.[367] According to UNHCR,

> In determining whether a country is 'safe', states should take into account the following factors: its respect for human rights and the rule of law, its record of not producing refugees, its ratification and compliance with human rights instruments and its accessibility to independent national or international organisations for the purpose of verifying and supervising respect for human rights.[368]

365 According to R. Bruin and K. Wouters (2003: 20–21), this conclusion summarises the two positions held by legal theorists: 'it can be concluded that Article 33 (2) Refugee Convention allows deportation if a provable danger to the national security of the country of refuge exists or if the refugee is convicted for a particularly serious crime and constitutes a provable danger to the community of the country of refuge, irrespective of the persecution the refugee might be subjected to, unless the persecution can be qualified as torture or inhuman or degrading treatment or punishment. In those cases, deportation is not permitted'.
366 J. C. Hathaway (2005: 293).
367 During the *travaux préparatoires* the Swedish proposal to incorporate in Article 33 (then Article 28) the mention 'or where he would be exposed to the risk of being sent to a territory where his life or freedom would thereby be endangered' was explicitly rejected (see Conference of Plenipotentiaries on the Status of Refugees and Stateless Persons: Summary Record of the Sixteenth Meeting, especially pp. 4–5, containing the declarations against by the French and British delegates). Today, however, it is clear that the principle of *non-refoulement* extends to the indirect involvement of the State: see G. S. Goodwin-Gill and J. McAdam (2007: 252) and C. W. Wouters (2009: 140).
368 UNHCR (1992b). At a later date UNHCR added that, 'As for the general question of "safety", this cannot be answered solely on the basis of formal criteria, such as whether or not the third State is a party to the 1951 Convention and 1967 Protocol and/or relevant international human rights treaties. The third State needs actually

The practice of States in this respect follows three lines, according to the purpose for which a country is designated safe. The term used is 'burden sharing' when the purpose of designating a safe State is 'to distribute' among the participants in an agreement (under the provisions of the agreement itself or of related instruments) the task of examining an application for asylum, and the applicant is sent to the country selected on that basis. Instead, 'safe third country', in the narrowest sense, is used when States unilaterally fix the conditions under which the applicant is sent to the country with which he or she has the closest links, assuming that country offers similar protection to the one in which the asylum application was made. Last, 'safe country of origin' is the term used when States draw up a list of countries of origin where the applicant does not fear persecution and to which he or she can therefore be sent. In all these situations the assessment of the 'safety' of the country of destination is positive, although its purpose differs. In the first, the objective is to rationalise the examination of asylum applications within the context of regional or sub-regional cooperation. In the second, the assessment aims more directly to prevent the entry of an asylum-seeker who could equally obtain protection in another State. The last type of assessment undermines the asylum application because its purpose, in substance, is to establish that the asylum-seeker is not a refugee.[369]

The practice of burden sharing is not in itself unlawful in terms of the obligations deriving from the Refugee Convention, and particularly the obligation enshrined in Article 33(1). In fact, UNHCR

> generally favours the adoption between States of agreements aimed at identifying the country responsible for examining an asylum request, as such agreements may constitute the most satisfactory way to address the problem of 'refugees in orbit' and provide guarantees that an asylum request will be examined in substance.[370]

Indeed, one of the aims of the Dublin Convention, which will be discussed in Chapter 3, was to prevent the problem of refugees being 'in orbit',[371] just as the same objective lies behind the more recent agreement signed between Canada and the United States.[372] What, clearly, the Refugee Convention does not permit

to implement appropriate asylum procedures and systems fairly. Any list-based general assessment of safety of the third country needs to be applied flexibly, and ensure due consideration of that country's safety for the individual asylum-seeker' (UNHCR (2001b: para. 14)).

369 It is no accident that the criteria of citizenship and residence are only used to designate the safe country of origin. See Article 31 of the Asylum Procedures Directive, and also Article 36 of the new Procedures Directive 2013/32/EU.

370 UNHCR (1998: 1).

371 See footnote 30, Chapter 3.

372 Agreement between the Government of Canada and the Government of the United States of America for Cooperation in the Examination of Refugee Status Claims from Nationals of Third Countries, available online at www.cic.gc.ca. The agreement, of

is that a decision to remove should be made without a careful examination of the applicant's situation.[373] Thus, it is not the abstract notion of the 'distribution' of responsibility for examining asylum applications that may be in conflict with the Refugee Convention, but its concrete application, particularly if it entails conclusive presumptions regarding the 'safety' of the country of destination.[374] This is not the case of the Dublin II Regulation,[375] which replaces the Dublin Convention, insofar as, according to the European Court of Justice (ECJ),

> an application of Regulation No 343/2003 on the basis of the conclusive presumption that the asylum seeker's fundamental rights will be observed in the Member State primarily responsible for his application is incompatible with the duty of the Member States to interpret and apply Regulation No 343/2003 in a manner consistent with fundamental rights.[376]

which a first draft was approved on 30 August 2002, was adopted by the two countries on 5 December 2002 and entered into force on 29 December 2004. An amendment was introduced on 23 July 2009: see 'Minister Kenney announces removal of exception relating to Safe Third Country Agreement', available online at www.cic.gc.ca. The agreement, like the Dublin Convention, did not meet with any objections, at least in principle, on the part of UNHCR: see UNHCR (2002c).

373 C. W. Wouters (2009: 146). Similarly, see also UNHCR (2001b: para. 13).

374 Of course, the risk that the country of destination is not truly safe is just the most important of the many risks associated with a system of burden sharing: UNHCR has underlined that such a system must rest on the premise that the destination country, designated according to the rules to be in charge of the asylum application, respects all the provisions of the Refugee Convention. In fact, UNHCR had already emphasised, in connection with the Dublin Convention, 'that the credibility of any mechanism for transfer of responsibility is contingent upon the existence of harmonised standards in several other substantive and procedural areas of asylum. These include: the interpretation of the 1951 Convention refugee definition and the scope of complementary forms of protection; fair and expeditious asylum procedures; conditions for the reception of asylum-seekers; and the balance of effort among Member States. . . . The disparity of national standards in these key areas challenges many of the assumptions on which the Dublin Convention is implicitly based' (UNHCR (2001a)).

375 Council Regulation (EC) No 343/2003 of 18 February 2003 establishing the criteria and mechanisms for determining the Member State responsible for examining an asylum application lodged in one of the Member States by a third-country national, OJ L 50 of 25 February 2003, p. 1 ff. Regulation 343/2003 has been replaced recently by Regulation (EU) No 604/2013 (Dublin III) of the European Parliament and of the Council of 26 June 2013 establishing the criteria and mechanisms for determining the Member State responsible for examining an application for international protection lodged in one of the Member States by a third-country national or a stateless person, OJ L 180 of 29 June 2013, p. 31 ff., which maintains, even if with some modifications, the rule provided for in Article 3(2) of the Dublin II Regulation. See further, § 4.11.

376 European Court of Justice, judgment of 21 December 2011 in the Joined Cases C-411/10 and C-493/10, *N. S. v. Secretary of State for the Home Department* and *M.E. and others v. Refugee Applications Commissioner, Minister of Justice, Equality and Law Reform (N. S.)*, not yet published, para. 99. It is likely that the ECJ's position reflected the earlier

States required to apply the Regulation may in fact rebut the presumption, according to the Court,[377] on the basis of the so-called sovereignty clause contained in Article 3(2), which states:

> By way of derogation from paragraph 1, each Member State may examine an application for asylum lodged with it by a third-country national, even if such examination is not its responsibility under the criteria laid down in this Regulation. In such an event, that Member State shall become the Member State responsible within the meaning of this Regulation and shall assume the obligations associated with that responsibility.[378]

Similar considerations can be made regarding the Agreement between Canada and the United States. Under Article 4 the country responsible for examining the application is that of 'last presence' and therefore a person who entered first the US (or Canada) cannot apply for asylum in Canada (or the US) and will be sent away.[379] Although there are some exceptions to the rule, which reflect the rationale mentioned earlier (safeguarding family unity, protection of minors, and so on[380]), the Agreement has been strongly criticised for allowing asylum-seekers to be transferred from Canada to the US, where they are likely to be sent away again, this time to a persecutory State.[381] Some human rights associations (including Amnesty International) took up these concerns and brought a case in the Canadian Federal Court against the Canadian provisions implementing the Agreement (and in fact against the provisions of the Agreement itself). After the court of first instance had ruled against the provisions,[382] they were subsequently found to be

judgment of the ECtHR of 21 January 2011, Application No. 30696/09, *M. S. S.* v. *Belgium and Greece*, available online at www.echr.coe.int, in which Belgium was held to have violated Article 3 of the ECHR for having transferred some asylum-seekers to Greece in application of the Dublin II Regulation.

377 *N. S.*, para. 104.

378 UNHCR has also described the sovereignty clause as a loophole allowing States to get round the problem of burden sharing and comply with the prohibition on *refoulement*: 'In practice, the use by a Member State of its discretionary power under Article 3(4) [which later became 3(2)] may, in some cases, provide the only effective safeguard against indirect refoulement or against denial of access to the benefits of the 1951 Convention' (UNHCR (2001a)).

379 Under Article 4, the Agreement applies only to requests for asylum made at a 'land border port of entry'.

380 See, respectively, Article 4(2)(a) and (b) of the Agreement.

381 This is the result of the extremely intransigent attitude of the US to asylum-seekers, particularly since 11 September 2001, which in fact prompted the parties to resume negotiations for an agreement such as the one signed in 2002. For a critical comment see E. Carasco (2003: 305 ff.), C. D. Cutler (2004–2005: 121 ff.) and A. F. Moore (2007: 201 ff.).

382 Federal Court of Canada, decision of 29 November 2007, *Canadian Council for Refugees, Canadian Council of Churches, Amnesty International and John Doe* v. *Her Majesty the Queen*, on which see S. J. Glen (2007–2008: 587 ff.).

lawful, among other under the Canadian Charter of Rights and Freedoms.[383] On appeal, the Court found that the Canadian authorities' designation of the United States as a 'safe' country was not unreasonable, but left completely open the possibility that actually sending an asylum-seeker to the US might violate human rights legislation.[384] Although the Court does not mention this point, the refugee's return to the US is not the automatic consequence of it being a safe country because, as with the Dublin II Regulation, the Safe Third Country Agreement also contains a sovereignty clause stating that 'Notwithstanding any provision of this Agreement, either Party may at its own discretion examine any refugee status claim made to that Party where it determines that it is in its public interest to do so' (Article 6).[385]

It is not contrary to the Refugee Convention for a State where a request for asylum has been made to unilaterally designate a safe third country, provided this is not based on a conclusive presumption. At a much earlier time UNHCR had clearly stated that where a country is among those deemed safe,

> the claimant should be given the possibility to rebut the presumption. For this rebuttal to be effective it should in turn be surrounded by procedural safeguards similar to those required for manifestly unfounded procedures, including an appeal or review possibility.[386]

383 Federal Court of Appeal of Canada, decision of 29 June 2008, *The Queen v. Canadian Council for Refugees, Canadian Council of Churches, Amnesty International and John Doe (Canadian Council for Refugees)*. An appeal to the Supreme Court was proposed but it was declared inadmissible on 5 February 2009: see Supreme Court of Canada, *Bulletin of Proceedings*, 6 February 2009, p. 160.
384 It should be recalled that the Federal Court judge had recognised the associations as having legal capacity to sue (*locus standi*) because they represented a public interest in a situation in which an applicant refused entry to Canada would be unable to dispute the provisions of the Agreement, which would thus be immune to any challenge. The Federal Court of Appeal found this assumption to be incorrect (decision in *Canadian Council for Refugees*, para. 101) and affirmed that the 'border officer's lack of discretion to forgo returning a claimant to the U.S. for reasons other than the enumerated exception . . . should be assessed in a proper factual context – that is, when advanced by a refugee who has been denied asylum in Canada pursuant to the Regulations and faces a real risk of refoulement in being sent back to the U.S. pursuant to the Safe Third Country Agreement' (ibid., para 103). The Court did not rule out, therefore, that the refugee's return to the US might violate his or her human rights.
385 C. D. Cutler (2004–2005: 141) refers to precisely this possibility, albeit with a certain degree of scepticism.
386 UNHCR (1992b). The concept is reaffirmed by UNHCR Executive Committee, which stressed 'the need for decisions to exclude asylum-seekers from access to procedures to be treated as substantive and accompanied by appropriate procedural safeguards, including the opportunity to rebut the presumption that a particular country is "safe" with respect to the individual concerned' (UNHCR EXCOM Note on International Protection, 31 August 1993, A/AC.96/815, available online at www.refworld.org, para. 21). In the literature see, among others, S. H. Legomsky (2003: 567 ff., especially 669), S. Taylor (2006: 293) and C. W. Wouters (2009: 135–6 and 146).

Standard practice generally, though not always, follows the recommendations of UNHCR.[387] Under Article 27(2)(c) of the Asylum Procedures Directive the concept of safe third country depends, among other things, on

> rules in accordance with international law, allowing an *individual examination* of whether the third country concerned is safe for a particular applicant which, as a minimum, shall permit the applicant to challenge the application of the safe third country concept on the grounds that he/she would be subjected to torture, cruel, inhuman or degrading treatment or punishment.[388]

This essential procedural requirement is not the only condition for application of the safe third country concept. Apart from the obvious need to verify the safety of the country on the basis of precisely the elements listed above,[389] UNHCR has always insisted that the expelling State should make sure that the third country has a reasonable connection with the asylum-seeker,[390] is willing to take him or her in, and will examine the application by means of a fair procedure.[391]

387 Australia, as J. C. Hathaway (2005: 295) correctly notes, does not follow the prevailing practice. Refugees are virtually automatically returned to neighbouring States without any individual assessment of whether they would be at risk in the country of destination. Although this practice has been partly rectified following a High Court decision (2 March 2005, *NAGV and NAGW of 2002* v. *Minister for Immigration and Multicultural and Indigenous Affairs (NAGV)*, in favour of which see H. Hadaway (2005: 727 ff.)), the new conduct continues to raise questions, on which see S. Taylor (2006: 309 ff.). For a critique of Australian legislation before the reform prompted by the decision in *NAGV*, see S. Taylor (1996: 198 ff.).

388 Emphasis added. See also Article 38 of the new Procedures Directive.

389 See footnote 368.

390 UNHCR (2001b: para. 16).

391 See, among several others, UNHCR (1996): 'Governments should apply the "safe third country" notion only if they have received, on a bilateral basis, the explicit or implicit consent of the third State to take back the asylum-seeker and to grant him/her access to a fair asylum procedure, so as to ensure that the application will be examined on its merits'. UNHCR expresses the same opinion elsewhere (2001b: para. 15). Clearly, this condition is also included in agreements and instruments relating to burden sharing: see Article 16 of the Dublin II Regulation, which obligates the Member State responsible for examining the application to take in (or take back) the asylum-seeker; or, now, Article 18 of Dublin III Regulation. This condition is unnecessary where a safe third country is concerned because, as explained (see footnote 369), the criteria used are citizenship and residence; the close link is therefore sufficient in itself, according to established practice (see footnote 315), to obligate the destination country (that is, the country of citizenship or habitual residence) to take in the asylum-seeker. Article 31 of the Asylum Procedures Directive (which covers the safe country of origin notion) in fact does not mention this condition, while Article 27(4), relating to the safe third country concept, provides that 'Where the third country does not permit the applicant for asylum to enter its territory, Member States shall ensure that access to a procedure is given in accordance with the basic principles and guarantees described in Chapter II'. See, respectively, Articles 36 and 38 of the new Procedures Directive.

This requirement has often led States not party to a burden-sharing agreement to make sure, by means of *ad hoc* treaties, that they have the prior consent of the safe States to which they normally send part of the influx of asylum-seekers (usually neighbouring countries). These arrangements are generally known as re-admission agreements and they include numerous instruments signed by the EU.[392] Such agreements also exist outside the EU, both in Europe and elsewhere. For example, a number of European States have entered into such pacts with Kosovo,[393] while a recent agreement of the kind has been signed by Australia and Malaysia.[394] Re-admission agreements obligate the States parties to take in not only their own citizens (an obligation enshrined, as explained earlier, in general international law[395]) but above all the citizens of third countries with whom there exists a link, generally a fairly tenuous one: possession of a visa or of a permit to stay or even the fact of having transited through the country.[396] Clearly, the purpose of such agreements is to guarantee repatriation to neighbouring States. Migrants often reach their final destination after transiting through just one State: if they are refugees, the re-admission agreement 'shifts' the responsibility for their protection onto the third country that has undertaken to admit them; if they are not refugees, the State does not have to arrange repatriation to each country of origin as this will be handled exclusively by the (safe) country of transit. However, these arrangements do not relieve the State repatriating the migrants of the duty to verify, case by case, the safety of the country of destination. In States in which the Asylum Procedures Directive applies, this obligation is not only provided for in the Directive itself, it is also (more generally) enshrined in Article 3(3) of the Dublin II Regulation, according to which an asylum-seeker can only be sent to a third

392 See the references in footnote 252, Chapter 4.
393 Kosovo signed re-admission agreements with eleven European countries: with Albania on 6 October 2009, France on 2 December 2009, Switzerland on 3 February 2010, Germany on 14 April 2010, Denmark on 8 June 2010, Norway on 15 October 2010, Austria on 30 September 2010, Slovenia on 10 May 2011, the Benelux countries on 12 May 2011, the Czech Republic on 24 June 2011 and Sweden on 4 October 2011. On other re-admission agreements signed by European countries see J.-P. Cassarino (2010a: 1 ff.).
394 The text of the agreement, which was signed on 25 July 2011, is available online at www.immi.gov.au. It provides for the transfer of asylum-seekers from Australia to Malaysia, and in the opposite direction of persons recognised as refugees in Malaysia by UNHCR (Malaysia is not a signatory to the Refugee Convention).
395 See footnote 391.
396 The link usually consists in possession of a visa or a permit to stay, previous residence or transit through the country to which re-admission is sought, or the presence of family connections. This is the case, to cite just a few examples, of Article 3 of the agreements between Kosovo and, respectively, Sweden, the Benelux countries, the Czech Republic (although here a permit to stay is not included and transit must be combined with illegal entry) and Slovenia. UNHCR is of the opinion that transit does not constitute a strong enough link and that the State in which the application for asylum is made should be the one to examine it: see UNHCR (2001b: para. 16).

country 'in compliance with the provisions of the Geneva Convention'.[397] The same cannot be said of the Agreement between Australia and Malaysia, which does not envisage a preliminary screening to reject asylum-seekers whose destination country, be it Australia or Malaysia, cannot be defined safe.[398]

The last type of safe country is the safe country of origin. Although this concept has been used in the past even outside the EU,[399] it mainly appears in Article 31 of the Asylum Procedures Directive, which provides that 'Member States shall, in accordance with paragraph 1, consider the application for asylum as unfounded where the third country is designated as safe pursuant to Article 29'. Designation as safe may occur in two ways: the first process, which takes place within the EU, has never been used because the Court of Justice nullified the provisions of Article 29 on the grounds that the procedure they stipulated for designating safe countries of origin was not the same as the procedure provided for in the EC Treaty.[400]

397 The Refugee Convention is mentioned in all the agreements signed with Kosovo: see, to give just one example, Article 12 of the Agreement with Albania. In reality, it is not so much the provisions of these agreements that may conflict with those of the Refugee Convention as the national legislation enacting them, in particular the procedural rules. Whereas in the case of the EU countries the provisions of the Asylum Procedures Directive and the Dublin II Regulation (which lays down procedural requirements that are in line with the obligations dictated by the Refugee Convention) apply, the problem may arise in respect of Kosovo's compliance with those obligations (the country not being a party to the Convention). In the new Dublin III Regulation, Article 3(3) does not refer to the Refugee Convention but directly to the new Procedures Directive.

398 See Australian Human Rights Commission, *Inquiry into Australia's agreement with Malaysia in relation to asylum seekers. Australian Human Rights Commission Submission to the Senate Standing Committees on Legal and Constitutional Affairs*, 14 September 2011, available online at www.hreoc.gov.au, especially para. 33 ff. As pointed out in footnote 387, the procedure adopted in Australia in respect of asylum-seekers has several flaws. On this point see also Amnesty International, *Refugee Campaign Factsheet. Australia's Refugee Determination Process*, 23 March 2009, available online at www.amnesty.org.au. Moreover, the Agreement between Australia and Malaysia does not require any type of link between asylum-seekers and the State required to re-admit them.

399 Examples referring to countries outside the EU – for which see J. C. Hathaway (2005: 296) – nonetheless concern countries within Europe, such as France, Germany, UK (when not EU Members) and Switzerland.

400 European Court of Justice, judgment of 6 May 2008, Case C-133/06, *European Parliament v. Council of the European Union, Reports of Cases*, 2008, p. I-03189 ff. Article 29(1) and (2) of the Asylum Procedures Directive provided for the adoption and amendment of the list of safe countries of origin by means of consultation ('The Council shall, acting by a qualified majority on a proposal from the Commission and after consultation of the European Parliament, adopt a minimum common list of third countries . . .') while Article 67(5) of the EC Treaty stipulated that – provided the Council had already adopted 'Community legislation defining the common rules and basic principles governing these issues' – the co-decision procedure (now ordinary legislative procedure) should be used for measures on asylum, as part of 'minimum standards on procedures in Member States for granting or withdrawing refugee status' (Article 63(1)(d), TEC). Thus, on the one hand, the Treaty adopted the co-decision procedure while, on the other, the Directive required the consultation procedure, in

The second process is national and is adopted in some Member States, as documented by the European Commission in its report on the application of the Directive as prescribed in Article 42 of the same.[401] It is worth noting that Article 31(1) of the Directive requires, for the purpose of applying the concept of safe country of origin and in accordance with the recommendations of UNHCR,[402] an 'individual examination',[403] an obligation that is generally respected by the States to which the Directive applies.[404]

violation of Article 67 as the Council would thereby overstep the powers granted to it under the Treaty. According to Article 67, the co-decision procedure was only to be followed in the absence of 'common rules' and 'basic procedures', which is the reason why the Asylum Procedures Directive was adopted by consultation procedure, allowing the Council to insert the provisions contained in Article 29(1) and (2) despite the contrary opinion of the European Parliament. See the European Parliament legislative Resolution on the amended proposal for a Council directive on minimum standards on procedures in Member States for granting and withdrawing refugee status (14203/2004 – C6-0200/2004 – 2000/0238(CNS)), OJ C 277 of 21 September 2006, p. 42 ff., and for the reasons see Report (A6-0222/2005) by Wolfgang Kreissl-Dörfler of 29 June 2005 on the amended proposal for a Council directive on minimum standards on procedures in Member States for granting and withdrawing refugee status (2000/0238(CNS)). In the new Procedures Directive the 'European' designation has been eliminated.

401 Report from the Commission to the European Parliament and the Council on the application of Directive 2005/85/EC of 1 December 2005 on minimum standards on procedures in Member States for granting and withdrawing refugee status, COM (2010) 465 def., especially para. 5.2.5. The new Procedures Directive has retained the concept of nationally designated safe country of origin (see Article 36), including the safeguards already included in the text of the previous Procedures Directive.

402 UNHCR (2001b: para. 39): 'given the need for an individual assessment of the specific circumstances of the case and the complexities of such a decision, best State practice does not apply any designation of safety in a rigid manner or use it to deny access to procedures. Rather, it bases any presumption of safety on precise, impartial and up-to-date information and admits the applicant to the regular asylum procedure, so that s/he has an effective opportunity to rebut any general presumption of safety based on his/her particular circumstances'. UNHCR had already expressed a similar view: see UNHCR (1992b). For a practical application of these criteria see UNHCR (2003b).

403 Similarly, see Article 36 of the new Procedures Directive.

404 Report from the Commission COM (2010) 465 def., para. 5.2.5. Annex II of the Directive sets out the criteria that States and the Council – for which, as explained, the problem no longer exists – must apply in designating the safe country of origin: 'A country is considered as a safe country of origin where, on the basis of the legal situation, the application of the law within a democratic system and the general political circumstances, it can be shown that there is generally and consistently no persecution as defined in Article 9 of Directive 2004/83/EC, no torture or inhuman or degrading treatment or punishment and no threat by reason of indiscriminate violence in situations of international or internal armed conflict'. The Annex also lists some of the elements that should be taken into account when making the assessment: 'the extent to which protection is provided against persecution or mistreatment by: (a) the relevant laws and regulations of the country and the manner in which they are applied;

In the final analysis, it is clear from the foregoing considerations that the concept of safe country, whatever the context, does not constitute an exception to the prohibition on *refoulement*. It assumes that the country of destination is not one in which the asylum-seeker risks persecution as described in Article 33 of the Refugee Convention. Moreover, as we have seen, there exists no widespread practice in the opposite sense, either substantive or regarding the procedures for determining whether a State is truly safe for each individual asylum-seeker.

1.7 C) Mass influxes

In the course of the *travaux préparatoires* for the Refugee Convention the delegate for the Netherlands, Baron van Boetzelaer, taking up an earlier statement by the Swiss delegate Mr Zutter offering an interpretation of Article 33 that did not contemplate rejection at the border of 'large groups of persons',[405] expressed his country's reluctance 'about assuming unconditional obligations so far as mass influxes of refugees were concerned'.[406] His position was endorsed, at the same meeting, by the Italian, Swedish, German, Belgian and French delegates. The French delegate was particularly explicit, restricting the application of the prohibition on *refoulement* to the country 'in which the refugee is residing' and adding that 'The hypothesis of any large influx of refugees did not ... enter into question'.[407] Baron van Boetzelaer, clearly concerned about the possibility of deducing from the work of the Conference that the States were even vaguely in favour of including mass influxes within the scope of the principle of *non-refoulement*, insisted at a later meeting that,

> In order to dispel any possible ambiguity and to reassure his Government, ... to have it placed on record that the Conference was in agreement with the

(b) observance of the rights and freedoms laid down in the European Convention for the Protection of Human Rights and Fundamental Freedoms and/or the International Covenant for Civil and Political Rights and/or the Convention against Torture, in particular the rights from which derogation cannot be made under Article 15(2) of the said European Convention; (c) respect of the non-refoulement principle according to the Geneva Convention; (d) provision for a system of effective remedies against violations of these rights and freedoms'. According to the Commission Report there are five member states whose national rules 'do not fully and explicitly reflect the Directive's criteria'. Similarly, see Annex I of the new Procedures Directive.

405 See Conference of Plenipotentiaries on the Status of Refugees and Stateless Persons: Summary Record of the Sixteenth Meeting, p. 11. Mr Zutter had said that, 'in the present instance the word ["return"] applied solely to refugees who had already entered a country, but were not yet resident there. According to that interpretation, States were not compelled to allow large groups of persons claiming refugee status to cross its frontier' (ibid. p. 6).

406 Ibid. p. 11.

407 Ibid. p. 12. The French delegate's statement opened up the debate, prompted by the Chair of the Conference, that led to the replacement in Article 33(2) of the wording 'in which he is residing' with the broader expression 'in which he is'.

interpretation that the possibility of mass migrations across frontiers or of attempted mass migrations was not covered by article 33.[408]

In response, the Chair of the Conference noted that there were no objections to the request and put the States' position on official record.[409] As with other aspects of the Convention that have been extensively 'reshaped' during subsequent implementation, one may wonder whether the interpretation that emerged from the *travaux préparatoires* for the Refugee Convention has been faithfully followed in this field.

First we need to clarify exactly what is meant by mass influx of refugees (or asylum-seekers). This is defined as the movement of extremely large numbers of persons, prompted to abandon their country in haste as a result of war, revolution or natural disaster.[410] That said, more important for a correct assessment of this alleged exception to the principle of *non-refoulement* is not so much the reason for the mass influx as its dimensions. It would be illogical to assume that there exists an exception to the principle of *non-refoulement* based on substantive motives, for the prohibition 'fixes' the asylum seeker's presence (and indeed that of any individual coming 'into contact' with the territory of the State[411]) until it is clear, including from the reasons for that presence, whether or not he or she has the right to stay. In other words, the lawfulness of a rejection cannot be determined on the basis of something that is subject to an assessment, which, in turn, cannot be performed if the person is removed.

It is also apparent from the *travaux préparatoires* that none of the delegates was particularly keen to make it clear from the terminology whether the influx involved persons not included in the definition of Article 1A of the Refugee Convention.[412]

408 Conference of Plenipotentiaries on the Status of Refugees and Stateless Persons: Summary Record of the Thirty-Fifth Meeting, p. 21.
409 Ibid.
410 On this point see G. Carella (1992: 905), who uses the term 'displaced persons' to describe such people. Recently, UNHCR Executive Committee provided a more exhaustive explanation of the concept of mass influx: 'mass influx situations may, inter alia, have some or all of the following characteristics: (i) considerable numbers of people arriving over an international border; (ii) a rapid rate of arrival; (iii) inadequate absorption or response capacity in host States, particularly during the emergency; (iv) individual asylum procedures, where they exist, which are unable to deal with the assessment of such large numbers' (UNHCR EXCOM Conclusion on International Cooperation and Burden and Responsibility Sharing in Mass Influx No. 100 (LV), 2004, available online at www.refworld.org, para. a)).
411 See footnote 212.
412 Baron van Boetzelaer himself did not distinguish between 'mass influxes of refugees' (Conference of Plenipotentiaries on the Status of Refugees and Stateless Persons: Summary Record of the Sixteenth Meeting, p. 11) and 'mass migrations' (Conference of Plenipotentiaries on the Status of Refugees and Stateless Persons: Summary Record of the Thirty-Fifth Meeting, p. 21). The other delegates adopted the same attitude: see Conference of Plenipotentiaries on the Status of Refugees and Stateless Persons: Summary Record of the Sixteenth Meeting, p. 11 ff.

On the contrary, the concern voiced on that occasion related to the difficulties the State would encounter in processing such a large number of refugees (or asylum-seekers). Even the delegate for the Netherlands, apparently among the strongest supporters of this narrow interpretation of Article 33(1), seemed eager to assure any State concerned that they would receive staunch international cooperation.[413] Another question is whether the notion of refugee contained in the Refugee Convention has evolved to the extent that it now includes persons who, far from being at risk of persecution in their country of origin, have fled because of generalised violations of human rights.[414] This, however, does not impinge on the main obligation associated with the principle of *non-refoulement*, that is, the obligation to admit temporarily a person during the course of a fair procedure to determine whether (and on what basis) he or she can stay in the territory of the host country.

Having clarified this point, it can be shown that there is a tendency in standard practice, albeit with some exceptions,[415] to adopt (and even to consolidate) an interpretation of Article 33(1) whereby States are obligated to admit, temporarily, even persons arriving *en masse* at their borders. This obligation is accompanied, however, by a duty of other States, especially those in proximity, to assist in dealing with the emergency and to do everything they can to resolve it, mainly through dialogue and cooperation with the State of origin with a view to allowing the eventual repatriation of the refugees when the situation that caused the influx comes to an end.[416] This is based on a number of elements: legal theory generally

413 See Conference of Plenipotentiaries on the Status of Refugees and Stateless Persons: Summary Record of the Sixteenth Meeting, p. 11: 'the Netherlands was somewhat diffident about assuming unconditional obligations so far as mass influxes of refugees were concerned, unless international cooperation was sufficiently organized to deal with such a situation'.

414 Which I do not think is the case. Anyway, on this point see Chapter 2 below.

415 An example is Nepal's rejection of asylum-seekers from Tibet in 2011. According to J. C. Hathaway (2005: 360), there could have been some justification in the Nepalese authorities' fear of retaliation by China. Some newspapers (see, in particular, the article by S. Unnithan, 'Fleeing Tibet', *India Today*, 5 December 2011) reported that the Chinese authorities bribed Nepalese border officials with sums of about 10,000 yuan, just over 1,200 euros, for every Tibetan asylum-seeker handed over. Another example is the restrictions introduced from 1995 by Tanzania and other neighbouring African countries during the Rwanda genocide. See the article by S. Kiley, 'Tanzania closes border to 100,000 Rwanda refugees', *The Times*, 1 April 1995, and more generally the article by M. K. Juma (2000: 136–7). Last, there is the closure of Macedonia's frontiers against refugees from Kosovo in 1999 (on which see M. Barutciski and A. Suhrke (2001: 95 ff.)), although this did not last long, as in the face of pressure (and cooperation) from the international community the country re-opened its borders and made temporary arrangements for the refugees (see 'Macedonia accepts Kosovo refugees after UN plea', *Birmingham Evening Mail*, 24 May 1999).

416 As J. Fitzpatrick (2000: 305) underlines, repatriation is the most desirable solution and the one – I may add – that is generally preferred in practice. Of course, it goes without saying that among the mass of displaced persons there may be a few actual refugees

converges on this point and some writers have taken a very categorical position.[417] In addition, UNHCR has published numerous clarifications and the Executive Committee affirmed, as early as 1981, that,

> In situations of large-scale influx, asylum-seekers should be admitted to the State in which they first seek refuge and if that State is unable to admit them on a durable basis, it should always admit them at least on a temporary basis and provide them with protection according to the principles set out below. . . . In all cases the fundamental principle of *non-refoulement* – including non-rejection at the frontier – must be scrupulously observed.[418]

The OAU Refugee Convention includes the obligation of temporary protection, during which, 'in the spirit of African solidarity and international cooperation', a definitive solution must be found for the refugees.[419] The EU has adopted a specific directive (on which more in section 4.9), which sets out a complex mechanism for determining and managing refugee emergencies that the Council has not yet actually put into operation.[420] In the light of the foregoing and despite some continuing uncertainties,[421] there is a tendency to broaden the

who can still make an application for determination of that status in the country that has received them under the banner of international cooperation.

417   See E. Lauterpacht and D. Bethlehem (2003: 119 ff.), according to whom 'The requirement to focus on individual circumstances as a condition precedent to a denial of protection under Article 33(1) must not be taken as detracting in any way from the application of the principle of *non-refoulement* in cases of the mass influx of refugees or asylum seekers'. The same position is held by G. J. L. Coles (1978–1980: 189 ff.), G. Carella (1992: 916 ff.), I. Castrogiovanni (1994: 481–2), A. V. Eggli (2002: 168 ff.), J.-F. Durieux and J. McAdam (2004: 13) and F. Lenzerini (2009: 404 ff., especially 409), to which the reader is referred for the practice of States that follow the prevailing interpretation. More cautious are J. C. Hathaway (2005: 355 ff.) and G. S. Goodwin-Gill and J. McAdam (2007: 335 ff.). On the recent case of Syria, and also asserting that the principle of *non-refoulement* applies to mass influxes of persons, see Resolution of the Parliamentary Assembly of the Council of Europe No. 1902 (2012) and UNHCR (2013: *passim*).

418   UNHCR EXCOM Conclusion on protection of asylum-seekers in situations of large-scale influx No. 22 (XXXII), 1981, available online at www.refworld.org, para. II.A. See also, along the same lines, UNHCR EXCOM Conclusion on temporary refuge No. 19 (XXXI), 1981, para. a), and more fully, Conclusion on international cooperation and burden and responsibility sharing in mass influx No. 100, 1981, available online at www.refworld.org.

419   Article 2(4) and (5) of the Organization of African Unity Convention Governing the Specific Aspects of Refugee Problems in Africa.

420   Council Directive 2001/55/EC of 20 July 2001 on minimum standards for giving temporary protection in the event of a mass influx of displaced persons and on measures promoting a balance of efforts between Member States in receiving such persons and bearing the consequences thereof, OJ L 212 of 7 August 2001, p. 12 ff.

421   A more sceptical position appears to be taking hold, although there is certainly also a tendency to consolidate the application of the prohibition on *refoulement* to mass influxes: see J. Fitzpatrick (2000: 279 ff.). It is worth noting that UNHCR's insistence

guarantees offered under Article 33(1) to include mass influxes of displaced persons to which States must grant temporary entry. This will be conditional on the activation of international cooperation mechanisms to distribute the displaced persons among various States – bearing in mind the need to determine whether among them there are refugees in the true sense – and to undertake concrete attempts to resolve the causes of the influx, mainly through dialogue with the State (or in the territory) where it originated.[422]

The principle of *non-refoulement* has some exceptions, therefore, in that there exist cases in which a contracting State may send a refugee to a country where he or she is at risk of the type of persecution described in Article 1A and Article 33 of the Refugee Convention. This possibility is envisaged by the Convention itself (Article 33(2) as well as the specific exception of Article 1F) and may also be the case of a State faced with a mass influx of displaced persons without adequate cooperation from the international community, particularly neighbouring States. The exceptions do not operate in the same way, however. The exceptions of Article 33(2) and Article 1F in no case allow *refoulement* without a proper procedure to establish grounds for their application, during the course of which, in order to respect their purpose, the applicant must be allowed to stay in the territory of the State. It is less clear whether this procedural precaution, accompanied by temporary residence, must be observed in the case of a State faced with a mass influx. Indeed, it would appear that such a State only has an obligation when it receives appropriate cooperation from the rest of the international community, but not when it is left isolated and is unable, either because of the number of persons involved or the rapidity of their arrival, to manage the situation.

1.8 Other obligations of States in respect of refugees

Although *non-refoulement* is by far the most important obligation that the Refugee Convention imposes on the contracting States, it is not the only one. The others differ according to the category in which the refugee falls: refugee *tout court*, refugee lawfully present in the country, and refugee lawfully staying in the country (see section 1.1). Having already examined the principle of *non-refoulement*, I will now look at the other main rules enshrined in the Convention: the prohibition on imposing penalties on refugees who unlawfully enter the territory of the State (Article 31), a provision which, like the prohibition on *refoulement*, refers to refugees *tout court*; and the rules on freedom of movement (Article 26) and on

---

on drawing up an *ad hoc* instrument to extend the protection offered by the Refugee Convention by regulating the situation of mass influxes – the likely content of which is outlined by Fitzpatrick – suggests that that tendency is ongoing: see UNHCR (2003e: 38), in which UNHCR mentions exploring, in relation to mass influxes, 'the need for another authoritative text, in addition to the 1951 Convention and the 1969 OAU Convention'.

422 J.-P. L. Fonteyne (1978–1980: 162 ff., especially 187) is insistent on this aspect.

the expulsion of refugees 'lawfully in the country' (Article 32, also partly examined above).[423]

According to Article 31(1):

> The Contracting States shall not impose penalties, on account of their illegal entry or presence, on refugees who, coming directly from a territory where their life or freedom was threatened in the sense of article 1, enter or are present in their territory without authorization, provided they present themselves without delay to the authorities and show good cause for their illegal entry or presence.

This rule applies to refugees without specifying in any way the manner of their 'attachment' to the State receiving them. Hence, as borne out by standard practice,[424] its benefits apply to the broadest concept of 'refugee'.[425] Anyway, as I have shown earlier, the determination procedure does not create refugee status,

---

423   The other obligations are of minor importance in that they merely forbid discrimination and are normally 'overshadowed' by the more general human rights rules enshrined in universal or regional instruments. They are as follows: regarding refugees *tout court*, Article 3 (non-discrimination), on which see R. Marx and W. Staff (2011: 643 ff.); Article 4 (freedom of religion), on which see C. Walter (2011: 657 ff.); Article 13 (rights to moveable and immoveable property), on which see S. Leckie and E. Simperingham (2011a: 883 ff.); Article 16 (access to courts), on which see B. Elberling (2011: 931 ff.); Article 22 (right to education), on which see A. Zimmermann and J. Dörschner (2011: 1019 ff.); Article 25 (right to administrative assistance), on which see E. Lester (2011c: 1127 ff.); Article 27 (right to identity papers), on which see J. Vedsted-Hansen (2011a: 1163 ff.); Article 29 (fiscal charges) and Article 30 (transfer of assets), on which see B. Nagy (2011a: 1215 ff.; and 2011b: 1227 ff.). Regarding refugees lawfully present in the country the relevant article is Article 18 (self-employment), on which see A. Edwards (2011b: 973 ff.). For refugees lawfully staying the articles are: Article 14 (artistic rights and industrial property), on which see A. Metzger (2011: 895 ff.); Article 15 (rights of association), on which see M. Teichmann (2011: 909 ff.); Article 17 (wage-earning employment) and Article 19 (liberal professions), on which see A. Edwards (2011a: 951 ff.; and 2011c: 983 ff.); Article 21 (housing), on which see S. Leckie and E. Simperingham (2011b: 1003 ff.); Article 23 (public relief) and Article 24 (labour legislation and social security), on which see E. Lester (2011a: 1041 ff.; and 2011b: 1057 ff.); and Article 28 (travel documents), on which see J. Vedsted-Hansen (2011b: 1177 ff.). On all articles see also J. C. Hathaway (2005: *passim*).

424   See New Zealand Court of Appeal, decision of 18 November 2010, *X (CA746/2009)* v. *R*, especially para. 16 ff. In the opposite sense see also High Court of the Special Administrative Region of Hong Kong, decision of 10 March 2008, *RV* v. *Director of Immigration and another*, especially para. 92 ff., in which the judge did not deem that the imposition of penalties should be ruled out in the case of an asylum-seeker who had illegally entered the territory of the State on the grounds that 'In the present case, the applicant's challenge arises out of Hong Kong's obligations under the Convention Against Torture. The convention does not have an article equivalent to art. 31 of the Refugee Convention'. Note that China has not yet extended the application of the Refugee Convention to Hong Kong: on this point see K. Loper (2006) and footnote 280.

425   For the legal theory see J. C. Hathaway (2005: 388 ff.) and G. Noll (2011: 1253).

it merely declares it to exist. The rule in question excludes certain refugees for other reasons. It only applies to persons arriving *directly* from the country in which they are at risk of persecution, as stipulated in Article 1, and provided they present themselves to the authorities without delay and can show good reason for their illegal entry into the country.

The first requirement originates from an amendment proposed by France, which the country's delegate Mr Colemar advocated for the following reason:

> the right of asylum was implicit in the Convention, even if it was not explicitly proclaimed therein. . . . If a state were to refuse admission to refugees on the pretext that they had entered its territory irregularly, they would be sent back to their countries of origin and would no longer be refugees.[426]

The French delegate makes some very useful points, not so much by affirming a right of asylum, immediately disputed by the British delegate, as by clarifying that the protection of the Refugee Convention would fail if States were able to punish by *refoulement* asylum-seekers who entered the country illegally.[427] These are indeed in the majority, for in fleeing a present danger they are unlikely to have time to seek the documents required for lawful entry into the State of refuge. This means, in the first place, that even where the country from which the asylum-seekers have actually come is not the same as their country of origin, the rule still applies if they are at risk of persecution in that 'third' State.[428] Moreover, if asylum-seekers transit through places other than those where they risk persecution this should also be disregarded, as someone needing to flee from a persecutory State may not, indeed probably will not, always find a convenient route without 'stop-overs'.[429] Let it be clear, though, that if during the journey the refugee 'touches down' in 'safe' places, he or she may be sent back there, obviously following careful assessment. This rule, however, has absolutely nothing to do with removal, which is not among the penalties it precludes; and this is perhaps the most important consideration. The rationale for the rule does not envisage, as is clear from the *travaux préparatoires*, that lawful sanctions, in accordance with Article 31, may include *refoulement*.[430] An asylum-seeker who has illegally entered the territory of the State of refuge, and who has not come *directly* from a third country where he or she is at risk of persecution or who does not report immediately to the authorities, may be punished but may *never* be sent away, except under the conditions provided for in Article 33 of the Refugee Convention. The applicant must demonstrate good faith by reporting to the authorities without delay to prove that he or she entered the country illegally for

426 Conference of Plenipotentiaries on the Status of Refugees and Stateless Persons: Summary Record of the Thirteenth Meeting, 10 July 1951, A/CONF.2/SR.13, p. 13.
427 Ibid., p. 14.
428 According to J. C. Hathaway (2005: 393 ff.).
429 J. C. Hathaway (2005: 396 ff.). See also New Zealand High Court, decision of 4 April 2007, *Hassan* v. *Department of Labour (Hassan)*, para. 39.
430 J. C. Hathaway (2005: 412).

'good reasons'. This requirement should be interpreted flexibly, in the sense that there should be no strict time limit because the situation has to be assessed according to factors such as the 'effects of trauma, language problems, lack of information, previous experiences which often result in a suspicion of those in authority, feelings of insecurity . . .'.[431]

Article 31(2) adds that

> The Contracting States shall not apply to the movements of such refugees restrictions other than those which are necessary and such restrictions shall only be applied until their status in the country is regularized or they obtain admission into another country. The Contracting States shall allow such refugees a reasonable period and all the necessary facilities to obtain admission into another country.

This provision raises two problems: identifying the beneficiaries ('such refugees') and the matter of the restrictions, especially measures that limit personal freedom such as, first and foremost, detention. On the first problem, the question is whether refugees under Article 31(2) include all refugees who enter the country illegally or only the ones on whom no penalty can be imposed. The first option is supported by authoritative legal theory, according to which Article 31(2) 'not only *limits* States' prerogative to control the movements of refugees, but also *asserts* and *legitimizes* control over them. Therefore, it would make no sense to leave a larger group of unlawfully present refugees outside its scope'.[432] I believe the position taken in the literature to be the correct one, adding one further point: Article 31(2) does not represent an exception to Article 31(1) as the latter prohibits States from imposing penalties on some refugees, while the former *adds* a further, more specific prohibition (restrictions on freedom of movement) with certain exceptions ('other than those which are necessary . . . until their status in the country is regularized or they obtain admission into another country').[433] The restriction permitted by Article 31(2) is most often detention, to which many States resort.[434] The conditions under which they may exercise this power have been set out by UNHCR.[435] Citing the provisions of the 'main human rights instruments', it states, among other things, that detention must be an exceptional solution, adopted in the absence of viable alternatives (such as, for instance, the creation of 'open' residential centres), it must be prescribed by law, and it must be reasonable and proportional to the objectives pursued. These objectives are the need to identify the applicant, to verify the elements on which the application is based, to punish

---

431 UNHCR (1999: para. 4).
432 G. Noll (2011: 1267 ff.). The author cites other equally authoritative writers in support, particularly A. Grahl-Madsen (1966–1972, II: 420).
433 Some of the case law appears not to go in the same direction: see the decision in the case of *Hassan*, para. 35 ff., especially para. 43.
434 See J. Hughes and F. Liebaut (eds.) (1998: *passim*).
435 UNHCR (1999).

any instance of fraud in submitting the application, and to safeguard national security and public order. States must also observe specific safeguards in the case of applicants falling within one of the vulnerable categories.[436]

Articles 26 and 32 of the Refugee Convention, respectively on freedom of movement and limitations on expulsion, have a narrower field of application: both use the term 'refugees lawfully in the territories of States'.[437] It is unclear where exactly lies the line separating this category from refugees *tout court*. The problem arises in particular in connection with refugees arriving in the country of refuge without documents and it is resolved in the prevailing legal theory, although standard practice does not always follow the same line, by applying national laws.[438] Thus, in States where the rules on entry into their territory do not apply to asylum-seekers under national legislation, the latter will be 'lawfully' in the territory and therefore Articles 26 and 32 will apply to them, along with other specific provisions. Otherwise they can only enjoy the benefits granted to refugees *tout court*, above all the prohibition on *refoulement*.

Although this argument enjoys authoritative support, I do not think it is entirely convincing. It should be recalled that the main consequence of the prohibition on *refoulement* is to guarantee an applicant temporary residence, during which a fair procedure must take place. So, to declare that the applicant is lawfully in the territory when this is not in conflict with *national* laws on entry is completely irrelevant for the reason that those same laws *must* guarantee entry (subject to the outcome of a fair procedure) under Article 33(1). In other words, I do not consider an applicant's presence in the country to be lawful solely because it must be guaranteed temporarily under Article 33(1), as the lawfulness of the applicant's presence depends on the outcome of the procedure to determine status. This view appears to be borne out by the systematic interpretation given to the Refugee Convention. Consider that the other provision of the Convention, apart from Articles 26 and 32, that refers to 'lawfully in' the territory is Article 18, which obligates States to accord treatment as favourable as possible – and in any case

---

436 These are minors, elderly persons, victims of torture, persons with mental or physical disability, women, and stateless persons.

437 According to Article 26, 'Each Contracting State shall accord to refugees lawfully in its territory the right to choose their place of residence and to move freely within its territory subject to any regulations applicable to aliens generally in the same circumstance'. Article 32, on the other hand, states: '1. A Contracting State shall not expel a refugee lawfully in their territory save on grounds of national security or public order. 2. The expulsion of such a refugee shall be only in pursuance of a decision reached in accordance with due process of law. Except where compelling reasons of national security otherwise require, the refugee shall be allowed to submit evidence to clear himself, and to appeal to and be represented for the purpose before competent authority or a person or persons specially designated by the competent authority. 3. The Contracting States shall allow such a refugee a reasonable period within which to seek legal admission into another country. The Contracting States reserve the right to apply during that period such internal measures as they may deem necessary'.

438 For all see J. C. Hathaway (2005: 173 ff.).

no less favourable than that accorded to aliens generally – as regards 'the right to engage on his own account in agriculture, industry, handicrafts and commerce and to establish commercial and industrial companies'. The rights that the Convention associates with being lawfully in a country are based on a more solid 'attachment' between the refugee and the State than would appear realistic during determination of status.

An opposing argument, based on Article 31 examined above, also seems to concur with this interpretation; it refers explicitly to 'illegal entry or presence', and sets out at paragraph (2) the conditions under which States can restrict the freedom of movement of asylum-seekers. Were 'lawfully in' the territory, under Article 26, to signify the temporary residence of asylum-seekers who had entered the country without the necessary documents, it would be unclear to whom Article 31(2) might apply.[439] The provision would create a meaningless obligation because applicants 'lawfully in' the territory, allowed temporary entry without documents, would, as the argument goes, be subject to Article 26. It would be useless to object that this does not completely 'eliminate' the category of refugees to which Article 31(2) applies: the applicant who is without documents would either be allowed temporary entry (in which case his or her presence would become 'lawful' according to the theory) or not be admitted to the country, and hence the problem of restrictions on his or her freedom of movement would not arise, although there might be violation of the principle of *non-refoulement*.[440] Anyway, excluding people who are allowed into the country temporarily by virtue of that principle does not deprive them of the chief safeguard, which is the protection it offers.

Last, some convincing arguments are adduced in case law against the theory prevailing in legal literature. To quote Lord Burnton,

> I would . . . interpret Article 32 as inapplicable to a person who has been allowed in to a Contracting State for the sole purpose of its investigating and determining his claim to be a refugee and entitled to a right to reside. Otherwise, Article 32 would have the irrational effect of conferring on a person a right to remain in a Contracting State merely because he claims . . . his right to remain in the state in question. It is Article 33 that protects all refugees from being expelled to a country where they would be persecuted.[441]

---

439 Unless it is assumed to apply only to refugees who have entered the country unlawfully, coming directly from a place where they are at risk of persecution, and who have reported to the authorities without delay, showing good reason. But I have ruled out this interpretation (see above), including on the basis of the theory criticised here.

440 Nor is it possible to maintain that the applicant's temporary residence outside the territory of the State but within its jurisdiction is not equivalent to 'lawful presence' without destroying the argument upheld in § 1.3, as well as the theory now being criticised.

441 Decision of the Court of Appeal (Civil Division) of England and Wales, *Secretary of State for the Home Department* v. *ST*, para. 29.

It follows from the foregoing that the term 'lawfully in' refers to applicants who have entered the territory of the host country legally, and therefore have the documents required for entry by any other alien. There is not much to be said about the benefit accorded by Article 26, except that it grants refugees (lawfully present) 'the right to choose their place of residence, to move freely within its territory, subject to any regulations applicable to aliens generally in the same circumstances'.

Article 32 has already been discussed, particularly as regards its field of application. There remain a few remarks to add concerning the notion of expulsion, its limits and the procedure to be followed. Expulsion is any measure taken by the State that terminates the refugee's presence in its territory against the latter's will. Exceptions should be interpreted narrowly and are 'grounds of national security and public order'. In general, national security here is equivalent to the concept expressed in Article 33(2) and therefore includes any threats intended to overthrow a government, including spying, sabotage, and so on.[442] Grounds of public order are instead cited when the applicant has committed a crime, ranging from the possession of forged documents to murder and in some cases terrorism.[443] There is no need to add that if the applicant is expelled to a country where he or she is at risk of persecution, the host country must adhere to the strict requirements of Article 33(2), nor that if the crimes for which the State intends to issue an expulsion order are particularly serious refugee status can always be refused under Article 1F.

The procedure must follow due process of law, which includes allowing the refugee to submit evidence in his or her 'defence', to appeal a negative decision, and to obtain legal representation during the appeal process (not including free legal aid). These guarantees no longer exist in the face of 'compelling' reasons of national security. This provision is designed to allow a State that invokes reasons of national security to not reveal the source or content of vital information that could put the life of its agents in danger or assist the plans of its enemies. According to legal theory, however, which stresses the absolutely exceptional nature of this restriction, it does not absolve the State of certain minimum guarantees and does not permit an expulsion order to be issued without impartial judicial oversight to verify, at the very least, the reliability of the minimal information the State is nonetheless required to provide.[444]

---

442 One of the most frequent examples is terrorism: see Court of Appeal (Civil Division) of England and Wales, decision of 27 July 2011, *XX* v. *Secretary of State for the Home Department*. It is not surprising that there is little case law in regard, as when States are faced with a threat caused by membership of or proximity to terrorist organisations they intervene at an earlier stage under Article 1F.

443 U. Davy (2011: 1311 ff.).

444 Ibid.: 1320.

2 The 1950 Rome Convention and its Protocols

2.1 Protection *par ricochet* in the case law of the European Court of Human Rights: A) Prohibition on torture and inhuman or degrading treatment or punishment

The Rome Convention contains no provisions relating to asylum,[1] merely imposing, in two of its Protocols, some restrictions on the power of States to expel aliens in the general sense.[2] Nonetheless, the European Court of Human

1 Convention for the Protection of Human Rights and Fundamental Freedoms, signed in Rome on 4 November 1950 and entered into force on 3 September 1953, 213 UNTS 221 ff. (ECHR). The Parliamentary Assembly put forward a proposal (Recommendation 293 (1961) of 26 September 1961, *Right of Asylum*, available online at www.assembly.coe. int) to include a provision on the right of asylum in the text of the Second Additional Protocol to the ECHR, having already begun drafting a Second Protocol following Recommendation 234 (1960) of 22 January 1960, Second Protocol to the Convention on Human Rights, ibid., which contained no mention of the right of asylum. The Assembly made its proposal only when the *travaux préparatoires* for the Second Protocol were already under way; accordingly, the Committee of Experts charged with reviewing the draft of the Second Protocol proposed by the Assembly in Recommendation 234 remarked that 'The complex nature of the problems raised by those proposals [on the right of asylum and the rights of minorities] prohibits any possibility of concluding examination of them in the near future. The Committee therefore considers that it is preferable to continue to study them in a legal context other than that of the Second Protocol to the Convention. It will give its views at a later stage on the action which should be taken upon them': see Committee of Experts on the problems relating to the European Convention on the Protection of Human Rights and Fundamental Freedoms, Second Protocol to the Convention, Draft Report to the Committee of Ministers, Introduction (DH/Exp/ Misc (62) 31 of 27 October 1962), in Council of Europe, *Collected Edition of the 'Travaux préparatoires' of the Protocol n. 4*, Strasbourg, 1976, ibid., p. 566. The Protocol (by then No. 4, following the adoption on 6 May 1963 of two amendment protocols) was adopted on 16 September 1963 with no clause on the right of asylum. The Assembly tried again later to promote the adoption of a convention on the right of asylum but gave up after a few years. I believe one of the last attempts was in Recommendation 1236 (1994) of 12 April 1994, available online at www.assembly.coe.int., para. 8.3 (a).
2 In Article 4 of Protocol No. 4 and Article 1 of Protocol No. 7, on which see below.

Rights (ECtHR) has managed to extract from the provisions of the Convention, notably Article 3, a sort of safeguard for persons at risk of serious violation of their human rights if sent to a given country (not necessarily that of origin). The outcome is not to give such persons a right of asylum but to prevent their removal, 'fixing' their presence in the territory of the State concerned until they can be sent to a country where they are not at risk or until they are granted leave to stay in the host State. The mechanism works very much like that of Article 33 of the Refugee Convention, which does not itself recognise a right of asylum but (save for exceptions) prevents a contracting State from removing an asylum-seeker to a persecutory country. Article 3 of the European Convention on Human Rights (ECHR) is not formulated in the same terms as Article 33, however, 'merely' stipulating that 'No one shall be subjected to torture or to inhuman or degrading treatment or punishment'. Because of this difference of wording the ECtHR has had to make some effort on the technical front to obtain a result similar to that of Article 33 of the Refugee Convention.

The means by which the ECtHR has imposed this interpretation is usually denoted as protection *par ricochet*,[3] a technique used first and most famously in the case of *Soering* on 7 July 1989.[4] On that occasion the Court ruled that the extradition of a German citizen by the UK violated the ECHR because in the country to which he was being sent (the United States) he would have been at serious risk of a treatment prohibited by Article 3. The applicant was suspected of a crime that in Virginia carried (and still carries) the death penalty and would therefore have been in danger of experiencing death row syndrome. The Court did not rule that Article 3 prohibited the death penalty as such, only that the expectation of such a penalty would amount to a form of torture.

The Court's ruling followed a long series of decisions by the European Commission of Human Rights (still functioning at the time) in which it had applied that very same reasoning. The ruling in the case of *Soering* had a far wider impact, however, as although in previous cases the Commission had upheld the principle of protection *par ricochet* in abstract, it had not found that a violation had been committed. Indeed, in what was probably the earliest case of the kind the Commission had used this principle not in relation to Article 3 ECHR, but to Article 6: the applicant argued that the respondent (Sweden) violated this provision by continuing to refuse him entry, thereby preventing him from appearing before the Swedish judge in the case to determine his right to visit his son.[5]

---

3 See G. Cohen-Jonathan (1989: 84).
4 Judgment of the ECtHR of 7 July 1989, Application 14038/88, *Soering* v. *United Kingdom (Soering)*, on which see, among others, S. Breitenmoser and G. E. Wilms (1989–1990: 845 ff.), C. Warbrick (1989–1990: 1073 ff.), A. Damato (1991: 648 ff.), R. B. Lillich (1991: 128 ff.) and M. P. Shea (1992: 85 ff.). For further references see A. Saccucci (2011: 151). Where not specified, judgments and decisions of the Commission and of the ECtHR are available online at www.echr.coe.int.
5 The applicant also alleged violation of Article 8 ECHR because by denying him an entry permit Sweden was preventing him from joining his son. On this point see § 2.3.

The Commission declared the application inadmissible because the petitioner had not exhausted all the internal remedies, but pronounced that

> a State which signs and ratifies the European Convention on Human Rights ... must be understood as agreeing to restrict the free exercise of its rights under general international law, including its right to control the entry and exit of foreigners, to the extent and within the limits of obligations which it has accepted under that Convention.[6]

Of particular interest is the Commission's decision in the case of *Kirkwood*: as would later happen before the ECtHR in the case of *Soering*, the allegation that extradition violated Article 3 (a US request of extradition from the UK) was based on death row syndrome. The Commission, after recalling that a 'decision to deport, extradite or expel an individual to face such conditions incurs the responsibility under Article I of the Convention of the contracting State which so decides',[7] nonetheless found that owing to a series of procedural and substantive elements the risk was not serious enough to warrant protection *par ricochet*.

Therefore, when the case of *Soering* came before the Court it had behind it a fairly solid body of decisions by the Commission, based on a highly innovative interpretation of Article 1 ECHR but also requiring that, where the connection with one of the provisions of the ECHR (in this case Article 3) was only 'indirect', the risk of exposing the applicant to violation of the article by means of removal had to be particularly serious. The Court based its decision in *Soering* on similar

---

6 Decision of the European Commission of Human Rights of 26 March 1960, Application 434/58, *X* v. *Sweden, Yearbook of the European Commission for Human Rights*, 1958–1959, p. 354 ff., especially p. 372. This case was the first of many decided by the Commission, which always ruled against the applicant: see the decision of 30 June 1964, Application 2143/64, *X* v. *Austria and Yugoslavia*, ibid., 1964, p. 328 ff., in which the Commission, having reaffirmed that it was not competent to decide in the matter of Yugoslavia's alleged violation (the State not being a member of the ECHR), ruled that the extradition of a Yugoslav citizen from Austria did not violate Article 3. See also the decision of 15 December 1971, Application 5012/71, *X* v. *Belgium, Collection of Decisions of the European Commission for Human Rights*, No. 40, p. 53 ff.: in this case, in which the applicant feared that extradition to Algeria would put him at risk of torture and death, the Commission based its decision on the fact that France had applied for extradition at the same time and if its request were accepted this would automatically rule out any violation of Article 3; decision of 26 March 1972, Application 1802/62, *X* v. *Germany, Yearbook of the European Commission for Human Rights*, 1963, p. 463 ff., concerning the applicant's extradition to Turkey, which according to the Commission would not put him at risk of the treatment listed in Article 3 ECHR. See also the decisions of 6 October 1962, Application 1465/62, *X* v. *Germany*, ibid., 1962, p. 256 ff.; 2 April 1971, Application 4763/71, *X* v. *Belgium, Collection of Decisions of the European Commission for Human Rights*, No. 37, p. 157 ff.; 30 September 1974, Application 6315/73, *X* v. *Germany*; 20 May 1976, Application 7216/75, *X* v. *Germany*; 6 October 1976, Application 7317/75, *Lynas* v. *Switzerland*; 3 May 1983, Application 10308/83, *Altun* v. *Germany*; and 6 March 1980, Application 8581/79, *X* v. *United Kingdom*.

7 Decision of 12 March 1984, Application 10479/83, *E. M. Kirkwood* v. *United Kingdom*.

arguments to those used by the Commission,[8] but with one, significant difference: briefly, it relied on the prime importance of the prohibition on torture ('one of the fundamental values of the democratic societies making up the Council of Europe'[9]) to justify extending the protection afforded in general by Article 1 ECHR to cover what the Court termed a 'potential' violation.[10] Where the ECtHR did not follow the Commission was in determining the threshold of risk required for the ECHR to be extended in this way. While it was the practice of the Commission, as borne out in the *Soering* case,[11] to require that the risk be serious and almost certain, the ECtHR lowered the threshold on the grounds that the assurances of the United States[12] were not sufficient to guarantee that there would be little likelihood or, in the words of the Court, to 'eliminate the risk' of a death sentence being handed down, in the face of which the petitioner would suffer death row syndrome.[13]

In subsequent decisions the ECtHR reiterated and elaborated on the principle of protection *par ricochet,* particularly with reference to Article 3 ECHR. The first point that needs to be clarified in the light of this case law is the specific nature of such protection. It has been argued, first and foremost by the defence counsel of the various respondent States,[14] that there is no basis for such protection in the ECHR insofar as violation would take place outside their *jurisdiction* (that is, in a third State) and so could not be attributed to them. I do not refer to the 'extraterritorial' nature of the obligations arising out of the ECHR, which is famously based on the interpretation of Article 1 ECHR that the ECtHR has adopted from the case of *Loizidou* onwards.[15] With protection *par ricochet* a sort of

---

8 The Court cited its judgment of 28 May 1985, Applications 9214/80, 9473/81 and 9474/81, *Abdulaziz, Cabales and Balkandali* v. *United Kingdom (Abdulaziz)*, especially para. 59, stating that, 'The Commission . . . confirmed . . . its established case law: the right of a foreigner to enter or remain in a country was not as such guaranteed by the Convention, but immigration controls had to be exercised consistently with Convention obligations, and the exclusion of a person from a State where members of his family were living might raise an issue under Article 8'.

9 *Soering* (ECtHR), para. 88.

10 Ibid., para. 90.

11 See the decision of the Commission of 19 January 1989, *Soering* v. *United Kingdom, Judgments and Decisions*, vol. 161, p. 53 ff., especially para. 162 ff.

12 The US gave an assurance that its 'own' judge would be informed that the UK had expressed the wish that a death sentence should not be handed down or at least not carried out.

13 *Soering* (ECtHR), para. 98. The reasons why the ECtHR diverged, here at least, from the established practice of the Commission probably relate, according to M. P. Shea (1992: 110), to the situation of the applicant, a young man with mental health problems.

14 See, for example, the UK's defence in *Soering* (ECtHR), para. 83. For a more recent example see the judgment of the ECtHR of 23 September 2010, Application 17185/05, *Iskandarov* v. *Russia*, para. 118. Legal theorists have rejected this interpretation: see P. De Sena (2002: 24 ff.). A contrary opinion, to my mind, is that of N. Mole and C. Meredith (2010: *passim*, especially pp. 9–10).

15 Judgment of the ECtHR of 18 December 1996, Application 15318/89, *Loizidou* v. *Turchia (Loizidou)*.

'dual' extraterritoriality may come into play, stemming on one side from the fact that removal occurs outside the territory of a contracting State but within its jurisdiction, as the ECtHR has reiterated in respect of the application of Article 3,[16] while the other (structural) aspect relates to the fact that Article 3 is (or may be) violated *owing to* the removal, but by and in the territory of a third State. I believe this second interpretation of 'extraterritoriality' has been promoted by the ECtHR, for although it has stated on several occasions that the actions of third States do not come within the field of application of the ECHR, and are therefore not within its own competence under the Convention,[17] on occasion it has debated whether such violations are potential or virtual.[18] This is a contradiction in terms: if there is indeed a violation it cannot be described as virtual; if instead the violation is defined as virtual, this is the same as affirming that it is committed (or may be committed) by entities or persons not belonging to the States parties to the Rome Convention and not within their jurisdiction, at some time following the removal. In other words, this simply confirms its extraterritorial nature.

It is clear from the case law of the ECtHR that an indirect violation is anything but virtual. On more than one occasion the Court has ruled that what will happen to the person removed is not a decisive factor, as the fact that he or she is (or is not) subjected to the treatment prohibited by Article 3 ECHR in the country of destination does not *per se* make the respondent State liable (or not liable). This position comes across very clearly in the case of *Vilvarajah*, in which the Court had to rule on the matter of several nationals of Sri Lanka of Tamil ethnic origin who were expelled from the UK and then subjected in their country of destination (Sri Lanka) to treatment prohibited by Article 3 ECHR. The ECtHR stated that

> there existed no special distinguishing features in their cases that could or ought to have enabled the Secretary of State to foresee that they would be treated in this way. . . . The Court also attaches importance to the knowledge and experience that the United Kingdom authorities had in dealing with large numbers of asylum seekers from Sri Lanka, many of whom were granted leave to stay, and to the fact that the personal circumstances of each applicant had been carefully considered by the Secretary of State in the light of a

16 For all, see the judgment of 23 February 2012, Application 27765/09, *Hirsi Jamaa et al. v. Italy (Hirsi Jamaa)*.

17 See, among many others, the judgment of the ECtHR of 28 February 2008, Application 37201/06, *Saadi v. Italy*, para. 126, on which see B. Concolino (2008: 627 ff.) and A. Gianelli (2008a: 449 ff.). Of course, the situation changes where the State of destination is a signatory to the ECHR, in which case the ECtHR can investigate what happens after removal: see the judgment of the ECtHR of 21 January 2011, Application 30696/09, *M. S. S. v. Belgium and Greece (M. S. S.)*.

18 Apart from the judgment in *Soering* (ECtHR), para. 90, see also the judgment of the ECtHR of 12 April 2005, Application 36378/02, *Shamayev and others v. Georgia and Russia (Shamayev)*, para. 339, on which see the brief comment by M. Gavouneli (2006: 674 ff.).

substantial body of material concerning the current situation in Sri Lanka and the position of the Tamil community within it.[19]

The Court was recently called upon to decide on the conduct of the Italian authorities, which had rejected several people to Libya under agreements with that country. Again, it did not give any particular weight to the circumstance that some of the applicants had been accorded refugee status by the Tripoli office of UNHCR – its presence in Libya being one of the factors, according to the Italian government, in favour of a positive evaluation of the country's safety[20] – but instead based its assessment on the '*foreseeable* consequences of the removal of an applicant to the receiving country in the light of the general situation there as well as his or her personal circumstances'.[21] In other decisions the Court has added that events taking place after removal are not entirely irrelevant. Thus, in the decision in the case of *Cruz Varas*, involving a citizen of Chile who was expelled from Sweden to his country of origin where he was then subjected to torture, the ECtHR found that it was not

> precluded, however, from having regard to information which comes to light subsequent to the expulsion. This may be of value in confirming or refuting the appreciation that has been made by the Contracting Party or the well-foundedness or otherwise of an applicant's fears.[22]

In other words, although the Court allowed that events taking place *after* a removal order issued by the respondent State was put into effect could help to 'confirm or refute' whether that decision was valid, it ruled out once and for all that they could confirm or refute that a violation had been committed. Despite some uncertainty on the part of the Court,[23] I believe this argument is decisive: actions taking place outside the jurisdiction of the contracting States cannot be construed as a violation of the ECHR; any violation must occur at the time of the removal, well within the jurisdiction of the State. This approach provides a clearer frame of reference for the obligation that States must fulfil to avoid violating the provisions of the ECHR.

The decision in the *Cruz Varas* case also provides an important indication. The ECtHR held that there was no alleged violation of Article 3 by Sweden because, despite medical evidence of past torture, there was only the applicant's testimony that this had been inflicted by the Chilean authorities. Since the existence of a risk of torture was based only on the applicant's claim, the Court focused on his

19 Judgment of the ECtHR of 30 October 1991, Applications 13163/87, 13164/87, 13165/87, 13447/87, 13448/87, *Vilvarajah and others* v. *United Kingdom (Vilvarajah)*, paras 112 and 114.
20 *Hirsi Jamaa*, para. 97.
21 Ibid., para. 117 (emphasis added).
22 Judgment of the ECtHR of 20 March 1991, Application 15576/89, *Cruz Varas and others* v. *Sweden (Cruz Varas)*, para. 76.
23 On this point see A. Saccucci (2011: 166–7).

credibility from the viewpoint of the Swedish authorities, and as he did not appear credible attributed importance to the fact that

> the Swedish authorities had particular knowledge and experience in evaluating claims of the present nature by virtue of the large number of Chilean asylum-seekers who had arrived in Sweden since 1973. The final decision to expel the applicant was taken after thorough examinations of his case by the National Immigration Board and by the Government.[24]

Ultimately, what the Court ruled on was how the State came to formulate its prognosis concerning the risk to the applicant in the country of destination. Thus, the first implication of Article 3 ECHR and, more generally, of protection *par ricochet* is a positive obligation of the contracting State to put in place a *procedure* designed, on the one hand, to collect all the information needed to reach a decision about the level of risk and, on the other, to make reasonable use of it in taking that decision. The Court could not have been clearer on this point. By setting out the circumstances in which the mechanism of protection *par ricochet* comes into play it has created an abstract formula whereby there is a violation of the provision every time the facts known to a State, or which should be known to it, when the removal takes place offer 'substantial grounds for believing in the existence of a real risk'.[25] The obligation concerns the means not the result, as States do not have to guarantee that every time a risk exists it will be detected.

Although this obligation is at the heart of protection *par ricochet*, failure to observe it is of course not enough to constitute a violation: the seriousness of the risk must be above a given threshold and, at least for Article 3, it must relate to the rights safeguarded by that provision, principally a person's physical and moral integrity, his or her human dignity. Hence, as the ECtHR's decision in *Soering* has shown, Article 3 cannot be used to safeguard the right to life; this and other rights may give rise to a separate form of protection (*par ricochet*), based on other provisions of the ECHR, in this case Article 2 (see below, section 2.2). The established case law of the ECtHR is extensive and it offers some indications of a general nature. First, there is little to be said about the types of treatment that qualify as torture or inhuman or degrading punishment: as noted in the literature,[26] the same general concept is found in the case law of the Court regarding Article 3 ECHR, including decisions not relating to its 'indirect' application.[27] The difference lies in the approach to seeking proof of violation, for it should not be forgotten that the violation does not stem from the treatment that the person removed (or about to be removed) is at risk of suffering in the country where he or she is sent, but is based on the contracting State's ability to foresee it. The cases of indirect

---

24 *Cruz Varas*, para. 81. See also *Vilvarajah*, para. 114.
25 *Cruz Varas*, para. 75.
26 C. W. Wouters (2009: 242–3).
27 On this point see P. Pustorino (2012: 63 ff.).

application of Article 3 largely concern what is traditionally protected by the prohibition on torture. Thus, the Court recognised that the prohibition extends not only to the cases mentioned but also to that of an Iranian woman wanted for adultery in her country of origin, an offence for which she risked lapidation,[28] the case of a man sentenced in Iran to one hundred lashes for the crime of fornication;[29] and the case of two Nigerian women, mother and daughter, at risk of female genital mutilation.[30]

In some circumstances the ECtHR has gone further and expanded the notion of torture for the purpose of the indirect application of Article 3 ECHR: it has extended it to cases of indirect *refoulement*, starting with the well-known decision in the case of *T. I.* v. *United Kingdom*.[31] The Court has also allowed, very exceptionally, that alleged damage to 'equivalent goods' may be admissible for the purpose of protection *par ricochet*, as with the right to health: in the case of *D.* v. *United Kingdom*, the ECtHR ruled that expelling a person in the terminal stage of AIDS would prevent him from obtaining suitable treatment.[32] Moreover, I believe that the Court has not in principle excluded from protection *par ricochet* even the breaching of second generation rights: in the case of *Tomic*, in which the applicant (a Serbian) complained that return to Croatia would put him at risk of being unable to regain possession of his property and of not obtaining recognition of several documents needed in order to find work and receive a pension, the Court remarked that

> The applicant has not specified any particular difficulty that would face him on his return, regarding, for example, property or pensions. Insofar as he relies therefore on the general hardship and difficulty of the situation facing those in a war-affected region, *the Court is not persuaded that this reaches the level of minimum severity* required to engage Article 3 of the Convention.[33]

28 Judgment of the ECtHR of 11 July 2000, Application 40035/98, *Jabari* v. *Turkey*.
29 Judgment of the ECtHR of 22 June 2006, Application 24245/03, *D. and others* v. *Turkey*.
30 Decision of the ECtHR of 8 March 2007, Application 23944/05, *Emily Collins and Ashley Akaziebie* v. *Sweden*.
31 Judgment of the ECtHR of 7 March 2000, Application 43844/98, *T. I.* v. *United Kingdom*. For more recent cases see *M. S. S.*, para. 286, and *Hirsi Jamaa*, para. 146.
32 Judgment of the ECtHR of 2 May 1997, Application 30240/96, *D.* v. *United Kingdom*. However, the Court sets a particularly high risk threshold in such cases. Its position is completely coherent because, as will be explained later, this is a situation in which the country of destination does not comply with the positive obligation of protection, as typically happens when the threat comes from private individuals. The judgment of the ECtHR of 20 October 2011, Application 55463/09, *Samina* v. *Sweden*, especially para. 56 ff., is a good example: rejecting the argument based on the health of the applicant, the Court stated that, 'having regard to the high threshold set by Article 3, particularly where the case does not concern the direct responsibility of the Contracting State for the possible harm, in the Court's view, the present case does not disclose the very exceptional circumstances established by its case-law'.
33 Decision of the ECtHR of 14 October 2003, Application 17837/03, *Tomic* v. *United Kingdom*. C. W. Wouters (2009: 240–1) holds a sceptical view of the Court's allegedly more open stance.

The threshold of risk was based on the notion of probability, the Court ruling that it was not necessary to be certain something would happen but that an abstract possibility was not enough. Typically, the threshold is not passed when the risk does not depend on the applicant's personal circumstances but on the general situation of the country of destination. In *Vilvarajah*, the ECtHR decided that the evidence relating to the applicants' past and the general situation in the country was insufficient to prove 'that their personal position was any worse than the generality of other members of the Tamil community or other young male Tamils who were returning to their country'.[34] Recently, the Court has apparently taken a more liberal position when the applicants belong to a group (or a minority) that is systematically subjected, in the country of destination, to the treatment prohibited by Article 3 ECHR. In the case of *Salah Sheekh*, the Court, after reaffirming the view it had expressed in *Vilvarajah*, added,

> on the basis of the applicant's account and the information about the situation in the 'relatively unsafe' areas of Somalia in so far as members of the Ashraf minority are concerned, that it is foreseeable that on his return the applicant would be exposed to treatment in breach of Article 3.[35]

In fact the ECtHR went even further, remarking that, at least in theory, in 'extreme cases of general violence' it is possible that a removal will violate Article 3 ECHR 'simply by virtue of an individual being exposed to such violence on return'.[36] The

---

34 *Vilvarajah*, para. 111, in which the Court added that, 'Since the situation was still unsettled there existed the possibility that they might be detained and ill-treated as appears to have occurred previously in the cases of some of the applicants. . . . A mere possibility of ill-treatment, however, in such circumstances, is not in itself sufficient to give rise to a breach of Article 3'. For a more recent case see the judgment of the ECtHR of 1 June 2010, Application 29031/04, *Mawaka v. The Netherlands*, in which the judges ruled that a citizen of the Congo, who had fled his country in the past because he had refused to kill his employer (a leading member of the opposition party Union pour la Démocratie et le Progrès Social), had not shown that he ran a personal risk because of his earlier activities even though the general situation in the country was not yet entirely safe. By contrast see the judgment of the ECtHR of 26 July 2005, Application 38885/02, *N. v. Finland*, in which the judges came to the opposite conclusion in the case of another citizen of the Congo who had worked as an agent and informer of the special guard of former president Mobutu.

35 Judgment of the ECtHR of 11 January 2007, Application 1948/04, *Salah Sheekh v. The Netherlands (Salah Sheekh)*, para. 148. According to A. Hurwitz (2009: 193), the Court was influenced by Directive 2004/83/EC, Article 15 of which, as will be discussed (see below § 4.5), contemplates the possibility of 'serious and individual threat to a civilian's life or person by reason of indiscriminate violence in situations of international or internal armed conflict'. For a more recent case see the judgment of the ECtHR of 3 July 2012, Application 11209/10, *Rustamov v. Russia*, especially para. 128, concerning a member of the Islamic organisation Hizb ut-Tahrir.

36 See the judgment of the ECtHR of 17 July 2008, Application 25904/07, *Na. v. United Kingdom*, para. 115. The exceptional nature of this conjecture has recently been confirmed by the Court, which held that the situation in Iraq in recent years 'will not

threshold must be extremely high, on the other hand, when the risk does not come from the authorities of the country of destination but from individuals. While affirming that the circumstances may entail a violation of Article 3, the Court was of the opinion that in such cases 'it must be shown that the risk is real and that the authorities of the receiving State are not able to obviate the risk by providing appropriate protection'.[37] This position is, I believe, consistent with the Court's earlier decisions regarding Article 3 and more generally on the subject of positive obligations.[38] As far as protection *par ricochet* is concerned, proof is notoriously difficult, for it must be shown that the receiving State is unable, according to the Court, to afford sufficient protection.[39]

Finally, it should be noted that in the established case law of the ECtHR there are two specific situations in which no risk exists. The first is where the State of destination provides satisfactory assurances as to the treatment that the person removed will receive.[40] These guarantees must of course be substantive, not just nominal, in accordance with the requirement to ascertain the 'safety' of any destination. In other words, the 'value' of diplomatic assurances will be assessed in the light of the actual observance of fundamental human rights in the receiving country, including on the basis of independent information (for example, reports by NGOs).[41] Second, there can be no violation if the applicant can be repatriated to an area of the country where there is no risk, applying the concept of internal

---

normally in itself entail a violation of Article 3' (judgment of 19 December 2013, Application 1231/11, *T. K. H.* v. *Sweden*, para. 46; along the same lines, see the judgment of the same date, Application 48866/10, *T. A.* v. *Sweden*).

37 Judgment of the ECtHR of 29 April 1997, Application 24573/94, *H. L. R.* v. *France*, para. 40. Note that as with the Refugee Convention (see above § 1.1) the Court has allowed that the prohibition under Article 3 ECHR remains in place where the destination is a failed State: see *Salah Sheekh*, especially para. 147, concerning precisely the case of Somalia. In this instance, however, the Court did not encounter the hurdles that domestic judges get round in connection with the Refugee Convention, as Article 3 ECHR contains no mention of 'country of nationality'.

38 On this see, in general, D. Xenos (2011).

39 The Court did not appear to exclude entirely the possibility that the entity which may afford protection (and therefore whose inability to prevent unlawful treatment by individuals must be investigated) may be an international organisation: see the judgment of the ECtHR of 19 February 2004, Application 14513/03, *Muratovic* v. *Denmark*. The Court's position does not provide a clear indication in regard, as noted by H. Battjes (2006: 249).

40 On the dangers of excluding the application of the principle of *non-refoulement* for this reason see A. Tancredi (2010: 41 ff.). On the need to limit the use of this reason to restrict violation of Article 3 ECHR to exceptional cases only, particularly where there is no question of extradition (in which case diplomatic assurances may be supported by actual legal guarantees), see C. W. Wouters (2009: 293 ff.).

41 However, on the apparent abandonment of this 'substantive' criterion in the recent case of *Hirsi Jamaa* see U. Villani (2012: 9 ff.).

flight alternative, which as we have seen is fairly common within the context of the Refugee Convention.[42]

One further element that must be present for there to be a violation of Article 3, given the protection *par ricochet* it offers, is the enforcement of the removal order. If the State fails in its positive obligation to properly assess the existence of a risk, it only commits a violation when its decision is implemented.[43] This is an obligation of result: the nature of the removal order is irrelevant and may involve extradition, expulsion or a similar measure that exposes the person to the risk of the treatment in Article 3 ECHR. In line with the Court's decisions regarding the notion of 'jurisdiction' in Article 1 ECHR,[44] removal includes rejection at the frontier, as well as at sea and even in the territory of a third State.[45] In such instances the persons subjected to the measures prohibited by Article 3 must be under the control of the authorities of the accused State. Evidently, the removal order must be carried out before there can be a violation whenever the Court has been able to issue a judgment *before* the order is carried out – either for reasons of procedure under the national legislation of the respondent State or because that State has been forced to take precautionary measures (usually suspension of the removal order) under Article 39 of the Court's Rules of Procedure. In such cases the Court issues a hypothetical decision, noting that were the order to be carried out 'there would be a violation'.[46]

In similar cases the Court has always maintained that it can also assess the risk in the light of events taking place between the time the respondent State makes the decision and the moment it carries it out. In my opinion this confirms the 'composite' nature of the obligation of indirect protection: an obligation of means, in determining the risk, and an obligation of result, in carrying out an order that makes the risk real. Indeed, any assessment of States' prediction about risk must be based on what they know or should know at the time the removal is carried out: if, in the course of the proceedings before the Court, something happens

---

42 The limitations on this alternative are generally the same as the ones which, according to UNHCR, apply in respect of the Refugee Convention (see above § 1.3). On this point see C. W. Wouters (2009: 288 ff.). For recent case law, see the judgment of 19 December 2013, Application 11161/11, *B. K. A. v. Sweden.*

43 In fact, on only one occasion did the ECtHR independently evaluate the positive obligation on States to make a proper predictive assessment, regardless of whether the removal order had been carried out: see the judgment of 7 June 2007, Application 38411/02, *Garabayev* v. *Russia.* However, legal theorists (notably A. Tancredi (2010: 41 ff., especially 50)) are of the opinion, correctly I believe, that this is just a 'sporadic divergence from the main approach' (trans. added).

44 The prohibition is extended to expulsion and similar measures *directly* as a result of the decisions of the Court regarding the notion of *jurisdiction* in Article 1 ECHR (see above, Chapter 1, footnotes 254–5). According to legal theorists, commenting the case of *Hirsi Jamaa* in which the ECtHR decided that the ECHR applied to the actions of States outside their territorial waters, the decision was not unexpected: see U. Villani (2012: 9).

45 See the judgment of the ECtHR of 2 March 2010, Application 61498/08, *Al-Saadoon and Mufdhi* v. *United Kingdom (Al-Saadoon).*

46 To give just one example, see *Shamayev*, Application No. 36378/02, para. 8.

that makes it necessary to revise that prediction, the likelihood that the removal will expose the applicant to the risk of the treatment in Article 3 ECHR must be evaluated in the light of the changed circumstances.[47]

2.2 B) Other instances of protection *par ricochet*

Although probably the most important use of protection *par ricochet* is in connection with Article 3 ECHR, it is not its only application. Indeed, the first time the Commission interpreted Article 1 in this way, Article 6 was also involved. It was in connection with the latter, as well as Article 2, that the Court built up a series of decisions mirroring those relating to Article 3, but fewer in number. Article 2, as we know, safeguards the right to life, but does not go so far as to prohibit the death penalty.[48] This is instead the object of a 'relative' prohibition in Article 1 of Protocol No. 6, which only becomes an absolute prohibition in Article 1 of Protocol No. 13.[49] The protection *par ricochet* afforded by Article 2 ECHR was first contemplated almost ten years after *Soering*, again on the initiative of the Commission: in the case of *Bahaddar*, in which the Court eventually declared the application inadmissible because not all the domestic remedies had been exhausted,[50] the Commission, in its decision of 13 September 1996, after recalling that protection *par ricochet* was already allowed in connection with Article 3 ECHR, asked

> whether analogous considerations apply to Article 2, in particular whether this provision can also engage the responsibility of a Contracting State where, upon expulsion or other removal, the person's life is in danger.[51]

---

47 According to legal theory, this is the main basis for the obligation of *non-refoulement* upheld by the ECtHR in respect of Article 3: see H. Battjes (2009: 583 ff.) and C. W. Wouters (2009: 315 ff.). For the opposite view see A. Gianelli (2008b: 363 ff.).

48 '1. Everyone's right to life shall be protected by law. No one shall be deprived of his life intentionally save in the execution of a sentence of a court following his conviction of a crime for which this penalty is provided by law. 2. Deprivation of life shall not be regarded as inflicted in contravention of this Article when it results from the use of force which is no more than absolutely necessary: (a) in defence of any person from unlawful violence; (b) in order to effect a lawful arrest or to prevent the escape of a person lawfully detained; (c) in action lawfully taken for the purpose of quelling a riot or insurrection'.

49 According to Article 2 of Protocol No. 6 'A State may make provision in its law for the death penalty in respect of acts committed in time of war or of imminent threat of war; such penalty shall be applied only in the instances laid down in the law and in accordance with its provisions . . .', while no derogation to the prohibition enshrined in Article 1 of Protocol No. 13 is allowed, not even, per Article 2 of that Protocol, under Article 15 of the ECHR.

50 Judgment of the ECtHR of 19 February 1998, Application 25894/94, *Bahaddar* v. *The Netherlands*.

51 Decision of the Commission of 13 September 1996, *Bahaddar* v. *The Netherlands*, para. 75. The salient passages are reported in *European Human Rights Reports*, 1998, p. 286 ff.

After answering in the negative in relation to the first sentence of Article 2(1) ('Everyone's right to life shall be protected by law'), the Commission did not rule out, in relation to the second sentence ('No one shall be deprived of his life intentionally'),

> that an issue might be raised under Article 2 in circumstances in which the expelling State knowingly puts the person concerned at such high risk of losing his life as for the outcome to be a near-certainty.[52]

For many years, in the established case law of the ECtHR the possibility that Article 2 could automatically apply *par ricochet* in relation to the death penalty was never contemplated, although it was never ruled out in theory. The Court always believed that alleged violations of Article 2 could not be separated from those of Article 3, so that the latter article 'embraced' the former. It took a similar view regarding the prohibitions enshrined in Protocols Nos 6 and 13.[53] It was only in the case of *Bader*, in which the Court had to decide, among other points, whether the expulsion of a Syrian citizen who had been sentenced to death by the regional Court of Aleppo violated Article 2 ECHR, that it adopted the same argument as the Commission in *Bahaddar*. Initially, it relied on the Commission's decision to reaffirm that, in principle, the indirect application of Article 2 could not be ruled out where the person to be expelled risked the death penalty in the receiving country. However, citing its earlier decision in *Öcalan*,[54] the Court did not allow that

---

52 Ibid. para. 78. Note that the Commission found there was no violation of Article 2 because the applicant's expulsion to Bangladesh would not have entailed any risk: the crime of which he was accused did not carry the death penalty. The Commission added, however, 'that a "real risk" – within the meaning of the case law concerning Article 3 – of loss of life would not as such necessarily suffice to make expulsion an "intentional deprivation of life" prohibited by Article 2, although it would amount to inhuman treatment within the meaning of Article 3', and found that there had been a violation of Article 3.

53 For reports of the relative practice see C. W. Wouters (2009: 346).

54 Judgment of 12 May 2005, Application 46221/99, *Öcalan v. Turkey (Öcalan)*, paras 164–5, in which the Grand Chamber recalled what had been stated previously in the judgment of the Chamber of 12 March 2003, paras 195–6: 'Equally the Court observes that the legal position as regards the death penalty has undergone a considerable evolution since the *Soering* case was decided. The *de facto* abolition noted in that case in respect of twenty-two Contracting States in 1989 has developed into a *de jure* abolition in forty-three of the forty-four Contracting States – most recently in the respondent State – and a moratorium in the remaining State which has not yet abolished the penalty, namely Russia. This almost complete abandonment of the death penalty in times of peace in Europe is reflected in the fact that all the Contracting States have signed Protocol No. 6 and forty-one States have ratified it, that is to say, all except Turkey, Armenia and Russia. It is further reflected in the policy of the Council of Europe which requires that new member States undertake to abolish capital punishment as a condition of their admission into the organisation. As a result of these developments the territories encompassed by the member States of the Council of Europe have become a zone free of capital punishment. . . . Such a marked

Article 2 had been 'modified' in the meantime as a result of events relating to Protocol No. 13 to the extent that it contained an absolute prohibition of the death penalty. Instead, the Court suggested that such situations might give rise to two separate violations of the ECHR: violation of Article 2, insofar as the death penalty is handed down following an unfair trial and so becomes 'an arbitrary deprivation of life';[55] and violation of Article 3, insofar as

> to impose a death sentence on a person after an unfair trial would generate, in circumstances where there exists a real possibility that the sentence will be enforced, a significant degree of human anguish and fear.[56]

The ECtHR found that these principles applied to the case in question and concluded that the expulsion order, were it to be carried out, would be in breach of Articles 2 and 3.

Interestingly, although Sweden itself had asked the Court to examine *also* Protocol No. 13, which it had already ratified,[57] the Court did not consider it necessary to verify this point, apparently wishing to avoid an enquiry into the application *par ricochet* of the Protocol. This apparent restraint can probably be put down to uncertainty about the effects that standard practice regarding Protocol No. 13 had had on Article 2 ECHR. In the later case of *Al-Saadoon* the Court stated, on the one hand, that events after *Öcalan* were 'strongly indicative that Article 2 has been amended so as to prohibit the death penalty in all circumstances'[58] and, on the other, that the delivery of the applicants to the Iraqi authorities

---

development could now be taken as signalling the agreement of the Contracting States to abrogate, or at the very least to modify, the second sentence of Article 2 § 1, particularly when regard is had to the fact that all Contracting States have now signed Protocol No. 6 and that it has been ratified by forty-one States. It may be questioned whether it is necessary to await ratification of Protocol No. 6 by the three remaining States before concluding that the death penalty exception in Article 2 has been significantly modified. Against such a consistent background, it can be said that capital punishment in peacetime has come to be regarded as an unacceptable, if not inhuman, form of punishment which is no longer permissible under Article 2'. A different conclusion was reached, however, in relation to Protocol No. 13: see *Öcalan* (Grand Chamber), paras. 164–5.

55 Judgment of the ECtHR of 8 November 2005, Application 13284/04, *Bader and Kanbor v. Sweden (Bader)*, para. 42; again the Court referred to *Öcalan* (Grand Chamber), para. 165 ff.

56 *Bader*, para. 42.

57 This took place on 2 April 2003 and the Protocol entered into force in Sweden on 1 August 2003. In view of these dates, the application of Article 1 of the Protocol in the case before the Court did not raise any problems of competence *ratione temporis*: the Swedish authorities' decision to expel the applicant had become final on 7 April 2004.

58 *Al-Saadoon*, para. 120. The consequence of this 'passage' is that according to the Court there is no possibility that 'the wording of the second sentence of Article 2 § 1 continues to act as a bar to its interpreting the words "inhuman or degrading treatment or punishment" in Article 3 as including the death penalty'.

failed to take proper account of the United Kingdom's obligations under Articles 2 and 3 of the Convention and Article 1 of Protocol No. 13 since, throughout the period in question, there were substantial grounds for believing that the applicants would face a real risk of being sentenced to death and executed.[59]

Thus, although removal to a country where the applicant risks the death penalty can still entail violations that are not always distinguishable from violation of Article 3, on one hand, and Article 2 ECHR and Article 1 of Protocol No. 13, on the other, the Court has extended protection *par ricochet* to include the last two provisions.[60]

As soon as the Commission mentioned the principle of protection *par ricochet* attention turned immediately to other provisions of the ECHR. Article 6, which establishes the right to a fair trial,[61] was considered in the case of *X* v. *Sweden*, and in fact in the *Soering* case the ECtHR had not ruled out that it might apply indirectly.[62] That said, there are two obstacles to transposing the case law on

---

59 Ibid., para. 143. Since events after the delivery of the applicants might suggest that there was no longer a risk of the death penalty being handed down and carried out, the Court decided not to investigate further regarding the violation of Article 2 ECHR and Article 1 of Protocol No. 13, declaring itself 'satisfied' with violation of Article 3 ECHR.

60 On this see also C. W. Wouters (2009: 345 ff.). More briefly, but in the same direction, see M. W. Janis, R. S. Kay and A. W. Bradley (2008: 163).

61 '1. In the determination of his civil rights and obligations or of any criminal charge against him, everyone is entitled to a fair and public hearing within a reasonable time by an independent and impartial tribunal established by law. Judgment shall be pronounced publicly but the press and public may be excluded from all or part of the trial in the interests of morals, public order or national security in a democratic society, where the interests of juveniles or the protection of the private life of the parties so require, or to the extent strictly necessary in the opinion of the court in special circumstances where publicity would prejudice the interests of justice. 2. Everyone charged with a criminal offence shall be presumed innocent until proved guilty according to law. 3. Everyone charged with a criminal offence has the following minimum rights: (a) to be informed promptly, in a language which he understands and in detail, of the nature and cause of the accusation against him; (b) to have adequate time and facilities for the preparation of his defence; (c) to defend himself in person or through legal assistance of his own choosing or, if he has not sufficient means to pay for legal assistance, to be given it free when the interests of justice so require; (d) to examine or have examined witnesses against him and to obtain the attendance and examination of witnesses on his behalf under the same conditions as witnesses against him; (e) to have the free assistance of an interpreter if he cannot understand or speak the language used in court'.

62 *Soering* (ECtHR), para. 113: 'The right to a fair trial in criminal proceedings, as embodied in Article 6 (Article 6), holds a prominent place in a democratic society. . . . The Court does not exclude that an issue might exceptionally be raised under Article 6 . . . by an extradition decision in circumstances where the fugitive has suffered or risks suffering a flagrant denial of a fair trial in the requesting country'. Note that the ECtHR has always ruled out any direct relevance of Article 6 in proceedings generally relating to the removal of foreign nationals from the territory of a Member State. In other

protection *par ricochet* to Article 6. The Court does not consider any violation of Article 6 to be sufficient, but requires a much more 'exceptional' violation: 'flagrant denial of a fair trial'. According to legal theory, this is due to the nature of the right enshrined in Article 6:[63] although the Court accords it 'a prominent place in a democratic society',[64] it does not use the more incisive expressions reserved for Article 3.[65] Moreover, as with Article 2, the Court rarely examines Article 6 separately from Article 3. Indeed, often when the Court either finds there has been a violation of Article 3 (occasionally combined with Article 2) or rules it out, a *separate* assessment of Article 6 is excluded. This often happens where the applicant's expulsion might lead to an unfair trial during which he or she is at risk of the treatment prohibited by Article 3 or at the end of which there is a risk of the death penalty. For example, in the case of *Kaboulov* the Court declared that the applicant was not at risk of receiving the death penalty – thus ruling out a violation of *both* Article 2 *and* Article 3 – and then found on the contrary that there was a risk of indirect violation of Article 3 on other grounds, ruling out separate examination of Article 6.[66] Similarly, in *N. M. and M. M.* v. *United Kingdom* the Court ruled out that there had been a violation of Article 6 as there had been no violation of Articles 2 and/or 3, in the latter case because 'the applicants have [not] demonstrated that they would come to the adverse attention of the Uzbek authorities or face any criminal proceedings upon return'.[67] Ultimately, the possibility that Article 6 might find a place of its own in the case law on protection *par ricochet* has been squashed by the fairly predictable outcome of such complaints, given the extremely high threshold imposed by the Court,[68] and by the 'gravitational' pull of Article 2 and above all Article 3 ECHR.

---

words, it has never held that a removal order needs to comply with the principle of fair trial insofar as, according to the Court, such orders do not affect either 'civil rights and obligations' or 'any criminal charge' (see judgment of 5 October 2000, Application 39652/98, *Maaouia* v. *France*, especially para. 33 ff., and, for a more recent case, judgment of 16 January 2014, Application 43611/11, *F. G.* v. *Sweden*, para. 43).

63 C. W. Wouters (2009: 348), who recalls that Article 6, unlike Article 3, is subject to the derogation clause of Article 15 ECHR.

64 *Soering* (ECtHR), para. 113.

65 'One of the fundamental values of the democratic societies making up the Council of Europe' (ibid., para. 88).

66 Judgment of the ECtHR of 19 November 2009, Application 41015/04, *Kaboulov* v. *Ukraine*, especially para. 121 ff. For a previous and possibly more explicit case see the judgment of the ECtHR of 24 April 2008, Application 2947/06, *Ismoilov and others* v. *Russia*, especially para. 153 ff.

67 Judgment of the ECtHR of 25 January 2011, Applications 38851/09 and 39128/09, *N. M. and M. M.* v. *United Kingdom*, para. 76.

68 There are many circumstances in which a violation of Article 6 has been examined separately, although the outcome for the applicant has always been negative: see the judgment of the ECtHR of 14 September 2010, Applications 21022/08 and 51946/08, *Anzor Chadidovich Chentiev and Ali Nurdinovich Ibragimov* v. *Slovakia*, especially para. 3, and the judgment of 21 October 2010, Application 25404/09, *Gaforov* v. *Russia*, especially para. 206 ff.

A recent exception can be found in a decision of 2012 in which the Court found for the first time that there had been a separate indirect violation of Article 6. The case was that of a citizen of Jordan about to be expelled to his country of origin, who complained that he would be subjected to torture there. He also claimed that in Jordan he would risk being sentenced following a trial in which it would have been virtually impossible for him to refute the evidence against him, obtained through torture of other parties. The Court, having rejected the claim that the applicant was personally at risk of torture in the receiving country, gave a brief outline, based on its own case law, of the situations that would exceed the threshold for indirect violation of Article 6: sentencing *in absentia* without the possibility of obtaining at a later time 'a fresh determination of the merits of the charge'; a summary trial conducted 'with a total disregard for the rights of the defence'; the impossibility of having the grounds for detention heard by a judge; and deliberate and systematic refusal to provide legal assistance.[69] Finally, the Court concluded that impossibility for the applicant to refute, at the new trial, the testimony obtained by torture would constitute, were he expelled, a violation of Article 6.[70]

To conclude, it would appear from the foregoing explanation of how the principle of protection *par ricochet* of the rights enshrined in Articles 2, 3 and 6 ECHR became established that nothing can prevent the same reasoning being applied to all the other rights granted by the Convention. As legal theorists have not failed to point out,[71] this *modus operandi* of the Court is slowly spreading to other provisions of the ECHR. In the *Othman* case cited above, the applicant complained, among other things, that his return to Jordan would put him at risk of serious violations of the rights safeguarded by Article 5 ECHR: isolation in prison for up to 50 days and denial of legal assistance during the period of detention. He also complained that an unfair trial awaited him in his home country and said he believed that the punishment he would receive following sentence would also breach Article 5.[72] The Court, responding to these grounds of appeal, argued convincingly that the article in question was not excluded from the mechanism of indirect application; after citing its own, as yet uncertain, case law on Article 5,[73] the Court declared

> that it would be illogical if an applicant who faced imprisonment in a receiving State after a flagrantly unfair trial could rely on Article 6 to prevent

---

69 Judgment of the ECtHR of 17 January 2012, Application 8139/09, *Othman (Abu Qatada) v. United Kingdom (Othman)*, para. 259.

70 Ibid., para. 285.

71 A. Saccucci (2011: 175).

72 *Othman*, para. 226.

73 See A. Saccucci (2011: 174). The Court recognised that in its earlier case law it had expressed 'doubts' about the indirect application of Article 5: see *Othman*, para. 233.

his expulsion to that State but an applicant who faced imprisonment without any trial whatsoever could not rely on Article 5 to prevent his expulsion.[74]

The conclusion reached by the ECtHR was of course cushioned by a well-known set of caveats. The judges were of the opinion that in such cases violation of Article 5 required a particularly high risk threshold, which they did not consider had been reached in this instance. Thus, to quote the examples used by the Court, a 'flagrant breach' might occur where the applicant was detained in the receiving country without the authorities ever having shown they intended to hold a trial, or – an alternative that is destined to carry weight – where the applicant would be sentenced to a punishment of some 'gravity' as a result of an unfair trial as above.[75]

Article 5 is not the only provision of the ECHR that has undergone this sort of extension of the principle of protection *par ricochet*. The Court has come to a similar conclusion regarding Article 9.[76] In the case of two nationals of Pakistan of Christian faith who complained that returning them to their country of origin where they would not be able to practice their religion freely was a violation of that article, the Court rejected the application because it was clearly unfounded but did not rule out 'the possibility that the responsibility of the returning State might in *exceptional* circumstances be engaged under Article 9 of the Convention'.[77] In fact the judges found it difficult 'to visualise a case in which a sufficiently flagrant violation of Article 9 would not also involve treatment in violation of Article 3 of the Convention' and ruled that the gravitational pull of the provisions on which the principle of protection *par ricochet* was well established should prevail. On a more general level, I believe that this case gave the ECtHR an opportunity to express a view in favour of 'limiting' the indirect application of the provisions of the ECHR. After reaffirming that this interpretation does not allow States to remove asylum-seekers only when 'the conditions [in the receiving country] are

---

74 Ibid., para. 232. The Court added other logical arguments: 'Equally, there may well be a situation where an applicant has already been convicted in the receiving State after a flagrantly unfair trial and is to be extradited to that State to serve a sentence of imprisonment. If there were no possibility of those criminal proceedings being reopened on his return, he could not rely on Article 6 because he would not be at risk of a further flagrant denial of justice. It would be unreasonable if that applicant could not then rely on Article 5 to prevent his extradition'.

75 Ibid., para. 233.

76 '1. Everyone has the right to freedom of thought, conscience and religion; this right includes freedom to change his religion or belief and freedom, either alone or in community with others and in public or private, to manifest his religion or belief, in worship, teaching, practice and observance. 2. Freedom to manifest one's religion or beliefs shall be subject only to such limitations as are prescribed by law and are necessary in a democratic society in the interests of public safety, for the protection of public order, health or morals, or for the protection of the rights and freedoms of others'.

77 Decision of the ECtHR of 28 February 2006, Application 27034/05, *Z. and T. v. United Kingdom* (emphasis added).

in full and effective accord with *each* of the safeguards of the rights and freedoms set out in the Convention' (emphasis added), the Court limited the situations in which States must become indirect guarantors of the safeguards enjoyed in the rest of the world to cases where 'persecution, prosecution, deprivation of liberty or ill-treatment' sought to dismantle them. In other words, except in the context of Articles 2, 3, 5 and 6 there should be no scope for protection *par ricochet* other than in 'exceptional' – and, I might add, purely academic – circumstances. The implications of this pronouncement are borne out by a more recent decision of the Court, this time in the case of a woman from Nepal who claimed that her return there would, because of her husband's political activities, put her at risk of violation of the rights enshrined in Articles 2, 3, 5, 6, 8 (right to respect of private and family life), 10 (freedom of expression), 11 (freedom of assembly and association) and 14 (prohibition of discrimination) ECHR and Article 1 of Protocol No. 1 (protection of property). While the Court carefully examined the potential violations of Articles 2 and 3, the negative outcome of which 'overflowed' onto Articles 5 and 6, regarding the remaining provisions it simply noted that

> the applicant's complaints . . . appear to relate to the alleged activities of the Nepalese authorities and cannot be imputed to the Government of the United Kingdom. . . . It follows that these complaints are incompatible *ratione personae* with the provisions of the Convention. . . . In so far as the applicant makes these allegations in support of the alleged risk to her life and physical integrity if removed to Nepal, the Court does not find that they add anything to her Articles 2 and 3 complaints.[78]

2.3 Other major obligations deriving from the European Convention on Human Rights

Protection *par ricochet*, which is more or less equivalent to the principle of *non-refoulement*, is certainly the most important of the safeguards of the ECHR for our purposes. It should not be forgotten, however, that all the other provisions of the Convention of Rome may also apply, within limits, to asylum-seekers. While some of these provisions, as in the Refugee Convention, regulate situations that are ancillary to the main matter or 'cornerstone', which is governed by the principle of *non-refoulement*, others are of more specific interest. This is because, as we will see, a far from secondary part of EU asylum law has developed precisely out of these provisions and it is therefore worth making a few observations in this regard. The first consideration relates to Article 8 ECHR protecting private and family life.[79] The Court has used this article to limit the power of States to

---

78 Decision of the ECtHR of 24 June 2008, Application 43136/02, *Milan Basnet* v. *United Kingdom*, paras 78–9.

79 '1. Everyone has the right to respect for his private and family life, his home and his correspondence. 2. There shall be no interference by a public authority with the

regulate the entry and removal of aliens because it might separate, unlawfully, an individual from his or her family.

It should be pointed out immediately that there has been no significant case of indirect application of this provision. Once the State refuses entry or removes the person, no event in the receiving country can fall within the scope of Article 8; on the contrary, the State's action already constitutes a direct violation of the provision, assuming that the requirements for this are met. The decisions of the Court reveal various ways in which a State's power over the entry and removal of aliens can be limited under Article 8, and very few of the cases concern people fleeing their country of origin for the reasons that have emerged in the case law of the ECtHR regarding Articles 2, 3, 5 and 6 (or asylum-seekers in general).[80] Often the situations involve aliens not afforded protection, even indirectly,[81] by the host State and these can be divided into two groups: preventing entry or refusing permanent residence in the country where the alien's family live;[82] and removal.[83] In the first case, the Court makes a preliminary assessment as to whether the matter it is called to decide upon effectively falls within the concept of family life. This concept is different from the one found in national legislation and, according to the Court, its scope is fairly broad, including not only links *de iure*, but also *de facto*, such as prolonged cohabitation or natural children; it also extends to adoption and polygamous marriage.[84] Second, the Court examines

exercise of this right except such as is in accordance with the law and is necessary in a democratic society in the interests of national security, public safety or the economic well-being of the country, for the prevention of disorder or crime, for the protection of health or morals, or for the protection of the rights and freedoms of others'.

80 In the majority of cases these are people who have had their refugee status revoked for having committed some crime and who are expelled from the country as a result: see the judgment of the ECtHR of 12 June 2012, Application 54131/10, *Bajsultanov* v. *Austria*.

81 In the sense that the person has neither a 'primary' right to stay in the host State because 'at risk' in his or her country of origin, nor a secondary right as a relative of a person accorded the protection of the host country.

82 In another case, the Court declared that the Netherlands' refusal to grant a temporary permit to stay to a Turkish married couple seeking reunion with their eldest daughter, born in Turkey where she had lived with a relative, violated Article 8 because, given the couple's roots in the host country, where their other children had been born and were living, the respondent State 'En ne laissant aux deux premiers requérants que le choix d'abandonner la situation qu'ils avaient acquise aux Pays-Bas ou de renoncer à la compagnie de leur fille aînée, . . . a omis de ménager un juste équilibre entre les intérêts des requérants, d'une part, et son propre intérêt à contrôler l'immigration, de l'autre': see the judgment of the ECtHR of 21 December 2001, Application 31465/96, *Şen* v. *The Netherlands*, para. 41.

83 Thus, in the case of a citizen of Morocco expelled from Belgium for having committed, when a minor, various not particularly serious offences, the Court found that there had been a violation of Article 8 ECHR and that while the authorities' measure sought to achieve a legitimate objective it was unnecessary in a democratic society: see the judgment of 18 February 1991, Application 12313/86, *Moustaquim* v. *Belgium*.

84 For the other situations see A. W. Heringa and L. Zwaak (2006: 690 ff.). See also H. Lambert (2006b: 39 ff.), M. W. Janis, R. S. Kay and A. W. Bradley (2008: 426 ff.),

whether there has been any interference by the State, while nonetheless allowing it wide discretionary power.[85] There exist a number of factors that will rule out, at source, any possibility that there has been State interference; they include, first and foremost, the possibility of continuing family life in a third State, normally the country of origin.[86] This, however, must be assessed in the light of several elements, which may become impediments: an example is the presence of other children in the receiving State,[87] or the age and conditions of the child for which reunion is requested.[88]

Instead, in cases of removal, the Court, assuming it has found there to have been interference and again excluding that this has taken place where there is a possibility of conducting family life in a third country,[89] will examine the exceptions provided in Article 8(2). The reason for this assessment in cases of removal is simple: such a measure usually follows a final judgment and it is therefore necessary to ascertain whether the commission of certain crimes is among the reasons that 'in a democratic society' make such a measure necessary. The Court has drawn up some brief guidelines that it uses to make assessments on the basis of Article 8(2).[90] However, although the Council of Europe has

D. Harris, M. O'Boyle and C. Warbrick (2009: 392 ff.) and F. G. Jacobs, R. C. A. White and C. Ovey (2010: 335 ff.). As pointed out by A. Del Guercio (2010: 392–3), the Court has broadened the range of interests that may be affected by the removal of an alien to include not just family, but also private life. On this point see the extensive arguments set out in C. Steinorth (2008: 185 ff.) and D. Thym (2008: 87 ff.).

85 *Abdulaziz*, para. 67. On the difference between the Court's review to establish whether there has been interference and its challenge, *once interference has been ascertained*, of the lawfulness of the State's action in the light of Article 8(2) see the incisive arguments in M. Evola (2010: 293 ff.).

86 See the judgment of the ECtHR of 19 February 1996, Application 23218/94, *Gül* v. *Switzerland*, especially para. 41 ff., in which the decisive factor that made the possibility of creating a family life in the country of destination (Turkey) 'not easy . . . but all the more real' was the circumstance that the daughter which the couple had applied to join them in Switzerland had always lived there.

87 See footnote 82.

88 See the judgment of the ECtHR of 1 December 2005, Application 60665/00, *Tuquabo-Tekle and others* v. *The Netherlands*, especially para. 50 ff. For other cases the reader is referred to A. W. Heringa and L. Zwaak (2006: 705 ff.).

89 See the judgment of the ECtHR of 5 October 2000, Application 54273/00, *Abdelouahab Boultif* v. *Switzerland*.

90 See the judgment of the ECtHR of 18 October 2006, Application 46410, *Üner* v. *The Netherlands*, para. 57: 'the nature and seriousness of the offence committed by the applicant; . . . the length of the applicant's stay in the country from which he or she is to be expelled; . . . the time elapsed since the offence was committed and the applicant's conduct during that period; . . . the nationalities of the various persons concerned; . . . the applicant's family situation, such as the length of the marriage, and other factors expressing the effectiveness of a couple's family life; . . . whether the spouse knew about the offence at the time when he or she entered into a family relationship; . . . whether there are children of the marriage, and if so, their age; and . . . the seriousness of the difficulties which the spouse is likely to encounter in the country to which the applicant is to be expelled'.

approved these guidelines, they by no means resolve all the doubts that the application of the provision raises.[91]

One provision of particular importance for asylum is Article 5 ECHR regarding the right to liberty and security. I do not intend here to explore its potential in terms of the theory of protection *par ricochet*, which has already been discussed above, but to analyse its application in relation to the detention, *in the receiving country*, of asylum-seekers who have requested protection, either in the form provided in the Refugee Convention, or in that envisaged by the ECHR. The relevant provision here is not Article 5 as a whole, but Article 5(1)(f), which states that a person can be deprived of liberty, in accordance with the law, where it involves

> the lawful arrest or detention of a person to prevent his effecting an unauthorised entry into the country or of a person against whom action is being taken with a view to deportation or extradition.

The first part of the provision applies to asylum-seekers who have entered the host country unlawfully, for it goes without saying that where they have entered by official means detention must comply with the higher standards of Article 5(1).[92] In the case of *Saadi* v. *United Kingdom* the Grand Chamber clarified that as regards Article 5(1)(f) the lawfulness of the detention should not be assessed also according to whether it is necessary in order to achieve its objective, among other elements; it is simply subject to the requirement of non-arbitrariness, assuming this to be provided for by the law.[93] The ECtHR also enumerated the requirements for detention not to be arbitrary: it must be imposed in good faith and must be strictly related to the need to prevent unlawful entry into the country. The Court added that the detention must not continue beyond the time reasonably needed to achieve the intended purpose and that the place and conditions of detention must be suitable.[94] As authoritative writers have pointed out,[95] in interpreting Article 5(1)(f) in this way the Court was fairly generous in the discretion granted to States. As subsequent decisions demonstrate,[96] the detention of asylum-seekers is justifiable

---

91 On this point see A. Del Guercio (2010: 395 ff.).
92 Judgment of the ECtHR (Chamber) of 11 July 2006, Application 13229/03, *Saadi* v. *United Kingdom*, para. 44, on which see E. Ocello (2009: 87 ff., especially 94).
93 Judgment of the ECtHR (Grand Chamber) of 29 January 2008, Application 13229/03, *Saadi* v. *United Kingdom*, para. 73.
94 Ibid., para. 74. The Court refers to its earlier judgment of 25 June 1996, Application 19776/92, *Amuur* v. *France*, especially para. 43.
95 E. Ocello (2009: 99 ff.), to which the reader is referred for other incongruities in the Court's position.
96 See the judgment of the ECtHR of 15 January 2011, Application 57229/09, *Longa Yonkeu* v. *Latvia*, in which the Court stated, very briefly, that the detention of an asylum-seeker was lawful insofar as it took place while (and because) the application was pending, and the judgment of 13 December 2011, Application 15297/09, *Kanagaratnam* v. *Belgium*, in which the ECtHR found that the detention was unlawful

in the light of the ECHR if it is in suitable premises and does not last overly long, the Court having eliminated the test of necessity almost as if detention were always necessary in order to combat illegal immigration.[97] The outcome of this approach is far removed from the solution offered by the Refugee Convention, discussed above (section 1.8): the detention of asylum-seekers is allowed according to established practice, not only of UNHCR, but Article 31 limits it to very specific cases and much narrower circumstances than those envisaged by the Grand Chamber in the case of *Saadi* v. *United Kingdom*.[98]

Two other provisions of some importance merit a final comment: they are Article 4 of Protocol No. 4 prohibiting the collective expulsion of aliens and Article 1 of Protocol No. 7 on procedural safeguards relating to the expulsion of aliens lawfully resident in the territory of the host State. The Court well illustrated the purpose of the first article in its judgment in the case of *Hirsi Jamaa*,[99] describing it as the need

> to prevent States being able to remove certain aliens without examining their personal circumstances and, consequently, without enabling them to put forward their arguments against the measure taken by the relevant authority.[100]

In other words, States are not allowed to deny aliens an individual assessment of their situation, from which elements may emerge that justify their presence in the host State. Clearly, these elements may include one or more of the circumstances that entail protection *par ricochet*, but the provision is not limited to these cases alone.[101] The provisions are independent of one another, so that using the derogation of Article 15(1) in relation to Article 4 would not affect, in accordance with Article 15(2), its application to Articles 2 and 3 – the principal instances of protection *par ricochet*.[102]

---

because it lasted too long and was also inappropriate because it involved three minors and their mother.

97 The Court stated explicitly in *Saadi* v. *United Kingdom* (Grand Chamber), para. 72, that 'where a person has been detained under Article 5 § 1(f), the Grand Chamber, interpreting the second limb of this sub-paragraph, held that, as long as a person was being detained "with a view to deportation", that is, as long as "action [was] being taken with a view to deportation", *there was no requirement that the detention be reasonably considered necessary*, for example to prevent the person concerned from committing an offence or fleeing' (emphasis added).

98 E. Ocello (2009: 95 ff.) is of the same opinion.

99 On this see J. Schokkenbroek (2006: 953 ff.) and D. Harris, M. O'Boyle and C. Warbrick (2009: 744 ff.).

100 *Hirsi Jamaa*, para. 177.

101 This is confirmed by the judgment of the ECtHR of 5 February 2002, Application 51564/99, *Čonka* v. *Belgium (Čonka)*, in which the Court found there had been a violation of Article 4 of Protocol No. 4 and not of Article 3, which the applicants did not, themselves, complain had been violated.

102 Of course, nor can States claim that the Court is not competent *ratione loci* where the removal takes place outside the territory of the State, for example outside its territorial waters: see *Hirsi Jamaa*, para. 166 ff.

According to the Commission, collective expulsion is

> any measure of the competent authority compelling aliens as a group to leave the country, except where such a measure is taken after and on the basis of a reasonable and objective examination of the particular cases of each individual alien of the group.[103]

Thus, collective expulsion itself is not prohibited, only if it does not follow a careful and objective individual assessment. In practice, this has occurred where the authorities have not put in place any procedure to identify the expelled aliens, or where the employees carrying out the expulsion were unqualified to conduct individual interviews,[104] or again where the expulsion order was drawn up in exactly the same terms for all the aliens concerned.[105] Article 1 of Protocol No. 7 sets out more clearly the rules that are already laid down, according to the Court, in Article 4 of Protocol No. 4.[106] The opinion of scholarly writers that the two provisions are procedurally almost identical is a valid one.[107] However, they are not identical as regards their beneficiaries: Article 1 does not apply to aliens who have entered the State unlawfully, similarly to Article 32 of the Refugee Convention,[108] nor does it apply to collective expulsions.

2.4 Some final remarks

The foregoing chapters provide a fairly structured description of the obligations imposed by the two Conventions examined. Central to both is, of course, the prohibition on *refoulement*, which in the ECtHR's interpretation of Articles 2, 3, 5 and 6 ECHR has a different sphere of application from Article 33(1) of the Refugee Convention.[109] In reality, the Conventions also have several elements in

---

103 Decision of the Commission of 3 October 1975, Application 7011/75, *Becker* v. *Denmark*.
104 See *Hirsi Jamaa*, para. 185.
105 *Čonka*, para. 62.
106 According to Article 1 of Protocol No. 7, '1. An alien lawfully resident in the territory of a State shall not be expelled therefrom except in pursuance of a decision reached in accordance with law and shall be allowed: (a) to submit reasons against his expulsion, (b) to have his case reviewed, and (c) to be represented for these purposes before the competent authority or a person or persons designated by that authority. 2. An alien may be expelled before the exercise of his rights under paragraph 1.a, b and c of this Article, when such expulsion is necessary in the interests of public order or is grounded on reasons of national security'.
107 J. Schokkenbroek (2006: 956). On the additional safeguards provided by Article 1 of Protocol No. 7, however, see C. Flinterman (2006: 965 ff.).
108 On this point see D. Harris, M. O'Boyle and C. Warbrick (2009: 747). It should be noted that according to these authors the provision does not apply even to aliens awaiting a decision regarding their permit to stay. Consequently, I believe it does not apply to asylum-seekers, in parallel with what is contended above (see § 1.8).
109 I do not consider here the connection between Article 3 ECHR and Article 33 of the Refugee Convention and *ius cogens*: the nature of the customary norm of *non-refoulement*

common: according to both, the receiving State must make a proper assessment of the existence of a risk (obligation of means), while the shape that risk takes has no bearing because any form of removal, be it extradition, expulsion or other, can give rise to a violation (obligation of result). This implies that the two Conventions share other features: the place where the State's action takes place is not important as the person concerned has only to be within the jurisdiction of the authorities. In other words, the provisions considered also apply to rejection at the frontier, as well as to any rejection outside territorial waters. However, while the Refugee Convention does not apply if rejection or refusal of entry takes place in the territory of the alleged refugee's State of origin, the same is not true of the ECHR, in which only the criterion of jurisdiction applies.[110]

Clearly, since they are required to serve a useful purpose, even the provisions of the ECHR require an asylum-seeker awaiting removal to be allowed to remain in the host State until the risk assessment procedure has been completed. The importance of this aspect is highlighted by the fact that where national legislation in the respondent State makes no provision for suspending removal, the ECtHR will request it on the basis of Article 39 of its Rules of Procedure. The significance of the precautionary measures, and hence of the guarantee that the applicant will not be removed from the territory of the respondent State while the proceedings are under way, is exemplified by the position that the Court, and more generally the other bodies of the ECHR, adopted in respect of Italy: in at least two cases,[111] Italy expelled applicants to countries where they were 'at risk' even though the ECtHR had clearly requested they be allowed to remain[112] pending the outcome of the case it was due to hear.[113] In both instances the Court found, at the end of the trial, that there had been a violation of Articles 3 and 34 ECHR,[114]

as enshrined in Article 33(1) of the Refugee Convention is not really the subject of debate, which its nature as a peremptory norm is. I believe that there is a convincing argument against this prohibition having become a peremptory norm, particularly in view of the various exceptions that exist: see A. Duffy (2008: 373 ff.). Instead, *non-refoulement* may become *ius cogens* when the rule from which it is indirectly derived itself belongs to the category of peremptory norms, as in the case of Article 3 ECHR: on this point see F. Lenzerini (2009: 378 ff.).

110   See footnote 278, Chapter 1.

111   The reference is to the Application of 3 January 2007, No. 246/07, *Khemais* v. *Italy (Khemais)*, and the Application of 17 May 2009, No. 25716/09, *Toumi* v. *Italy (Toumi)*, available online at www.echr.coe.int.

112   See the 'Exposé des faits' of 2 July 2008 in the *Khemais* case and similar document of 14 August 2009 relating to the case of *Toumi*.

113   There are other cases in which, according to the Report of UNHCR of 16 April 2009 issued following a visit to Italy from 13 to 15 January 2009, CommDH (2009) 16, available online at www.echr.coe.int, para. 94 ff., Italy actually carried out removals even before the asylum-seekers could ask the Court to rule on the provisional measures, thus preventing them from exercising a right recognised by Article 34 ECHR.

114   Judgment of the ECtHR of 24 February 2009, *Khemais*, para. 80 ff. Judgment of 5 April 2011, *Toumi*, para. 31 ff., on which see M. Guidi (2011: 109 ff.).

while during the course of the proceedings Italy was severely reprimanded by the Chair of the Committee on Legal Affairs and Human Rights and the rapporteur on the implementation of Strasbourg Court judgments, who declared that 'It is totally unacceptable to ignore binding interim measures ordered by the European Court of Human Rights' and that Italy's behaviour was 'intolerable'.[115]

Where the two provisions differ significantly is in relation to the object of the assessment that the State is required to make: while both impose such an assessment, its intended outcome is not the same. In the articles of the ECHR the only element assessed is the likelihood that the person awaiting removal will be subjected to torture or to inhuman or degrading treatment or punishment, or to the death penalty. Article 33(1), on the other hand, sets limits on the concept of risk in its various forms: minor limits aside,[116] the beneficiaries of the prohibition are 'selected' on the basis of their well-founded fear, the right that their persecution violates, and the reasons for that persecution. The first two elements do not create a tangible gap between the ECHR and the Refugee Convention: the risk of suffering persecution cannot be excluded, notwithstanding some resistance in practice, just because the applicant does not perceive it as such, in the same way as in the ECHR. Moreover, while the set of rights safeguarded by Article 33(1) is much broader insofar as persecution occurs not only in connection with acts of torture and the like but also when other things are harmed, such as freedom of opinion and religious freedom and even, as explained, the right to education,[117] the ECtHR does not restrict protection *par ricochet* to Article 3 only but extends it to some of the principal rights enshrined in the Convention. In other words, it cannot be ruled out that a risk falling outside the field of application of Article 3 ECHR (but within that of Article 33 of the Refugee Convention) will 'come in by the back door' via one of Articles 2, 5 or 6 ECHR.

The last difference concerns the reasons for persecution. Under the ECHR, the risk of being subjected to torture (or similar) is always taken into account regardless of the reasons for it, while under the Refugee Convention if it is not shown that the persecution is caused by one of the reasons listed then it falls outside the field of application. Considering the standard practice in this regard, I do not think the latter alternative is likely to enjoy much support, because with an 'exceptional' risk such as torture it is unlikely that one of the reasons enumerated in the Convention will not be present; some of these, for example membership of a particular social group, are open to fairly broad interpretation. In other words, a particularly serious violation, such as torture, often stems from political motives or membership of a specific social group, which in most cases should not prevent the application of the provisions of the Refugee Convention.

---

115 See Press Release 615 (2009), available online at www.echr.coe.int.
116 The *dies ad quem* of 1 January 1951 and the fact that the risk is connected with events that took place in Europe; as mentioned earlier (see § 1.1), both limits are virtually meaningless now.
117 See footnote 34, Chapter I.

The greatest difference between the two Conventions emerges from a comparison of Article 33(2) and Article 1F of the Refugee Convention, on one side, and Article 15(2) ECHR, on the other. As a consequence of the latter provision, Articles 2 and 3 ECHR contain a prohibition which, as expressly stipulated and confirmed by the case law of the ECtHR,[118] is absolute and allows for no exception. By contrast, the prohibition contained in Article 33(1) is subject to the exceptions listed in 33(2) as well as to the exclusion clauses of Article 1F.[119] Briefly, if the person awaiting removal is suspected of having committed a crime or is a threat to the State or its community, Articles 2 and 3 ECHR cannot be set aside in any circumstances. Instead, under the Refugee Convention a person in the same situation, even with a well-founded fear of suffering persecution, cannot *be* a refugee or, if a refugee, cannot enjoy the safeguards provided by the prohibition on *refoulement*. If the *procedure* for assessing all these complex elements is an obligation, either for the States parties to the Refugee Convention or for the contracting States of the ECHR, the outcome may be radically different even in identical circumstances. This difference clearly plays (and has played) a decisive role in EU legislation insofar as all the Member States are also signatories to the ECHR, apart from the fact that the EU itself is about to ratify the Convention *sui iuris*.

118 For a recent case see *Saadi* v. *Italy*, para. 137–8.
119 The case law of the ECtHR does not contain any significant references to what is apparently a further exception to the prohibition of Article 33(1) of the Refugee Convention: the case of mass influxes of displaced persons. In this regard I can only note the opinion of Justice Pinto de Albuquerque, who declared, in connection with *Hirsi Jamaa*, that 'Groups of refugees cannot be subject to a diminished status based on an "inherent" mass-influx exception to "genuine" refugee status. To provide reduced, subsidiary protection (for example, with less extensive entitlements regarding access to residence permits, employment, social welfare and health care) for people who arrive as part of a mass influx would be unjustified discrimination'.

3 Evolution of EC and EU competences for asylum

3.1 Absence of competences for asylum in the Treaty of Rome and partial reference in the provisions on workers' social security

Apart from some implied and dubious references to the broader issue of immigration,[1] the Treaty of Rome contained no provisions on the right

---

1 According to a first approach – on which see A. Adinolfi (1998: 124) and L. Manca (2003: 15) – the Council had the power to issue directives on the entry and residence of third-country nationals under Article 100 of the Treaty Establishing the European Economic Community (TEEC). To this day, Article 115 of the Treaty on the Functioning of the European Union (TFEU) empowers the Council to 'issue directives for the approximation of such laws, regulations or administrative provisions of the Member States as directly affect the establishment or functioning of the internal market'. It was thought that differences in immigration legislation might become an obstacle to the single market and therefore justify the Council's intervention. Any considerations about the soundness of this theory aside, it should be noted that this alleged competence resulted in just one proposal by the Commission for the harmonisation of national legislation to combat illegal immigration and illegal employment: see the proposal for a Council directive concerning the approximation of the legislation of the Member States, in order to combat illegal migration and illegal employment (Recast), COM (1978) 86 of 22 March 1978, OJ C 97, 22 April 1978, p. 9 ff., on which see L. Manca (2003: 16 ff.) and M. Condinanzi, A. Lang and B. Nascimbene (2006: 253). The proposal indicated as legal basis Article 100 TEEC, but as there was no follow-up by Council, the Commission withdrew it. In a second, more successful attempt the Commission based its proposal on Articles 117 and 118 TEEC. The first of these aimed 'to promote improved working conditions and an improved standard of living for workers', while the second gave the Commission the task 'of promoting close cooperation between Member States in the social field'. On this basis the Commission adopted Decision 85/381/EEC of 8 July 1985, OJ L 217, 14 August 1985, p. 25 ff., setting up a prior communication and consultation procedure on migration policies in relation to non-member countries. The Decision was appealed in the European Court of Justice (ECJ) by five Member States; the outcome – judgment of 9 July 1987, Joined Cases 281, 283, 284, 285 and 287/85, *Federal Republic of Germany, French Republic, Kingdom of the Netherlands, Kingdom of Denmark and United Kingdom of Great Britain and Northern Ireland* v. *Commission of the European Communities, Reports of Cases*, 1987, p. 3203 ff., on which see, among others, K. R. Simmonds (1988: 177 ff.), E. Traversa (1988: 5 ff.) and F. Mancini

of asylum.[2] However, this did not prevent European Economic Community (EEC) institutions from tethering the problem of asylum to some of the issues regulated by the Treaty. In particular, asylum 'benefited' from the typically heterogeneous purpose of the provisions establishing the single market, which brought some of the areas originally completely outside the scope of the Treaty of Rome within the competences of the EEC. Article 4(1) of Council Regulation 3/1958 on social security for migrant workers extended its benefits

> to workers who are or have been subject to the legislation of one or more Member States and who are . . . refugees residing within the territory of one of the Member States, as also to the members of their families and their survivors.[3]

The Regulation arose out of the European Convention on the Legal Status of Migrant Workers, which was drawn up within the framework of the European Coal and Steel Community (ECSC) and was based on Articles 227 and 51 of the Treaty Establishing the European Economic Community (TEEC). The latter entrusted the Council, in matters of social security, with the task of adopting, on a proposal from the Commission, 'measures required to bring about freedom of movement for workers'.[4] The impact on refugees was in reality very limited. As the European Court of Justice (ECJ) confirmed with regard to Regulation

(1989: 309 ff.) – was a statement that the migration policies of members regarding workers from third countries were not outside the scope of Article 118 TEEC. However, the Court acknowledged that the Commission had overstepped its authority by also imposing an obligation of result (para. 33 ff.). The Decision was repeated in a second case (Decision 88/384/EEC of the Commission, 8 June 1988, setting up a prior communication and consultation procedure on migration policies in relation to non-member countries, OJ L 183, 14 July 1988, p. 35 ff.) that reproduced the same content with the amendments requested by the Court. Instead, L. Manca (2003: 17 ff.) theorised that, apart from Articles 100, 117 and 118, the TEEC provided a further and pre-sumably sounder legal basis for EEC action in the field of immigration: Article 235 TEEC, now Article 352 TFEU. Manca was not the only one to uphold this theory (for a conflicting view see K. Hailbronner (2000: 120)), although there is no instance of it being followed by the EEC institutions.

2 Treaty Establishing the European Economic Community, adopted Rome 25 March 1957 and entered into force 1 January 1958, 294 UNTS 17 ff. For the first comments on asylum in the EEC, see M. Udina (1974: 5 ff.).

3 Regulation 3/1958 on the application of social security schemes to migrant workers, OJ 30, 16 December 1958, p. 561 ff. An identical provision appears in Council Regulation 36/63/EEC, 2 April 1963, on social security for cross-border workers, OJ 62, 20 April 1963, p. 1314 ff.

4 The Convention, which was signed on 9 December 1957, was drawn up by a committee of government experts with the assistance of the International Labour Organization (ILO): on its provisions, which would eventually apply also to refugees, see J. Doublet (1957: 574 ff.).

No. 1408/71[5] replacing Regulation No. 3, it could not apply to situations that were exclusively national, a circumstance that was bound to arise often as EEC law did not grant, and the Refugee Convention still does not recognise,[6] any right of refugees to freedom of movement as workers in the territory of Member States other than the receiving country.[7] The inclusion of a clause extending social security schemes to refugees came about less in the wake of the construction of the single market than as a consequence of the obligations on EEC Member States deriving from the Refugee Convention, to which they were also signatories. In fact, under Article 24 refugees should receive the same treatment as that accorded to nationals in respect of various matters, including social security.

3.2 How to link the creation of the single market and dismantling of internal frontiers to a common policy on asylum

A more effective means of tackling the problem of asylum as part of the completion of the single market was only developed some years later, when the dismantling of internal borders made it necessary to harmonise foreign policy, including policy on asylum. The single market could not be completed without first eliminating various 'encumbrances' such as internal border controls, a measure which implied the existence of a single external frontier and therefore at least convergent policies on the entry and residence of third-country nationals. This approach was not shared by all the members of the EEC,[8] however, with the result that a split developed even before the Single European Act[9] and was

5 Regulation (EEC) No. 1408/71 of the Council of 14 June 1971 on the application of social security schemes to employed persons and their families moving within the Community, OJ L 149, 5 July 1972, p. 2 ff. The ECJ, which initially appeared to interpret Article 4 of Regulation No. 3 fairly broadly (see judgment of 12 November 1969, Case 27/69, *Caisse de maladie des V.F.L. 'Entr'aide médicale' and Société nationale des chemins de fer luxembourgeois v. Compagnie belge d'assurances générales sur la vie et contre les accidents, Reports of Cases*, 1969, p. 405 ff., para. 4), later confirmed its case law on national situations involving Article 2 of Regulation No. 1408, which is identical to Article 4 of Regulation No. 3, in the judgment of 11 October 2001, Joined Cases C-95/99 to C-98/99 and C-180/99, *Mervett Khalil, Issa Chaaban and Hassan Osseili v. Bundesanstalt für Arbeit* and *Mohamad Nasser v. Landeshauptstadt Stuttgart* and *Meriem Addou v. Land Nordrhein-Westfalen, Reports of Cases*, 2001, p. I-7413 ff., para. 65 ff.
6 Convention Relating to the Status of Refugees (adopted Geneva 28 July 1951 and entered into force 22 April 1954), 189 UNTS 137 ff.
7 See E. Guild (2006: 633).
8 Ireland and the UK in particular (later joined by Greece) were firmly against abolishing internal border controls, chiefly for geographical reasons. Denmark's reluctance was also to some extent due to the fact that it was a member of the Nordic Passport Union. On this point see M. Fridegotto (1992: 48).
9 Adopted by nine Member States, Luxembourg 17 February 1986, and by a further three at The Hague 28 February 1986 and entered into force 1 July 1987; the text can be found in OJ L 169, 29 June 1987, p. 1 ff.

only partially mended by the Treaty of Amsterdam of 1997.[10] Some States continued to cooperate outside Community law, which had not evolved beyond the good intentions declared by the European Council and the Commission. The European Council had already advocated the abolition of internal border controls in its conclusions following the Fontainebleau meeting of 25 and 26 June 1984.[11] The Commission, for its part, published in 1985 a White Paper on the completion of the internal market,[12] in which for the first time[13] a link was established between the abolition of internal border controls, a necessary step in order to build the single market, and harmonisation of policies, including of asylum policy,[14] providing for proposals to be presented by the end of 1990. Because of resistance,[15] the Council, and the Commission too, were hesitant to comply with the Parliament's requests,[16] even though the Single European

10 Treaty of Amsterdam amending the Treaty on European Union, the Treaties Establishing the European Communities and Related Acts (adopted Amsterdam 2 October 1997), OJ C 340,10 November 1997, p. 1 ff.

11 Conclusions of the Fontainebleau European Council, 25–26 June 1984, 'A People's Europe', *Bulletin of the European Communities*, Supplement 7/85, p. 5. The Council laid the foundations for setting up an *ad hoc* committee that would prepare and coordinate suitable measures to strengthen and promote the identity of the Community for its citizens and for the rest of the world. The Committee on 'A People's Europe', also named the Adonnino Committee after its President, submitted a report to the President of the European Council, at the time Italian Prime Minister Bettino Craxi, prior to the meeting of March 1985, in which the Committee (ibid., p. 9 ff.) advocated that controls be transferred to the external borders.

12 *Completing the Internal Market: White Paper from the Commission to the European Council* (Milan, 28–29 June 1985), COM(85) 310, 14 June 1985, para. 55. The Milan European Council of 1985 also received the Adonnino Committee's final report, cited in the previous footnote. On the Commission's noteworthy efforts to extend the Community's competence regarding the treatment of non-EU citizens see S. Peers (1996: 9 ff.).

13 However, see the Resolution of the European Parliament of 9 June 1983 closing the procedure for consultation of the European Parliament on the communication from the Commission of the European Communities to the Council on a draft Council resolution on the easing of the formalities relating to checks on citizens of Member States at the Community's internal frontiers and on the passport union and the abolition of personal checks at the internal frontiers of the Community, OJ C 184, 11 July 1983, p. 112 ff. The Parliament, which until then had only occasionally considered the matter of asylum rights (see Resolution of the European Parliament of 18 April 1980 on the granting of asylum to Cuban citizens, OJ C 117, 12 May 1980, p. 75, and Resolution of 13 June 1985 on the political situation in Sri Lanka, OJ C 175, 15 July 1985, p. 219), called on the Council and the Commission 'to draw up proposals for the harmonization of . . . the rights of asylum', but gave no indications where a sound legal basis existed within the Treaty.

14 See also H. Staples (1999: 28).

15 The Commission's proposal (OJ C 197, 31 July 1982, p. 6 ff.), which contained no mention of harmonising asylum rights – later called for in the Resolution of the European Parliament (footnote 13) – was never taken up by the Council for the reasons described in footnote 8.

16 In its Resolution of 9 October 1986 on an initiative concerning negotiations within the Council on the drawing up of a common European policy on refugees the European

Act had endowed the Treaty with a slightly sounder legal basis for anchoring immigration policy to the establishment of the single market.[17]

3.3 The inevitability of intergovernmental cooperation: A) The Schengen Agreements

Initially, intergovernmental cooperation outside the Treaty of Rome produced greater results through multilateral cooperation over controls at common borders. Collaboration of this kind had in fact been taking place since the early days of the EEC, as in the Franco-German Agreement of April 1958.[18] After the lorry drivers' protest in the spring of 1984 against delays caused by border controls, Germany and France used the old pact as the basis for the Saarbrücken Agreement, progressively dismantling controls at their common borders.[19] Foreshadowing the European Commission's Green Paper issued almost a year later, Article 15 mentioned the need to combine the dismantling of controls at common frontiers with the harmonisation of policies on the entry and residence of aliens 'en vue de réunir les conditions nécessaires à la suppression de tout contrôle pour les ressortissants des pays membres des Communautés européennes'.

Shortly afterwards, the Netherlands (with which Germany was in negotiations to facilitate the transportation of goods) joined in the arrangements, along with

Parliament had highlighted the need for a common policy: OJ C 283, 10 November 1986, p. 74. This is very significant because by calling on the Council to start 'negotiations as soon as possible with the Member States' the European Parliament implied that the matter was outside the scope of the Treaty. Moreover, the Resolution mentioned two problems that would become a constant feature of common refugee policy: respect for human rights, on which the European Parliament 'considers that a common policy must be based', and reaching a general agreement on which States would be responsible for examining applications for refugee status. Finally, the Resolution proposed that a study should be made of the (somewhat unlikely) possibility 'of the Community acceding to the UN Convention on refugees'.

17 Article 13 of the Single European Act incorporated Article 8A into the TEEC, setting a deadline for the completion of the single market. According to F. Crépeau and J. Y. Carlier (1999: 959 ff.), A. Liguori (2000: 129), L. Manca (2003: 38 ff.) and M. Condinanzi, A. Lang and B. Nascimbene (2006: 254 ff.), the Commission immediately realised that Article 8A could provide a basis for its competence in matters of immigration: because the article aimed to establish a market without internal borders it assumed that the external borders would be strengthened as an indispensible step towards achieving its goal. It is significant, however, that the States could not agree whether Article 8A referred only to Community citizens or not. On this see M. Fridegotto (1992: 43 ff.) and S. Bertini (2003: 187 ff.).

18 Convention relative aux bureau de contrôles nationaux juxtaposés aux gares communes ou d'échange à la frontière franco-allemande, 746 UNTS 335 ff., adopted Paris 18 April 1958 by France and the Federal Republic of Germany.

19 Accord relatif à la suppression graduelle des contrôles à la frontière franco-allemande, 1401 UNTS 167 ff., adopted Saarbrücken 13 July 1984. On the origins of the Saarbrücken Agreement and on the Schengen Agreement in general, see M. Fridegotto (1992: 13 ff.), V. Hreblay (1998: 15) and S. Bellucci (2002: 21).

Belgium and Luxembourg as part of the same economic and customs union (Benelux).[20] The five States then signed, on 14 June 1985 at Schengen, a general agreement to progressively dismantle controls at their common frontiers.[21] The agreement confirmed the connection between the establishment of the single market, an essential element of which was the free movement of people, goods, services and capital, and the harmonisation of controls at external borders, which required a common policy on the entry of third-country nationals, including asylum-seekers. The paradigms of this assertion are Article 17 of the Agreement, which states that 'the Parties shall endeavour to abolish checks at common borders and *transfer* them to their external borders' (emphasis added),[22] and, following on from it, Article 20, according to which the Parties

> in so far as is necessary, . . . shall also prepare the harmonisation of their rules governing certain aspects of the law on aliens in regard to nationals of States that are not members of the European Communities.

The preamble to the Schengen Agreement very clearly reflects the view that to create the single European market internal border checks had to be abolished; it contains several references to the freedoms of the European Community, particularly in the first recital in which the Parties declare they are

> aware that the ever closer union of the peoples of the Member States of the European Communities should find its expression in the freedom to cross internal borders for all nationals of the Member States and in the free movement of goods and services.

The consequences of the commitments entered into under the Agreement were set out in the Schengen Implementation Convention, again signed in Schengen on 19 June 1990.[23] Because national measures adapting to the harmonised system of

20 Customs agreement signed in London on 5 September 1944, *Bulletin d'information du Grand-duché de Luxembourg*, 1947, p. 51 ff., and Treaty Establishing the Benelux Economic Union (adopted The Hague 3 February 1958), 381 UNTS 165 ff.

21 Agreement between the Governments of the States of the Benelux Economic Union, the Federal Republic of Germany and the French Republic on the gradual abolition of checks at their common borders (adopted Schengen 14 June 1985). An English version is available in OJ L 239, 22 September 2000, p. 13 ff.

22 M. Fridegotto (1992: 40) recounts the colourful metaphor used by the President of the Executive Committee set up under the Convention Implementing the Schengen Agreement, that the aim was to move the entry checks from the door of the apartment to the door of the building.

23 Convention Implementing the Schengen Agreement of 14 June 1985 between the Governments of the States of the Benelux Economic Union, the Federal Republic of Germany and the French Republic, on the gradual abolition of checks at their common borders ('Implementation Convention'), OJ L 239, 22 September 2000, p. 19 ff.

checks at common borders had to be introduced first,[24] the Implementation Convention did not come into force until 26 March 1995 for Belgium, France, Germany, Luxembourg, the Netherlands, Portugal and Spain.[25] For the other States parties to the Convention (Italy, Greece and Austria[26]), it entered into force following a decision of the Executive Committee set up under Article 131 of the Convention also 'to ensure that this Convention is implemented correctly'.[27] For Italy and Austria, the respective dates of entry into force were 26 October 1997 and 1 December 1997, while in the case of Greece the Convention only became operational following a series of decisions of the Executive Committee[28] after the entry into force of the Treaty of Amsterdam (see below, section 3.11).

Despite the very broad resolutions made five years earlier, at least as far as asylum-seekers were concerned the Implementation Convention merely repeated the intention expressed by the European Council of London in 1986,[29] i.e. to combat abuse of the right of asylum, especially by applying for recognition of refugee status under the Refugee Convention in several Member Countries at the same time to increase the chances of success (known as asylum shopping).[30] Thus,

24 Regarding these measures, which were the reason for Italy's delay (the Convention only entered into force on 26 October 1997), see 'Documento relativo all'indagine conoscitiva sullo stato di attuazione della Convenzione di applicazione dell'accordo di Schengen' drafted by the Parliamentary Committee on the adoption and operation of the Schengen Implementation Agreement, *Stato di attuazione della Convenzione di applicazione dell'accordo di Schengen*, Rome, 1997, p. 11 ff.

25 Decision of the Executive Committee of 22 December 1994 bringing into force the Convention Implementing the Schengen Agreement of 19 June 1990, OJ L 239, 22 September 2000, p. 130 ff. Portugal and Spain joined the Schengen Agreements at Bonn on 25 June 1991, OJ L 239, 22 September 2000, p. 69 ff.

26 Italy acceded by the Agreement adopted at Paris on 27 November 1990, OJ L 239, 22 September 2000, p. 63 ff.; Greece by the Agreement adopted at Madrid on 6 November 1992, OJ L 239, 22 September 2000, p. 83 ff.; and Austria by the Agreement adopted at Brussels on 28 April 1995, OJ L 239, 22 September 2000, p. 90 ff.

27 Questions were raised about the 'democraticness' and transparency of the Committee's activities: see M. Condinanzi, A. Lang and B. Nascimbene (2006: 257). A fairly bland oversight was already envisaged by the national parliaments, such as that of Italy's Parliamentary Committee, on which see B. Nascimbene (1999a: 731 ff.). On the oversight of the national parliaments of the States parties to the Convention see 'Documento relativo all'indagine conoscitiva', p. 15 ff.

28 Decision of the Executive Committee of 7 October 1997 on bringing into force the Convention implementing the Schengen Agreement in Greece, OJ L 239, 22 September 2000, pp. 135–6, and Decision of the Executive Committee of 16 December 1998 on bringing into force the Implementing Convention in Greece, OJ L 239, 22 September 2000, pp. 147–8.

29 See below, footnote 34.

30 Regarding this objective, which would be taken up again in the Dublin Convention, see 'Documento conclusivo dell'indagine conoscitiva sullo stato di attuazione della Convenzione di applicazione dell'accordo di Schengen' drafted by Italy's Parliamentary Committee on the adoption and operation of the Schengen Implementation Convention, *Stato di attuazione della Convenzione di applicazione dell'accordo di Schengen*, Rome,

Chapter 7 (Article 28 ff.) laid down the rules for identifying the State responsible for processing asylum applications; and Article 30 in particular prioritised the criterion of the applicant's proximity to the State issuing the visa or, failing that, to the State that had granted first entry.[31] The Implementation Convention regulated the matter of asylum-seekers for more general reasons as well. By abolishing internal border checks, it established common rules for the entry of third-country nationals at the area's common borders, although these did not apply to asylum-seekers. This factor, taken together with Article 29(1) and (2) obligating States to examine asylum applications except in cases of rejection and expulsion permitted under national law in compliance with international obligations, was the first building block of future Community legislation on asylum, separating the scope of the rules on the entry of asylum-seekers from that of the rules applying to third-country nationals *tout court*.

3.4 B) The Dublin Convention

A second route by which intergovernmental cooperation produced substantial results in the field of asylum was examined at the informal meeting of interior ministers in London on 20 October 1986,[32] at which it was decided to set up an *ad hoc* working group on immigration.[33] The group was to re-consider 'measures to achieve a common policy to eliminate asylum abuse, in consultation with the Council of Europe and UNHCR'.[34] The group's work was further assisted by The Palma Document, adopted by the European Council of Madrid in 1989,[35] and resulted in two draft conventions, one on the crossing of external borders, which was never adopted,[36] and one which led in 1990 to the Convention

1997, p. 13. One of the purposes of the provisions on refugees contained in the Convention is to make sure than an application for refugee status was always made to one Member State to avoid the problem of refugees 'in orbit', people whose applications are repeatedly rejected by Member States because none accept responsibility for examining them.

31 On this point see M. G. Garbagnati (1996: 59 ff.) and K. Hailbronner and V. Thiery (1997: 957 ff.).

32 *Bulletin of the European Communities*, No. 10/1986, p. 77 ff.

33 The working group would include members of the Commission if Community competences are involved. This was not an isolated case: on the activities of the other working groups see M. Fridegotto (1992: 51 ff.), F. Crépeau and J. Y. Carlier (1999: 961 ff.) and L. Manca (2003: 39 ff.).

34 The need to ensure that asylum was not abused was reiterated in the Conclusions of the President of the European Council, London, 5–6 December 1986, *Bulletin of the European Communities*, No. 12/1986, p. 7 ff.

35 On this point see M. Fridegotto (1992: 50 ff.). 'The Palma Document' was simply the report of the Coordinators' Group on the free movement of persons set up by the European Council of Rhodes in December 1988.

36 The project collapsed because of disagreement between the UK and Spain regarding the rules of territorial application because of the status of Gibraltar. See J. Niessen (1996: 34). For a commentary on the draft convention see M. G. Garbagnati (1996: 88 ff.).

determining the State responsible for examining applications for asylum lodged in one of the Member States of the European Communities, better known as the Dublin Convention.[37] It entered into force on 1 September 1997 and was signed between Belgium, Denmark, France, Germany, Greece, Ireland, Italy, Luxembourg, the Netherlands, Portugal, the UK and Spain, later joined by Austria and Sweden (entering into force on 1 October 1997) and Finland (1 January 1998). As the Dublin Convention had the same scope as Articles 28 ff. of the Schengen Implementation Convention and not all the States parties to the first were also parties to the second, on 26 April 1995 a Protocol was signed in Bonn establishing that the relevant provisions of the Convention would be replaced by those of the Dublin Convention as soon as it came into force.[38] However, the other provisions of the Implementation Convention naturally remained in place between the States parties, thus separating *ratione personarum* the field of application of the rules on the elimination of checks at common borders and the crossing of external borders from the field of application of the Dublin Convention.[39]

Apart from re-stating the relevant provisions of the Schengen Implementation Convention, the Dublin Convention added an element of importance for its own application.[40] Article 18 called for a committee to be set up to 'examine, at the request of one or more Member States, any question of a general nature concerning the application or interpretation of this Convention' and with the power to adopt any measures, including revisions and amendments (subject to ratification by the States), that prove necessary 'pursuant to the achievement of the objectives set out in Article 8a of the Treaty establishing the European Economic

37 Convention determining the State responsible for examining applications for asylum lodged in one of the Member States of the European Communities – Dublin Convention, OJ C 254, 19 August 1997, pp. 1 ff. For a general analysis see A. Hurwitz (1999: 646 ff.).
38 The Protocol was published in *Journal officiel du Grand-duché de Luxembourg, Recueil de la législation*, No. 30, 7 May 1996, pp. 1028–9. The overlapping of various parts of the two conventions could have created some problems of compatibility in the light of Article 30 of the Vienna Convention on the Law of Treaties, 1155 UNTS 331 ff. When the Dublin Convention entered into force on 1 September 1997 only for Belgium, France, Germany, Luxembourg, the Netherlands, Portugal and Spain, the Schengen Implementation Convention had already been in force since 26 March 1995. On this point see also K. Hailbronner and V. Thiery (1997: 957 ff., especially 960 ff.).
39 When the Treaty of Amsterdam entered into force (1 May 1999), revolutionising the whole matter by transposing the Schengen provisions into Community law, the Schengen Implementation Convention had not yet been applied and therefore the common frontiers of Austria, Denmark, Finland, Greece and Sweden (to which the Dublin Convention did apply) had not yet been dismantled.
40 Because the Dublin Convention contained no provisions on the crossing of internal and external borders – and therefore did not consider problems of immigration *tout court* – it contained more safeguards for asylum applicants. On this point see G. Barontini (1992: 334 ff.). For an analysis of the criteria adopted by the Dublin Convention see K. Hailbronner and V. Thiery (1997: 957 ff., especially 960).

Community'.[41] The hybrid nature of the Dublin Convention, being the outcome of intergovernmental cooperation with a large input from the EEC,[42] is further confirmed by the composition of the committee set up under Article 18: one representative of each Member State and one of the European Commission could take part and the committee was chaired by the Member State that held the Presidency of the Council. Finally, the Dublin Convention laid the foundations for an exchange of information between Member States, which was necessary to improve its application. Article 15 allowed the information to be computerised at a later date provided that certain conditions were met relating to the protection of personal information.

3.5 The Treaty of Maastricht and the Third Pillar

It was not until the signing of the Treaty of Maastricht, which entered into force on 1 November 1993, that the issue of asylum became part of the Treaties.[43] Apart from amending the Treaty of Rome, transforming the EEC into the European Community,[44] the Treaty of Maastricht also gave birth to the European Union (EU) and introduced its two 'new' pillars, the Common Foreign and Security Policy (CFSP) and Justice and Home Affairs (JHA).[45] The latter, in effect the Third

---

41 The Committee in fact took several decisions pursuant to Article 18 of the Dublin Convention: Decision No. 1/97 of 9 September 1997, concerning provisions for the implementation of the Convention, OJ L 281, 14 October 1997, p. 1 ff.; Decision No. 1/98 of 30 June 1998, concerning provisions for the implementation of the Convention, OJ L 196, 14 July 1998, pp. 49–50; and Decision No. 1/2000 of 31 October 2000, concerning the transfer of responsibility for family members in accordance with Article 3(4) and Article 9 of that Convention, OJ L 281, 7 November 2000, p. 1 ff.

42 It should be recalled (footnote 33) that the European Commission took part in the work of the *ad hoc* committee that drafted the Dublin Convention for matters within the competence of the Community.

43 Treaty on European Union (TEU), adopted Maastricht 7 February 1992, OJ C 191, 29 July 1992, p. 1 ff.

44 The Treaty introduced a provision into EU law that was to have enormous consequences for asylum. Article F(2), which set out the approach adopted by the ECJ in previous years, confirmed that the EU would respect 'fundamental rights, as guaranteed by the European Convention for the Protection of Human Rights and Fundamental Freedoms signed in Rome on 4 November 1950 and as they result from the constitutional traditions common to the Member States, as general principles of Community law'. The case law of the European Court of Human Rights (ECtHR) having already 'persuaded' the judges of the ECJ in Luxembourg, this reference to the convention created an opening for major consequences regarding the law on asylum, as we shall see below (§ 4.5). It was through this opening that the ECtHR's particular interpretation of Article 3 of the European Convention on Human Rights (ECHR) found its way into Community, and eventually EU, law.

45 The Treaty reiterated, with some amendments, Article 8A TEEC, which became Article 7A TEC, and the Commission resumed its earlier attempts based on Article 100 TEEC (see footnotes 12 and 16) to put forward another series of proposals, also unsuccessful (see the proposal for a Council directive on the right of third-country

Pillar, envisaged competence to regulate asylum, still largely a matter of intergovernmental cooperation despite a generalised, if somewhat hesitant, move by Member States to limit their competence for immigration:[46] in the Council unanimous voting was almost invariably required, whereas the Commission had the right of initiative, shared with the Member States only in certain areas, while in others it was 'fully associated with the work carried out' by the Council. The role of the ECJ was greatly reduced, having only competence to interpret convent-ions and resolve disputes on their application. As for the European Parliament, it was briefly mentioned in Article K.6 TEU, stating that it would be regularly informed about discussions, it would be consulted by the Presidency 'on the principal aspects of activities in the areas' of JHA, and that it could ask questions to the Council or make recommendations to it.[47] Moreover, there was some lack of transparency about the activities included in the JHA pillar, the results of which were not even published in the Official Journal before the Council's Decision of 23 November 1995.[48]

nationals to travel in the Community, OJ C 306, 17 November 1995, p. 5, later re-submitted as amended proposal for a Council directive on the right of third-country nationals to travel in the Community, OJ C 139, 6 May 1997, p. 6, and the proposal for a Council directive on the elimination of controls on persons crossing internal frontiers, OJ C 289, 31 October 1995, p. 16, later re-submitted as amended proposal for a Council directive on the elimination of controls on persons crossing internal frontiers, OJ C 140, 7 May 1997, p. 21).

46 These developments in matters of immigration concerned both the Third Pillar and, to a lesser extent, the Community Pillar. The TEC in fact incorporated Article 100C on the EC's competence for some aspects of visa policy, with the Council responsible for drawing up the list of third countries whose nationals require a visa in order to cross the external borders of Member States and for adopting measures relating to a uniform format for visas. This had several regulatory repercussions: Council Regulation (EC) No. 2317/95 of 25 September 1995 determining the third countries whose nationals must be in possession of visas when crossing the external borders of the Member States, OJ L 234, 3 October 1995, p. 1 ff., and Council Regulation (EC) No. 1638/95 of 29 May 1995 laying down a uniform format for visas, OJ L 164, 14 July 1995, p. 1 ff. The first was declared null by the ECJ, judgment of 10 June 1997, Case C-392/95, *European Parliament* v. *Council of the European Union, Reports of Cases*, 1997, p. I-3213 ff. It was later replaced by Council Regulation (EC) No. 574/1999 of 12 March 1999 determining the third countries whose nationals must be in possession of visas when crossing the external borders of the Member States, OJ L 72, 18 March 1999, p. 2 ff. (adopted on the basis of Article 100C TEC), and finally, after the amendments intro-duced by the Treaty of Amsterdam, notably the competence pursuant to Article 62(2)(b)(i) TEC, by Council Regulation (EC) No. 539/2001 of 15 March 2001 listing the third countries whose nationals must be in possession of visas when crossing the external borders and those nationals who are exempt from that requirement, OJ L 81, 21 March 2001, p. 2 ff., in turn amended on several occasions. Instead, Regulation 1638/95 remains in force, albeit with some amendments.

47 On this point see M. Missorici and C. Romano (1998: 74) and L. Manca (2003: 64).

48 Council Decision of 23 November 1995 on publication in the Official Journal of the European Communities of acts and other texts adopted by the Council in the field of asylum and immigration, OJ C 274, 19 September 1996, pp. 1–2. The Member States

There is no clearer evidence of the unwillingness of the Member States to abandon intergovernmentalism than the Council's failure to make use of Article K.9 TEU. Under this article, action in some of the areas referred to in Article K.1, including asylum, could be transferred within the Community Pillar, in particular to Article 100C of the Treaty Establishing the European Community (TEC). However, although Declaration No. 31 annexed to the Final Act of the TEU had already provided that the Council would consider 'by the end of 1993' the possibility of applying Article K.9, even in view of the contrary opinion of the Commission expressed in its Communication of 22 November 1995,[49] the question of the 'communitarisation' of some matters alluded to in Article K.1 was deferred to the intergovernmental conference that would draw up the Treaty of Amsterdam.[50]

3.6 Achievements in asylum through Third Pillar competences

Article K.1 TEU stated that

> For the purposes of achieving the objectives of the Union, in particular the free movement of persons, and without prejudice to the powers of the European Community, Member States shall regard the following areas as matters of common interest: 1. asylum policy. . . .

This objective was to be achieved not only through consultation among the Member States, but also, according to Article K.3, by the Council adopting joint positions and joint actions or drawing up conventions to be ratified by every Member State.[51] The results were not very encouraging. First, the Commission attempted to resurrect, with some changes, the old proposal for a convention on crossing external frontiers drafted by the *ad hoc* committee set up at the informal meeting of 26 October 1986 in London.[52] Despite the Commission's best efforts, the problems that had prevented any consensus being reached on the adoption of

were similarly reticent in matters of immigration even outside the various treaties (see footnote 27).

49 Communication from the Commission to the European Parliament and the Council on the possible application of Article K.9 of the Treaty on European Union, COM (95) 566 final.

50 See the Council Conclusions of 20 June 1994 concerning the possible application of Article K.9 of the Treaty on European Union to asylum policy.

51 These acts are binding only to a very limited extent, that is not always evident beforehand. On this point see N. Parisi (1996: 50).

52 Proposal for a decision, based on Article K.3 of the Treaty on European Union establishing the Convention on the crossing of the external frontiers of the Member States, OJ C 11, 15 January 1994, p. 6 ff.

the final text the first time round[53] persisted and the proposal was permanently withdrawn in 2004.[54]

More specifically on the matter of asylum, the Council adopted a Resolution on minimum procedural standards for examining asylum applications.[55] While re-stating some key principles based on Article 33 of the Refugee Convention, including that 'To ensure effectively the principle of "non-refoulement", no expulsion measure will be carried out as long as no decision has been taken on the asylum application', the Resolution again left the Member States broad scope for manoeuvre. Paragraph (3) stated that 'The regulations on access to the asylum procedure, the basic features of the asylum procedure itself and the designation of the authorities responsible for examination of asylum applications are to be laid down in the individual Member State's legislation'. A second attempt, this time successful, led to the adoption of a Joint Position on harmonising the definition of 'refugee' among the Member States.[56] In this document, as in the Dublin Convention, the Council not only adopted a concept of refugee based on that of the Refugee Convention, but also gave a detailed interpretation of Article 1, which the competent State authorities were requested to 'take as a basis', 'without prejudice to Member States' case law on asylum matters and their relevant constitutional positions'. Because of the Member States' unwillingness to take joint decisions, even if not always binding,[57] in an area so close to that of immigration,

53 See footnote 36. The European Parliament had already given its opinion on the Commission's proposal in the Resolution of 21 April 1994, OJ C 128, 9 May 1994, p. 351 ff.
54 Withdrawal of obsolete Commission proposals, OJ C 5, 9 January 1994, p. 2 ff. This was the proposal for a regulation based on Article 100C of the Treaty establishing the European Community, determining the third countries whose nationals must be in possession of a visa when crossing the external borders of the Member States, later adopted by the Council and transformed into Regulation No. 2317/95, on which see footnote 46 above.
55 Council Resolution of 20 June 1995 on minimum guarantees for asylum procedures, OJ C 274, 19 September 1996, p. 13 ff., for an analysis of which see P. Boeles and A. Terlouw (1997: 472). This Resolution had something of a precedent in the European Parliament Resolution on the right of asylum of 12 March 1987, OJ C 99, 13 April 1987, p. 167 ff., and Resolution on the harmonisation within the European Communities of asylum law and policies of 18 November 1992, OJ C 337, 21 December 1992, p. 97 ff.
56 Joint Position 96/196/JHA of 4 March 1996, defined by the Council on the basis of Article K.3 of the Treaty on European Union on the harmonised application of the definition of the term 'refugee' in Article 1 of the Geneva Convention of 28 July 1951 relating to the status of refugees, OJ L 63, 13 March 1996, p. 2 ff. The Joint Position came about as a result of the wish to harmonise asylum regulations within the Community, which the European Council had called for at previous meetings, notably the meetings in Strasbourg (8–9 December 1990), Maastricht (9–10 December 1991) and Brussels (10–11 December 1993).
57 Only joint positions were compulsory according to Article K.5 TEU: 'Within international organizations and at international conferences in which they take part, Member States shall defend the common positions adopted under the provisions of this Title'.

this harmonisation was never achieved, as evidenced by the practice of Member States, which continued to apply different substantive and procedural laws at national level.[58]

Although the TEU, in its original version, contained no provisions on establishing forms of solidarity to ensure that most of the costs of receiving asylum-seekers were not borne by only a few Member States, the Council issued a series of acts designed precisely to distribute the burden among the Member States, at least in the case of temporary influxes of displaced persons. Thus, following a Resolution of 25 September 1995,[59] the Council adopted Decision 96/198/JHA[60] allowing Member States to convene a meeting of the Coordinating Committee referred to in Article K.4 TEU. According to the indications provided by each Member State the Committee would draw up a proposal for burden sharing to be submitted to the Council for approval. It was not until later that the Council approved a number of proposals for direct financing of the costs of receiving displaced persons, for measures to cover educational facilities for persons under 18 years of age, vocational training, information on the economic and administrative set-up in their country of origin aimed at assisting their reintegration into their country, projects developed in connection with the twinning of local administrative areas, and aid to transport.[61]

58 According to R. Wallace (1996: 57). For a comparative analysis of the national laws on the recognition of refugee status see A. Beghè Loreti (1990: 101), R. Wallace (1996: 83) and various articles published in J.-Y. Carlier, D. Vanheule, K. Hullmann and C. Peña (1997: *passim*).

59 Council Resolution of 25 September 1995 on burden-sharing with regard to the admission and residence of displaced persons on a temporary basis, OJ C 262, 7 October 1995, p. 1 ff.

60 Council Decision of 4 March 1996 96/198/JHA on an alert and emergency procedure for burden sharing with regard to the admission and residence of displaced persons on a temporary basis, OJ L 63, 13 March 1996, pp. 10–11.

61 Joint Action 97/477/JHA of 22 July 1997 adopted by the Council on the basis of Article K.3 of the Treaty on European Union, concerning the financing of specific projects in favour of displaced persons who have found temporary protection in the Member States and asylum-seekers, OJ L 205, 31 July 1997, pp. 3–4. On the same date the Council also adopted a project directed more generally at asylum-seekers: see Joint Action 97/478/JHA of 22 July 1997 adopted by the Council on the basis of Article K.3 of the Treaty on European Union, concerning the financing of specific projects in favour of asylum-seekers and refugees, OJ L 205, 31 July 1997, pp. 5–6. For other projects see Joint Action 98/244/JHA of 19 March 1998, adopted by the Council on the basis of Article K.3 of the Treaty on European Union, introducing a programme of training, exchanges and cooperation in the field of asylum, immigration and crossing of external borders (Odysseus programme), OJ L 99, 31 March 1998, p. 2 ff.; Joint Action 98/304/JHA of 27 April 1998, adopted by the Council on the basis of Article K.3 of the Treaty on European Union, concerning the financing of specific projects in favour of displaced persons who have found temporary protection in the Member States and asylum-seekers, OJ L 138, 9 May 1998, pp. 6–7; Joint Action 98/305/JHA of 27 April 1998, adopted by the Council on the basis of Article K.3 of the Treaty on European Union, concerning the financing of specific projects in favour

3.7 Further developments in intergovernmental cooperation

Although the Treaty of Maastricht failed to give the institutions incisive powers in the area of asylum, governments continued to cooperate outside the Treaties. New developments included not only the entry into force of the Dublin Convention and the Convention Implementing the Schengen Agreement, mentioned above, but also the addition of other signatories to the Schengen Agreement. The original ten signatory States were joined on 19 December 1996 by Denmark, Finland and Sweden,[62] and on the same day but under a separate agreement by Iceland and Norway as associated States.[63] The position of the last two countries, which had to become associated with Schengen activities so that the other members of the Nordic Passport Union (Denmark, Finland and Sweden) could join, was unique in that they were the only States to take part in the meetings of the Schengen institutions – first and foremost, the Executive Committee – without having the right to vote. Moreover, a decision of the Executive Committee was required for the Agreement to enter into force in the five 'new' States as well as in Greece, for which it was still pending at the time (see below, section 3.11).

3.8 'Communitarisation' of the Schengen *acquis* and inclusion in Title IV TEC

The experiments in intergovernmental cooperation consisting in the Schengen agreements and the Dublin Convention did not become part of Community law until the signing of the Treaty of Amsterdam, which entered into force on 1 May 1999. It would not be too far-fetched to say that the Treaty represented a sort of Copernican Revolution[64] in the field of asylum and immigration. As predicted, and augured, by the Commission,[65] it performed the role that Article K.9 TEU attributed to the Council, transferring almost all the areas covered by the Third Pillar under Community law, specifically Title IV of the Treaty. As a consequence, it also incorporated the results of intergovernmental cooperation (through the

of asylum-seekers and refugees, OJ L 138, 9 May 1998, pp. 8–9; and Joint Action 1999/290/JHA of 26 April 1999, adopted by the Council on the basis of Article K.3 of the Treaty on European Union, establishing projects and measures to provide practical support in relation to the reception and voluntary repatriation of refugees, displaced persons and asylum-seekers, including emergency assistance to persons who have fled as a result of recent events in Kosovo, OJ L 114, 1 May 1999, p. 2 ff.

62 The agreements were signed in Luxembourg on 19 December 1996, OJ L 239, 22 September 2000, p. 97 ff.

63 The agreement is published in *Journal official du Grand-duché de Luxembourg. Recueil de la legislation*, No. 37, 15 April 1999, p. 958 ff.

64 According to M. Condinanzi, A. Lang and B. Nascimbene (2006: 263). See also K. Hailbronner (1998: 1047).

65 See footnote 49.

Schengen agreements) partly in Community law and partly in the new Third Pillar (from which asylum and immigration had been virtually stripped, leaving only competence for police and judicial cooperation in criminal matters). The Dublin Convention remained outside the field of Community law, but it was soon to be replaced by one of the first concrete outcomes of the 'new' competences attributed to Title IV: Regulation No. 343/2003 establishing the criteria and mechanisms for determining the Member State responsible for examining an asylum application lodged in one of the Member States by a third-country national.[66]

However, 'communitarisation' did not take place without some compromises having to be made.[67] The Community method was not adopted globally and some Member States that were particularly jealous of their competences were excluded from Title IV and/or the integration of the Schengen *acquis* by means of complex formulas that were the fruit of another Copernican Revolution enacted by the Treaty of Amsterdam,[68] a sort of institutionalisation of Europe *à la carte* by means of a system of enhanced cooperation.

Meanwhile, Article 62 TEC, reiterating word for word Article 14 TEC (itself nothing more than a re-phrasing of Article 7A TEC), laid down the principle that was the cornerstone of the Schengen Agreement, the elimination of checks at internal borders. It also put an end to the debate on the scope of Article 7A by stating that the measures to eliminate internal border checks applied to both EU citizens and third-country nationals.[69] In reality, this merely by-passed the obstacle of the interpretation of the provisions on free movement. The States that had maintained that Article 7A applied only to EU citizens were the very ones that benefited from differentiated integration: Denmark, Ireland and the UK. Instead, it was particularly significant that competence for asylum and immigration were now part of the framework of a market that was no longer strictly economic in character: Article 61 TEC attributed this competence to the institutions 'in order to establish progressively an area of freedom, security and justice'.[70] The journey which began with the first declaration of positions by the European Parliament and the Commission and progressed into an 'experimental workshop for achieving the objective set out in Article 7A'[71] that was the Schengen Agreement, now ended with the new Title IV of the Treaty. It is not surprising that the adoption of a broader notion of 'market' – as an area of freedom, security and justice – was accompanied by

---

66 Council Regulation (EC) No. 343/2003 of 18 February 2003 establishing the criteria and mechanisms for determining the Member State responsible for examining an asylum application lodged in one of the Member States by a third-country national, OJ L 50, 25 February 2003, p. 1 ff.
67 According to H. Labayle (1997: 843).
68 This time the expression is used by E. Wagner (1998: 35).
69 See footnote 17.
70 On this see H. Labayle (1997: 813).
71 S. Bertini (2003: 190, trans. added).

the attribution of new powers for asylum and immigration: by professing a liberal concept of 'market', one that had in fact been hypothesised long before 1997,[72] built on individual choices, the EU equipped itself accordingly with the powers to influence those choices.

The competences for asylum were set out in Article 63 TEC, and according to the prevailing legal theory they were shared.[73] They were founded, in line with previous practice, on the Refugee Convention, to which Article 63 made explicit reference, and the problem of displaced persons – which had already emerged from earlier activities of the Council – and they envisaged a new category of asylum-seekers, that of 'persons who otherwise need international protection'. This broader notion of asylum, no longer confined only to the concept of 'refugee' as understood by the Refugee Convention, had evolved out of the case law of the European Court of Human Rights (ECtHR). As explained earlier (Chapter 2), the Strasbourg Court had extended the principle of *non-refoulement* to people who did not necessarily come within the scope of the Refugee Convention. Article 63(1) listed four aspects of asylum for which the Council should adopt measures: criteria and mechanisms for determining which Member State was responsible for considering an application for asylum submitted by a third-country national in one of the Member States, a matter already covered outside EU law by the Dublin Convention; and minimum standards on the reception of asylum-seekers in Member States, with respect to the qualification of nationals of third countries as refugees, and on procedures in Member States for granting or withdrawing refugee status (on which the Council had previously issued several joint positions and resolutions within the framework of the original version of the Third Pillar). In addition to these were the competences listed in Article 63(2) on 'promoting a balance of effort between Member States in receiving and bearing the consequences of receiving refugees and displaced persons', also the object of earlier activities of the Council, and competences for adopting minimum standards for giving temporary protection to displaced persons from third countries who cannot return to their country of origin and for persons who otherwise need international protection. These competences were joined by another, listed in Article 63(3)(a) calling on the Council to adopt measures relating to the issue of 'long-term visas and residence permits, including those for the purpose of family reunion'. The article does not distinguish between third-country nationals *tout court* and refugees

72 The reference is to the theories of the Austrian School of economics, whose notion of market is best described by one of the leading exponents, L. von Mises (1949: *passim*).

73 See H. Labayle (1997: 846), K. Hailbronner (1998: 1051) who reiterated this view in (1999: 13), A. Adinolfi (2005b: 96), G. Cellamare (2006: 53) and M. Condinanzi, A. Lang and B. Nascimbene (2006: 289). This opinion is confirmed by the subsequent practice of Community institutions: almost all the binding acts issued under Title IV contain specific references to the principle of subsidiarity, the principle of proportionality and Article 5 TEC. See, for all, recital 16 of Council Regulation (EC) No. 343/2003, p. 1 ff.

and it was therefore used by the Council to adopt a 'general' directive on family reunion and on the status of long-term residents.

3.9 Title IV concessions to the intergovernmental cooperation method: A) Procedures for adopting secondary legislation

Although the Treaty of Amsterdam marked a significant step forward, introducing the new Title IV in the EC Treaty did entail some compromises: the method was not exactly the same as that of the First Pillar, being designed to allow Member States some concessions; and a diversified system of implementation was adopted to enable less committed Member States to opt out of Title IV or to not incorporate the Schengen *acquis*, offering them a variety of ways of opting in definitively or occasionally. On the first point, the differences with respect to the Community integration method were evident. One of the main ones concerned the procedures for adopting acts, already extensively covered by the Treaty of Amsterdam, which extended the co-decision procedure introduced by the Treaty of Maastricht to a large number of areas. Title IV leant in the opposite direction:[74] the European Parliament's role became marginal;[75] the Commission lost its exclusive power to initiate measures, albeit only for a transitional period of five years, and had to share the right of initiative with Member States;[76] and in the Council unanimous voting prevailed.[77] Although the Community integration method was to some

---

74 As soon as the Treaty of Amsterdam had been signed J. D. M. Steenbergen (1999: 31) and K. Hailbronner (2000: 1054) raised doubts about the decision-making system of Title IV.

75 For five years from the entry into force of the Treaty of Amsterdam, that is, until 1 May 2004, Article 67 TEC provided only for compulsory consultation. Once the five years were over, some measures relating to immigration became subject to the co-decision procedure, while for others a unanimous decision of the Council was required. The Council availed itself of this faculty to adopt Decision 2004/927/EC of 22 December 2004 providing for certain areas covered by Title IV of Part Three of the Treaty establishing the European Community to be governed by the procedure laid down in Article 251 of that Treaty, OJ L 396, 31 December 2004, pp. 45–6, effectively only allowing the co-decision procedure in matters of asylum for measures to promote a balance of efforts between Member States in receiving refugees and displaced persons.

76 According to Article 67(2) TEC, first indent, at the end of the transitional period the Commission 'shall examine any request made by a Member State' with a view to submitting a proposal to the Council. Of course, as A. Adinolfi (1998: 85) and L. Manca (2003: 172) admit, the Commission was not obliged either to submit the proposal or to follow its contents if it did decide to draft one.

77 The unanimity rule applied to all measures during the first five years of entry into force of the Amsterdam Treaty, except the measures (previously listed in Article 100C TEC) relating to the list of third countries for which there exists a visa requirement and to the uniform visa format, for which there is qualified majority voting. At the end of the transitional period, Article 67 merely laid down that 'the Council shall act on proposals from the Commission', which, combined with Article 205 TEC, is equivalent, strictly speaking, to adopting the rule of majority voting.

extent restored after the transitional period,[78] as a whole the institutions complied with the requirement of Article 63 TEC that all measures relating to asylum had to be passed within five years of the entry into force of the Treaty of Amsterdam, thus preventing the method from being used.

The measures in question were the most important passed as Community legislation and many of them[79] remain in force within the new framework of EU law. The main ones were drafted following the conclusions of the Tampere European Council of 15 and 16 October 1999 at which the first stage of European asylum policy was launched on the basis of the Vienna Action Plan.[80] They are discussed in detail in Chapter 4 and briefly comprise Regulation No. 2725/2000 establishing Eurodac;[81] Directive 2001/55/CE on minimum standards for giving temporary protection in the event of a mass influx of displaced persons and on measures promoting a balance of efforts between Member States in receiving such persons and bearing the consequences thereof;[82] Directive 2003/9/EC laying down minimum standards for the reception of asylum-seekers;[83] Regulation No. 343/2003 cited earlier; Directive 2003/86/EC on the right to family reunification;[84] Directive 2003/109/EC concerning the status of third-country nationals who are long-term residents;[85] and Directive 2004/83/EC on minimum standards for the qualification and status of third-country nationals or stateless persons as refugees or as persons who otherwise need international protection and the content of the protection granted.[86]

78 For all measures relating to asylum, except of course those subjected to the co-decision procedure by Council Decision 2004/927, the Treaty of Nice, which entered into force on 1 February 2003, OJ C 80, 10 March 2001, p. 1 ff., introduced paragraph (5) in Article 67 TEC, according to which 'the Council shall adopt, in accordance with the procedure referred to in Article 251: – the measures provided for in Article 63(1) and (2)(a) provided that the Council has previously adopted, in accordance with paragraph 1 of this Article, Community legislation defining the common rules and basic principles governing these issues'.

79 For further developments regarding the Asylum Package see below, § 3.13.

80 Council and Commission Action Plan of 3 December 1998 on how best to implement the provisions of the Treaty of Amsterdam on the creation of an area of freedom, security and justice.

81 Council Regulation (EC) No. 2725/2000 of 11 December 2000 concerning the establishment of 'Eurodac' for the comparison of fingerprints for the effective application of the Dublin Convention, OJ L 316, 15 December 2000, p. 1 ff.

82 Council Directive 2001/55/EC of 20 July 2001, OJ L 212, 7 August 2001, p. 12 ff.

83 Council Directive 2003/9/EC of 27 January 2003, OJ L 31, 6 February 2003, p. 18 ff.

84 Council Directive 2003/86/EC of 22 September 2003, OJ L 251, 3 October 2003, p. 12 ff.

85 Council Directive 2003/109/EC of 25 November 2003, OJ L 16, 23 January 2004, p. 4 ff.

86 Council Directive 2004/83/EC of 29 April 2004, OJ L 304, 30 September 2004, p. 12 ff.

3.10 B) Competences of the European Court of Justice

A second and far more significant deviation from the Community method concerns the competences of the ECJ.[87] Article 68(1) TEC eliminated part of the ECJ's competence to issue preliminary rulings and no longer permitted lower courts to refer to it questions of interpretation or validity. The rule did not clarify the position of the higher courts, however, even though most authoritative writers upheld the theory of an obligation to refer.[88] For its part, the Luxembourg Court appeared to lean in the opposite direction, albeit not always clearly, and in some decisions tentatively alluded to a faculty of higher courts to refer questions.[89] By contrast, several advocates general, in their opinions, declared themselves to be firmly in favour of the obligation to refer.[90]

Aside from this, Article 68 TEC left no room for doubt that lower courts were excluded from the possibility of referring questions for preliminary ruling. This created a major problem when such courts were faced with a patently invalid measure. The question was thus whether the principle asserted by the ECJ in the *Foto-Frost* decision applied, i.e. that it is the only court competent to rule on the invalidity of a Community (now EU) measure, with national courts merely competent to confirm its validity, or whether, in proceedings that relate to an application for interim measures, judgment should be deferred pending the

---

87 For the theory see H. Labayle (1997: 862 ff.), A. Albors-Llorens (1998: 1273 ff.), C. Curti Gialdino (1998: 41 ff.), N. Fennelly (1998: 185 ff.), P. Eeckhout (2000: 153 ff.), L. Garofalo (2000: 805 ff.), A. Adinolfi (2001: 315 ff.), J. J. Martín Arribas and P. Dembour van Overbergh (2001: 321 ff.), P. Ivaldi (2002: 273 ff.), S. Bertini (2003: 205 ff.), L. Daniele (2004: 460 ff.) and G. Cellamare (2006: 86 ff.).

88 See C. Curti Gialdino (1998: 59 ff.), P. Girerd (1999: 243), P. Eeckhout (2000: 155), L. Garofalo (2000: 809 ff.), A. Adinolfi (2001: 317 ff.), J. J. Martín Arribas and P. Dembour van Overbergh (2001: 339), G. Papagianni (2001–2002: 122), P. Ivaldi (2002: 274), L. Daniele (2004: 462) and G. Cellamare (2006: 90). For the contrasting view see H. Labayle (1997: 863), P. Biavati (1998: 821 ff.) and B. Nascimbene (1999b: 265).

89 See order of 31 March 2004, Case C-51/03, *Criminal proceedings against Nicoleta Maria Georgescu, Reports of Cases*, 2004, p. I-3203 ff., especially para. 30; order of 10 June 2004, Case C-555/03, *Magali Warbecq* v. *Ryanair Ltd.*, ibid., 2004, p. I-6041 ff., especially para. 13; judgment of 8 November 2005, Case C-443/03, *Götz Leffler* v. *Berlin Chemie AG*, ibid., 2005, p. I-9611 ff., especially para. 70; and judgment of 25 June 2009, Case C-14/08, *Roda Golf & Beach Resort SL (Roda)*, ibid., 2009, p. I-5439 ff., especially para. 24 ff. Less explicit, but still in favour of the non-compulsory nature of reference, is the order of 22 March 2002, Case C-24/02, *Marseille Fret SA* v. *Seatrano Shipping Company Ltd.*, ibid., 2002, p. I-3383 ff., especially para. 14.

90 Explicitly in favour of the compulsory reference theory were Advocate General Ruiz-Jarabo Colomer in his opinion of 28 June 2001, Case C-17/00, *François De Coster* v. *Collège des bourgmestres et échevins de Watermael-Boitsfort, Reports of Cases*, 2001, p. I-9445 ff., especially para. 68; Advocate General Kokott in her opinion of 18 July 2007, Case C-175/06, *Alessandro Tedesco* v. *Tomasoni Fittings Srl and RWO Marine Equipment Ltd.*, ibid., 2007, p. I-7929 ff., para. 21 ff.; and Advocate General Sharpston in her opinion of 20 May 2010, Case C-256/09, *Bianca Purrucker* v. *Guillermo Vallès Pérez*, ibid., 2010, p. I-7353 ff., para. 28.

decision of the ECJ to which the national court is clearly obliged to refer the matter.[91] Thus, if the national court refers the question to the ECJ or if it independently examines the (patent in)validity of the Community measure, it will fail to adhere to the letter of Article 68 TEC in the first instance and to observe the principle asserted in the *Foto-Frost* decision in the second.[92] It is clear that the purpose of Article 68 was to eliminate the premise of this argument, ensuring that Community measures were outside the jurisdiction of lower courts right up to the court of last instance. This resulted in a clear, twofold defect. On the one hand, it limited the jurisdictional safeguards for the individual in a field in which asylum-seekers generally still have difficulty gaining access to the higher courts.[93] On the other hand, it seriously jeopardised the uniform interpretation of Title IV.[94] This is one of the reasons why scholarly writers[95] hoped that the Council would use Article 67(2), second indent, TEC, allowing it, after consulting the European Parliament, to take a decision unanimously with a view to 'adapting the provisions relating to the powers of the Court of Justice'. Despite promptings from the Commission, among others, the Council has never taken advantage of this possibility.[96]

Article 68(2) placed a further limitation on the ECJ's jurisdiction, not allowing it to rule on measures or decisions taken pursuant to Article 62(1). This meant that the ECJ was not competent to evaluate measures ensuring the abolition of checks at internal borders to maintain law and order and safeguard internal security. Article 68(2) in fact appeared to contradict Article 64(1), which was without prejudice to the exercise of the 'responsibilities incumbent upon Member States with regard to the maintenance of law and order and the safeguarding of internal security'. It is unclear how the Treaty could exclude the Court's jurisdiction in respect of measures that the Community was probably not competent to adopt.[97] There is an explanation for this apparent contradiction, however: the aim of Article 68(2) was to prevent 'unorthodox' use of preliminary ruling on interpretation leading the Court to rule on the validity (*vis-à-vis* the Treaties) of those measures, taken by Member States, excluded by Article 64(1),[98] a point firmly upheld by the French delegation during the negotiations leading up to the Treaty of Amsterdam.[99] In fact, as the Treaty enshrined the principle of abolishing

---

91 ECJ, judgment of 22 October 1987, Case 314/85, *Foto-Frost* v. *Hauptzollamt Lübeck-Ost*, *Reports of Cases*, 1987, p. 4199 ff.
92 According to Advocate General Ruiz-Jarabo Colomer, opinion of 5 March 2009, *Roda*, especially para. 30.
93 See K. Hailbronner (2000: 19) and L. Daniele (2004: 461).
94 According to C. Curti Gialdino (1998: 61), S. Peers (1998: 353 ff.) and P. Eeckhout (2000: 157 ff.).
95 A. Albors-Llorens (1998: 1289), C. Curti-Gialdino (1998: 62) and G. Papagianni (2001–2002: 124).
96 See the summing up in *Roda*, para. 31.
97 See G. Papagianni (2001–2002: 123) and L. Daniele (2004: 463).
98 On the 'unorthodox' use of preliminary ruling see U. Villani (2013: 376 ff.).
99 G. Papagianni (2001–2002: 123).

checks at internal borders, this limitation on the ECJ's jurisdiction was bound to have little or no practical effect.[100] Considerably more significant was the similar restriction imposed by Article 2(1) of the Protocol Integrating the Schengen *Acquis* annexed to the Treaty of Amsterdam, which stated that the Court had no jurisdiction over measures and decisions 'relating to the maintenance of law and order and the safeguarding of internal security', without the limitation concerning measures on the abolition of internal borders, thus granting Member States virtual immunity concerning checks at external borders.

Although Article 68 TEC constituted a special rule with respect to Article 234 TEC, it was silent on the matter of the other competences of the ECJ. Some legal theorists[101] interpreted this as meaning that within the framework of Title IV these other competences had the same 'common' content (at that time) as Article 226 ff. TEC. In reality, the problem arose whether the exception regarding the competence to issue preliminary rulings provided in Article 68(2) also applied to the ECJ's other competences. Although Article 68 was not entirely clear on the point, legal theorists tended to take the literal wording of paragraph (2), especially the phrase 'In any event', as an implicit reference to Articles 226 ff. They therefore concluded that the ECJ could not, as part of its common competences, rule on the validity of Community measures to abolish checks at internal borders for the maintenance of law and order and the safeguarding of internal security.[102] If, as I believe, the rationale for Article 68(2) was to prevent the 'unorthodox' use of preliminary ruling on interpretation from encompassing Member States' measures, then it follows that the limitation established in that article should extend to the other competences of the Court, especially its jurisdiction in the infringement procedure.[103]

A competence of the ECJ, limited to this area, aimed to partly restore a uniform interpretation of Title IV.[104] Under Article 68(3) the Council, the Commission or a Member State could request the ECJ to interpret a clause of Title IV or of

---

100 The only possibility for a Member State to restore checks at internal borders – and therefore the only situation in which this limitation on the Court's jurisdiction would take effect – was that allowed by Article 2(2) of the Convention Implementing the Schengen Agreement, according to which 'where public policy or national security so require a Contracting Party may, after consulting the other Contracting Parties, decide that for a limited period national border checks appropriate to the situation shall be carried out at internal borders'.

101 See H. Labayle (1997: 862), S. Peers (1998: 352) and L. Garofalo (2000: 807).

102 See C. Curti Gialdino (1998: 65), L. Garofalo (2000: 808), L. Daniele (2004: 463) and G. Cellamare (2006: 91 ff.). According to Cellamare 'Article 2(1) [of the Protocol Integrating the Schengen *Acquis*] simply mentions the "competences" of the Court without elaborating further, thus referring not only to applications for preliminary rulings but also the other competences mentioned' (trans. added). This argument is sound, although possibly the reference itself alludes not so much to the common competences of the Court under Title IV as to that exercised under Title VI of the TEU.

103 For an argument against see A. Adinolfi (1998: 319).

104 According to K. Hailbronner (2000: 1055).

acts based on it.[105] In order to avoid non-uniform application of Title IV by national courts, particularly as lower courts could no longer refer matters to Luxembourg, the provision aimed to institute a mechanism, activated by the Community institutions or Member States,[106] which would in any case allow a ruling on interpretation to be obtained from the Court.

3.11 More compromises to 'communitarise' asylum: differentiated integration of Title IV and enhanced cooperation under the Schengen Agreements

The other compromises involved in drawing up the Treaty of Amsterdam were differentiated integration of the clauses of Title IV and enhanced cooperation under the Schengen *acquis*. Asylum was not entirely included in these two complex systems, and the only differentiated scheme applicable to it was that of Title IV. The Schengen *acquis* was in fact 'communitarised' after the only provisions of the Implementation Convention with direct relevance to asylum – those contained in Article 28 ff. on responsibility for examining asylum applications – had been superseded by the Dublin Convention. The Convention, to which the three States subject to the system of differentiated integration were party, was outside Community law, a fact that would become significant when the Council exercised its power under Article 63 TEC to adopt measures with the same field of application as the Convention (such as Regulation 343/2003, known as Dublin II because intended to replace the Dublin Convention) or somehow associated with it (such as the Eurodac Regulation).

It is nevertheless useful, for two reasons, to recall briefly how the 'communitarisation' of the Schengen *acquis* took place. First, the Schengen *acquis* contained rules, such as those on the crossing of external borders, with an impact on asylum. Second, as will be shown later, it is not easy to identify the differentiated integration system applying to each of the three States affected without a clear concept of how the integration mechanism worked. Integration took place by means of an *ad hoc* Protocol citing the sources of the Schengen *acquis*[107] and also setting out how they were incorporated into EC/EU law. Incorporation basically occurred in two stages: the Council identified the exact acts forming part of the *acquis* by Decision

---

105 Of course, this competence was also subject to the limitation laid down in Article 68(2) TEC.

106 But not, as H. Labayle (1997: 863) points out, activated by the European Parliament. Furthermore, although this competence was designed to restore a uniform interpretation of the relevant EC provisions, for obvious reasons it was not retro-active: according to Article 68(3) the Court's ruling would not apply to 'judgements of courts or tribunals of the Member States which have become *res judicata*'.

107 Briefly, these include the Agreement of 1985 and the Implementation Convention of 1990, all the subsequent agreements on association and implementing agreements, and all the decisions and declarations of the Executive Committee or delegated bodies.

1999/436/EC,[108] and the legal basis of *acquis* was determined, between Title IV TEC and Title VI TEU, by Decision 1999/436/EC.[109]

Starting from the system applied to Denmark within the framework of Title IV, the relevant rules were set out in a Protocol 'on the position of Denmark', Articles 1 and 2 of which excluded the country completely from that Title. Thus, Denmark did not take part in the adoption of measures pursuant to the Title; it was not bound by its provisions or by any measures adopted pursuant to it or by the provisions of any international agreement concluded pursuant to it, and not by the decisions of the ECJ. With few exceptions,[110] Denmark simply stayed outside both the drafting and the implementation of Title IV.

Ireland and the UK were in a different position altogether (neither, it should be recalled, being parties to the Schengen agreements). First, under Articles 1 and 2

108 Council Decision 1999/436/EC of 20 May 1999 determining, in conformity with the relevant provisions of the Treaty establishing the European Community and the Treaty on European Union, the legal basis for each of the provisions or decisions which constitute the Schengen *acquis*, OJ L 176, 10 July 1999, p. 1 ff.

109 Council Decision 1999/436/EC of 20 May 1999 determining, in conformity with the relevant provisions of the Treaty establishing the European Community and the Treaty on European Union, the legal basis for each of the provisions or decisions which constitute the Schengen *acquis*, OJ L 176, 10 July 1999, p. 17 ff. Article 2(1), paragraph (4), of the Protocol Integrating the Schengen *Acquis* established that until determination by the Council Title VI TEU should be regarded as the basis for the *acquis*. According to A. Adinolfi (1998: 101) this solution continued to apply, despite the Council's determination, to provisions of the *acquis* still without an established legal basis (for instance, the provisions on the Schengen Information System, SIS). B. Nascimbene (1999a: 735) pointed out that 'the referral to Title VI should be temporary and exceptional, and it should be the rule that the legal basis is to be found in Title IV' (trans. added). This better reflected the proximity between the subject of the *acquis* and the subject of Title IV, and anyway Title VI was probably adopted as a provisional legal basis out of prudence in the face of the possible immediate 'communitarisation' of the whole *acquis*.

110 The first exception was laid down in Article 7 of the Protocol on the Position of Denmark, and allowed Denmark at any time to decide no longer to avail itself of all or part of the differentiated integration system by simply notifying the other Member States. A second exception was provided in Article 4, bringing Denmark's position into line with that of all the other Member States in respect of measures concerning third countries for which there existed a visa requirement when crossing external borders and in respect of measures concerning the adoption of a uniform visa format. These were the Community competences set out in Article 62(2)(b)(i) and (iii) TEC, which eventually incorporated the competences previously covered by Article 100C TEC (see footnote 46). The third exception concerned the Schengen rules that Council Decision 1999/436/EC determined had their legal basis in Title IV TEC. Regarding these rules, Article 3 of the Protocol Integrating the Schengen *Acquis* provided that Denmark 'shall maintain the same rights and obligations in relation to the other signatories to the Schengen Agreements as before said determination'. In other words, Denmark remained bound by the rules only under international law. Regarding the *acquis* that the Council Decision determined to have a legal basis in Title VI TEU, Article 3 of the Protocol used a slightly different wording, stating that 'Denmark shall continue to have the same rights and obligations as the other

of the Protocol on the application of certain aspects of Article 14 TEC, they continued to carry out checks on persons at their borders with other Member States,[111] while for their part the other Member States had a reciprocal right to carry out checks on persons coming from the two countries.[112] Second, under the terms of Articles 1 and 2 of the Protocol on the Position of Ireland and the United Kingdom, the two countries, like Denmark, were not bound by Title IV or by any acts adopted pursuant to it, or by any decision of the ECJ.

Once again there were exceptions to the general rule, but broader ones than in the case of Denmark. First, Ireland and the UK could opt in to measures based on Title IV TEC under different rules according to the case.[113] There was then

signatories to the Schengen agreements'. Legal theorists are divided between those who maintain that Denmark was bound by the whole of the *acquis* under international law and those who limit this to the *acquis* based on Title IV TEC. On the first school of thought see M. Condinanzi, A. Lang and B. Nascimbene (2006: 271), as well as K. Hailbronner (1997a: 204) and A. Adinolfi (1998: 103). On the second school see A. G. Toth (1998: 240) and K. Pollet (2000: 70). I believe that the way Article 3 is formulated is irrelevant to this debate, being due to the fact that pursuant to Article 2(1)(4) of the Protocol Integrating the Schengen *Acquis*, the whole of the *acquis* was automatically based on Title VI TEU pending the Council's determination regarding its legal basis, so that the expression 'as before' was unnecessary. There are other reasons for preferring the view that Denmark's position regarding the Schengen *acquis* based on Title VI TEU was no different from that of the other Member States. To begin, it did not enjoy a 'privileged' position similar to the one in respect of Title IV TEC. Moreover, if that had been the case, an unusual situation would have arisen: on the one hand, Denmark would have been bound, under international law, by the *acquis* based on Title VI TEU and, on the other, it would have been in the same position as the other Member States (with the exception of Ireland and the UK) regarding the progressive development of the Schengen *acquis* within that Title. This interpretation is confirmed indirectly by the Protocol on Denmark incorporated in the Treaty of Lisbon. The last exception was set out in Article 5 of the Protocol on the Position of Denmark: within six months of a Council decision to adopt a measure building on the Schengen *acquis* that Decision 1999/436/EC had determined as having a legal basis in Title IV TEC, Denmark could choose whether to implement the measure in its national law. In that case it would be bound by the decisions under international law both in respect of the twelve EU Member States parties to the Schengen Agreements and of Ireland and/or the UK if one or both had chosen to opt in.

111 In fact, only the UK was the subject of Article 1 of the Protocol, although its effects extended to Ireland as well insofar as both countries maintained 'arrangements between themselves relating to the movement of persons between their territories'.

112 It has rightly been observed that 'the result of this is that the borders between the United Kingdom and Ireland, on the one hand, and the other Member States, on the other, are basically regarded as external frontiers' (A. Adinolfi (1998: 98, trans. added)).

113 For measures based on Title IV that did not build on the Schengen *acquis* there were two possibilities: under Article 3 of the Protocol on the Position of Ireland and the United Kingdom, the two countries' participation in the adoption of measures was not subject to control by the institutions (see A. G. Toth (1998: 233) and E. Wagner (1998: 38); for the contrary opinion see G. Cellamare (2006: 58)); this is confirmed by the Council's practice of merely noting that the UK and/or Ireland wished to take part (see recital 20 to Regulation No. 2725/2000, p. 1 ff.). To take part in measures

a second exception regarding the Schengen *acquis*, in the sense of the set of rules for which the Council established a legal basis in Title IV TEC (and Title VI TEU) and of measures already adopted that build on the *acquis*.[114] A third exception concerned participation in measures building on the *acquis* (again, regardless of whether the legal basis was Title IV TEC or Title VI TEU), to which the general rules on enhanced cooperation applied, as explicitly stated in Article 5(1) of the Protocol Integrating the Schengen *Acquis*.[115] The fourth and last exception

already adopted, Article 4 of the Protocol on their position explicitly indicated the rules on enhanced cooperation, especially Article 5A(3) TEC (to be read as a reference to Article 11A following the amendments introduced by the Treaty of Nice), requiring the filter of the Commission: see Commission Decision 2003/690/EC of 2 October 2003 on the request by Ireland to accept Council Directive 2001/55/EC on minimum standards for giving temporary protection in the event of a mass influx of displaced persons and on measures promoting a balance of efforts between Member States in receiving such persons and bearing the consequences thereof, OJ L 251, 3 October 2003, p. 23 ff., a directive that did not build on the Schengen *acquis*. Regarding the legal theory, see H. Kortenberg (1998: 838) and A. G. Toth (1998: 234). In both cases, Ireland and the UK were bound by the measure adopted and by the application of Article 68 TEC on the competences of the ECJ: see Article 6 of the Protocol on the Position of Ireland and the United Kingdom.

114 According to Article 4 of the Protocol Integrating the Schengen *Acquis*, Ireland and the UK could request to join at any time. In line with the solution adopted in respect of measures (already) adopted under Title IV (but not forming part of the *acquis*), the Council was required to decide on the request and could therefore authorise the two countries to join. The provisions of the *acquis* in which Ireland and the UK take part are set out, in general, in Council Decision 2000/365/EC of 29 May 2000 concerning the request of the United Kingdom of Great Britain and Northern Ireland to take part in some of the provisions of the Schengen *acquis*, OJ L 131, 1 June 2000, p. 43 ff., later followed by Council Decision 2004/926/EC of 22 December 2004 on the putting into effect of parts of the Schengen *acquis* by the United Kingdom of Great Britain and Northern Ireland, OJ L 395, 31 December 2004, p. 70 ff., as well as by Council Decision 2002/192/EC of 28 February 2002 concerning Ireland's request to take part in some of the provisions of the Schengen *acquis*, OJ L 64, 7 March 2002, p. 20 ff.

115 However, the provision contained a variation with respect to the rules laid down in the Treaties by instituting a system of silent consent that effectively side-stepped the usual Council authorisation. The consequence of this was to allow Ireland and the UK to join automatically if they notified their intention to do so. In reality, as borne out by later practice, the Council retained its power of authorisation pursuant to the rules on enhanced cooperation even in respect of requests by Ireland and the UK. The two countries were in fact excluded from taking part in the adoption of some measures that were connected with or based on a part of the *acquis* in which Ireland and the UK did not participate. The question actually went before the ECJ, which held the Council's view to be valid: see judgment of 18 December 2007, Case 77/05, *United Kingdom of Great Britain and Northern Ireland* v. *Council of the European Union (United Kingdom* v. *Council I)*, *Reports of Cases*, 2007, p. I-11459 ff., and judgment of the same date, Case C-137/05, *United Kingdom of Great Britain and Northern Ireland* v. *Council of the European Union*, ibid., p. I-11593 ff. For a more recent case, see judgment of 26 October 2010, Case C-482/08, *United Kingdom of Great Britain and Northern Ireland* v. *Council of the European Union*, ibid., 2010, p. I-10413 ff.

concerned only Ireland, which was allowed to no longer avail itself of the provisions of the Protocol on its position and that of the UK.[116]

Considering that, on the whole, the rules on asylum were not included in the Schengen *acquis* and therefore could not be part of the Schengen-building measures,[117] the general content of the provisions was that Denmark remained completely excluded from the Community asylum system (although it could renounce the Protocol on its position), while Ireland and the UK could, case by case, either join in the adoption of measures or accept the application of secondary legislation (which in fact happened on several occasions, discussed in Chapter 4). It should not be forgotten that all three countries were still parties to the Dublin Convention, which continued to apply until Dublin II entered into force. Because of the differences between the systems it was particularly important to define a measure as building on the Schengen *acquis*, as this determined whether it could be joined and what procedure should apply. The ECJ debated on more than one occasion the notion of 'proposal or initiative based on the Schengen *acquis*', underlining that it should rest 'on objective factors which are amenable to judicial review, including in particular the aim and the content of the act'.[118]

As mentioned above, problems concerning the position of the three countries arose when the Council adopted measures that were part of the 'Dublin system' (in which Denmark, Ireland and the UK participated under international law). While Ireland and the UK could, and did, opt in to measures, a solution used to overcome the problem of their relations with the Member States bound by acts such as Dublin II and Eurodac, for Denmark this was not possible because it could only adopt such measures if they built upon the Schengen *acquis*, which they did not. Therefore, it was necessary to enter into an agreement to coordinate Denmark's position, as a State party to the Dublin Convention, with that of the other EU Member States to which the measures applied (including Ireland and the UK, which had opted in).[119] As a result of this agreement, Denmark was

---

116 According to Article 8, which, unlike the Protocol on the Position of Denmark, only considered the possibility of a total opt out not a partial one. Another difference with respect to the position of Denmark was that even after notification in accordance with Article 8, the system of differentiated integration would continue to apply to Ireland in respect of the Schengen rules, evidently because it was not part of the relative agreements.

117 In Council Decision 1999/436/EC determining the legal basis of the *acquis* virtually no provision was based on Article 63 TEC setting out the competences in the field of asylum. The only provisions that were based on it – Article 17(3)(g), Article 23(2)–(5), Articles 24–26, Article 27(1) of the Schengen Implementation Convention and a few decisions of the Executive Committee (SCH/Com-ex (97) 34 rev. of 15 December 1997, SCH/Com-ex (98) 10 of 21 April 1998, SCH/Com-ex (98) 37 def. 2 of 16 September 1998, SCH/Com-ex (98) 59 rev. of 16 December 1998 – mainly concerned illegal immigration, which is dealt with in Article 63(3)(b) TEC.

118 *United Kingdom v. Council I*, para. 77.

119 See Agreement between the European Community and the Kingdom of Denmark on the criteria and mechanisms for establishing the State responsible for examining a request for asylum lodged in Denmark or any other Member State of the European

bound by the whole of the 'communitarised' Dublin system (Dublin II and Eurodac), although with some important variations mainly relating to the ECJ.[120]

The conjunction of Title IV differentiated integration and enhanced cooperation in the Schengen area, on the one hand, with the new competences assigned to the institutions, on the other, had further consequences as well. With the entry into force of the Treaty of Amsterdam, the Council had replaced the Executive Committee in the Convention Implementing the Schengen Agreement, thus 'inheriting' the decision still pending on the implementation of the Schengen Agreements for Greece, Denmark, Finland and Sweden.[121] The Council fixed the date of 26 March 2000 for Greece and 25 March 2001 for the other countries.[122] The same happened with the States that joined the EU later, thus accepting the Schengen system as provided in Article 8 of the Protocol on the *acquis*.[123] For nine

Union and Eurodac for the comparison of fingerprints for the effective application of the Dublin Convention, OJ L 66, 8 March 2006, p. 38 ff.

120　In particular, under Article 6(1) of the Agreement only a Danish upper court can request the ECJ to give a ruling on the provisions of the Dublin II and Eurodac Regulations. According to Article 6(2) 'the courts in Denmark shall, when interpreting this Agreement, take due account of the rulings contained in the case law of the Court of Justice in respect of provisions of the Dublin II Regulation and the Eurodac Regulation and any implementing Community measures'.

121　According to Article 2(1), paragraph (1), of the Protocol Integrating the Schengen *Acquis* into the Framework of the European Union, annexed to the Treaty of Amsterdam. Naturally, the Council also replaced the Executive Committee regarding other aspects of the Implementation Convention and adopted some acts (of unspecified nature) in the exercise of these functions: see Means of proof in the framework of the Dublin Convention of 20 June 1994, OJ C 274, 19 September 1996, p. 35 ff., and Form of a laissez-passer for the transfer of an asylum applicant from one Member State to another of 20 June 1994, OJ C 274, 19 September 1996, p. 42.

122　Respectively, by Council Decision 1999/848/EC of 13 December 1999 on the full application of the Schengen *acquis* in Greece, OJ L 327, 21 December 1999, p. 58, and Council Decision 2000/777/EC of 1 December 2000 on the application of the Schengen *acquis* in Denmark, Finland and Sweden and in Iceland and Norway, OJ L 309, 9 December 2000, p. 24 ff. These dates were also important for determining which EU Members would vote in the Council on the incorporation of the *acquis*. According to Article 2(2) of the Protocol, the provisions on Council decisions applied to the Member States that had signed accession protocols to the Schengen agreements from the dates decided by the Council, acting with the unanimity of its Members (with the exception of Ireland and the UK) unless the conditions for one of the States joining in the Schengen *acquis* were fulfilled before the Treaty of Amsterdam entered into force, which did not happen in the case of Greece, Denmark, Finland or Sweden.

123　Article 3 of the Treaty of Accession (Treaty of Athens) on the accession of ten new Member States of the European Union, OJ L 236, 23 September 2003, p. 17 ff., provided that part of the *acquis* would apply to the countries from the date of their accession while the rest of the *acquis*, although binding on them, would only apply after a decision of the Council in regard. The provisions that did not depend for their application on a decision of the Council were listed in Annex 1 to the Treaty of Accession, OJ L 236, 23 September 2003, p. 50 ff. On this point see M. den Boer (2002: 139 ff.) and A. Adinolfi (2005a: 469 ff.). Similar provisions applied to Bulgaria and Romania: see Article 4 of the Protocol concerning the conditions and arrangements for admission of the Republic of

of the ten members acceding in 2003 the Council set the date of 21 December 2007 (Cyprus was not included),[124] while the position of Bulgaria, Romania and Croatia remains unaligned to this day.[125]

Still to be resolved was the situation of Iceland and Norway. Not only had no decision been taken on the application of the Schengen system,[126] but as non-Member States of the EU the framework for the two countries' participation had yet to be defined. Article 6 of the Protocol on the *acquis* entrusted this to three agreements. The first, between the Council and Iceland and Norway, would establish the manner of their participation in the *acquis*, while the other agreements would regulate relations between Iceland and Norway, on the one side, and Ireland and the UK, on the other, should the latter two States decide to opt in. All the agreements were signed,[127] although this raised some doubts about their compliance with the Treaties.[128] Moreover, Article 7 of the Agreement on the association of Iceland and Norway required an 'appropriate' arrangement to be reached on the criteria and mechanisms for establishing the State responsible for

Bulgaria and Romania to the EU, OJ L 157, 21 June 2005, p. 29 ff. An annex similar to the one attached to the Treaty of Accession was also attached to the Treaty of Accession of Romania and Bulgaria, OJ L 157, 21 June 2005, p. 49 ff. See also Article 4 of the Act concerning the conditions of accession of the Republic of Croatia and the adjustments to the Treaty on European Union, the Treaty on the Functioning of the European Union and the Treaty establishing the European Atomic Energy Community, OJ L 112, 24 April 2012, p. 21 ff., and Annex II, List of provisions of the Schengen *acquis* as integrated into the framework of the European Union and the acts building upon it or otherwise related to it, to be binding on, and applicable in, the Republic of Croatia as of accession (referred to in Article 4(1) of the Act of Accession), OJ L 112, 24 April 2012, p. 36 ff.

124 Council Decision 2007/801/EC of 6 December 2007 on the full application of the Schengen *acquis* in the Czech Republic, the Republic of Estonia, the Republic of Latvia, the Republic of Lithuania, the Republic of Hungary, the Republic of Malta, the Republic of Poland, the Republic of Slovenia and the Slovak Republic, OJ L 323, 8 December 2007, p. 34 ff.

125 Only the *acquis* for which no decision of the Council is required and the rules on the SIS apply to the first two countries: see Council Decision 2010/365 of 29 June 2010 on the application of the provisions of the Schengen *acquis* relating to the Schengen Information System in the Republic of Bulgaria and Romania. On the position of the two countries I refer the reader to F. Cherubini (2010b: 111 ff.).

126 The date would be set to coincide with that chosen for the other three members of the Nordic Union: see Council Decision 2000/777/EC, p. 24 ff.

127 Agreement concluded by the Council of the European Union, the Republic of Iceland and the Kingdom of Norway on the association of these two States to the implementation, to the application and to the development of the *acquis de Schengen*, OJ L 176, 10 July 1999, p. 36 ff, and Agreement concluded by the Council of the European Union and the Republic of Iceland and the Kingdom of Norway on the establishment of rights and obligations between Ireland and the United Kingdom of Great Britain and Northern Ireland, on the one hand, and the Republic of Iceland and the Kingdom of Norway, on the other, in areas of the Schengen *acquis* which apply to these States, OJ L 15, 20 January 2000, p. 22 ff. On these agreements see P. J. Kuijper (2000: 350 ff.) and K. Pollet (2000: 73).

128 See A. Tizzano (1999: 521 ff.).

examining an asylum application 'lodged in any of the Member States or in Iceland or Norway'; the arrangement was concluded with the Council in the form of an agreement dated 12 January 2001.[129] Article 12 allowed Denmark to request to participate; in fact, because that country was excluded from Title IV under the rules on differentiated application, its participation in the Dublin system had to be coordinated with the agreement that Iceland and Norway had signed with the Council.[130]

A further consequence of this combination of factors resulting from the Treaty of Amsterdam was that the association of any other countries in the Schengen system and the agreements this would entail concerning participation in secondary legislation on asylum could no longer be negotiated and concluded under international law, but fell within the scope of EU law. Thus, in addition to the agreement implementing the Schengen *acquis* signed with Switzerland on 26 October 2004,[131] on the same date the Council concluded an agreement on the country's participation in some of the rules on asylum, including the Dublin II Regulation.[132] Liechtenstein then took part in the same process, but in this case by joining the two agreements already concluded with Switzerland.[133] The position

---

129 Agreement between the European Community and the Republic of Iceland and the Kingdom of Norway concerning the criteria and mechanisms for establishing the State responsible for examining a request for asylum lodged in a Member State or in Iceland or Norway, OJ L 93, 3 April 2001, p. 40 ff.

130 Protocol to the Agreement between the European Community and the Republic of Iceland and the Kingdom of Norway concerning the criteria and mechanisms for establishing the State responsible for examining a request for asylum lodged in a Member State or in Iceland or Norway, OJ L 57, 28 February 2006, p. 16 ff.

131 Agreement between the European Union, the European Community and the Swiss Confederation on the Swiss Confederation's association with the implementation, application and development of the Schengen *acquis*, OJ L 53, 27 February 2008, p. 52 ff. Once again, it was necessary to await the effective application of the *acquis*, on 12 December 2008, pursuant to Council Decision 2008/903/EC of 27 November 2008 on the full application of the provisions of the Schengen *acquis* in the Swiss Confederation, OJ L 327, 5 December 2008, p. 15 ff.

132 Agreement between the European Union and the Swiss Confederation concerning the criteria and mechanisms for establishing the State responsible for examining a request for asylum lodged in a Member State or in Switzerland, OJ L 53, 27 February 2008, p. 5 ff.

133 Protocol between the European Union, the European Community and the Swiss Confederation and the Principality of Liechtenstein on the accession of the Principality of Liechtenstein to the Agreement between the European Union, the European Community and the Swiss Confederation on the Swiss Confederation's association with the implementation, application and development of the Schengen *acquis*, OJ L 160, 18 June 2011, p. 3 ff. The protocol entered into force on 7 April 2011 but the Council's final decision on its effective application is still pending, with the exception (as for Bulgaria and Romania; see footnote 125) of the SIS (see Council Decision 2011/352/EC of 9 June 2011 on the application of the provisions of the Schengen *acquis* relating to the Schengen Information System in the Principality of Liechtenstein, OJ L 160, 18 June 2011, p. 84 ff.). Regarding asylum see instead the Protocol between the European Union, the European Community and the Swiss Confederation and the

of both States had to be coordinated with that of Denmark, Iceland and Norway, as had been the case in the past for other countries wishing to join the Dublin system. Accordingly, Article 11 of the Agreement with Switzerland allowed Denmark to opt in and called for separate agreements to be concluded with Iceland and Norway, as in fact happened shortly afterwards.[134]

3.12 The Treaty of Lisbon reforms: communitarising (definitively) the rules on asylum

The Treaty of Lisbon, which entered into force on 1 December 2009,[135] definitively communitarised the field of asylum. In particular, it introduced some radical changes to the aspects that diverged from the Community method (see above section 3.9 ff.). It also eliminated the Third Pillar (previously Title VI TEU) and incorporated police and judicial cooperation in criminal matters within a new Title V of the Treaty on the Functioning of the European Union (TFEU), uniting these competences with those for visas, asylum and immigration. As to the adoption of measures, Article 78 TFEU states that this must follow the ordinary legislative procedure, which generally reproduces the 'old' co-decision procedure. This is an enormous step forward, considering that despite the hesitant progress made with the Treaty of Nice[136] almost all the measures discussed in Chapter 4, which combine to form the body of European rules on asylum, were adopted with a minor contribution from the European Parliament, which was merely consulted at the time. Although European legislation on asylum was thus virtually complete, the institutions, including the European Parliament (but this time in a leading role), have nonetheless been called upon to intervene in order to draw up part of the Hague Programme, embodying European policy in the sector.[137] Accordingly,

Principality of Liechtenstein concerning the criteria and mechanisms for establishing the State responsible for examining a request for asylum lodged in a Member State or in Switzerland, OJ L 160, 18 June 2011, p. 39 ff.

134 The different treatment was due to the different positions of the three countries, as only Denmark was part of the EU. All the agreements in question were concluded: see Agreement of 17 December 2004 between the Swiss Confederation, the Republic of Iceland and the Kingdom of Norway on the implementation, application and development of the Schengen *acquis* and concerning the criteria and mechanisms for establishing the State responsible for examining a request for asylum lodged in Switzerland, in Iceland or in Norway, and Agreement of 28 April 2005 between the Swiss Confederation, the Republic of Iceland and the Kingdom of Norway on the implementation, application and development of the parts of the Schengen *acquis* based on the provisions of Title IV of the Treaty establishing the European Community (both available online at www.admin.ch).

135 Treaty of Lisbon amending the Treaty on European Union and the Treaty establishing the European Community, signed Lisbon, 13 December 2007, OJ C 306, 17 December 2007, p. 1 ff.

136 See footnote 78.

137 The Programme was adopted by the European Council of Brussels, 4–5 November 2004: *The Hague Programme: strengthening freedom, security and justice in the European Union*, OJ C 53, 3 March 2005, p. 1 ff. It was followed by the Communication from the

the European Parliament's new role assigned by Article 78 TFEU was recently put into practice when it became necessary to review the general framework adopted in the first five years from the entry into force of the Treaty of Amsterdam.

The Treaty of Lisbon also abolished the restrictions on the competences of the ECJ previously laid down in Article 68 TEC. Article 267 TFEU (replacing Article 234 TEC) now applies in full to asylum and therefore also allows lower courts to refer questions of interpretation or validity to the ECJ.[138] In some ways the Court actually speeded up the 'communitarisation' of the system of referral for preliminary ruling in the field of asylum, anticipating its effects to all references for preliminary ruling made before the entry into force of the Lisbon Treaty but dealt with afterwards by the Court. In the recent decision in the case of *Weryński*,[139] the ECJ allowed the reference made by a lower court even though it was received before the entry into force of the Treaty of Lisbon. The ECJ cited as grounds the efficiency of judicial proceedings because, according to the judgment,

> rejection on the ground of inadmissibility would, in those circumstances, only lead the referring court, which would in the meantime have acquired the right to make a reference, to refer the same question for a preliminary ruling once more, resulting in excessive procedural formalities and unnecessary lengthening of the duration of the main proceedings.[140]

The Court also cited the purpose of Article 267 TFEU, an argument that Advocate General Kokott developed further, reaching the same conclusion: in her opinion, in which she remarked on the change that the Treaty of Lisbon had introduced in regard to reference for a preliminary ruling in the area of asylum, she deduced that this was proof of a difference in Member States' attitude to the dangers of extending the right to refer to the lower courts as well.[141] She asserted that, in general, when determining whether the provisions applying were those of Article 68 TEC or of Article 267 TFEU, 'It is not the time when the reference

---

Commission to the Council and the European Parliament – *The Hague Programme: ten priorities for the next five years. The Partnership for European renewal in the field of Freedom, Security and Justice*, COM (2005) 184 final.

138 Correspondingly, the competence once granted under Article 68(3), according to which the Court could be asked by the Council, the Commission or a Member State to rule on the interpretation of Title IV or of any acts based on it, disappeared from the Treaty. This confirms that the competence was closely related to the rule allowing upper courts to request a preliminary ruling.

139 ECJ, judgment of 17 February 2011, Case C-283/09, *Artur Weryński v. Mediatel 4B spółka z o. o. (Weryński)*, *Reports of Cases*, 2011, p. I-601 ff.

140 Ibid., para. 30. Only a few days before the entry into force of the Treaty of Lisbon, in an identical situation the ECJ did not allow reference for preliminary ruling: see ECJ, order of 20 November 2009, Case C-278/09, *Olivier Martinez and Robert Martinez v. Société MGN Ltd.*, *Reports of Cases*, 2009, p. I-11099 ff.

141 Opinion of Advocate General Kokott of 2 September 2010, *Weryński*, para. 23 ff.

for a preliminary ruling is lodged which should be decisive . . . but the time when a decision on that reference is made.'[142]

Together with the limitations on preliminary rulings, the restrictions imposed by Article 68(2) TEC and Article 2(1)(3) of the Protocol Integrating the Schengen *Acquis* attached to the Treaty of Amsterdam were also eliminated. The former concerned only controls at internal borders and therefore were actually applied very infrequently. The abolition of the equivalent restriction imposed by Article 2(1)(3) was instead of much greater significance. It should be noted, however, that the Treaty of Lisbon re-instituted in the TFEU the restriction contained in Article 35(5) TEU, according to which, within the framework of the Third Pillar only, the ECJ had no jurisdiction

> to review the validity of proportionality of operations carried out by the policy or other law enforcement services of a Member State or the exercise of the responsibilities incumbent upon Member States with regard to the maintenance of law and order and the safeguarding of internal security.

A similar provision is now contained in Article 276 TFEU, which states that the limitation applies to the exercise of 'powers regarding the provisions of Chapters 4 and 5 of Title V', that is to say, competences relating to police and judicial cooperation in criminal matters, precisely the ones left in the Third Pillar by the Treaty of Amsterdam.[143] Although, formally at least, the restriction does not concern the provisions on asylum (which are included in Chapter 2 of Title V), it cannot be stated that it will not have an indirect impact, particularly on such a delicate phase as the actual entry of asylum-seekers, which is the watershed between the legislation applying specifically to them and the legislation applying to all third-country nationals. Take, as an example, the matter of removals: if these are within the field of application of the Article 276 TFEU limitation, they will be outside the jurisdiction of the ECJ, including its power to issue preliminary rulings, even in the 'unorthodox' version.

The Treaty of Lisbon did not affect asylum only from the institutional point of view. As a result of it, the Nice Charter became part of the Treaties (Article 6(1) TEU) and at the end of a long process finally became

---

142 Ibid., para. 22.

143 The 'communitarisation' of the Third Pillar relating to police and judicial cooperation in criminal matters was incomplete in other respects as well. According to Article
10 of Protocol 36 on transitional provisions introduced by the Treaty of Lisbon, the
ECJ would continue to exercise its jurisdiction in respect of acts adopted pursuant to
the Third Pillar (prior to 1 December 2009, of course) under the 'old' rules of Article
35 TEU for a period of no more than five years from the entry into force of the Treaty.
This is a very clear restriction, given that according to Article 35 TEU the Court's
jurisdiction is optional because it depends on a declaration of acceptance by the
Member States. Moreover, Article 10 also excludes, for the same acts, jurisdiction in
the infringement procedure.

binding.[144] The Charter re-asserts rights that were already part of EU law pursuant to Article 6 TEU in the version introduced by the Treaty of Maastricht. Thus, regarding the right of asylum, Article 7 states that there must be respect for private and family life, as does Article 8 of the European Convention on Human Rights (ECHR) – explicitly mentioned in the Explanations relating to Article 7 of the Charter – which the ECtHR cited in order to rule that removal measures did not comply with the ECHR under certain conditions. More directly, Article 18 of the Charter, following Article 78 TFEU and before that Article 63 TEC, guarantees the right to asylum as established by the Refugee Convention of 1951 and its Protocol. Finally, Article 19 refers to the prohibition on *refoulement* where there is a serious risk that the person concerned will undergo the death penalty, torture or other inhuman or degrading punishment or treatment in the country of destination.[145] However, perhaps the main innovation in terms of human rights introduced by the Treaty of Lisbon is contained in Article 6(2) TEU, according to which 'The Union shall accede to the European Convention for the Protection of Human Rights and Fundamental Freedoms'. This innovation is of fundamental importance for, while the Nice Charter, although of great symbolic value, does not alter substantially the set of provisions binding the EU institutions and, to a different degree, also the Member States, the forthcoming accession to the ECHR will replace the existing reciprocal influence between the two systems with a formal relationship, with all the legal consequences this entails (see below, section 4.2).

3.13 Developments in asylum law in the light of Article 78 TFEU

Article 78 TFEU does not just reprise the competences originally envisaged by Article 63 TEC, it also gives them a broader and more structured content, although without changing their shared nature.[146] Article 78(1) states that

> The Union shall develop a common policy on asylum, subsidiary protection and temporary protection with a view to offering appropriate status to any third-country national requiring international protection and ensuring compliance with the principle of *non-refoulement*.

144 See U. Villani (2004: 73 ff.). Even for the Charter a system of differentiated application has been set: see Protocol (No 30) on the application of the Charter of Fundamental Rights of the European Union to Poland and to the United Kingdom.

145 On this point the Explanations relating to Article 19 explicitly refer to the judgment of the ECtHR inaugurating the case law to the effect that Article 3 ECHR contains a prohibition on *refoulement*: ECtHR, judgment of 7 July 1989, Case No. 14038/88, *Soering* v. *United Kingdom*, available online at www.echr.coe.int.

146 Nowadays, competences in the area of freedom, security and justice are explicitly described as shared in Article 4(2)(j) TFEU. Nonetheless, it should be noted that Article 78 TFEU no longer mentions 'minimum standards', as Article 63 TEC once did. For a comparison of the two provisions, see B. Nascimbene (2011a: 25 ff., especially 38).

This common policy in the field of asylum includes measures relating to a uniform status of asylum and subsidiary protection for third-country nationals, a common system of temporary protection, the now outdated measures on the criteria for determining the State responsible for examining an asylum application and on common procedures, and measures on reception and on partnership with third countries to manage influxes of asylum-seekers.

The new wording of Article 78 TFEU followed the launch, even before the Treaty of Lisbon, of a second phase of European policy on asylum after the one inaugurated by the European Council of Tampere in the wake of the provisions introduced by the Treaty of Amsterdam. This phase was known as the Hague Programme, which among other things called on the Council to adopt the Procedures Directive without delay and, more generally, indicated as objective of the second phase the creation of a uniform status for refugees and persons under international protection. To this end the European Council invited the Commission

> to conclude the evaluation of first-phase legal instruments in 2007 and to submit the second-phase instruments and measures to the Council and the European Parliament for their adoption before the end of 2010.

The Programme was followed by an Action Plan,[147] in which the Commission and the Council set out the objectives already achieved, including the approval of the Procedures Directive,[148] and confirmed that the second-phase measures would be adopted by the end of 2010. The Commission then sent a communication to the Council and the Parliament on the implementation of the Programme,[149] in which it specified the deadlines for the single activities set out in the Programme and the Action Plan: evaluation of the existing legislative framework resulting from the first phase, and a Green Paper and Policy Plan on asylum policy detailing the steps of the second phase of completion of the Common European Asylum System (CEAS). Regarding the first activity, the Commission would present general evaluations on the adoption of a common system and some evaluations on the application of individual acts in the Member States. While the findings of the latter evaluations were on balance positive,[150] the opinion expressed by the Commission

---

147 Council and Commission Action Plan implementing the Hague Programme on strengthening freedom, security and justice in the European Union, OJ C 198, 12 August 2005, p. 1 ff.

148 Council Directive 2005/85/EC of 1 December 2005 on minimum standards on procedures in Member States for granting and withdrawing refugee status, OJ L 326, 13 December 2005, p. 13 ff.

149 Communication from the Commission to the Council and the European Parliament of 28 June 2006 – *Implementing the Hague Programme: The Way Forward*, COM (2006) 331 final.

150 See, respectively, the Report from the Commission to the European Parliament and the Council on the evaluation of the Dublin system of 6 June 2007, COM (2007) 299 final, and the Report from the Commission to the Council and the European Parliament on the application of Council Directive 2003/9/EC, COM (2007) 745 final.

in its various evaluations on the implementation of the Hague Programme was not. In the first report, dated 2006,[151] the general situation was found to be not entirely satisfactory, even though the first phase had been completed with the adoption of the Procedures Directive. The Commission regretted that a proposal could not be presented for a directive extending the status of long-term resident also to beneficiaries of subsidiary protection. As noted in the 2007 evaluation,[152] such a proposal was not presented until later,[153] prompting the Commission once again to give a not entirely positive evaluation.[154]

In the meantime, the Green Paper on a common asylum system was also adopted. Its enormous political importance resided in the fact that the Commission detailed the work to be carried out in respect of existing legislation by the deadline (at that time) of 2010. This included reducing the wide margin of discretion left to Member States regarding procedural rules, already harmonised by Directive 2005/85, with a view to adopting a uniform procedure for all Member States; increasing the level of harmonisation of reception conditions regulated by Directive 2003/9 given the enormous divergences between Member States regarding access to the labour market and healthcare, among other things; reducing the wide margin for divergent interpretations of the concept of 'asylum' and 'subsidiary protection'; evaluating the possibility of extending this status also to other persons 'protected' against removal (such as people in ill health and unaccompanied minors); possibly creating a single uniform status to reduce the incentive for 'applicants to appeal the decisions granting subsidiary protection, in order to seek refugee status'; examining possible *ad hoc* measures for vulnerable people; and, last, improving the management of mixed influxes made up of people in need of protection and illegal immigrants so as not to 'deprive the right to asylum of its practical meaning', particularly as tighter rules on immigration could overlap with those on the reception of asylum-seekers.

According to the Commission, the aim of the Green Paper was to launch a wide-ranging debate on the CEAS. After gathering the results it drew up a policy plan[155] containing concrete proposals based on a monitoring of the application of existing legislation. In view of the imminent reform that would

151 Communication from the Commission to the Council and the European Parliament of 28 June 2006 – *Report on the implementation of the Hague Programme for 2005*, COM (2006) 333 final.
152 Communication from the Commission to the Council and the European Parliament of 28 June 2006 – *Report on the implementation of the Hague Programme for 2006*, COM (2007) 373 final.
153 Proposal for a Council Directive amending Directive 2003/109/EC establishing a long-term residence status to extend its scope to beneficiaries of international protection, COM (2007) 298 final.
154 The following report took the same line: see Communication from the Commission to the Council and the European Parliament of 2 July 2008 – *Report on the implementation of the Hague Programme for 2007*, COM (2008) 373 final.
155 Communication from the Commission to the European Parliament, the Council, the European Economic and Social Committee and the Committee of the Regions of

be brought about by the Treaty of Lisbon, the Commission decided to postpone adopting the proposals, possibly until 2012;[156] they consisted in a partial recasting of existing legislation, especially Directive 2003/9 on reception,[157] Directive 2005/85 on procedures,[158] Directive 2004/83 on qualification,[159] and the Dublin system comprising Dublin II and Eurodac.[160]

17 June 2008 – *Policy Plan on Asylum: an integrated approach to protection across the EU*, COM (2008) 360 final.

156 See the European Pact on Immigration and Asylum (Doc. 13440/08) attached to the Conclusions of the Presidency of the Brussels European Council of 15 and 16 October 2008.

157 'To this end, the Commission will propose amendments in the course of 2008, in order to: cover persons seeking subsidiary protection, ensuring consistency with the rest of the asylum *acquis*; ensure greater equality and improved standards of treatment with regard to the level and form of material reception conditions; provide for simplified and more harmonised access to the labour market, ensuring that actual access to employment is not hindered by additional unnecessary administrative restrictions, without prejudice to Member States' competences; incorporate procedural guarantees on detention; and guarantee that the special needs of vulnerable persons, such as children, women, victims of torture or person with medical needs, are identified immediately and that adequate care is available for them'.

158 These proposals, to be presented in 2009, would aim at the 'setting up of a single, common asylum procedure leaving no space for the proliferation of disparate procedural arrangements in Member States, thus providing for a comprehensive examination of protection needs under both the Geneva Convention and the EU's subsidiary protection regime; establishing obligatory procedural safeguards as well as common notions and devices, which will consolidate the asylum process and ensure equal access to procedures throughout the Union; accommodating the particular situation of mixed arrivals, including where persons seeking international protection are present at the external borders of the EU; and enhancing gender equality in the asylum process and providing for additional safeguards for vulnerable applicants'.

159 '. . . the Commission will propose, in the course of 2009, to: amend the criteria for qualifying for international protection under this Directive. To this effect, it may be necessary inter alia to clarify further the eligibility conditions for subsidiary protection, since the wording of the current relevant provisions allows for substantial divergences in the interpretation and the application of the concept across Member States; define with more precision when non-state parties may be considered as actors of protection. In particular, the Commission will consider the need to stipulate in greater detail the criteria to be used by Member States authorities in order to assess the capacity of a potential actor of protection to provide effective, accessible and durable protection; clarify the conditions for the application of the concept of internal flight alternative i.e. the conditions under which it may be considered that an applicant for asylum has a genuine protection alternative in a certain part of his/her country of origin, taking into account recent developments in the case law of the European Court of Human Rights; and reconsider the level of rights and benefits to be secured for beneficiaries of subsidiary protection, in order to enhance their access to social and economic entitlements which are crucial for their successful integration, whilst ensuring respect for the principle of family unity across the EU'.

160 'As regards the amendments specific to the Dublin Regulation, the Commission will: strengthen and clarify several provisions in order to ensure better compliance and uniform application by the Member States (in particular the provisions on the

The Action Plan has been implemented very recently. Given that the Treaty of Lisbon entered into force at the same time, all the measures envisaged are now part of the new system, and hence they have their legal basis in Article 78 TFEU. Thus, the Action Plan has been implemented according to the ordinary legislative procedure, in which the European Parliament plays a much greater role than in the past. Following the adoption of the amendments to the Directive on long-term residence,[161] which had long been pending, the Council and the European Parliament have adopted the new Asylum Package, represented by the recast Qualification,[162] Reception,[163] Procedures[164] Directives and the new Dublin system.[165]

humanitarian and sovereignty clause and those relating to family unity); and introduce amendments to enhance the efficiency of the system (notably as regards deadlines). Concerning the amendments specific to EURODAC, as already announced in the Dublin system evaluation, the Commission will propose: to unblock data on recognised refugees and to make them searchable by national asylum authorities, in order to avoid that a recognised refugee in one Member State applies for protection in another Member State; to clarify deadlines for transmission of data and rules for their deletion, in order to improve the efficiency of the system; and to introduce more information in the system in order to ensure a better determination of the Member State responsible'.

161 Directive 2011/51/EU of the European Parliament and the Council of 11 May 2011 amending Council Directive 2003/109/EC extending its scope to beneficiaries of international protection, OJ L 132, 19 May 2011, p. 1 ff.

162 Directive 2011/95/EU of the European Parliament and of the Council of 13 December 2011 on standards for the qualification of third-country nationals or stateless persons as beneficiaries of international protection, for a uniform status for refugees or for persons eligible for subsidiary protection, and for the content of the protection granted, OJ L 337, 20 December 2011, p. 9 ff. The deadline for its implementation expired on 21 December 2013.

163 Directive 2013/33/EU of the European Parliament and of the Council of 26 June 2013 laying down standards for the reception of applicants for international protection, OJ L 180, 29 June 2013, p. 96 ff. The deadline for its implementation will expire on 20 July 2015.

164 Directive 2013/32/EU of the European Parliament and of the Council of 26 June 2013 on common procedures for granting and withdrawing international protection, OJ L 180, 29 June 2013, p. 60 ff. The deadline for its implementation will expire on 20 July 2015.

165 Regulation (EU) No 604/2013 of the European Parliament and of the Council of 26 June 2013 establishing the criteria and mechanisms for determining the Member State responsible for examining an application for international protection lodged in one of the Member States by a third-country national or a stateless person ('Dublin III'), OJ L 180, 29 June 2013, p. 31 ff., which replaced, from 1 January 2014, Dublin II Regulation. For the Eurodac system, see Regulation (EU) No 603/2013 of the European Parliament and of the Council of 26 June 2013 on the establishment of 'Eurodac' for the comparison of fingerprints for the effective application of Regulation (EU) No 604/2013 establishing the criteria and mechanisms for determining the Member State responsible for examining an application for international protection lodged in one of the Member States by a third-country national or a stateless person and on requests for the comparison with Eurodac data by Member

3.14 The new system of differentiated integration

The Treaty of Lisbon also dealt with the positions of Denmark, Ireland and the UK, introducing amendments to tighten the system of differentiated integration. One of the reasons was that with the elimination of the Third Pillar all the matters previously covered by Title IV TEC and Title VI TEU became part of Title V TFEU on the area of freedom, security and justice. The new Protocol on the position of Denmark excludes the country from the whole of Title V, where it was once excluded only from Title IV TEC, with the result that it is now subject to the system of differentiated integration also in respect of police and judicial cooperation in criminal matters. The new Protocol does envisage some exceptions, which reprise almost all of the previous ones.[166] It also introduces a major innovation, although this depends on a decision by Denmark that appears unlikely for the time being: according to Article 8 Denmark can simply notify the other Member States that it wishes to 'replace' part of the provisions of the Protocol with those contained in its Annex. Six months after the date on which the notification takes effect, 'all the Schengen *acquis* and measures adopted to build upon this *acquis*, which until then have been binding on Denmark as obligations under international law, shall be binding upon Denmark as Union law'.[167]

States' law enforcement authorities and Europol for law enforcement purposes, and amending Regulation (EU) No 1077/2011 establishing a European Agency for the operational management of large-scale systems in the area of freedom, security and justice, OJ L 180, 29 June 2013, p. 1 ff.

166 According to Article 7, Denmark can notify the other Member States that it does not wish to avail itself of the differentiated system. Under Article 6, Denmark's position is exactly the same as that of the other Member States regarding the measures determining the third countries whose nationals must have a visa when crossing external frontiers and the measures relating to the adoption of a uniform format for visas. A third exception, not actually mentioned in the Protocol but 'inherited' by Denmark from the previous rules, concerns the Schengen *acquis*, once with their legal basis in Title IV TEC, to which Denmark remains bound under international law. This is borne out by the fact that Denmark continues to be bound by EU law to the *acquis* once based on Title VI TEU (although – see footnote 143 – these acts come under the transitional system for the competences of the ECJ). The fourth exception concerns measures to build on the *acquis*; according to Article 4 of the present Protocol Denmark can implement a measure in its national law and be bound by it under international law. Now that there is no longer any difference between Title IV TEC and Title VI TEU, Denmark's option also extends to acts relating to policy and judicial cooperation in criminal matters, from which it is excluded under the general rule.

167 The wording is not very felicitous and might suggest that when the six months are up and without any notification on the part of Denmark all the *acquis*, as well as the measures building on it, would bind Denmark under international law. In reality, the phrase 'which until then have been binding on Denmark as obligations under international law' should be interpreted 'selectively' as referring only to the *acquis* (including building-on measures) based on Title IV TEC. Any other interpretation would not conform with previous practice. The rules envisaged in the Annex make Denmark's position more flexible: apart from retaining the exceptions of Articles 6 and 7 of the Protocol, which would still apply, and 'communitarising' Denmark's

The position of Ireland and the UK remains virtually unchanged, although the elimination of the Third Pillar has extended the field of application of the differentiated system. Their position in relation to Article 26 TFEU (replacing Article 14 TEC) remains unchanged because they continue to carry out checks at common external borders at the same conditions, not being bound by the rule on the elimination of internal frontiers contained in Article 26 TFEU. The Protocol on the application of the article makes reference not only to the provision in question but also to Article 77 TFEU, replacing Article 62 TEC, both containing a clear reference to the abolition of checks at internal borders.[168]

As far as the rest is concerned, Ireland and the UK are not part of Title V TFEU and therefore, unlike in the past, they do not participate (either) in police and judicial cooperation in criminal matters. The exceptions to the differentiated integration system are therefore virtually the same as before: participation in acts adopted pursuant to Title V that do not build on the Schengen *acquis* is automatic, following notification by one or both countries. Participation in measures already adopted is subject to the common rules of enhanced cooperation, especially Article 331(1) TFEU.[169] The Council's approval is still needed for the *acquis*, including measures built on it, but for participation in measures to develop the *acquis* the rules on enhanced cooperation (still) apply. The Protocol on the position of Ireland and the UK also confirms that Ireland can opt out, becoming subject to Title V, except of course regarding the Schengen rules, for which

position regarding all the parts of the *acquis* to which the country was previously bound by international law, the Annex introduces a new rule on opting-in. According to Article 3, within three months of a proposal being presented, Denmark can notify that it wishes to accept an act based on Title V TFEU, in which case it will have its participation confirmed; as with Ireland and the UK, participation in the measure is automatic. In the case of measures that have already been adopted, Article 4 of the Annex allows Denmark to opt in according to the common rules on enhanced cooperation set out in Article 331(1) TFEU. In other words, Denmark's request is assessed by the Commission and then subject to the final decision of the Council. The Annex also envisages that, where Denmark's failure to participate in a measure pursuant to Title V, amending a measure by which it is bound, means that its application is 'inoperable', the Council can 'urge' Denmark to make a notification, and if it has not done so after a period of two months the amended measures will no longer be binding on the country. If Denmark remains bound by any measure pursuant to Title V, either under the new opting-in mechanisms or by notification in accordance with Article 8 of the Protocol, its position will become one of full acceptance of the mechanisms of EU law, including the jurisdiction of the ECJ. However, measures adopted pursuant to the old Title VI TEU, as well as all the *acquis* developed on the basis of it, are subject to the restrictions of Article 10 of Protocol No. 36 on transitional provisions (see footnote 143).

168 The reason why the reference to Article 77 TFEU, not included in the old version of the Protocol, was left out was that Article 62 TEC, unlike Article 77 TFEU, made explicit mention of Article 14, then covered by the Protocol on Ireland and the UK, which has now become Article 26 TFEU.

169 Note that, unlike Article 11A TEC, which required only the Commission's confirmation, Article 331(1) provides for ultimate confirmation by the Council.

Ireland, not being a contracting party, is subject to the provisions of the Protocol on the *acquis*.

The novelties affecting these two countries are few. For Ireland alone, there is an exception to Article 9 of the Protocol on its position and that of the UK, which does not apply to Article 75 TFEU. Notoriously, this provision was introduced to specify the competence of the institutions regarding financial measures to combat terrorism and it therefore applies to Ireland, which will participate in the measures taken pursuant to it. A second reform was introduced to prevent Ireland and/or the UK from blocking the adoption of a measure amending a provision in force that is binding on one or both of them. This is the same as the system applying to Denmark (should it notify a wish to replace part of the Protocol on its position by the Annex[170]) and it is designed to bring Ireland's and/or the UK's participation in an existing measure to a halt upon expiry of the period of two months from the Council's invitation to take part in the application of an otherwise 'inoperable' measure.

170 See footnote 167.

4 International protection in EU legislation

4.1 EU legislation and the Refugee Convention

Before examining the measures adopted by the European Union as part of its competences in the field of asylum, it is worth considering briefly the relationship between EU legal system and both the Refugee Convention[1] and the European Convention on Human Rights (ECHR).[2] There are few data on which to base an analysis of the role of the Refugee Convention in the EU legal system but their content is clear: the signatory is not the EU but its Member States, which ratified it from different dates. Some tentative doubts have been voiced about this assumption, however. In theory, powers could be transferred from the Member States to the EU in respect of the Refugee Convention in the same way, according to the European Court of Justice (ECJ), as with the General Agreement on Tariffs and Trade (GATT).[3] The ECJ has ruled that this is conditional on two requirements being met: exclusive competence for the subject matter of the previous agreement and recognition by third States.[4] Consequently, the EU can in no way replace the Member States in the Refugee Convention, if only because, as explained earlier, competence for asylum is shared. Nonetheless, in a recent decision the EU Court of First Instance held that such an effect did exist, whereby the EU assumed the 'powers previously exercised by Member States in the area governed by the Charter of the United Nations'.[5] Because these were powers to implement

1 Convention Relating to the Status of Refugees, adopted Geneva 28 July 1951, entered into force 22 April 1954, 189 UNTS 137 ff. See also footnote 1, Chapter 1.
2 Convention for the Protection of Human Rights and Fundamental Freedoms, adopted Rome 4 November 1950, entered into force 3 September 1953, 213 UNTS 221 ff. See also footnote 1, Chapter 2.
3 Judgment of the Court of Justice of 12 December 1972, Joined Cases 21 to 24–72, *International Fruit Company NV and others* v. *Produktschap voor Groenten en Fruit, EC Reports,*1972, p. 1219 ff., on which see, among others, A. Del Vecchio (1973: 274 ff.) and A. Giardina (1973: 582 ff.).
4 On this point see U. Villani (2013: 259 ff.).
5 Judgment of the Court of First Instance of 21 September 2005, Case T-306/01, *Ahmed Ali Yusuf and Al Barakaat International Foundation* v. *Council of the European Union and Commission of the European Community, EC Reports*, 2005, p. II-3533 ff., para. 253. The Court followed

the resolutions of the UN Security Council imposing pecuniary sanctions on individuals or groups of persons (smart sanctions) – and were only partly exclusive because both foreign policy and trade policy were concerned – the decision might have resulted from a reconsideration of the necessary conditions for a transfer of powers. It does not seem that this change of mind on the part of the Court of First Instance, which the ECJ appears not to have upheld (or rejected, for that matter[6]), warrants any conclusion other than the one suggested.

While this satisfactorily interprets the rulings of the ECJ, excluding any succession or replacement effect, as far as just the relationship between international agreements is concerned – the EU Treaties on one side and the Refugee Convention on the other – the matter is regulated by Article 30 of the 1969 Vienna Convention on the Law of Treaties setting out the general principles of international law.[7] Article 30(2) establishes the overarching rule[8] that 'When a treaty specifies that it is subject to, or that it is not to be considered as incompatible with, an earlier or later treaty, the provisions of that other treaty prevail.' As far as the EU Treaties are concerned, Article 351 TFEU contains a general clause (also present until 1957 in Article 234 TEEC) concerning only agreements between Member States and third States in force before 1 January 1958, or before the date of accession for States joining later.[9] It would not appear to function as a subordination clause, however, because, in line with general international law, it states that the Treaties shall be without prejudice to previous agreements and provides that in the event of incompatibility the 'Member State or States concerned shall take

a similar reasoning in the 'twin' judgment of the same date, Case T-315/01, *Yassin Abdullah Kadi* v. *Council of the European Union and Commission of the European Community*, ibid., p. II-3649 ff., para. 203.

6 See the judgment of the Court of Justice of 3 September 2008, Joined Cases C-402/05 P and C-415/05 P, *Yassin Abdullah Kadi and Al Barakaat International Foundation* v. *Council of the European Union and Commission of the European Community (Kadi and Al Barakaat)*, *EC Reports*, 2008, p. I-6351 ff., especially para. 281 ff., in which the Court asserted that the (then) EC had an obligation to implement the relevant resolutions of the Security Council without clarifying the relationship between EC legal order and that of the UN. On this point see F. Cherubini (2010a: 39 ff.) and bibliography.

7 Vienna Convention on the Law of Treaties, adopted Vienna 23 May 1969, entered into force 27 January 1980, 1155 UNTS 331 ff.

8 On the 'residual' nature of the rules imposed by the Article 30(3) and (4) see S. A. Sadat-Akhavi (2003: 61 f.).

9 Article 351 TFEU applies because all the EU Member States were parties to the Refugee Convention or its Protocol from before 1 January 1958 or, in the case of acceding States, from the date of their accession. For the founding Member States of the EU (or EEC as it was) the 1967 Protocol actually entered into force after 1 January 1958. However, at the time asylum was not yet a subject of EEC law and therefore there was no question of any incompatibility. When amendments were made, starting with the Treaty of Maastricht, to make competence for asylum part of EU law, the 1967 Protocol had already entered into force for the founding Members and therefore the relationship between the Protocol and the Treaties was subject to the earlier versions of Article 351 TFEU (starting, after Maastricht, with Article 234 TEC, later Article 307 TEC).

all appropriate steps to eliminate the incompatibilities established'.[10] Were it regarded as a subordination clause, then the relationship with the Refugee Convention, being *leges speciales*, would be governed by the provisions of Article 18 of the Charter of Fundamental Rights of the European Union, which recognises the right of asylum and underlines that it 'shall be guaranteed with due respect for the rules of the Geneva Convention',[11] and of Article 78 TFEU stating, specifically with regard to EU competence for asylum, that the common policy 'must be in accordance with the Geneva Convention'. This has two very important consequences. First, the criteria for resolving any incompatibility between the Treaties and the Refugee Convention are still to be found in the provisions of Article 30(2) of the Vienna Convention on the Law of Treaties, according to which the Refugee Convention must prevail.[12] Second, on the basis of the references to the Refugee Convention, any secondary legislation that is not compatible will be invalid because it infringes the rules of the Treaties, particularly those referring to the Convention. Some clarifications are necessary regarding both these consequences.

First, the only possible incompatibility between the Refugee Convention and the Treaties concerns the provisions of the latter giving the EU power to adopt criteria and mechanisms for determining the Member State responsible for examining an application for asylum (Article 78(2)(e) TFEU). This allows a Member State to evade its obligation to examine an asylum application for reasons, such as those laid down in the EU rules, not contemplated by the Refugee Convention. The Council of State of the Netherlands came to this conclusion in an opinion issued on 8 April 1991 concerning the initial method of determining the State responsible for examining an asylum application, which was laid down in Articles 28 ff. of the Convention Implementing the Schengen Agreement. The Raad van State found that 'it would be unlawful to delegate to another State the task of determining whether an individual is a refugee'.[13]

The only certain obligation imposed by the Refugee Convention is that of *non-refoulement*, requiring the States parties not to remove asylum-seekers to countries in which they are at risk of persecution (including by indirect *refoulement*). Where that risk does not exist because the country of destination – the Member State determined according to EU rules as being responsible for examining the asylum application – is considered 'safe', then there can be no violation of the prohibition on *refoulement*. In other words, a competence such as that assigned by

---

10 According to the ECJ such conflicts can be eliminated by various means: from uniform interpretation, to re-negotiation, and even to denouncing the previous agreement. On this point see U. Villani (2013: 261 f.) and the case law cited therein.

11 See M.-T. Gil-Bazo (2008: 33 ff.).

12 It is accepted in legal theory this effect of the application of the rule contained in Article 30(2) of the Vienna Convention on the Law of Treaties: see E. Sciso (1986: 127 ff.) and more recently S. A. Sadat-Akhavi (2003: 92).

13 Opinion of the Raad van State (Council of State) of 8 April 1991, N. WO2.91.0013, 8, quoted in A. Hurwitz (2009: 183).

Article 78(2)(e) TFEU, the purpose of which is to create rules 'distributing' responsibility for the examination of asylum applications among EU Member States, is not itself in conflict with the Refugee Convention, as UNHCR has confirmed.[14] Another issue is whether both the law implementing Article 78(2)(e) TFEU and its application by Member States are compatible with the Refugee Convention, and therefore also with the Treaties, particularly as that legislation allows room for manoeuvre, including in the determination whether a Member State is 'safe'. This is an area in which there are potentially greater reasons for concern, as we shall see below (section 4.11).

It would seem that the same argument cannot be made regarding a rule similar to that of Article 78 TFEU. This is the single article of Protocol No. 24, which Article 51 TEU accorded the same status as the Treaties, along with all the other protocols. The article states that 'Given the level of protection of fundamental rights and freedoms by the Member States of the European Union, Member States shall be regarded as constituting safe countries of origin in respect of each other for all legal and practical purposes in relation to asylum matters'. The Protocol concerns only asylum for nationals of EU Member States – and therefore excludes third-country nationals or stateless persons, who are the people most likely to apply for asylum – but despite this the rule would appear to be incompatible with the Refugee Convention. Yet, the (questionable) assumption that all EU Member States are 'safe' is not absolute. The single article of Protocol No. 24 lists some situations in which 'any application for asylum made by a national of a Member State may be taken into consideration or declared admissible for processing by another Member State'. These include the case where 'a Member State should so decide unilaterally',[15] which, although involving a series of

---

14 See above § 1.6. If we accept the theory that the EU replaces its Member States with respect to the Refugee Convention, the terms of the problem change and the EU will also be bound under international law by the rules of the Refugee Convention. The same should apply in the case of the EU's accession to the Convention. In both cases there is still the problem of establishing which rule is in conflict with the Refugee Convention: the European rule, in which case the EU is responsible, or the national implementing rule, in which case the Member States are responsible.

15 There are three other situations: one in which the Member State of which the applicant is a national has used the derogation clause of Article 15(1) ECHR ('In time of war or other public emergency threatening the life of the nation any High Contracting Party may take measures derogating from its obligations under this Convention to the extent strictly required by the exigencies of the situation, provided that such measures are not inconsistent with its other obligations under international law'); a second situation in which the procedure pursuant to Article 7 TEU has been initiated (existence of a clear risk of a serious breach or of a serious and persistent breach by the Member State of which the applicant is a national of one of the values set out in Article 2 TEU); and the situation in which the Article 7 TEU procedure has revealed the existence of a clear risk of a serious breach (with a decision made by the Council), or the existence of a serious and persistent breach (with a decision of the European Council).

procedural requirements,[16] tends to contradict the above assumption. In other words, a Member State faced with an application for asylum from a national of another Member State can examine and accept that application if it considers the Member State of provenance not to be 'safe' without violating the prohibition on *refoulement* of Article 33 of the Refugee Convention or the obligations imposed by the Treaties.

The primacy of the Refugee Convention over the Treaties yields in the face of 'counter limits', as the ECJ recently clarified in defence of the founding principles of the EU legal system, which it asserted were inviolable in respect of obligations arising under international law.[17] Indeed, it is hypothetical that a conflict might exist between the Refugee Convention and the founding principles of EU law. Even in the more likely case that those principles envisage greater protection than the Refugee Convention, conflict is impossible because it is stated in Article 5 that 'Nothing in this Convention shall be deemed to impair any rights and benefits granted by a Contracting State to refugees apart from this Convention'. Thus, the Refugee Convention in no way affects the possibility of 'greater protection', as I believe is offered by the Treaties, bearing in mind that the Treaty of Lisbon grants equivalent legal value to the EU Charter of fundamental rights.

Regarding the second consequence – that is, the relationship between the provisions of the Refugee Convention and EU secondary legislation – it should be noted that the former cannot be a parameter of legitimacy because part of an EU agreement, as the EU cannot assume the Member States' rights and obligations under the Refugee Convention. Instead, the provisions of the Refugee Convention are relevant because of the reference to them in various articles of the Treaties.[18] Thus, the illegitimacy of a rule of secondary legislation that is incompatible with those provisions will not depend, as the ECJ has held,[19] on the fact that the rules of the Refugee Convention have direct effect (which in fact they do not). The reference 'opens up' the Treaties to the Refugee Convention, endowing them with the same legal value.

16 In this case the Member State must 'immediately' notify the Council and must examine the application 'on the basis of the presumption that it is manifestly unfounded without affecting in any way . . . [its] decision-making power . . .'.

17 *Kadi and Al Barakaat*, para. 278 ff., especially para. 285, which states that 'the obligations imposed by an international agreement cannot have the effect of prejudicing the constitutional principles of the EC Treaty, which include the principle that all Community acts must respect fundamental rights'.

18 See also ECJ, judgment of 10 December 2013, Case C-394/12, *Shamso Abdullahi v. Bundesasylamt*, not yet published, especially para. 4, which states that 'The European Union is not a contracting party to the Geneva Convention or to the 1967 Protocol, but Article 78 TFEU and Article 18 of the Charter of Fundamental Rights of the European Union . . . provide that the right of asylum is to be guaranteed with due respect for the Geneva Convention and the 1967 Protocol'.

19 For all see ECJ, judgment of 5 October 1994, Case C-280/93, *Federal Republic of Germany v. Council of the European Union, EC Reports*, 1994, p. I-4973 ff. This approach, which is sometimes ambiguous, has been criticised by legal theorists: see U. Villani (2013: 355–6).

The ECJ has not yet ruled on a question of conflict between a provision of secondary legislation (or its implementation by a Member State) and the Refugee Convention. It has merely asserted on more than one occasion that EU rules on asylum must be interpreted in conformity with the Convention. In 2010, the ECJ, called on by the Bundesverwaltungsgericht to give a preliminary ruling regarding Article 11 of the Qualification Directive,[20] having taken note of the references to the Refugee Convention contained in Article 63 TEC (then the legal basis for the Directive) and in some of the recitals of the Directive, asserted without further explanation that 'The provisions of the Directive must for that reason [the said references] be interpreted in the light of its general scheme and purpose, while respecting the Geneva Convention and the other relevant treaties . . .'.[21]

The case law of the ECJ also contains references to a more significant role of the Refugee Convention. In one case it was suggested (and later ruled out) by Advocate General Bot that secondary legislation (this was Council Decision No. 1/80 of the Association Council of the Agreement establishing an Association between the European Economic Community and Turkey[22]) might be in conflict with the Refugee Convention.[23] However, the Court's decision of 18 December 2008 did not use the same language as Advocate General Bot, who had suggested that the alleged conflict with the Refugee Convention had the effect of 'preventing' the decision. The Court's decision in the case of *Bolbol* clarified that a consistent interpretation should be sought even if it conflicted with similar concepts embodied in other provisions of EU law. The case in question, concerning exclusion from protection, involved assessing whether the applicant was a member of one of the

---

20 Council Directive 2004/83/EC of 29 April 2004, OJ L 304, 30 September 2004, p. 12 ff.

21 ECJ, judgment of 2 March 2010, Joined Cases C-175/08, C-176/08, C-178/08, *Aydin Salahadin Abdulla, Kamil Hasan, Ahmed Adem, Hamrin Mosa Rashi and Dler Jamal* v. *Bundesrepublik Deutschland (Abdulla)*, *EC Reports*, 2010, p. I-1493 ff., para. 53, in which the Court followed the opinion of Advocate General Mazák of 15 September 2009, ibid., para. 43. This case law was confirmed later: see judgment of 17 June 2010, Case C-31/09, *Nawras Bolbol* v. *Bevándorlási és Állampolgársági Hivatal (Bolbol)*, ibid., 2010, p. I-5539 ff., para. 36 ff.; judgment of 9 November 2010, Joined Cases C-57/09 and C-101/09, *Bundesrepublik Deutschland* v. *B and D (B and D)*, ibid., p. I-10979 ff., para. 76 ff.; judgment of 5 September 2012, Joined Cases C-71/11 and C-99/11, *Bundesrepublik Deutschland* v. *Y and Z (Y and Z)*, not yet published, para. 47 f.; judgment of 19 December 2012, Case C-364/11, *Mostafa Abed El Karem El Kott, Chadi Amin A Radi, Hazem Kamel Ismail* v. *Bevándorlási és Állampolgársági Hivatal (El Kott)*, not yet published, para. 42 f.; and judgment of 7 November 2013, Joined Cases from C-199/12 to C-201/12, *Minister voor Immigratie en Asiel* v. *X, Y* and *Z* v. *Minister voor Immigratie en Asiel (X, Y and Z)*, not yet published, especially para. 40.

22 Agreement establishing an Association between the European Economic Community and Turkey, signed Ankara 12 September 1963; the English version can be found in OJ C 113, 24 December 1973, p. 1 ff.

23 See the opinion of 11 September 2008, Case C-337/07, *Ibrahim Altun* v. *Stadt Böblingen*, *EC Reports*, 2008, p. I-10323 ff., especially para. 36.

terrorist organisations included in the lists drawn up by the EU institutions. Advocate General Mengozzi, in his opinion of 1 June 2010, stated clearly that

> It is necessary, therefore, to treat with extreme caution the Commission's argument that, in order to assess whether membership of a terrorist organisation constitutes a 'serious non-political crime' for the purposes of Article 12(2)(b), it is necessary to refer to the provisions of Framework Decision 2002/475/JHA. The reason is that that decision was adopted as part of the fight against terrorism, a context with different requirements from the – essentially humanitarian – requirements that inform the international protection of refugees. Although dictated by the desire to encourage the development of uniform criteria at EU level for the application of the 1951 Geneva Convention, the Commission's argument fails to acknowledge that, on the basis of Directive 2004/83 itself, the approximation of the laws and practices of the Member States in this area must proceed in compliance with the Convention, account being taken of the international nature of its provisions.[24]

In other words, an interpretation that complies with the Refugee Convention should take precedence over an argument reflecting the aims of the EU, based on acts not adopted as part of the powers granted by Article 78 TFEU. Thus, in the case in question, a member of an association listed as a terrorist organisation on the basis of measures adopted within the framework of cooperation in criminal matters should not necessarily be excluded from protection, as the exclusion clause of Article 12 of the Qualification Directive must be assessed independently.

4.2 The European Union, fundamental rights and the European Convention on Human Rights

The history of the relationship between EU law and the ECHR is a more complex one. Originally, Community law contained no mention of fundamental human rights and their later inclusion was due entirely to the 'juridical' work of the ECJ. No doubt eager to safeguard the unity and efficiency of its 'new legal order',[25] the

---

24 Opinion *B and D*, para. 66.
25 The words are from the ECJ judgment of 5 February 1963, Case 26–62, *NV Algemene Transport – en Expeditie Onderneming van Gend & Loos* v. *Netherlands Inland Revenue, EC Reports*, 1963, p. 3 ff. As U. Villani (2004: 73 ff., especially 74) suggests, the first 'warning signs' that national courts, especially Italy's Constitutional Court in the judgment of 27 December 1965, No. 98, *Acciaierie S. Michele*, were developing a theory of 'counter limits' probably persuaded the ECJ to change its original stance (see the judgment of 4 February 1959, Case 1–58, *Friedrich Stork & Co.* v. *the High Authority of the European Coal and Steel Community, EC Reports*, 1959, p. 43 ff.), firmly ruling out that human rights had a place in the law of the EEC. On the evolution of human rights in the EU see also the more recent work by N. Napoletano (2010: 33 ff.).

Court assumed the task of assessing the legitimacy of secondary legislation from the point of view of human rights and then extended this power to the measures taken by Member States implementing the law of the EC (now the EU).[26] The path that the EU then took in the field of human rights is well documented and only the main stages need be recalled here: the entire body of human rights has been updated on several occasions by the ECJ; the Treaty of Maastricht recognised them as 'general principles of Community law' and included an explicit reference to the ECHR; and human rights were enshrined in the Charter of Nice. The Charter only became binding, with some amendments, with the reform enacted by the Treaty of Lisbon, which consolidated the reference to the ECHR in Article 6(3) TEU stating that its fundamental rights 'shall constitute general principles of the Union's law'.[27]

The relationship between the EU Treaties and the ECHR retraces only in part the relationship between those same Treaties and the Refugee Convention. Clearly, the relationship is not dissimilar: like the Refugee Convention, the ECHR is a parameter of legitimacy for secondary legislation,[28] which must be interpreted in the light of its provisions.[29] Moreover, the circumstance that fundamental rights

---

26 See ECJ, judgment of 18 June 1991, Case C-260/89, *Elliniki Radiophonia Tiléorassi AE* v. *Dimotiki Etairia Pliroforissis and Sotirios Kouvelas, EC Reports*, 1991, p. I-2925 ff., especially para. 42. The Member States are simply bound by the human rights recognised by the EU from a more strictly political point of view: Article 2 TEU includes them among the 'values' on which the EU is founded and which are subject to a specific, and well-known, system of monitoring pursuant to Article 7 TEU. Correspondingly, pursuant to Article 49 TEU, these values are a necessary condition for accession to the EU. The political nature of this instrument is clear from the provisions of Article 269 TFEU, which state that 'The Court of Justice shall have jurisdiction to decide on the legality of an act adopted by the European Council or by the Council pursuant to Article 7 of the Treaty on European Union solely at the request of the Member State concerned by a determination of the European Council or of the Council and in respect solely of the procedural stipulations contained in that Article'.

27 See U. Villani (2004: 73 ff.). According to Article 6(1)(2) TEU, 'The provisions of the Charter shall not extend in any way the competences of the Union as defined in the Treaties'. This concern, reiterated in Protocol No. 8 TEU and TFEU relating to Article 6(2) of the Treaty on European Union on the accession of the Union to the European Convention for the Protection of Human Rights and Fundamental Freedoms, was heightened by the prospect of accession to the ECHR: some writers noted in fact that a potential 'loophole' to evade the provision could be offered by European Court of Human Rights (ECtHR) case law on positive obligations (see A. Gianelli (2009: 686 f.)).

28 See U. Villani (2013: 47).

29 Article 78 TFEU imitates Article 6(3) TEU, which states that 'Fundamental rights, as guaranteed by the European Convention for the Protection of Human Rights and Fundamental Freedoms and as they result from the constitutional traditions common to the Member States, shall constitute general principles of the Union's law'. There are further references to the ECHR elsewhere in the Treaties: see the second recital of Protocol No. 24 on asylum for nationals of Member States, which specifically refers to Article 6(3). Declaration No. 1 concerning the Charter of Fundamental Rights of the European Union states 'The Charter of Fundamental Rights of the European Union,

are already observed by the EU as general principles does not create any significant differences either: if, as the ECJ has stressed, such rights bind not only the institutions but also the Member States, the same conclusion must hold in respect of the Refugee Convention. There is nonetheless a major difference between the Convention and the ECHR, one potentially entailing more serious effects: the ECHR possesses a judicial control body that is usually the most efficient means of safeguarding human rights available in international law, the Court of Strasbourg.

The result is that although, as things stand, the relationship between the ECHR and the EU Treaties is clearly not unlike the one between the Treaties and the Refugee Convention, the ECHR 'permeates', as it were, EU law much more thoroughly.[30] It has been pointed out[31] that while this ensures better protection for human rights in the EU now than immediately after the Treaties establishing it came into force, it is still a source of uncertainty. In particular, the relationship between the Convention signed in Rome and the Charter is unclear because Article 52(3)[32] of the latter does not rule out potential conflicts between the two. More importantly, it should not be forgotten that the recognition of human rights in the EU is an 'internal' matter, as indeed is the legislation of the Member States, almost all of whose Constitutions contain rules on fundamental rights. Thus, only 'external' control, such as that offered by the ECHR, can supplement national protection,[33] and the ploys developed by the European Court of Human Rights (ECtHR) to exercise indirect control over EU law cannot make up for the EU's absence among the signatories to the ECHR.[34] Hence, although there is still much to be done, the Treaty of Lisbon has paved the way for progress by

which has legally binding force, confirms the fundamental rights guaranteed by the European Convention for the Protection of Human Rights and Fundamental Freedoms and as they result from the constitutional traditions common to the Member States'. On the fact (and its consequences) that Article 6 retains the references to the rights of the ECHR and to the rights arising, as 'general principles', from the constitutional traditions of the Member States, as well as on the reference to the Charter, see G. Strozzi (2011: 840 ff.).

30 Like the Refugee Convention, the ECHR is a parameter of legitimacy of the rules contained in secondary legislation, with the difference (a substantial one, but which does not change the terms of the problem) that the latter has this function *tout court*, while the Refugee Convention only binds measures relating to asylum policy, according to Article 78 TFEU. In reality, it seems unlikely that a rule of secondary legislation contained in an act relating to other matters could get round the limits on EU asylum policy imposed by the Refugee Convention.

31 See U. Villani (2004: 95 ff.).

32 'In so far as this Charter contains rights which correspond to rights guaranteed by the Convention for the Protection of Human Rights and Fundamental Freedoms, the meaning and scope of those rights shall be the same as those laid down by the said Convention. This provision shall not prevent Union law providing more extensive protection'.

33 As A. Tizzano (2011: 33) correctly points out, this does not mean that the need for external control of the observance of human rights is the same in the EU as in its Member States.

34 On this point see the persuasive arguments put forward by A. Gianelli (2009: 680 ff.).

introducing in Article 6(2) TEU a rule that 'The Union shall accede to the European Convention for the Protection of Human Rights and Fundamental Freedoms ...'.[35] This rule could have a considerable impact on the weight of ECtHR case law in EU law and it is therefore worth taking some time to look at it more closely and the developments that have ensued.

One development has already taken place: after Russia had ratified Protocol No. 14 ECHR on 18 February 2010 (which entered into force on 1 June 2010, in accordance with its Article 19) and another paragraph (2) had been added to Article 59 ECHR according to which 'The European Union may accede to this Convention', on 17 March 2010, observing the procedure laid down in Article 218 TFEU,[36] the European Commission issued a recommendation requesting authorisation from the Council to begin negotiations (which it obtained on 4 June). In July 2011 the outcome of the negotiations between the Council of Europe's Steering Committee for Human Rights (CDDH), to which the Committee of Ministers had given a mandate to negotiate,[37] and the European Commission was published. Finally, after further negotiations, in April 2013 the draft agreement was published and then submitted to the ECJ for its opinion in accordance with Article 218(11) TFEU.[38]

35 Accession was not the only solution to the problems outlined here: see J. P. Jacqué (2011: 998 ff.), who also recalls (ibid.: 995) that Article 6(2) TEU imposes a clear obligation on the institutions of the EU, so that their failure to act could be grounds for appeal (proceedings for failure to act).

36 According to Article 218 TFEU, the procedure to be followed in order for the EU to accede to the ECHR was as follows: the Commission makes a recommendation to the Council, 'which shall adopt a decision authorising the opening of negotiations and ... nominating the Union negotiator or the head of the Union's negotiating team'. When negotiations are over, the Council adopts the decision authorising the agreement to be signed, on a proposal from the negotiator. Article 218(6)(2)(ii) requires the consent of the European Parliament, which is therefore called upon to deliver its decision when the accession agreement is concluded. Article 218(8)(2) states that the Council must act unanimously throughout the procedure to conclude the accession agreement and also that 'the decision concluding this agreement shall enter into force after it has been approved by the Member States in accordance with their respective constitutional requirements'. Thus, if every Member State has effectively power of veto in the Council, for the agreement to enter into force it must be ratified – and as this normally involves national parliaments, the fact that the vote has been unanimous in the Council does not necessarily mean that all the ratifications will be forthcoming.

37 Decision of the Committee of Ministers of 26 May 2010, CM/882/26052010, *Ad hoc terms of reference for the Steering Committee for Human Rights (CDDH) to elaborate a legal instrument setting out the modalities of accession of the European Union to the European Convention on Human Rights*, available online at www.coe.int.

38 'Draft revised agreement on the accession of the European Union to the Convention for the Protection of Human Rights and Fundamental Freedoms', in *Fifth Negotiation Meeting between the CDDH Ad Hoc Negotiation Group and the European Commission on the Accession of the European Union to the European Convention on Human Rights*, 10 June 2013, 47+1(2013) 008rev2. See also *Request for an opinion submitted by the European Commission pursuant to Article 218(11) TFEU* (Opinion 2/13), OJ C 260, 07 September 2013, p. 19.

Without going into the various solutions to the problems of accession that were proposed in the course of the negotiations – including inappropriate references in the ECHR to Member States only,[39] the EU's presence in ECHR bodies,[40] its position in respect of the ECHR Protocols,[41] the relationship between the jurisdiction of the two courts,[42] the question of the ECtHR's intervention in the division of competences between the EU and its Member States,[43] and the relationship between the competence of the ECJ to issue preliminary rulings and

39 These were covered by Articles 1 and 4 of the draft agreement amending, respectively, Article 59 and Articles 29 and 33 ECHR.

40 Article 6 of the draft agreement made the necessary changes to the method of election of judges of the ECtHR: a delegation of the European Parliament would take part in sittings of the Parliamentary Assembly when exercising its functions relating to the election of judges of the ECtHR. Regarding the Committee of Ministers, Article 7 states that the EU will participate in the decisions made by the Committee in accordance with ECHR (such as supervising the execution of ECtHR judgments) and in decisions on which ECHR is silent (such as approval of protocols containing amendments or supplements).

41 Under the agreement the EU accedes only to Protocols Nos. 1 and 6, being the only ones ratified by all its Member States. As far as the other protocols are concerned, Article 1(2) of the draft agreement provides for an amendment to Article 59(2) ECHR, to be replaced by the provision that 'The European Union may accede to this Convention and the Protocols thereto. Accession of the European Union to the Protocols shall be governed, *mutatis mutandis*, by Article 6 of the Protocol, Article 7 of Protocol No. 4, Articles 7 to 9 of Protocol No. 6, Articles 8 to 10 of Protocol No. 7, Articles 4 to 6 of Protocol No. 12 and Articles 6 to 8 of Protocol No. 13'.

42 This is regulated by Article 5 of the draft agreement, according to which proceedings before the ECJ will not be considered, for the purposes of Articles 35(2) and 55 ECHR, as constituting procedures of international investigation or settlement. Thus, actions relating to matters already decided by the ECJ (for instance by an action for annulment) would not be declared inadmissible by the ECtHR, while proceedings before the ECJ involving the EU and/or its Member States (for instance, an infringement procedure under Article 258 ff. TFEU; the same does not apply to proceedings pursuant to Article 7 TEU because its political nature suggests, as noted by A. Gianelli (2009: 693 f.), that the initiation of proceedings by a EU Member State does not infringe Article 55 ECHR) might not entail a violation of Article 55 ECHR.

43 The possibility that the ECtHR might be able to interfere in the division of competences between the EU and its Member States was a far more delicate and complex issue. The proposed solution, which had already been put forward by scholarly writers (lately by T. Lock (2010: 777 ff.)), was that of the 'co-respondent': in order to prevent the Court intervening in the division of competences, it would issue judgment in respect of the EU and the Member State(s) as 'jointly responsible' making both equally responsible for implementing the decision, so that it would not be up to the ECtHR to identify which one was effectively responsible according to their respective competences. The presence of a co-respondent has several implications. These range from (ostensibly) 'secondary' effects, such as the fact that an amicable settlement must be reached with the agreement of all the parties, including the co-respondent, while either party can apply for a review by the Grand Chamber without the agreement of the other, to the principal consequence that where the violation is established all the parties involved will be jointly responsible, leaving them with the thorny problem of deciding which one will take responsibility. Article 3 of the draft agreement amends Article 34 ECHR

the subsidiary nature of the ECtHR's competence[44] – once the agreement entered into force[45] it would have significant effects on human rights protection within the EU.[46] The agreement introduced, under the principle of subsidiarity, a system of external control that has proved increasingly effective over the years, forcing the

making the co-respondent a party to the case and therefore extending to it the obligation set out in Article 46 ECHR to abide by the Court's decision.
44 Of particular interest is the problem of the subsidiary nature of the ECHR protection mechanism that emerged with the prospect of the EU's accession and to which several solutions had already been suggested; see A. Tizzano (2011: 39). According to the Report ('Draft explanatory report to the Agreement on the Accession of the European Union to the Convention for the Protection of Human Rights and Fundamental Freedoms', in *Fifth Negotiation Meeting between the CDDH Ad Hoc Negotiation Group and the European Commission on the Accession of the European Union to the European Convention on Human Rights*, para. 65 ff.), the national courts, in which the applicant must first institute proceedings before being able to access the ECHR mechanism, may not refer the matter for preliminary ruling, with the result that the ECtHR may be called to rule on acts of the EU that the ECJ has not been able to adjudicate. In order to respect the subsidiary nature of the ECtHR's jurisdiction, the national courts must have adjudicated on the matter beforehand; here the 'internal' court is the ECJ, which is not always called on directly to give its opinion, but often indirectly through reference for a preliminary ruling by the national courts. Such reference is not compulsory in the case of the lower courts and even, in some cases, for the upper courts, although where it is compulsory there is always the possibility that the judge will rule the matter not relevant and therefore not refer it for preliminary ruling (on this point see U. Villani (2013: 373 ff.). For this reason, the ECJ must be allowed to express its opinion, even (and above all) where the ECHR mechanism has already been triggered. Article 3(6) of the draft agreement states that in proceedings in which the EU is co-respondent before the ECtHR issues a judgment 'if the Court of Justice of the European Union has not yet assessed the compatibility with the rights at issue . . . of the provision of European Union law . . ., sufficient time shall be afforded for the Court of Justice of the European Union to make such an assessment, and thereafter for the parties to make observations to the Court' (if the EU is the respondent, the problem of not referring for a preliminary ruling does not arise, although that of not exhausting domestic remedies might; where there has been no action by a State giving rise to a complaint to the ECtHR, and unless the States become co-respondents as authors of the primary law that the EU institutions are obligated to implement in violation of a provision of ECHR, the Union's action may be judged directly by the ECJ instead of by referral for a preliminary ruling; on this point, however, see footnote 50). Of course, the ECtHR is not bound by the decision of the ECJ (see 'Draft explanatory report to the Agreement on the Accession of the European Union to the Convention for the Protection of Human Rights and Fundamental Freedoms', para. 68).
45 Pursuant to Article 10, the Agreement enters into force on the first day of the month following the expiry of the period of three months from the last ratification either by a Member State or by the EU.
46 See A. Gianelli (2009: *passim* but especially 679) and U. Villani (2013: 51 f.). G. Strozzi (2011: 838 ff., especially 865) believes that accession has less of an impact and asserts that 'the relationship between the legislations is a horizontal one and that shared levels of protection help to create a potentially unitary system that nonetheless respects the unique features and areas of independence that continue to exist within it' (trans. added).

Member States to align their legislation with the ECtHR's standards and remedy any previous violations of human rights. Of course, the gap it has filled is not a substantive one: human rights – and this applies to the Member States, too – are already part of EU law. It has remedied a procedural shortcoming by supplementing 'internal' control with control by an 'external' body guaranteeing human rights. Considering that some matters are completely outside the 'internal' control of the ECJ, on occasion the agreement serves to fill a very serious gap. An example of this is the Common Foreign and Security Policy (CFSP) and the ECJ's lack of power in this area,[47] as well as its limited competence in respect of agencies such as Frontex.[48] Finally, the ECtHR's contribution could 'shift' the ECJ from some of its firmly established and heavily criticised positions regarding the interpretation of several primary laws, such as the one contained in Article 263(4) TFEU on proceedings instituted by an individual,[49] which in my opinion could conflict with Article 6 ECHR,[50] or the one restricting the direct effect of the rules of a directive to vertical relationships only. In the field of asylum there is another reason why the agreement could have a considerable impact. As mentioned, the ECtHR has developed a substantial case law regarding Article 3 ECHR (and others), most of it confirming the existence of a prohibition on *refoulement*, which is in some respects even stricter than the one contained in Article 33(1) of the Refugee Convention. As defined by the ECtHR, EU law can now no longer escape it on the grounds that the Union is not party to the ECHR. In addition, the effect of the Treaty of Lisbon of 'extending' referral for preliminary ruling to the ECJ (as explained in section 3.12 above), bringing the whole matter of asylum within the Court's power to refer, has been to create a framework not only for greater protection but also for a potentially richer case law that can be of assistance in interpreting international (and European) rules on asylum.

---

47 See A. Ciucă (2011: 62), J. P. Jacqué (2011: 1005) and A. Tizzano (2011: 36).

48 Regarding Frontex see below § 4.8. On the role that the ECtHR could play in respect of the Agency, I take the liberty of referring the reader to F. Cherubini (2014: 39 ff.).

49 This case law has received much criticism; for an overview see U. Villani (2013: 342 ff.).

50 A possible scenario, one which does not appear to benefit from the amendment introduced by the Treaty of Lisbon (see U. Villani (2013: 348 f.)), is that where a person, owing to an incorrect interpretation of ECJ case law on individual active legitimation, fails to challenge within the prescribed period of two months an act that he or she theoretically has the right to contest. Because that person cannot apply for a preliminary ruling, he or she could bring an action against the EU in the ECtHR where, pursuant to Article 6(3) of the draft agreement, the mechanism for the involvement of the ECJ might not operate, with the result that the ECtHR could declare the application to be inadmissible because domestic remedies have not been exhausted (referring not so much to a preliminary ruling as to an action for annulment not presented within the two-month deadline). Equally, it could find that those domestic remedies (again, an action for annulment pursuant to Article 263(4) TFEU) were not efficacious or effective because of the uncertainty generated by ECJ case law.

4.3 Some features of the Qualification Directive

As will be recalled, Directive 2004/83/EU, also known as the Qualification Directive, was adopted under the asylum system introduced by the Treaty of Amsterdam[51] and has recently been replaced by the new Qualification Directive 2011/95/EU,[52] the deadline for its implementation having expired on 21 December 2013.[53] Like its predecessor, the new Qualification Directive refers to the notion of people in need of international protection and it therefore represents an important element of EU secondary legislation, to be set against the rules of international law analysed in Chapters 1 and 2. Before examining its content, however, some introductory remarks are necessary. To begin with, because of the differentiated system described in Chapter 3, the Directive does not apply to Denmark, as re-stated in Recital No. 51.[54] Moreover, unlike the old Qualification Directive, it does not apply to Ireland and the UK either, because at the time they did not notify their intention to adhere.[55] It is also worth noting that in this Directive, unlike other secondary legislation on asylum, the partner States (Iceland, Liechtenstein, Norway and Switzerland) do not have particular positions and are therefore not affected.

The purposes of the new Qualification Directive are set out in Recital No. 6, which mentions the need to ensure

> on the one hand, . . . that Member States apply common criteria for the identification of persons genuinely in need of international protection, and,

---

51 Thus, it is the product of a procedure in which the Council has had the main role and the European Parliament was relegated to a merely advisory position.
52 Directive 2011/95/EU of the European Parliament and of the Council of 13 December 2011 on standards for the qualification of third-country nationals or stateless persons as beneficiaries of international protection, for a uniform status for refugees or for persons eligible for subsidiary protection, and for the content of the protection granted, OJ L 337, 20 December 2011, p. 9 ff. Unlike the earlier Directive it was adopted by ordinary legislative procedure per Article 78 TFEU (as amended by the Treaty of Lisbon).
53 According to Recital No. 52, 'The obligation to transpose this Directive into national law should be confined to those provisions which represent a substantive change as compared with Directive 2004/83/EU. The obligation to transpose the provisions which are unchanged arises under that Directive'.
54 'In accordance with Articles 1 and 2 of the Protocol (No. 22) on the position of Denmark, annexed to the TEU and to the TFEU, Denmark is not taking part in the adoption of this Directive and is not bound by it or subject to its application'. Recital No. 40 of the old Qualification Directive contained the same provision.
55 See Recital No. 50. There is still the possibility that one or both States will opt in later, but in that case, which differs from immediate participation in the adoption of the act, the general rules on enhanced cooperation are followed, according to which the Commission, and possibly also the Council, act as filters: on this point see § 3.14 and especially footnote 169, Chapter 3. As mentioned, Ireland and the UK had instead decided to join in the adoption of the old Qualification Directive (see Recitals Nos. 38 and 39), by which they remain bound also, and above all, regarding the competence of the ECJ, especially for preliminary ruling.

on the other hand, . . . that a minimum level of benefits is available for those persons in all Member States.[56]

Recital No. 7 adds that this harmonisation 'should help to limit the secondary movement'.[57] This objective, it will be recalled, appeared in the first documents on asylum policy coordination in Europe before it came within the ambit of the EEC. The purpose was to prevent Member States 'exchanging' asylum-seekers under divergent rules regarding competence to examine the application without this actually being done. The Directive contains numerous references to the Refugee Convention, particularly those contained in Recitals Nos. 4, 23 and 24. These, in turn, define the Refugee Convention as 'the cornerstone of the international legal regime for the protection of refugees' and stress the need for minimum standards to direct Member States 'in the application of the Geneva Convention' and for 'common criteria . . . within the meaning of Article 1' of the Convention.[58] The ECJ considered that such references were sufficient to assert an obligation to interpret the provisions of the Directive in the same way as those of the Refugee Convention,[59] based, I believe, on the reference to the Convention contained in Article 78 TFEU. On the other hand, there are virtually no references to the ECHR,[60] even though the report accompanying the Commission's proposal states that it was one of the instruments on which the Directive was based.[61] In view of the enormous impact that the ECHR had on the drafting of the new

56 See Recital No. 6 of Directive 2004/83/EU.
57 As does Recital No. 7 of Directive 2004/83/EU.
58 See Recitals Nos. 3, 16 and 17 of Directive 2004/83/EU. Directive 2011/95/EU, as its name suggests, and especially Recital No. 23, eliminates all references to 'minimum standards', replacing them with mentions of 'standards' or 'criteria'. As G. Morgese (2012a: 259) has pointed out, these changes do not alter the aim of the Directive, which is to achieve minimum harmonisation. Article 3 (which is the same as in the old version; K. Hailbronner and S. Alt (2010: 1021 ff.)) states that 'Member States may introduce or retain more favourable standards for determining who qualifies as a refugee or as a person eligible for subsidiary protection, and for determining the content of international protection, in so far as those standards are compatible with this Directive'. More specific references to the provisions of the Refugee Convention are few; for a criticism of this aspect, at least as regards Directive 2004/83/EC, see J. McAdam (2005: 467).
59 *Abdulla*. Of course, the ECJ was referring to the old Qualification Directive, which contained exactly the same rules.
60 The only reference is in Article 9, but it is in relation to the concept of persecution that is valid for recognition of refugee status.
61 Proposal for a directive of the European Parliament and of the Council on minimum standards for the qualification and status of third country nationals or stateless persons as beneficiaries of international protection and the content of the protection granted of 21 October 2009, COM (2009) 551 final, p. 6. See also the proposal for a Council directive on minimum standards for the qualification and status of third country nationals and stateless persons as refugees or as persons who otherwise need international protection of 12 September 2001, COM (2001) 510 final, p. 6.

(and previously, the old) Qualification Directive (see below, section 4.5), a clearer reference to it would have been appropriate.[62]

The substance of the Directive basically suggests that it was intended not only to harmonise the Refugee Convention's application in the EU, but also for the first time to codify the system of subsidiary protection in international law. This particular form of protection 'binds' a person to a State other than that of nationality because he or she cannot be sent to a country where there is a risk of torture, death penalty or another threat, and it was developed by the ECtHR mainly, though not only, on the basis of Article 3 ECHR. It should be noted, however, that although the Qualification Directive represents a significant innovation, the Refugee Convention remains nonetheless central. This is apparent from the continuous references to the Convention, as well as from Recital No. 33, according to which 'Subsidiary protection should be complementary and additional to the refugee protection enshrined in the Geneva Convention'.[63] Thus, the protection that derives from the need to comply with the ECHR is *subsidiary* because it completes the framework of protection offered by the Refugee Convention.

In general, the Directive applies only to third-country nationals or stateless persons and therefore excludes EU citizens. It has been pointed out that this restriction is not in line with Article 42 of the Refugee Convention, which does not allow reservations to be made in respect of Article 1 containing the definition of refugee.[64] In reality, this does not prevent a national of an EU Member State from applying for asylum in another Member State. Recital No. 20 states that the Directive applies 'without prejudice to the Protocol on asylum for nationals of Member States of the European Union . . .', which we have seen (section 4.1 above) allows such an application to be examined and even accepted.[65] The only consequence of some significance is that in such cases the Member State in which the application is made will not be required to enforce the provision of the Directive, being directly bound by the Refugee Convention.

---

62 This was also the opinion of the European Parliament regarding the old Qualification Directive. See the Report on the proposal for a directive of the European Parliament and of the Council on minimum standards for the qualification and status of third country nationals or stateless persons as beneficiaries of international protection and the content of the protection granted, 8 October 2002, A5-333/2002, especially amendment No. 6 inserting a reference to the ECHR in Recital No. 7. This Recital, which then became Recital No. 12, contains in its final version a reference to the Charter of Fundamental Rights of the European Union, as does, in more precise form, Recital No. 16 of Directive 2011/95/EU.

63 See also Recital No. 24 of Directive 2004/83/EC.

64 On this point, regarding the identical provision contained in Directive 2004/83/EC, see G. Gilbert (2004: 975) and H. Lambert (2006a: 178), as well as J. McAdam (2007: 60 f.), who rightly stresses that the exclusion does not affect the system of subsidiary protection. See also UNHCR (2001c: para. 11).

65 According to K. Hailbronner and S. Alt (2010: 1015 f.).

As the literature suggests,[66] the problem is another. It is possible for a national of an EU Member State to have an application for asylum in a third country rejected on the grounds that being *also* an EU citizen and enjoying freedom of movement and establishment there, he or she will receive protection from any EU Member State. In my opinion the problem falls within the framework of the rules governing the identification of a safe third country; this is not illegal on condition that the applicant is not at risk there and also has some real link with the country (see section 1.6 above). For EU citizens, the courts of third countries – although, as we have seen,[67] the risk is implicit in the concept of safe third country – seem happy to accept a very tenuous link, or even no link at all except, of course, that of the rights conferred by European citizenship. This was the reasoning applied by Australia's Refugee Review Tribunal when ruling that a Czech national, of Roma ethnicity, did not have a right to protection because this was readily available in Spain,[68] despite the fact that 'the applicant has never visited Spain and is not familiar with the language or culture'.[69]

The new Qualification Directive contains other transversal rules regarding three problems that have already emerged in applying the Refugee Convention: the problem of people whose need for protection arises outside their country of origin (refugees *sur place* in the Convention); the problem of the people who are the source of the threat and of the people from whom protection is sought; and finally the problem of internal flight alternative. The first, now regulated by Article 5 of Directive 2011/95/EU, was split into two situations in the version (Article 8) contained in the Commission proposal regarding the old Qualification Directive: the case where the risk arises as a result of 'external' events, such as sudden regime change in the country of origin (para. 1),[70] and the case in which it is due to a change of behaviour, as when a person begins to criticise the government's policy once out of the country (para. 2).[71] During the preparation of the old Directive,

---

66 S. Boutillon (2003–2004: 140 f.).
67 See footnotes 396 and 398, Chapter 1.
68 Spain was used as an example because, according to the Australian court (see Refugee Review Tribunal, decision of 12 June 2009, *RRT Case No. 901933*, available online at www.refworld.org, para. 90 ff.), no conditions attached to residence of over three months, contrary to the requirements of Directive 2004/38/EC. See Real Decreto 240/2007, de 16 de febrero, sobre entrada, libre circulación y residencia en España de ciudadanos de los Estados miembros de la Unión Europea y de otros Estados parte en el Acuerdo sobre el Espacio Económico Europeo.
69 *RRT Case No. 901933*, para. 116.
70 See the Commission's proposal, COM (2001) 510, p. 50: 'A well-founded fear of being persecuted or otherwise suffering serious unjustified harm may be based on events which have taken place since the applicant left his country of origin'.
71 Ibid.: 'A well-founded fear of being persecuted or otherwise suffering serious unjustified harm may be based on activities which have been engaged in by the applicant since he left his country of origin, save where it is established that such activities were engaged in for the sole purpose of creating the necessary conditions for making an application for international protection. That is not the case where the activities relied upon constitute the expression and continuation of convictions held in the country of origin,

the European Parliament suggested eliminating the second case so that it would become a matter for objective assessment pursuant only to para. 1. The argument put forward in its report was based on the absence of a 'logical or empirical connection between the well-foundedness of the fear of being persecuted or of suffering serious unjustified harm, and the fact that the person may have acted in a manner designed to create a refugee claim'.[72] In the end, the final text of the Directive upheld the position of the Commission, with some small amendments, and the two cases in question were dealt with, respectively, in Article 5(1) and (2), which remain unchanged in the new Qualification Directive.

There is little to comment on in the case of people whose need for protection arises outside their country of origin[73] as it concerns a change of situation that must be assessed in the same way as if the applicant's move had been motivated from the very beginning by a need to flee his or her country of origin. There are few examples to be found in the practical application of the two Directives and those that do exist contain a combination of factors. The Administrative Court of Stuttgart ruled that a Lebanese woman, who at first had been denied refugee status, should obtain it on the grounds that by divorcing during her stay in Germany she risked the revenge of her brother who planned to kill her because her lifestyle did not follow the dictates of Islam.[74]

It is a more complex matter to assess the situation covered by Article 5(2), which states that

> A well-founded fear of being persecuted or a real risk of suffering serious harm may be based on activities which the applicant has engaged in since he or she left the country of origin, in particular where it is established that the activities relied upon constitute the expression and continuation of convictions or orientations held in the country of origin.

To this must be added the provision of Article 5(3), which in the case only of (alleged) refugees – excluding, therefore, people seeking subsidiary protection – allows States 'normally' to reject any subsequent application[75] 'if the risk of persecution is based on circumstances which the applicant has created by his or her own decision since leaving the country of origin' (i.e. bootstrap refugees). In other words, if the applicant

and they are related to the grounds for recognition of the need for international protection'.

72 See Report A5-333/2002, p. 20.

73 'A well-founded fear of being persecuted or a real risk of suffering serious harm may be based on events which have taken place since the applicant left the country of origin'.

74 Administrative Court of Stuttgart, decision of 8 September 2008, A 10 K 13/07. More recently, following the changed situation in Syria, see the Spanish Tribunal Supremo, decision of 10 October 2012, 6761/2012. Unless specified otherwise, the decisions are available online at www.asylumlawdatabase.eu.

75 Note that a subsequent application is an application submitted after a previous one has been rejected: see G. Morgese (2012a: 262).

deliberately engages in behaviour that is likely to 'create' a risk of persecution under the terms of the Refugee Convention alone, States can assume that a subsequent application is unfounded. Otherwise, the applicant's credibility must always be assessed, *in primis*[76] on the basis of his or her conduct prior to leaving the country of origin – a rule that applies without exception to subsidiary protection.

In its proposal regarding Directive 2004/83/EC, which was more restrictive from the viewpoint of the Member States, the Commission made it clear that, aside from 'fraudulent' intent on the part of the applicant, where an objective risk of persecution exists recognition of refugee status cannot be precluded.[77] In the final version of the Directive, as several writers have pointed out,[78] 'calculated' conduct by the applicant can hinder assessment of the risk, a situation that would appear out of line with the prohibition on *refoulement* as set out in Article 33 of the Refugee Convention and in the version adopted by the ECtHR. Some national courts do appear to follow the recommendations of UNHCR more faithfully than the uncertain wording of Article 5(2) and (3) and the UK Court of Appeal has clearly stated that

> A relevant difference is thus recognised between activities . . . which, while not necessary, are legitimately pursued by a political dissident against his or her own government and may expose him or her to a risk of ill-treatment on return, and activities which are pursued with the motive not of expressing dissent but of creating or aggravating such a risk. But the difference, while relevant, is not critical, because all . . . formulations recognise that opportunistic activity sur place *is not an automatic bar* to asylum.[79]

76 This is not the only criterion, as the use of the expression 'in particular' clearly indicates. On this point see also V. Teitgen-Colly (2006: 1522).
77 See COM (2001) 510, p. 20: 'The fact that a fear of persecution or otherwise suffering serious harm was manufactured, does not in itself necessarily mean that such a fear cannot be well founded and therefore sufficient to warrant the grant of a international protection status. However, where it can be established to a reasonable degree of certainty that the activities since leaving the country of origin were engaged in for the purpose of manufacturing the necessary conditions for being granted an international protection status, Member States are entitled to start from the premise that these activities do not in principle furnish grounds for such a grant and shall have serious grounds for questioning the credibility of the applicant. Member States should ensure though that the competent authorities recognise applicants as persons in need of international protection if the activities of the kind referred to in this paragraph may reasonably be expected to come to the notice of the authorities of the individual's country of origin, be treated by them as demonstrative of an adverse political or other protected opinion or characteristic, and give rise to a well-founded fear of being persecuted or suffering serious and unjustified harm'.
78 H. Lambert (2006a: 172) and H. Storey (2008: 26 ff.). For additional arguments see also S. Da Lomba (2011: 61 ff.).
79 Court of Appeal (civil division) of England and Wales, decision of 15 April 2008, *YB* v. *Secretary of State for the Home Department*, para. 11 (emphasis added). In the same vein see also the Council of State of the Netherlands, decision of 13 January 2010,

In Germany, a more literal interpretation of Article 5(3) has been adopted, according to which a subsequent application made after 'calculated' activities by the applicant does not preclude the granting of refugee status, although he or she has the duty (and the right) to prove that the risk of harm objectively exists.[80] In other EU States, the application of Article 5(2)(f) is determined on the basis of the applicant's credibility, in the sense that activities such as those described are more generally indicative that the reasons on which the application is based (the applicant's 'account' of his or her situation in the country of origin) are *also* not true. Most of such cases relate to applicants of Islamic faith who 'convert' to Christianity when they arrive in the EU, often without giving any proof of sincerity, who are then excluded from protection not because of fraudulent conduct but because their actions will not expose them to any risk in their country of origin.[81]

Articles 6 and 7 instead regulate the questions, respectively, of the persons responsible for the persecution and the persons or bodies offering protection. The two have much in common as the activities of non-state actors may have a bearing on the recognition of protection depending on the conduct of the other actors called upon to provide protection.[82] Article 6 identifies the actors responsible for the persecution (for refugee status) or the harm provoked (for subsidiary protection) as being

> (a) the State; (b) parties or organisations controlling the State or a substantial part of the territory of the State; (c) non-State actors, if it can be demonstrated that the actors mentioned in points (a) and (b), including international organisations, are unable or unwilling to provide protection against persecution or serious harm as defined in Article 7.[83]

200904515/1/V1, confirming that continuing activities previously undertaken in the country of origin is not a necessary condition for the recognition of protection *sur place*.

80 Federal Administrative Court of Germany, decision of 24 September 2009, 10 C 25.08.
81 See Aliens Appeal Board of Sweden, decision of 30 November 2011, UM 7850-10, which held the applicant's conduct to be scarcely credible in the case of an Afghan national who converted to Christianity on arrival in Sweden, and was even baptised, without showing he knew anything at all about his new religion, being unable to mention any passage of the Scriptures or even one Christian religious festivity. The case law is full of such examples, in which the national courts invariably raise the problem of credibility: see also High Court of Ireland, decision of 21 January 2011, *H. M.* v. *Minister for Justice, Equality, Law Reform*, and Administrative Court of Helsinki, decision of 7 April 2011, 11/0425/3.
82 In the Commission's proposal regarding the old Qualification Directive the two matters were dealt with together in Article 9: COM (2001) 510, p. 50.
83 The text of Article 6 of Directive 2004/83/EC is identical. Note that the list is absolute, in the sense that any other actor not mentioned in Article 6 is excluded from the group of those eligible to afford protection. The practice is not always uniform, however, and differences are often encountered, particularly regarding the actors in control of part of a territory, such as clans. On this point see the Report of the Commission to the European Parliament and the Council on the application of Directive 2004/83/EC, 16 June 2010, COM (2010) 314 final, p. 7.

The rule therefore envisages three cases. Leaving aside the first two as they do not raise particular problems and can be resolved according to the common rules on international responsibility, Article 6(c) is more problematic. In accepting the protection theory (see above, section 1.1), the Qualification Directive confirms that non-state actors can be a source of risk not only when they have links with the authorities under the normal rules of international responsibility, but also when, more controversially, that authority is unable (or unwilling) to prevent them from engaging in the activities in question, i.e. when it cannot or will not offer protection. The path taken by the EU has had some effect here: while the approach taken by the Directive was already widely adopted, it clearly encouraged the adoption of the protection theory in the Member States (France and Germany[84]) that had followed a more restrictive line.[85]

Considering all these factors, there is one problematic aspect: the gap between the actors that may be the source of the risk and the actors that are supposed to offer protection. Logically, it is the authority controlling a country that should be the main source of the risk and, according to the protection theory, if it does not offer protection then the source could be private individuals. Whereas Article 6 does not mention international organisations among the potential sources of risk, it does name them when listing the actors required to provide adequate protection from the actions of private individuals. In parallel, Article 7(1) does mention international organisations when listing the actors that provide protection.

The outcome is to create two areas of uncertainty. The first, which has been highlighted by legal theorists and by UNHCR,[86] concerns whether it is right to involve actors, such as international organisations, that in abstract cannot afford sufficient protection or at least the same protection as an authority like a State. As a result the system put in place by the Directive could exclude individuals eligible for a lower level of protection in their country of origin, such as that afforded by an international organisation. I do not think this is a real danger: the presence of an international organisation does not, in itself, imply that protection is available because that condition needs to be objectively verified on the basis of the criteria set out in Article 7(3)[87] and, as the ECJ has stated, an international organisation

---

84 See footnote 41, Chapter 1.
85 See K. Hailbronner and S. Alt (2010: 1047 f.).
86 For the legal theory see G. Gilbert (2004: 976) and H. Battjes (2006: 247 ff.); see also UNHCR (2001c: para. 31) and UNHCR (2007b: 10). Note that during the preparatory work the Parliament had suggested eliminating all references to international organisations: 'With regard to the role of international organisations providing "state" protection, recent history has highlighted the ineffectiveness of such organisations in maintaining peace and security and guaranteeing human rights in conflict areas. This is far from surprising to the extent that to date no international organisation has been given the broad political mandate that is necessary for guaranteeing the protection of human rights and fully ensuring law and order. The problems in Kosovo provide the most current example' (Report A5-0333/2002, p. 22).
87 'When assessing whether an international organisation controls a State or a substantial part of its territory and provides protection as described in paragraph 2, Member

must be 'entitled' to be present because for the rule to apply it must control 'the State or a substantial part of the territory of the State'.[88]

A second – and in my opinion more valid – concern stems from the (questionable) assumption that international organisations cannot be potentially responsible for the risk because they are not mentioned in Article 6(b). Not only is their exclusion in complete contrast with the reality of the situation, given the cases in which agents of an international organisation have been guilty of actions likely to 'produce' persons eligible for protection,[89] it is illogical. There is no reason why, if international organisations are deemed 'equivalent' (*de iure* or *de facto*) to an authority for the purpose of determining the actor offering protection, they should not be so as a source of risk. This inconsistency cannot be remedied by referring to Article 6(c) and including international organisations among non-state actors, for I believe it is impossible to reconcile this categorisation with the reference to international organisations as bodies affording protection. The reference is ambiguous – 'if it can be demonstrated that the actors mentioned in points (a) and (b), *including* international organisations . . .' – which could justify interpreting (b) as meaning that international organisations are among the actors controlling the State or a large part of its territory. If that was the intention, it remains to be clarified why international organisations were not expressly included in (b): I believe the omission arose from the fact that the matter was deliberately ignored, as evidenced by the fact that it is nowhere mentioned in the *travaux préparatoires*.

A second, less problematical aspect of the old Qualification Directive concerns the failure to set out protection theory explicitly; as a result the risk of persecution can come from private individuals even in the case of failed States. The earlier Article 7, however, which mentioned only States, political parties and organisations, including international organisations, apparently did not apply to situations in

States shall take into account any guidance which may be provided in relevant Union acts'.

88 *Abdulla*, para. 74. The ECJ added (para. 75) that 'As regards the latter point, it must be acknowledged that Article 7(1) of the Directive does not preclude the protection from being guaranteed by international organisations, including protection ensured through the presence of a multinational force in the territory of the third country'. Advocate General Mazák took a slightly more restrictive stance in his opinion of 15 September 2009, *Abdulla*, especially para. 58, suggesting that protection by an international organisation can only occur when the multinational troops operating under its aegis provide support to the State: 'In my view, where the assistance of multinational troops is employed by a State such employment could be viewed as a reasonable step to prevent persecution in the country of nationality of a refugee. I consider however that in order to comply with the terms of Article 7 of Directive 2004/83, a State may only rely on the assistance of multinational troops provided such troops operate under the mandate of the international community, for example under the auspices of the United Nations'. The ECtHR does not exclude the possibility of an international organisation offering protection: see footnote 39, Chapter 2.

89 On this point see R. A. Opie (2006: 1 ff.).

which one of these actors was completely absent. According to legal theory,[90] by referring to the fact of being 'unable' to provide protection, Article 6(c) covered situations in which there was no State authority.[91] The root of the problem has now been solved by Directive 2011/95/EU, which appropriately makes express mention of the ability 'to offer protection' in the new Article 7.

Instead, the new Directive does not change the criteria for determining whether the *de iure* or *de facto* authority is willing or able to provide protection. This is dealt with in Article 7(2), which mentions

> reasonable steps to prevent the persecution or suffering of serious harm, inter alia, by operating an effective legal system for the detection, prosecution and punishment of acts constituting persecution or serious harm . . .[92]

The article adds that the applicant must have access to such protection. The ECJ has already expressed its opinion on these measures, stating that they must be assessed in respect of,

> in particular, the conditions of operation of, on the one hand, the institutions, authorities and security forces and, on the other, all groups or bodies of the third country which may, by their action or inaction, be responsible for acts of persecution . . .[93]

Further indications can be obtained from the Commission's original proposal, which detailed the factors that should be taken into account when assessing whether the measures were sufficient and accessible.[94]

---

90 H. Battjes (2006: 245 f.).
91 This interpretation is confirmed by the case law. For cases relating specifically to Somalia in which the court found in favour of the application see the Migration söverdomstolen of Sweden, decision of 21 April 2011, UM 7851-10; the Conseil du Contentieux des Etrangers of Belgium, decision of 19 May 2011, *A. Abdi Madnek* v. *Commissaire général aux réfugiés et aux apatrides*; and the Administrative Court of Monaco, decision of 21 September 2011, M 11 K 11.30081.
92 The new Article 7 only adds what in reality was already implicit in the case law, that 'protection against persecution or serious harm must be effective and of a non-temporary nature'.
93 *Abdulla*, para. 71.
94 See COM (2001) 510, p. 20 ff.: '(a) General conditions in the country of origin; (b) The State's complicity with respect to the infliction of harm at stake; (c) The nature of State's policies with respect to the harm at stake, including whether there in force a criminal law which makes violent attacks by persecutors punishable by sentences commensurate with the gravity of their crimes; (d) The influence the alleged persecutors have with State officials; (e) Whether any official action taken is meaningful or merely perfunctory, including an evaluation of the willingness of law enforcement agencies to detect, prosecute and punish offenders; (f) Whether there is a pattern of State unresponsiveness; (g) A denial of State's services; (h) Whether any steps have been taken by the State to prevent infliction of harm'. Regarding accessibility, '(i) Evidence by the

Lastly, Article 8 deals with internal flight alternative. The old article immediately appeared inconsistent with the ruling of the ECtHR and with the unquestioned interpretation of the Refugee Convention. While, on the one hand, it mentioned briefly the elements that would justify considering an internal area to be safe – as borne out by practices relating to the application of the two acts – and made the applicant's return conditional on the existence of a link with the safe internal zone such as would allow him or her to move there,[95] on the other hand, at paragraph (3) it stated expressly that the internal flight alternative could apply 'notwithstanding technical obstacles to return to the country of origin'. This addition went beyond what was allowed by the ECHR and the Refugee Convention, evading the requirement that the internal zone should be accessible.[96] It was therefore appropriate that the new Qualification Directive introduce substantial amendments. It contains a more satisfactory description of the elements used to assess the safety of the internal zone[97] and above all it eliminates the 'incriminated' paragraph (3),[98] explicitly providing in paragraph (2) that the applicant can 'safely and legally travel to and gain admittance to that part of the country and can reasonably be expected to settle there'. This is the amendment that has also satisfied UNHCR.[99]

applicant that the alleged persecutors are not subject to the State's control; (j) The qualitative nature of the access the applicant has to whatever protection is available, bearing in mind that applicants as a class must not be exempt from protection by the law; (k) Steps, if any, by the applicant to obtain protection from State officials and the State response to these attempts'.

95 '1. As part of the assessment of the application for international protection, Member States may determine that an applicant is not in need of international protection if in a part of the country of origin there is no well-founded fear of being persecuted or no real risk of suffering serious harm and the applicant can reasonably be expected to stay in that part of the country. 2. In examining whether a part of the country of origin is in accordance with paragraph 1, Member States shall at the time of taking the decision on the application have regard to the general circumstances prevailing in that part of the country and to the personal circumstances of the applicant'.

96 See UNHCR (2007b: 10 f.). Among scholarly writers C. Favilli (2011: 133) takes a critical stance.

97 The new Article 8 not only mentions the absence of any risk in the safe zone (whether of persecution or of serious harm) but contains the express requirement that the applicant must have 'access to protection against persecution or serious harm' there. It then provides that when assessing whether or not there exists a risk 'Member States shall at the time of taking the decision on the application have regard to the general circumstances prevailing in that part of the country and to the personal circumstances of the applicant in accordance with Article 4. To that end, Member States shall ensure that precise and up-to-date information is obtained from relevant sources, such as the United Nations High Commissioner for Refugees and the European Asylum Support Office'.

98 According to G. Gilbert (2004: 976).

99 UNHCR (2010: 6 f.). UNHCR had also voiced some concerns about the elimination of the reference to reasonable grounds for believing the applicant will settle in the safe internal zone. The new version of the Commission's proposal (COM (2009) 551 final) was recast according to the suggestions of UNHCR.

4.4 Beneficiaries of international protection:
A) Refugees

Article 2 of the new Qualification Directive gives a definition of persons benefiting from international protection based on the two categories outlined in the Refugee Convention and ECHR: refugees in the first and persons eligible for subsidiary protection in the second. As far as refugees are concerned, Article 2(d) of the Directive simply reprises the text of Article 1(A)(2) of the Refugee Convention.[100] As is the practice regarding the Convention, Recital No. 21 of the Directive states that 'The recognition of refugee status is a declaratory act'.[101] This assertion, which would otherwise have no consequences of importance, entails several obligations for States (first and foremost, those deriving from the principle of *non-refoulement*) designed effectively to ensure the protection of refugees (see below, section 4.7 ff.).

On a general level, there are nonetheless differences in the wording of the two instruments. To begin with, the new Qualification Directive contains no time or geographical limitations. The obvious reason for this is that all the EU Member States had acceded to the Refugee Convention without the geographical limitation and also ratified the 1967 Protocol eliminating the time limitation.[102] Moreover, the new Qualification Directive does not differentiate between different categories of refugees in the same way as the Refugee Convention: according to Article 2(e) refugee status is obtained through 'recognition by a Member State of a third-country national or a stateless person as a refugee', while the Directive uses the expression 'beneficiaries of refugee status' to denote refugees.[103] The only rule applying to all refugees is that of Article 21(2), which, in setting out the

---

100 This defines a refugee as 'a third-country national who, owing to a well-founded fear of being persecuted for reasons of race, religion, nationality, political opinion or membership of a particular social group, is outside the country of nationality and is unable or, owing to such fear, is unwilling to avail himself or herself of the protection of that country, or a stateless person, who, being outside of the country of former habitual residence for the same reasons as mentioned above, is unable or, owing to such fear, unwilling to return to it, and to whom Article 12 does not apply'. Note that the new Qualification Directive integrates the concept of refugee with a reference to the cessation exclusion clauses of Article 12, unlike the Refugee Convention, which instead incorporates them in the provision (Article 1 D-F) containing the definition. Directive 2004/83/EC reproduced the same text: see Article 2(c).

101 The same is true of Recital No. 14 of Directive 2004/83/EC, according to which 'The recognition of refugee status is a declaratory act'.

102 Turkey is not (yet) a Member State of the EU but it ratified the 1967 Protocol with the geographical limitation, which it had opted for when ratifying the Refugee Convention (see above § 1.1).

103 Unlike the old Qualification Directive, the new Directive also specifies at Article 2(b) what is understood by 'beneficiary of international protection': 'a person who has been granted refugee status or subsidiary protection status . . .'.

exceptions to the principle of *non-refoulement*, indicates instead that the prohibition applies to a 'refugee, whether formally recognised or not'.[104]

The cornerstone of the definition is set out in Articles 9 and 10 of the Directive detailing what constitutes an act of persecution and when the reasons for it are present. One aspect the articles do not deal with is the notion of well-founded fear, although it is mentioned in Article 2(d). In the application of the Refugee Convention the concept is often interpreted as requiring an assessment of both subjective and objective elements, although this is widely criticised by legal theorists.[105] The new Qualification Directive appears to favour eliminating any assessment of the applicant's subjective perception of the risk of persecution.[106] This is borne out by the fact that Article 9 lists only the objective elements on which a decision regarding the determination of refugee status should be based. European case law, notably that of France, Germany and to some extent also the UK, has always taken this approach.[107]

As scholarly writers have noted,[108] the Directive favours an objective approach, in line with the argument put forward earlier (section 1.1), but without neglecting the potential role that personal factors may play in the assessment. Although it is not necessary for the applicant to perceive the risk personally, elements relating

---

104 Additionally, in the case of people who, because they represent a threat to the security of the host State or its population, do not or no longer have refugee status, Article 14(6) provides for an extension of the rights enshrined 'in Articles 3, 4, 16, 22, 31, 32 and 33 of the Geneva Convention in so far as they are present in the Member State'. According to the Refugee Convention, these are rights to which *de facto* refugees (in Article 32, only those legally present) are entitled. In reality, although the rights are the same ('set out in or similar to those'), the beneficiaries are not: in Article 14(6) the beneficiaries are people who do not have refugee status (any longer), and in fact the provision refers to 'persons', while for the Refugee Convention they are still refugees. Hence the apparent inconsistency between the Directive and the Convention, because while Article 14(6) refers to Article 32 of the Refugee Convention, which instead applies only to refugees legally present, it does not mention Articles 5, 13, 25, 27, 29 and 30 of the Convention, which apply to refugees *tout court*. Ultimately, it extends some of the rules of the Refugee Convention beyond the limits imposed by it. The extension of Article 33 is somewhat incongruous, given that it sets out the prohibition on *refoulement*: it is difficult to see why it should be extended to persons for whom States have already determined, by appropriate procedure, exclusion from or cessation of refugee status. It may have been included as an allusion to the part of the prohibition, as it has evolved under general international law, which is of an absolute nature and so admits no exclusion (subsidiary protection). However, in my opinion the rule applies in full to subsidiary protection and therefore the reference in Article 14(6) to Article 33 is excessive, if not actually incorrect. For similar considerations (regarding the identical provision contained in the old Qualification Directive) see K. Hailbronner and S. Alt (2010: 1136 f.).

105 See footnote 24, Chapter 1.

106 Legal theorists are of the same opinion: see S. Boutillon (2003–2004: 139). On the fact that the old Qualification Directive, like the new one, did not adopt the 'subjective' approach, see K. Hailbronner and S. Alt (2010: 1069).

107 A. Zimmermann and C. Mahler (2011: 340 f.).

108 J. McAdam (2005: 472).

to an individual person may be significant. Article 4(3)(c) requires States to take account, among other things, of 'the individual position and personal circumstances of the applicant, including factors such as background, gender and age'. Thus, the Administrative Court of Münster ruled that the risk of suffering genital mutilation and forced marriage was greater for a single woman whose return to Nigeria was under consideration.[109]

Article 9 of the Directive deals with the concept of persecution 'within the meaning of Article 1A of the Geneva Convention', to which it makes specific reference. The provision covers two different situations depending on the rights involved. According to Article 9(1)(a) the act must be

> sufficiently serious by its nature or repetition as to constitute a severe violation of basic human rights, in particular the rights from which derogation cannot be made under Article 15(2) of the European Convention for the Protection of Human Rights and Fundamental Freedoms.[110]

Two elements must be present for persecution to exist: the rights violated must be basic human rights and the acts infringing them must be severe beyond a given threshold. The first element is deduced from the international instruments safeguarding human rights: the reference to Article 15(2) ECHR is certainly useful as it clearly identifies the right to live, the prohibition on torture, the prohibition on slavery and forced labour, and the principle of legality in criminal matters. Moreover, the Directive's use of the term 'in particular' does not, as legal theorists have pointed out,[111] limit the rights whose serious violation may give rise to persecution to just the ones mentioned in Article 15. There are other agreements containing a longer list of rights from which derogation cannot be made,[112] just as the fact of being non-derogable is not a necessary condition for Article 9(1)(a) to apply. The Federal Administrative Court of Germany ruled to that effect, remarking that

> die Religionsfreiheit gehört nicht zu den gemäß Art. 15 Abs. 2 EMRK notstandsfesten Rechten; auch bei ihr handelt es sich jedoch um eines der in Art. 9 Abs. 1 Buchst. a der Richtlinie – über die notstandsfesten Rechte hinaus – geschützten grundlegenden Menschenrechte.[113]

---

109 Decision of 15 March 2010, 11 K 413/09.A.
110 A similar rule was contained in Directive 2004/83/EC.
111 K. Hailbronner and S. Alt (2010: 1071).
112 See Article 4(2) of the International Covenant on Civil and Political Rights (signed New York 16 December 1966, and entered into force 23 March 1976, 999 UNTS 171 ff.), which extends non-derogation to the prohibition on imprisonment for inability to fulfil an obligation, the right to recognition of legal status, and freedom of thought, conscience and religion.
113 Decision of 5 March 2009, 10 C 51.07, para. 13. See also the same court's decision of 29 February 2009, 10 C 50.07.

The other element required is the seriousness of the violation, which can be deduced from its nature and its frequency. There is always persecution when the right violated is strongly protected, as with the right to life, the prohibition on torture, and so on.[114] In the case of rights that are still basic, but not a cornerstone of international rules, there is only persecution when the violation is repeated. This is very similar to the scheme described in Chapter 1, which allows a flexible approach to be taken because the link between the assessment of serious risk and the nature of the rights protected is not rigid. In my opinion, discrimination affecting the enjoyment of protected rights is not itself serious beyond the minimum threshold. Indeed, reference to this was removed from the Commission's original proposal, where it appeared even though the accompanying report clarified that only repeated and systematic discrimination could constitute persecution.[115]

Article 9(1)(b) sets out the other (and alternative) requirements for persecution: specifically, when there is 'an accumulation of various measures, including violations of human rights which is sufficiently severe as to affect an individual in a similar manner as mentioned in point (a)'.[116] The provision protects all human rights, with no distinction as to their nature or, if preferred, their 'weight'. However, a repetition of the same violation is not sufficient to constitute persecution – as may be the case in point (a) – as there must be an '*accumulation* of *various* measures' (emphasis added). Only in these terms is it possible to uphold the theory that repeated discrimination can be included under point (b).[117] According to the letter of the rule, the acts to which the risk refers can only amount to persecution if they are 'measures, *including* violations of human rights' (emphasis added). It would

---

114 K. Hailbronner and S. Alt (2010: 1072).
115 See COM (2001) 510, p. 51. In the rule suggested by the Commission, 'the term persecution shall be considered to cover as a minimum any of the following situations: (a) the infliction of serious and unjustified harm or *discrimination* on the grounds of race, religion, nationality, political opinion or membership of a particular social group, sufficiently serious by its nature or repetition as to constitute a significant risk to the applicant's life, freedom or security or to preclude the applicant from living in his or her country of origin' (emphasis added). According to the Commission, 'The repetition of discriminatory measures which, taken separately, may not be serious enough to constitute persecution, may give rise to a valid claim for refugee status on cumulative grounds' (ibid., 23). For the case law see the Spanish Audiencia Nacional, decision of 3 November 2010, Nº Recurso 555/2009, which found that 'el señor Juan Alberto [applicant] no ha acreditado que recaigan sobre él medidas, actuaciones o comportamientos contrarios a la Convención de Ginebra, en los concretos términos que ésta establece, y aunque puede afirmarse que en su caso existe discriminación, ello no supone necesariamente que sea víctima de persecución'.
116 Directive 2004/83/EC contained the same provision.
117 K. Hailbronner and S. Alt (2010: 1074). It is a convincing argument, being based on an amendment made during the *travaux préparatoires* of the Council that was designed to replace the wording 'accumulation of violations of human rights' with the longer phrase 'accumulation of various measures, including violations of human rights', which was eventually adopted. This interpretation is confirmed by the case law: see High Court of Ireland, decision of 1 July 2011, *G. V. and I. V.* v. *Refugee Appeals Tribunal and Minister for Justice, Equality and Law Reform.*

appear contradictory to maintain that systematic discrimination relating to any one of the human rights mentioned at point (b) constitutes persecution when, according to point (a), it is excluded in respect of *fundamental* human rights. Nonetheless, Article 9(2) confirms that discrimination, *together* with other measures, can constitute persecution. In listing examples of some of the forms that persecutory acts can take, it makes several references to discrimination: point (b) mentions 'legal, administrative, police, and/or judicial measures which are in themselves discriminatory or which are implemented in a discriminatory manner', while point (c) instead refers to 'prosecution or punishment which is disproportionate or discriminatory'.[118]

The existence of persecution is not in itself sufficient grounds for an application for recognition of refugee status; it must be linked to one of the reasons indicated in the Refugee Convention: race, religion, nationality, membership of a particular social group or political opinion. This was stated in Article 9(3) of the old Directive, which referred to Article 10 for a definition of the reasons of the persecution.[119] In the new Qualification Directive, the wording of Article 9(3) rightly extends it to situations, covered by protection theory, in which persecution is by private individuals, in which case the reasons set out in Article 10 must be connected to the State authority's inability or unwillingness to provide protection.[120] This requirement had to be added because often the actions of private individuals that constitute persecution are not connected to the reasons listed and therefore fall outside the scope of the rule, even though the State fails to provide protection for reasons linked to race, religion and so on.[121] Instead, neither of the Directives offers a solution to a widely debated problem, left unresolved by the Refugee Convention: the problem of the nature of the connection between the persecution and the reasons for it. Some indications can be found in the Commission's original report: commenting on the rule on generalised oppression,[122] it appears to favour

---

118 The others, all of which, together with those cited in the body of the text, were already contained in Directive 2004/83/EC, are '(a) acts of physical or mental violence, including acts of sexual violence; . . . (d) denial of judicial redress resulting in a disproportionate or discriminatory punishment; (e) prosecution or punishment for refusal to perform military service in a conflict, where performing military service would include crimes or acts falling within the scope of the grounds for exclusion as set out in Article 12(2)'.

119 'In accordance with Article 2(c), there must be a connection between the reasons mentioned in Article 10 and the acts of persecution as qualified in paragraph 1'.

120 'In accordance with point (d) of Article 2, there must be a connection between the reasons mentioned in Article 10 and the acts of persecution as qualified in paragraph 1 of this Article *or the absence of protection against such acts*' (emphasis added).

121 See G. Morgese (2012a: 265). For the case law, see the German Federal Administrative Court, decision of 19 January 2009, 10 C 52.07.

122 'The following principles shall, as a minimum, govern the determination of whether a well-founded fear of being persecuted should result in the recognition of an applicant as a refugee: . . . (c) it is immaterial whether the applicant comes from a country in which many or all persons face the risk of generalised oppression': see Article 11(2) (c) of the Commission's proposal, COM (2001) 510.

the approach usually followed in practice that none of the reasons listed in the Refugee Convention should be either the only one or the decisive one in establishing a connection: according to the report, 'Only when one of these five reasons is not significantly implicated in relation to the fear of persecution are Member States justified in granting subsidiary protection status instead'.[123]

Article 10(2) takes a clearer position on another controversial issue, stating that,

> When assessing if an applicant has a well-founded fear of being persecuted it is immaterial whether the applicant actually possesses the racial, religious, national, social or political characteristic which attracts the persecution, provided that such a characteristic is attributed to the applicant by the actor of persecution.[124]

This provides two important indications. The first is that, consistently with the interpretation of the Refugee Convention, the applicant does not have to possess, objectively, the characteristics that are the cause of his or her persecution. The second, decisive, element is the persecutor's intention, which is governed by the reasons set out in the Refugee Convention.[125] This is in line with practices as regards the Refugee Convention, although the position is, with justification, strongly criticised by legal theorists.[126]

Clarification of the individual reasons can be found in Article 10, which at (2)(a) states that race 'shall, in particular, include considerations of colour, descent, or membership of a particular ethnic group'. In its report the Commission underlined that the concept should be interpreted broadly 'to include all kinds of ethnic groups and the full range of sociological understandings of the term'.[127] It also confirmed the decisive role of the persecutor's intentions, adding that the persecutor was often motivated by a conviction that 'the victim of persecution . . . [belongs] to a different racial group other than his own, by reason of real or supposed difference'.[128]

Religion is defined at point (b), which adds little to the indications already provided in practice regarding the Refugee Convention, particularly by UNHCR.[129] As mentioned earlier, persecution for religious reasons often affects religious freedom; since this is a basic right, but not one of the cornerstones of

---

123 Ibid., 25.
124 Directive 2004/83/EC contains the same provision.
125 See K. Hailbronner and S. Alt (2010: 1078). For a contrary opinion, although without citing specific reasons, see H. Battjes (2006: 255).
126 See footnote 54, Chapter 1.
127 COM (2001) 510, p. 25.
128 Ibid.
129 According to Article 10(2)(b), 'the concept of religion shall in particular include the holding of theistic, non-theistic and atheistic beliefs, the participation in, or abstention from, formal worship in private or in public, either alone or in community with others, other religious acts or expressions of view, or forms of personal or communal conduct based on or mandated by any religious belief'.

human rights, it means that acts which violate it must be repetitive in order to be persecutory, as persecution is ruled out unless the discrimination is sufficiently systematic. The Oberverwaltungsgericht für das Land Nordrhein-Westfalen ruled thus regarding acts performed against Afghan Hindus,[130] while the same court for Baden-Wurttemberg, though not upholding the complaint of a Pakistani applicant belonging to the Ahmadiyya movement, ruled that the acts performed by the authorities against members of the movement were sufficient to constitute persecution.[131] Of course, persecution must be ruled out not only when the right in question is not severely violated but also when it is lawfully restricted under the provisions of international rules. This is because it is important, as the Federal Administrative Court of Germany has asserted, to make a distinction between the reasons for persecution and the right that is violated.[132]

In accordance with the Refugee Convention, Article 10(2)(c) uses a concept of nationality that is not limited to the applicant's citizenship (or lack thereof) but includes 'membership of a group determined by its cultural, ethnic, or linguistic identity, common geographical or political origins or its relationship with the population of another State'. This concept overlaps in part with that of race and also allows the possibility of a relationship or affinity with persons of another nationality, as in the case of 'mixed' families. It is mainly employed in connection with minorities, such as the Chechens in Russia[133] or the Eritreans in Ethiopia.[134]

Membership of a particular social group – the only reason in which the new Qualification Directive intervenes – is regulated more fully by Article 10(2)(d), which applies a very different criterion compared with the approach taken as regards the Refugee Convention: it requires the group to be identified, *cumulatively*, by objective innate or essential characteristics and by external perception.[135] This approach, which has arisen out of an amendment to the Commission's original proposal,[136] has been strongly criticised by legal theorists and in the case law[137] because it sets much more stringent conditions than the

---

130 Decision of 19 June 2008, 20 A 4676/06.A.
131 Decision of 20 May 2008, A 10 S 72/08.
132 Decision of 5 March 2009, 10 C 51.07, on which see K. Hailbronner and S. Alt (2010: 1083) in favour. The ECJ was of the same opinion: see *Y and Z*, especially para. 60 ff.
133 See the Commission permanente de recours des réfugiés, decision of 4 March 2005, No. 04-3388/F1755, available online at www.refworld.org.
134 Court of Appeal (civil division) of England and Wales, decision of 31 July 2007, *EB* v. *Secretary of State for the Home Department*, available online at www.refugeecaselaw.org.
135 This is confirmed by the ECJ in the recent case of *X, Y and Z*, para. 45.
136 According to the Commission's proposal, COM (2001) 510, 'the concept of social group shall include a group which may be defined in terms of certain fundamental characteristics, such as sexual orientation, age or gender, as well as groups comprised of persons who share a common background or characteristic that is so fundamental to identity or conscience that those persons should not be forced to renounce their membership. The concept shall also include groups of individuals who are treated as "inferior" in the eyes of the law'.
137 A. Zimmermann and C. Mahler (2011: 394), including for the appropriate references. UNHCR (2005: 23) has explicitly recommended that 'To avoid any protection gaps

Refugee Convention. As a result, because the Directive should be interpreted in accordance with the rules of the Convention, national courts tend to follow a mixed approach, identifying social groups on the basis of objective *or* subjective elements. In a 2006 decision of the House of Lords, Lord Brown of Eaton-under-Heywood declared that he was fully in agreement with UNHCR's particular definition of social group and then concluded that the Directive had 'to be interpreted consistently with this definition'.[138] Of course, the one criterion does not usually produce widely differing solutions from the other, and so the adoption of this cumulative approach, which differs from that of the Refugee Convention, in reality has only a minor impact.

Instead, it would seem that the Directive rules out any possibility that persecution itself might point to the existence of a particular social group, even though this approach is sometimes found in practice. The *travaux préparatoires*[139] indicate that the drafters of the Directive wished to eliminate reference to any identifying elements, such as 'different treatment', that could have this effect. In my opinion, persecution occurs in these cases *on the basis* of the group's identification, so that logically the former takes place after the latter. For example, a rule prohibiting unmarried men from voting, imposed in a general climate unfavourable to them and in which other violations take place, does not make them a particular social group, but it does clearly point to an existing perception of them as separate from the rest of society. Thus, the adoption of this approach is merely a consequence of the relationship between the two different criteria applied in practice (which the Directive applies together, raising questions among legal theorists[140]). This, it seems to me, is the position recently taken by the ECJ when ruling that criminal legislation targeting homosexuals 'supports a finding that those persons form a separate group which is perceived by the surrounding society as being different'.[141]

The criteria were also the subject of much discussion during the *travaux préparatoires* for the old Qualification Directive, particularly as some States were unwilling to include express references to sexual orientation, age and gender.[142] In the end a clarification was added, on the one hand, that sexual orientation could be the basis for identifying the group, taking account of 'circumstances in the

---

... Member States reconcile the two approaches to permit alternative, rather than cumulative, application of the two concepts'.

138 House of Lords, decision of 18 October 2006, *Secretary of State for the Home Department v. K*, para. 118. See also Spain's Tribunal supremo, decision of 14 December 2006, N° 8233/2003, in which a particular social group was identified by emphasising only the social perception aspect. However, even before Directive 2004/83/EC the Aliens Appeal Board of Sweden had applied a different reasoning in the decision of 18 February 2001, UM 9899–09.

139 See the reconstruction by A. Zimmermann and C. Mahler (2011: 1086 f.).

140 This is why I believe that the position of those who criticise the cumulative approach of the Directive while denying that persecution can affect the identification of a social group is a contradictory one: see H. Battjes (2006: respectively, 256 and 257).

141 *X, Y and Z*, para. 48.

142 A. Zimmermann and C. Mahler (2011: 1088 ff.).

country of origin' but not including criminal conduct,[143] and, on the other hand, that gender could be considered for the same purpose, but without being a decisive factor.[144] The rule has been amended by the new Qualification Directive, which makes it compulsory (or almost: 'a particular social group *might* include a group based on a common characteristic of sexual orientation. . . . Gender related aspects, including gender identity, *shall be given due consideration*' (emphasis added)) to take sexual orientation and gender into account.[145] Under the old Qualification Directive the ECJ itself had stated that sexual orientation could define membership of a particular social group for the purpose of applying the regulation.[146]

Finally, political opinion is defined as 'the holding of an opinion, thought or belief on a matter related to the potential actors of persecution . . . and to their policies or methods'. It includes the assessment of all acts that come under the responsibility of the State, as in the Refugee Convention. Moreover, Directive 2011/95/EU does not take into account whether or not the applicant has already expressed such opinions. This is in line with the provisions of Article 10(2), according to which the decisive criterion is the persecutor's intention: if an

143 Criminal conduct would in any case rule out recognition of refugee status as acts designed to prevent it cannot be regarded as persecutory if they are within the limits imposed by human rights rules. This provision eliminates the problem by tackling it at its root, although the solution would in any case be the same because of the evident difficulty of having to recognise as a particular social group a set of people guilty or suspected of particularly heinous sexual crimes, such as paedophile pornography.

144 UNHCR has been highly critical in its assessment, not only of the partial inclusion of gender elements but also of the elimination of the criterion of age, which is essential in many forms of persecution, such as 'forcible or under-age recruitment into military service, (forced) child marriage, female genital mutilation, child trafficking, or child pornography or abuse': see UNHCR (2005: 23 f.).

145 The uncertain letter of the Directive has not prevented national courts from recognising a particular social group in cases of women at risk of genital mutilation in a country, such as Somalia, where it is practised on 98% of the female population (Belgium's Conseil du Contentieux des Etrangers, decision of 19 May 2011, No. 61.832); women from a specific area of Nigeria (the Delta) where large numbers are forced into the sex trade (France's Cour nationale du droit d'asile, decision of 29 July 2011, No. 10020534); and homosexuals from Islamic countries (Administrative Court of Köln, decision of 15 September 2011, 18 K 6103/10.A). In one case it was not even ruled out in abstract that the particular social group might consist of men: see Administrative Court of Berlin, decision of 9 June 2011, 33 K 285.10 A, although the required objective and subjective factors were not found to be present.

146 *X, Y and Z*. The ECJ took the opportunity to rule on a matter not always handled in a uniform manner in the case law relating to the Refugee Convention: the fairly infrequent issue of reasonable tolerability (see § 1.1). According to the Court, 'none of those rules contained in Article 10 of the old Qualification Directive states that, in assessing the extent of the risk of actual acts of persecution in a particular situation, it is necessary to take account of the possibility open to the applicant of avoiding the risk of persecution by abstaining from the religious practice in question and, consequently, renouncing the protection which the Directive is intended to afford the applicant by conferring refugee status' (ibid., para. 74).

individual is attributed with a given political opinion, it is clearly irrelevant whether he or she has actually expressed it. Hence, where the applicant has engaged in political activity that has not or cannot reach potential persecutors, he or she will not be granted protection. Cases of this type arise frequently and are often associated with activities carried on by the applicant after leaving his or her country (refugees *sur place*).[147]

4.5 B) People eligible for subsidiary protection

Article 2(f) of the new Qualification Directive defines a person eligible for subsidiary protection as

> a third-country national or a stateless person who does not qualify as a refugee but in respect of whom substantial grounds have been shown for believing that the person concerned, if returned to his or her country of origin, or in the case of a stateless person, to his or her country of former habitual residence, would face a real risk of suffering serious harm as defined in Article 15, and to whom Article 17(1) and (2) does not apply, and is unable, or, owing to such risk, unwilling to avail himself or herself of the protection of that country.[148]

This definition has a few similarities and some major differences with respect to the definition of refugee in Article 2(d). The elements in common are the exclusion of nationals of EU Member States and the application of the rules on the need for protection *sur place*, on the actors offering protection, on the actors responsible for providing protection, and on the internal flight alternative: for these aspects the considerations made above apply (see section 4.3). Cases of exclusion are similarly included in Article 2(f), which contains a reference to Article 17(1) and (2) (see below, section 4.6).

The premises, however, are widely divergent. There are two evident points of difference: one is the relationship between the risk of persecution and the person exposed to it because, contrary to the 'well-founded fear' of persecution that marks the refugee, Article 2(f) refers to 'substantial grounds . . . for believing'. Scholarly writers have remarked that the wording of point (f) clearly rules out the existence of subjective elements, which are present instead in the notion of 'well-founded fear', and concluded that point (f) 'demands a higher threshold than the well-founded fear test for persecution'.[149] I do not think this position is entirely justified as it again confuses the concept of fear and the concept of risk: to make it unnecessary for a person to show a deep fear of persecution in order to be

---

147 See the Swedish Migrationsöverdomstolens, decision of 16 September 2011, UM 4801-10.
148 Article 2(e) of Directive 2004/83/EC is identical.
149 J. McAdam (2007: 62).

eligible for protection is not the same as disregarding his or her personal situation. In fact, in assessing refugee status, not only is the requirement of well-founded fear questionable – as part of case law and the literature maintain[150] – but, again according to both, personal characteristics, such as temperament, disposition or social position, may also be taken into account in accordance with Article 4(3)(c) of the Directive. This provision completes the definition of 'person eligible for subsidiary protection' so that the phrase 'substantial grounds . . . for believing' does not rule out assessing the risk of persecution on the basis of the individual applicant. This, according to the writers criticised here,[151] is borne out by the case law regarding the ECHR, on which the notion of subsidiary protection is based. In reality, although the two wordings differ, I do not think their outcome is very different. In the Commission's original proposal the same formula ('well-founded fear'[152]) was used for both types of protection; during the *travaux préparatoires* the wording of subsidiary protection was then changed, but only to link up with the case law of the ECtHR[153] from which it had become apparent that another form of protection was needed to supplement the Refugee Convention.

Article 15, to which Article 2(f) refers, defines the notion of serious harm and requires 'substantial grounds' for believing the person concerned is at risk. It lists three potential situations of serious harm, which constitute the other, more evident difference between beneficiary of subsidiary protection and refugee: a) 'death penalty or execution', b) 'torture or inhuman or degrading treatment or punishment of an applicant in the country of origin', and c) 'serious and individual threat to a civilian's life or person by reason of indiscriminate violence in situations of international or internal armed conflict'.[154] The three situations echo the case law of the ECtHR although they do not incorporate some recent developments in the theory of protection *par ricochet*. Several writers had already pointed out that setting in stone the ECtHR's conclusions regarding some provisions of the ECHR could make it impossible to accommodate later developments.[155] An 'open' formulation would be a better way to take account of new interpretations of human rights, particularly those arising out of ECtHR case law. This was the sense of the Commission's original proposal, which added to the situations envisaged by Article 15 the 'violation of a human right, sufficiently severe to engage the Member State's international obligations'. As many writers noted,[156] the suggestion was strongly opposed by several Member States because its vagueness would allow too much scope for interpretation and it was therefore eliminated by the Council.

As a result, unless the cases of protection *par ricochet* resulting from the provisions of the ECHR other than Articles 2 and 3 (for instance, Article 6) are 'given a place'

---

150 See footnote 24, Chapter 1.
151 J. McAdam (2007: 63).
152 Article 5 of the Commission's proposal, COM (2001) 510.
153 See A. Zimmermann and C. Mahler (2011: 1017).
154 An identical version is found in Directive 2004/83/EC.
155 J. McAdam (2007: 65).
156 K. Hailbronner and S. Alt (2010: 1143).

within the framework of the other possible form of protection (refugee status) they will be excluded from subsidiary protection. This need not create a conflict with the ECHR: under Article 21(1) of Directive 2011/95/EU, 'Member States shall respect the principle of *non-refoulement* in accordance with their international obligations'. In other words, Article 21(1) prohibits removal in the other cases of protection *par ricochet* not included in the definition given in Article 15 of the new Qualification Directive. This does have a major consequence, however, insofar as people who do not come under Article 15 and cannot be removed pursuant to Article 21(1) are excluded from subsidiary protection and left in a sort of limbo, as was the case of beneficiaries of indirect protection before the Qualification Directive.

Article 15(a) reprises the ECtHR's interpretation of Articles 2 and 3 ECHR preventing a person being sent back to a country where he or she is at risk of the death penalty, which is prohibited by the first article, as it has evolved, and by the second article in connection with death row syndrome or an 'unjust' conviction (to the death penalty). Article 15(a) thus asserts, once and for all, the non-existence of the death penalty in all EU Member States. According to the literature, the Directive goes even further than the ECHR, because 'by focusing on the concept of "execution", it includes within the scope of this protection killings without preliminary trial. . .'.[157] This interpretation is not often upheld in practice (relating to the identical Article 15 of Directive 2004/83/EC),[158] partly because such an extension noted in the literature would normally be covered by the other situations envisaged in Article 15: the French Cour nationale du droit d'asile ruled thus in the case of an Albanian applicant who, if repatriated to Kosovo, would risk the vengeance to which the relatives of the victim of a murder committed by a relative (in this case, the applicant's uncle) were entitled in accordance with the Kanun.[159]

Article 15(b) lists the better-known situation covered by Article 3 ECHR. The wording is not identical to that used in the case law of the ECtHR and, according to scholarly writers,[160] excludes two situations: protection for humanitarian reasons, that is the cases referred to in the ECtHR's decision in *D.* v. *United Kingdom*;[161] and indirect *refoulement*, that is, the risk that the applicant will be sent from the third country of destination to another country where he or she would suffer serious harm. The exclusion of protection for humanitarian reasons is endorsed by Recital No. 15 of the new Qualification Directive, according to which it does not apply to

157 C. Teitgen-Colly (2006: 1534), who of course is referring to the identical version of the old Qualification Directive.
158 See High Court of England and Wales, decision of 17 February 2010, *R (on the application of Boroumand)* v. *Secretary of State for the Home Department*, available online at www.refworld.org, which dealt rather with the problem of exclusion clauses.
159 Decision of 17 December 2009, No. 641626, in which the situation in question was attributed to the risk defined in Article 15(b).
160 K. Hailbronner and S. Alt (2010: 1140 ff.). See also J. McAdam (2007: 69).
161 ECtHR, judgment of 2 May 1997, Application No. 30240/96, *D.* v. *United Kingdom*, available online at www.echr.coe.int. In this case the Court extended the protection granted under Article 3 ECHR to a person who would not have received suitable treatment for his terminal illness in the country of destination.

persons 'who are allowed to remain in the territories of the Member States for reasons not due to a need for international protection but on a discretionary basis on compassionate or humanitarian grounds'. There remains the problem of relating this exclusion, which concerns situations very rarely found in the case law of the ECtHR, to Article 21(1) of the Directive calling on States to comply with the prohibition on *refoulement*. The same should apply to the exclusion of indirect *refoulement*, which instead is included among the situations of protection *par ricochet* regularly ascribed to the ECHR. However, I believe that the provision in question should be interpreted in the light of the Procedures Directive, which specifically states that a country can only be designated safe if it respects the principle of *non-refoulement*, thus clearly including indirect *refoulement*.[162]

Article 15(b) not only betrays the rules on which it is based but encroaches on the field of application of the Refugee Convention, as the acts to which it refers generally come within the concept of refugee.[163] That said, point (b) can easily incorporate situations not covered by the Refugee Convention because unrelated to one of the reasons listed in Article 1A(2). National case law has signalled clearly that it follows this approach, as in the decision of the French Cour nationale du droit d'asile, in which the applicant had been unable to demonstrate that the risk of vengeance was linked to one of the reasons cited in the Convention. Moreover, point (b) serves a useful purpose when, for whatever reason, the Refugee Convention cannot apply, either because the acts that might give rise to persecution have not come to the attention of the potential persecutors,[164] or because refugee status is excluded for one of the reasons listed in Article 1F of the Refugee Convention, or again because the applicant is not outside his or her country of origin.[165]

Finally, Article 15(c) deals with the newest situation,[166] which is barely hinted at in the case law of the ECtHR: a 'serious and individual threat to a civilian's life or person by reason of indiscriminate violence in situations of international or internal armed conflict'. The rule raises a number of problems, some of which were solved by the ECJ in a judgment of 2009.[167] The first issue is to establish how the situation described at point (c) relates to the other situations considered in Article 15. The ECJ ruled that point (c) provides additional protection, points (a) and (b) being intended to deal with the situations described, respectively, in Articles 2 and 3 ECHR.[168] The Court's position does not seem correct: to

---

162 Council Directive 2005/85/EC of 1 December 2005 on minimum standards on procedures in Member States for granting and withdrawing refugee status, OJ L 326, 13 December 2005, p. 13 ff., in particular Appendix II.
163 C. Teitgen-Colly (2006: 1535 f.).
164 Helsinki Administrative Court, decision of 29 June 2010, 10/0868/1.
165 See footnote 110, Chapter 2.
166 See C. Favilli (2011: 136).
167 Judgment of 17 February 2009, Case C-465/07, *Meki Elgafaji and Noor Elgafaji* v. *Staatssecretaris van Justitie (Elgafaji)*, *EC Reports*, 2009, p. I-921 ff. For an early comment see R. Errera (2011: 93 ff.).
168 *Elgafaji*, para. 27 f.

begin, the two do not correspond exactly according to the rules of the Directive, on the one hand, and the case law of the ECtHR, on the other, as there may be cases in which point (b) is not applicable but Article 3 ECHR is. Furthermore, the ECtHR has not ruled out, in theory, that the rules of the ECHR may offer indirect protection in situations of indiscriminate violence.[169] Thus, it is possible that the situation in point (c) is already 'envisaged' by the ECHR.

The main problem facing the ECJ has been that of the type of threat that will trigger subsidiary protection according to point (c). The 'individual' threat required by the provision appears to contradict the reference to a situation of indiscriminate violence – in which the threat is, by definition, generalised – as well as the contents of Recital No. 35, according to which 'risks to which a population of a country or a section of the population is generally exposed do normally not create in themselves an individual threat which would qualify as serious harm'. The Court successfully reconciled these provisions. On the one hand, it ruled out that point (c) required exposure 'specifically . . . to the risk of a particular type of harm',[170] which is instead necessary in the situations considered at points (a) and (b), while, on the other hand, it stated that Recital No. 35 excludes *as a rule* that 'the objective finding alone of a risk linked to the general situation in a country' can constitute sufficient proof to meet the conditions of point (c), although admitting that this might happen in 'an exceptional situation which would be characterised by such a high degree of risk that substantial grounds would be shown for believing that that person would be subject individually to the risk in question'.[171] The ECJ therefore found that point (c) applies in situations where the threat is 'individual' insofar as it concerns 'harm to civilians irrespective of their identity'.[172] I think this approach of the Court provides a satisfactory answer to the questions raised by legal theorists regarding the individual nature of the threat.[173] The new Qualification Directive (and the old one) does not rule out the possibility that an indiscriminate threat will justify the granting of subsidiary protection, but it does require the level of threat to be greater in such cases. We can add to the Court's arguments the fact that, despite several opinions to the contrary,[174] point (c) does not appear to contradict the Directive on Temporary Protection.[175] The latter contains no mention of individual factors because its purpose is to ensure that applications for protection are properly assessed in situations, such as a mass influx of refugees, in which

169 See ECtHR, judgment of 17 July 2008, Application No. 25904/07, *Na.* v. *United Kingdom*, available online at www.echr.coe.int.
170 *Elgafaji*, para. 32.
171 Ibid., para. 37.
172 Ibid., para. 35.
173 J. McAdam (2007: 71 ff.).
174 Ibid.: 74.
175 Council Directive 2001/55/EC of 20 July 2001 on minimum standards for giving temporary protection in the event of a mass influx of displaced persons and on measures promoting a balance of efforts between Member States in receiving such persons and bearing the consequences thereof, OJ L 212, 7 August 2001, p. 12 ff.

several practical difficulties may arise. The Directive on Temporary Protection uses a very broad notion, one that in fact is only properly defined by a Council decision (see below, section 4.9), precisely in order to prevent exclusion *from the procedure* (not from recognition of status) of individuals who might be eligible for international protection.

Lastly, the serious and individual threat must be to a civilian in a situation of internal or international armed conflict. These concepts are part of *ius in bello* and must therefore be defined in those terms. Although there are several instances in which the case law has adhered rigidly to the rules of armed conflict law, particularly where it proved difficult to identify an internal conflict and it was necessary to refer to Article 3 of the four Geneva Conventions,[176] it is unlikely that Article 15(c) depends, in the strict sense, on the rules of *ius in bello*. An explicit reference to these rules was removed during the *travaux préparatoires*.[177] Moreover, in the case of *Elgafaji*, the ECJ left an opening that allowed the requirements of the rules to be avoided, particularly in relation to the level of indiscriminate violence;[178] this criterion was subsequently adopted in internal case law, as several decisions following that of the ECJ have demonstrated.[179] The interpretation was then explicitly confirmed by the ECJ in a very recent decision, in which it ruled that the notion of internal armed conflict should be formed independently of humanitarian law, which has a different purpose, as the Court emphasised.[180] The Court thus applied the notion identifying as internal armed conflict a situation in which 'a State's armed forces confront one or more armed groups or . . . two or more armed groups confront each other', without referring either to the rules of humanitarian law or to 'a separate assessment of the intensity of the armed confrontations, the level of organisation of the armed forces involved or the duration of the conflict',[181] the decisive factor being instead the assessment of the level of pervading violence in the territory in question.

The threat must also be serious and therefore at a higher threshold than contemplated by points (a) and (b). The ECJ did not spend time on this aspect, merely indicating that the seriousness of the threat should be assessed in the light of the degree of indiscriminate violence.[182] The internal case law suggests that the assessment of the seriousness of the harm is, as it were, transferred to the level of violence, so that there is always need for protection when any civilian involved may be affected. Considering only some of the more recent cases, this would apply to the Ivory Coast (the Spanish court refused refugee status because there was

---

176 See the Council of State of the Netherlands, decision of 20 July 2007, 200608939/1, especially para. 2.10.
177 See J. McAdam (2007: 76).
178 *Elgafaji*, para. 35.
179 See K. Hailbronner and S. Alt (2010: 1145 f.).
180 ECJ, judgment of 30 January 2014, Case C-285/12, *Aboubacar Diakité v. Commissaire général aux réfugiés et aux apatrides (Diakité)*, not yet published.
181 Ibid., para. 35.
182 *Elgafaji*, para. 43.

no individual threat);[183] to the Afghan provinces of Lowgar[184] and Khazni;[185] and to Somalia, particularly the areas around Mogadishu.[186] By contrast, the application of point (c) was rejected in connection with the situation in the Iraqi region of Mosul,[187] the northern part of Sri Lanka,[188] and the ghettos of Zimbabwe.[189] The German courts apparently found a more precise measure of the seriousness of the threat by using statistics on the civilian victims of attacks. In one case concerning an applicant's return to Iraq (the same country involved in the ECJ's judgment in the case of *Elgafaji*), they calculated that in the space of one year 288 civilians had been killed in attacks of various types in the province of destination (Al-Ta'mīm, now Kirkuk). Considering that in such events a further five civilians usually suffer serious injury, the North-Rhine Westphalia Oberverwaltungsgericht calculated a serious threat of 1 in 520, which was deemed too low.[190]

The notion of civilian also raises problems of interpretation. However, in this case the rules of *ius in bello* can only offer an indication as the authorities are not bound by them and retain a certain amount of discretion. For its part, humanitarian law, as Belgium's Conseil du Contentieux des Etrangers has confirmed, states that there should be a bias in *favour*, so that if there is any doubt the person must be recognised as a civilian.[191]

183 Audiencia Nacional of Spain, decision of 8 July 2011, 302/2010.
184 Oberverwaltungsgericht of Hessen, decision of 25 August 2011, 8 A 1657/10.A.
185 Fővárosi Bíróság of Hungary, decision of 22 April 2011, 17.K30.064/2010/18, in this case the court had refused the protection of the Refugee Convention because there was no individual threat.
186 France's Cour nationale du droit d'asile, decision of 31 March 2011, No. 100013192.
187 Federal Administrative Court of Germany, decision of 17 November 2011, 10 C 13.10.
188 Cour nationale du droit d'asile, decisions of 18 October 2011, No. 11007041, No. 11007040, No. 11007042, in which it was ruled that two applicants of Tamil origin could not invoke point (c) because the conflict with the Sri Lankan army had ended in May 2009. The Court deemed it had a duty to examine the possibility of granting refugee status, but denied this owing to the absence of an individual threat.
189 Council of State of the Netherlands, decision of 8 September 2011, 201009178/1/V2.
190 Decision of 29 October 2010, 9 A 3642/06.A. For a similar case, also before the German courts, see Verwaltungsgerichtshof of Bavaria, decision of 21 October 2010, 13a B 08.30304. However, see also the Federal Administrative Court of Germany, decision of 17 November 2011, 10 C 13.10, especially para. 23, which criticised the purely statistical approach, believing it should be accompanied by an assessment of the general situation in the country, including as regards health and hygiene.
191 Decision of 17 August 2007, No. 1.244, especially para. 6.4, in which the Belgian court referred, by analogy, to Article 50(1) of the Protocol I Additional to the Geneva Conventions of 8 June 1977 relating to the protection of victims of international armed conflicts, 1125 UNTS 33 ff.

4.6 Cessation and exclusion clauses

The cessation and exclusion clauses of the Qualification Directive contain some significant differences with respect to the Refugee Convention, as well as the ECHR. Beginning with the matter of refugee status, these clauses are contained in Article 11(1)[192] of the new Directive, which reprises, almost word for word, Article 1C of the Refugee Convention. In general, they are applied according to the practice relating to Article 1C, and similarly the European rule is applied just as infrequently. Sweden's Migrationsöverdomstolens has confirmed the recommendations of UNHCR regarding applications for a passport from the country of origin: in the case of an Iraqi national who asserted that he had applied to his country for a passport in order to travel briefly to Iran to get married because the papers provided by Sweden were insufficient to obtain a visa, the court referred exclusively to the *Handbook on Procedures*,[193] merely noting that 'under vissa

---

192 'A third-country national or a stateless person shall cease to be a refugee if he or she: (a) has voluntarily re-availed himself or herself of the protection of the country of nationality; or (b) having lost his or her nationality, has voluntarily re-acquired it; or (c) has acquired a new nationality, and enjoys the protection of the country of his or her new nationality; or (d) has voluntarily re-established himself or herself in the country which he or she left or outside which he or she remained owing to fear of persecution; or (e) can no longer, because the circumstances in connection with which he or she has been recognised as a refugee have ceased to exist, continue to refuse to avail himself or herself of the protection of the country of nationality; or (f) being a stateless person, he or she is able, because the circumstances in connection with which he or she has been recognised as a refugee have ceased to exist, to return to the country of former habitual residence'. Article 11(1) of the old Qualification Directive contained the same provision. However, Directive 2011/95/EU added a point (3), according to which 'points (e) and (f) of paragraph 1 shall not apply to a refugee who is able to invoke compelling reasons arising out of previous persecution for refusing to avail himself or herself of the protection of the country of nationality or, being a stateless person, of the country of former habitual residence'. The purpose of the exception was to implement (with some delay) the exceptions provided in Article 1C(5) and (6) regarding history or statutory refugees (on which see footnote 137, Chapter 1). The rule was included to prevent the return to Germany of Jews who had been sent to the concentration camps because although the threat no longer existed it was decided to impede their return to places that evoked such profound and dramatic memories: see S. Kneebone and M. O'Sullivan (2011: 530 ff.). In reality, the inclusion of this provision goes far beyond the scope of the Refugee Convention, as it is not limited to the refugees in question but extends to all refugees. I believe it would impose an excessive protection duty on States, even though a similar provision has been added regarding the clauses on the cessation of subsidiary protection. It would probably have been more than sufficient to confine the extension to statutory refugees, thus correctly implementing the Refugee Convention, and to allow States the option (not impose on them the obligation) to grant an extension of refugee status on humanitarian grounds, as already implied by Recital No. 15 of the new Qualification Directive.

193 UNHCR (1992a).

exceptionella omständigheter behöver det förhållandet att en flykting erhållit ett hemlandspass inte innebära att han upphör att vara flykting'.[194]

The United Kingdom High Court has taken a very questionable position regarding the cessation of refugee status following the acquisition of a new nationality (point c). In deciding whether a refugee who had obtained British citizenship was subject to the rules on family reunification for refugees or to the less favourable rules for family members of British citizens, the Court produced a very contorted interpretation of the internal rule implementing the Directive. As the rule defines the person being joined as the person who 'has been granted asylum', the Court decided that it could not be interpreted as referring to the person who 'has been granted asylum and *remains a refugee*',[195] opting instead to apply the (more favourable) rules for refugees' family members. Although concerned that the family members might also be at risk of persecution, the Court misinterpreted the content of the cessation clauses; the correct route, given the Court's concerns, would have been to assess whether the family members were themselves refugees and therefore eligible for protection in their own right.

There is more case law concerning cessation clauses relating to the objective disappearance of risk in the country of origin; they are set out in Article 11(1)(e) and (f). Regarding (only) these clauses, Article 11(2) requires an assessment of the nature of the change of circumstances, which must be 'significant and non-temporary' and sufficient to end a well-founded fear of persecution.[196] The provision echoes UNHCR's statement concerning the corresponding rules of the Refugee Convention.[197] The ECJ was called upon to issue a preliminary ruling on the matter following a referral by the German Bundesverwaltungsgericht, which required some clarification about the link between Article 11(1)(e) and, respectively, Article 2(c) of Directive 2004/83/EC (now Article 2(d) of Directive 2011/95/EU) defining the term refugee and Article 15 defining serious harm for the purpose of granting subsidiary protection. The ECJ confirmed that the cessation clauses at points (e) and (f) were symmetrical to the 'inclusion' clauses, as

> the circumstances which demonstrate the country of origin's inability or, conversely, its ability to ensure protection against acts of persecution constitute a crucial element in the assessment which leads to the granting of, or, as the

---

194 Decision of 13 June 2011, UM 5495-10: 'only in exceptional circumstance can the fact that a refugee has obtained a national passport not constitute cause for cessation of status' (trans. added). On this point see above, § 1.2, especially footnote 125, Chapter 1.

195 Decision of 12 May 2010, *ZN and Others* v. *Entry Clearance Officer (Karachi) and one other action*, para. 27.

196 As these cessation clauses are usually linked to radical changes of circumstances in the State of origin, such as the end of a conflict, it is a little 'disconcerting', in the words of G. Gilbert (2004: 977), that the Directive does not envisage a role of UNHCR.

197 Contained in Article 1C(5) and (6): see UNHCR (1997b: para. 19).

case may be, by means of the opposite conclusion, to the cessation of refugee status.[198]

The Court thus used Article 7(2) of the old Qualification Directive to re-state the criteria for assessing whether the need for protection has ceased, also pinpointing, as mentioned earlier,[199] the elements on which the authorities should focus. Finally, the Court noted that, while unlikely, it is possible for a person who has lived for many years as a refugee outside his or her country of origin, and whose *original* reasons for being granted refugee status no longer exist, to keep that status because other reasons have emerged; the new reasons must be assessed as for a 'first' application.[200] Given the different systems of international protection, it is possible that after cessation of refugee status an applicant may be entitled to subsidiary protection (pursuant to Article 15, which the Court considered for this purpose), although this protection is due to the fact that the conditions for applying the Refugee Convention do not exist (any longer).

The clauses on exclusion from refugee status are contained in Article 12, reprising Article 1D–F of the Refugee Convention. Leaving aside situations of minor importance, one of which has already been the subject of two rulings by the ECJ,[201] Article 1F is transposed into EU law by Article 12(2), which reproduces its content with some slight variations. All the exclusion clauses begin with a common element: 'serious reasons for considering'. This is supplemented by the provisions of Article 12(3), which states that the exclusion clauses apply not only to those who have committed or become guilty of the acts listed at point (2), but also to persons 'who incite or otherwise participate in the commission of the crimes or acts mentioned therein'. The clarification was added in order to underline that the person concerned need not necessarily be the actual author of the crime but may take part in other ways, particularly in the case of criminal enterprises such as terrorism.

The ECJ has ruled on this very point, having been asked whether the presence of a given organisation in the list of terrorist organisations drawn up by the EU institutions entailed the exclusion from refugee status of any person that had been a member.[202] The Court reaffirmed the earlier conclusion concerning Article 1F of the Refugee Convention: exclusion must always follow an individual assessment,

---

198 *Abdulla*, para. 68. For examples of the consequences of this decision for the internal courts, see the Federal Administrative Court of Germany, decision of 24 February 2011, 10 C 3.10, and decision of 1 June 2011, 10 C 10.10.

199 See above, footnote 93.

200 *Abdulla*, para. 86 ff.

201 *Bolbol*. On the decision and the situations envisaged in Article 12(1), see M. Guidi (2010: 155 ff.) and K. Hailbronner and S. Alt (2010: 1109 ff.). The other judgment is that of 19 December 2012, Case C-364/11, *Mostafa Abed El Karem El Kott, Chadi Amin A Radi, Hazem Kamel Ismail* v. *Bevándorlási és Állampolgársági Hivatal*, not yet published.

202 See Council Common Position 2001/931/CFSP of 27 December 2001 on the application of specific measures to combat terrorism, OJ L 344, 28 December 2001, p. 93 ff.

designed to reveal *personal* responsibility for the crimes through objective and subjective criteria applicable to an individual, such as

> the true role played by the person concerned in the perpetration of the acts in question; his position within the organisation; the extent of the knowledge he had, or was deemed to have, of its activities; any pressure to which he was exposed; or other factors likely to have influenced his conduct.[203]

Internal case law also seems to take a somewhat rigid position, although this is because of the need to interpret the exclusion clauses narrowly. Thus, the French Conseil d'Etat did not find that there existed 'serious reasons for considering' that a person who 'avait pris la fuite en remettant aux autorités locales les clés des bâtiments où se trouvaient les réfugiés, les livrant ainsi à leurs assassins' and

> n'avait pas entrepris toutes les diligences nécessaires pour tenter d'assurer la sécurité des réfugiés et qu'il ne pouvait ignorer ni l'appartenance des autorités locales à un mouvement politique dont la responsabilité dans le génocide serait ultérieurement établie, ni le fait que la présence de miliciens vouait à une mort certaine les réfugiés qu'il avait accueillis,[204]

had committed acts of genocide, thereby excluding the application of Article 12(2). As pointed out in connection with Article 1F of the Refugee Convention, full proof is not required. Spain's Audiencia nacional, dealing similarly with a person belonging to one of the EU listed terrorist organisations,[205] after noting the evidence of his direct participation in acts covered by Article 12(2) of the old Qualification Directive, deemed that evidence sufficient insofar as

> Y el precepto de la Convención de Ginebra no demanda, para la aplicación de esta causa de exclusión, pruebas cumplidas, ni tampoco exige previas condenas firmes de los Tribunales de Justicia, sino que establece como bastante la existencia de 'motivos fundados', esto es, indicios.[206]

In its decision in the case of *B and D*, the ECJ also clarified an extremely controversial aspect of the application of exclusion clauses. Contrary to the advice

---

203 *B and D*, para. 97. The Court followed the advice of Advocate General Mengozzi, contained in his opinion of 1 June 2010, para. 72 ff. The Conseil du Contentieux des Etrangers of Belgium followed the ECJ's approach faithfully in a decision of 13 January 2011, No. 54.335.

204 Decision of 26 January 2011, No. 312833.

205 See the Council Common Position 2009/468/CFSP of 15 June 2009 updating Common Position 2001/931/CFSP on the application of specific measures to combat terrorism and repealing Common Position 2009/67/CFSP, OJ L 151, 16 June 2009, p. 45 ff.

206 Decision of 17 January 2011, 680/2009.

of Advocate General Mengozzi,[207] the Court asserted that assessment of the clauses did not involve a proportionality test and therefore the national authorities were not required to balance the seriousness of the acts committed (*recte*: there were 'serious reasons' for considering had been committed) against the nature of the risk faced by the applicant in the country of destination. The Court's position would appear to confirm the earlier contention, that 'the circumstances surrounding those acts and the situation of that person' are already examined by the competent authority 'in its assessment of the seriousness of the acts committed by the person concerned and of that person's individual responsibility',[208] and therefore the authority has no need to make a second assessment, as would happen instead in the event of a proportionality test. However, the ECJ does not rule out the possibility that a particularly serious threat (for example, the death penalty or torture) might prevent the removal of an applicant 'undeserving' of refugee status.[209] This hints at the situations covered by Articles 2 and 3 ECHR, although because the (subsidiary) protection on which they are based may be subject to the same exclusion from refugee status, the only relevant element, according to the words of the ECJ ('whether that person can be deported'), is the prohibition on *refoulement* contained in Article 21(1) of the Directive.

Article 12(2) clarifies some aspects of the rules of the Refugee Convention in order to regulate several principles that have become established practice in applying the Convention. Point (b), in particular, states that the applicant must have committed a serious common law crime 'prior to his or her admission as a refugee, which means the time of issuing a residence permit based on the granting of refugee status'.[210] Moreover, such crime must involve 'particularly cruel actions, even if committed with an allegedly political objective, which may be classified as serious non-political crimes'. The rule not only increases the period of time in which the serious crime may have been committed, which does not end when the applicant enters the country but extends to the period of assessment or rather of issue of the residence permit. According to some scholarly writers,[211] the rule thus disregards the fact that recognition is a declaratory act. I believe that, generally speaking, the Refugee Convention does not prevent emphasis being placed on

---

207 Opinion in *B and D*, para. 89 ff.

208 *B and D*, para. 109.

209 Ibid., para. 110 ('It is important to note that the exclusion of a person from refugee status pursuant to Article 12(2) of Directive 2004/83 does not imply the adoption of a position on the separate question of whether that person can be deported to his country of origin').

210 According to the French Conseil d'Etat, if the applicant has been found guilty but has completed the whole of his or her sentence then Article 12(2)(b) cannot apply and instead there may be grounds for applying Article 14(4)–(5) (which in the new Qualification Directive identify the exceptions to the prohibition on *refoulement* per Article 33(2) of the Refugee Convention as causes for cessation or exclusion of refugee status): see the decision of 4 May 2011, No. 320910.

211 G. Gilbert (2004: 977) and K. Hailbronner and S. Alt (2010: 1116 f.).

recognition,[212] but rather the problem of the rule's compatibility with the letter of point (F), which refers to 'admission to that country as a refugee'. As the same writers have acknowledged, the problem is overcome by the fact that any crimes committed after the applicant's entry into the country do not take place 'outside the country of refuge', which is also a necessary condition for point (b) to apply.

The clarification regarding serious common law crimes is certainly more significant. The Directive aims to follow the recommendations of UNHCR, that because a crime has a political objective it is not disregarded if disproportionate means are used to achieve it. This was the ECJ's position in the case of *B and D* regarding acts of terrorism which, because 'characterised by their violence towards civilian populations, even if committed with a purportedly political objective, fall to be regarded as serious non-political crimes'.[213] There remains the problem of defining such crimes, which neither the ECJ nor the Advocate General solve for the very good reason, according to the latter, that 'the national court alone is aware of all the circumstances of the particular cases before it' and the 'Directive . . . does not introduce a uniform body of rules to govern that area'.[214]

A further clarification in this regard concerns point (c), which mentions acts contrary to the purposes and principles of the UN 'as set out in the Preamble and Articles 1 and 2 of the Charter of the United Nations'. It should be read in conjunction with Recital No. 31, which identifies these purposes and principles with reference to the UN resolutions concerning measures to combat terrorism. The link between the two is not immune to interference from the national authorities, however, as Advocate General Mengozzi remarked in the case of *B and D*:

> It must be pointed out, on the one hand, that the Security Council resolutions are not always binding in their entirety and that the Security Council itself is, in any event, required to act in conformity with the UN Charter and its principles and purposes.[215]

The Court, instead, tended to infer automatically that an organisation was a terrorist organisation, and that any acts attributable to it were contrary to the purposes and principles of the UN, from the mere fact of its inclusion in the resolutions of the Security Council or in EU acts implementing them. However, as mentioned, it left the question of the exclusion of individual persons from refugee status as members of such organisations to a case-by-case assessment.

---

212 The nature of recognition of status as a declaration does not prevent the rules of the Refugee Convention being applied selectively. As we have seen, some apply only to people who have a stronger link with the host State, which probably only happens after status has been recognised.
213 *B and D*, para. 81. See also the opinion in *B and D*, para. 69.
214 Ibid., para. 81 f.
215 Ibid., para. 63.

Although the ECJ's position is not absolutely unequivocal,[216] I believe that the acts of the UN, like those of the EU, should not decisively attribute certain crimes to a person belonging to one of the listed organisations (as indeed the Court maintains), but nor should they categorically identify such organisations as terrorist. Trusting unconditionally in the assessments of UN and EU bodies creates a twofold risk. To begin, it should not be forgotten that these lists also contain the names and surnames of individuals in respect of whom, according to the Court, the lists should be deemed to have the same value as evidence, thus automatically excluding them from refugee status without any verification of the motive for their inclusion – about which there may be considerable doubt, as is apparent from some well-known cases brought before the ECJ.[217] Second, this irrefutable assumption prevents the national authorities from independently assessing whether an organisation is of a terrorist nature whereas, merely looking at the organisations cited in the Annex to the Council Common Position 2001/931/CFSP,[218] such an assessment might reveal that many are in fact movements in favour of self-determination. This would not prevent the acts ascribable to them being defined terrorist, nor would it stop a person who had taken part being excluded from refugee status, but it would shift the problem into the sphere of *ius in bello*, which is the basis, in my opinion, on which the nature (terrorist or otherwise) of such acts should be assessed.

The clauses on cessation and exclusion of refugee status are completed by Article 14(3)–(5), containing some major differences with respect to the Refugee Convention. There is little to be said about point (3)(a), which simply clarifies that once refugee status has been recognised it must be revoked if the Member State establishes that 'he or she should have been or is excluded from being a refugee in accordance with Article 12'. As mentioned earlier, it is a practice relating to the Convention that exclusion clauses can constitute a motive for revoking or not renewing refugee status and therefore Article 14(3) does not add anything new. I would just underline the use of the present tense ('is excluded'), suggesting once again that the acts in Article 12(2) can be performed even after the applicant's admission to the host country, with the exception of those expressly excluded at point (b).[219] Article 14(3)(b) lays down the reverse procedure, specifying that if the refugee committed fraud at the time of his or her application that status may end

---

216 According to the ECJ, 'the inclusion of an organisation on a list such as that which forms the Annex to Common Position 2001/931 makes it possible to establish the terrorist nature of the group of which the person concerned was a member, which is a factor which the competent authority must take into account when determining, initially, whether that group has committed acts falling within the scope of Article 12(2)(b) or (c)' (*B and D*, para. 90).
217 The reference is to the well-known matter of *Kadi*.
218 They include Hamas (the majority party in the Palestinian Territories) and the Kurdistan Workers' Party (PKK).
219 See also UNHCR (2005: 29).

if the misrepresentation or omission 'was decisive for the granting of refugee status'.[220]

A significant difference is found in Article 14(4), which combines the cessation clauses with the exceptions to the principle of *non-refoulement* laid down in Article 33(2) of the Refugee Convention.[221] The following paragraph (5) states further that where one of the situations described in paragraph (4) exists, refugee status may be excluded *ab initio*. As a consequence of this, the fact that a person constitutes a danger to the security of the State or its community will prevent him or her gaining refugee status, effectively acting as an exclusion clause, or will entail cessation of refugee status, thus taking the Directive well beyond the limits of the Refugee Convention. This approach has been strongly criticised and calls for several comments.[222] To begin, it has already been noted that the situations described in Article 33(2) of the Refugee Convention exclude 'only' the application of the principle of *non-refoulement*, leaving unaltered the status of refugee; in fact, they assume the existence of refugee status as without it I do not think that Article 33(2) could apply. The rationale for this provision is very different from that of the cessation and exclusion clauses, and therefore the procedure designed to assess its application should remain separate from the one relating to Articles 11 and 12(2) of the Directive.

That said, in the practical implementation of the Refugee Convention the inclusion procedure 'attracts' the assessment procedure for exclusion clauses and exceptions to the principle of *non-refoulement* and therefore the new Qualification Directive differs little in its approach from this general trend. The inclusion procedure's power to attract is evidence of the key importance of *non-refoulement*, which States regard as underpinning refugee status, as the whole system of the Refugee Convention demonstrates. Although in theory recognition of refugee status and *non-refoulement* remain separate, in practice exceptions to *non-refoulement* demolish the whole edifice of the Convention *because* the whole of the Convention

---

220 According to the High Court of Ireland, to assess whether the misrepresentation of facts was decisive the question to ask is 'whether the application for protection would have been determined differently had the information in question not been concealed' (decision of 1 December 2010, *G. v. Minister of Justice and Law Reform*, available online at www.refworld.org, para. 25).

221 As K. Hailbronner and S. Alt (2010: 1133 f.) point out, Article 14(4) is based on Article 33(2) of the Refugee Convention but does not reprise it word for word. It states that 'Member States may revoke, end or refuse to renew the status granted to a refugee by a governmental, administrative, judicial or quasi-judicial body, when: (a) there are reasonable grounds for regarding him or her as a danger to the security of the Member State in which he or she is present; (b) he or she, having been convicted by a final judgment of a particularly serious crime, constitutes a danger to the community of that Member State'. Anyway, according to the Court of Appeal (civil division) of England and Wales, Article 14(4) should be interpreted in the light of Article 33(2) of the Refugee Convention: see the decision of 26 September 2009, *EN v. Secretary of State for the Home Department*.

222 UNHCR (2005: para. 30).

is embodied in the prohibition. This is clearly explained by the UK Special Immigration Appeal Commission, according to which

> There can be little doubt that a person who fosters or supports terrorism is a danger to the security of the country in which he is. There can also be little doubt that fostering or supporting international terrorism are acts contrary to the purposes and principles of the United Nations. . . . If therefore there are serious reasons or reasonable grounds for considering that a person has taken part in fostering or supporting international terrorism, therefore, it may not matter very much whether his case is considered under Article 1(F) or 33: the outcome is that he is not entitled to protection from refoulement.[223]

The mistaken, but now well-established, practice of pooling together cessation and exclusion clauses and exceptions to the principle of *non-refoulement* is mitigated by its non-compulsory nature. Paragraphs (4) and (5) both allow States to equate such exceptions with the reasons for cessation and for exclusion, respectively, which they in fact do.[224]

Article 16(1) of the Directive concerns the cessation of subsidiary protection. This happens when 'the circumstances which led to the granting of subsidiary protection status have ceased to exist or have changed to such a degree that protection is no longer required'. The wording differs from that of Article 11 in more than one respect. Article 16 appears to consider only the situation in which the risk of harm no longer exists as a result of a change of circumstances in the country of origin (Article 11(1)(e) and (f)) omitting all those (points (a)–(d) of the same article) with which the link affording the applicant the protection of a third country (not necessarily the country of origin) is (re-)established. The provision is expressed in very broad terms, referring to the 'circumstances which led' to the recognition of refugee status. Some scholarly writers affirm,[225] correctly I believe, that these circumstances may well include the various situations in which protection is not provided and is then later obtained by acquiring a new nationality or re-acquiring a nationality previously lost, and so on.

Also unclear is the link between the change in circumstances and the fact that protection is no longer needed, as Article 16(1) uses a different wording, at least compared with points (e) and (f) above. Once again, the elements linking the risk – whether of persecution or of serious harm – to one person should be assessed objectively, although this does not rule out also an assessment less of the

---

223 Decision of 29 October 2003, *C. v. Secretary of State for the Home Department*, available online at www.refworld.org, para. 31. See also the Verwaltungsgerichtshof of Hesse, decision of 15 September 2010, 5 A 1985/08A.

224 See the Report from the Commission to the European Parliament and the Council on the application of Directive 2004/83/EC, 16 June 2010, p. 10.

225 K. Hailbronner and S. Alt (2010: 1154), regarding the identical rule contained in Directive 2004/83/EC.

person's character than of his or her personal circumstances. The clauses governing the cessation of subsidiary protection offer a further element in support of this: Article 16(2), informing States of the types of changes in circumstances that may eliminate the need for protection, uses exactly the same wording as Article 11(2) regarding the cessation of refugee status.[226]

Exclusion clauses also exist for subsidiary protection and are found in Article 17 of the Directive. This may seem strange insofar as the purpose of subsidiary protection is generally to give a status to the persons protected (indirectly) by the provisions of the ECHR, almost all of which admit no exception. In reality, there are some differences between Article 15 of the Qualification Directive and the ECtHR case law on protection *par ricochet*. There are cases in which the first protection is broader than the second (consider point (c) on cases of indiscriminate violence, which for the time being does not appear to have a sound basis in ECtHR case law) and other cases in which the opposite is true (for instance, indirect protection per Articles 5 and 6 ECHR). For the former, it is absolutely lawful for the EU to introduce exclusion clauses as this does not conflict with the ECHR. For the latter, the problem is rather one of violating the ECHR by a minor extension of the reasons for 'inclusion'; once this is solved, the existence of the Article 17 exclusion clauses would not conflict with the ECtHR's interpretation of Articles 5 and 6 as they allow derogation.

In the areas where the two systems overlap (those covered by Articles 2 and 3 ECHR) a substantial difference remains as the Directive introduces exclusion clauses for prohibitions that the ECtHR deems to be absolute. This anomaly is overcome by Article 21(1) of the Directive requiring States to respect the principle of *non-refoulement*. Significantly, there are also exceptions to this, but they only apply to refugees.[227] Thus, people who are excluded from subsidiary protection for the reasons listed in Article 17 could (or rather, do) fall within the scope of Article 21(1). The Czech Republic's Nejvyšší správní soud held that removing an applicant who had been refused refugee status because of insufficient proof regarding his political opinions and who had been excluded from subsidiary protection because there were sufficient reasons for believing he had committed acts contrary to the UN Charter (spying in the Communist Czech Republic on behalf of Cuba) might be prohibited under Article 3 ECHR.[228] Similarly, the Swedish Migrationsöverdomstolens granted a residence permit of one year to a former officer in the Iraqi security forces under Saddam Hussein, who had been

---

226 See also K. Hailbronner and S. Alt (2010: 1154).

227 The exceptions are among those listed in Article 14(4) and (5), which in turn reprise those of Article 33(2) of the Refugee Convention. Given what has been said in respect of Article 14, I believe that the best place to insert exceptions to the prohibition on *refoulement* is Article 21(2). The result is that the exceptions can operate on more levels: as cessation clauses (Article 14(4)) or as exclusion clauses (Article 14(5)) of refugee status, or as reasons permitting *refoulement* (Article 21(2), in line with the Refugee Convention).

228 Decision of 23 March 2011, 6 Azs 40/2010-70.

excluded from international protection on suspicion of having committed crimes against humanity and benefited from the prohibition on *refoulement*.[229]

The content of the clauses excluding from subsidiary protection is not identical to the provisions of Article 12 regarding refugee status. Leaving aside situations of minor importance (dealt with in Article 1D–E of the Refugee Convention), some major differences are apparent. Parallel to those of Article 12(2)(a) and (c) are the situations listed in Article 17(1)(a) and (c): for subsidiary protection, too, exclusion comes about as a result of 'serious reasons'[230] for believing the applicant has committed a crime against peace, a war crime, or an act contrary to the purposes and principles of the UN. Article 17(1)(b) instead contains no reference to the time or place when the serious crime was committed, and it does not require the crime to be non-political. Consequently, the commission of any crime, if serious, regardless of where it was committed and whether before or after recognition of subsidiary protection status, is sufficient to trigger exclusion.[231] Furthermore, point (d) adds the condition of serious reasons for considering that the person 'constitutes a danger to the community or to the security of the Member State in which he or she is present'. Although the rule is apparently based on Article 33(2) of the Refugee Convention,[232] it in fact employs a different standard: the danger to the community must be the result of having been found guilty of a particularly serious crime, a condition that does not appear in Article 17(1)(d).

Finally, Article 17(3) allows Member States an option to exclude a person if, before being admitted to the State,[233] he or she had committed 'one or more crimes outside the scope of paragraph 1 which would be punishable by imprisonment, had they been committed in the Member State concerned', assuming that the person 'left his or her country of origin solely in order to avoid sanctions resulting from those crimes'. This rule was included to cover minor crimes and therefore requires higher standards: there is no mention of 'serious reasons' but of having committed a crime, which means there must be sufficient proof for criminal sanctions to be imposed. I also believe that this reason for exclusion can only be applied when the person fled for no reason other than to attempt to avoid criminal sanctions. If other motives also played a role, particularly

229 Decision of 9 September 2011, UM 3891-10.
230 For subsidiary protection, Article 17(2) extends the application of the exclusion clauses 'to persons who incite or otherwise participate in the commission of the crimes or acts' mentioned in paragraph (1) of the same Article.
231 See the Supreme Administrative Court of Finland, decision of 18 February 2014, KHO:2014: 35.
232 K. Hailbronner and S. Alt (2010: 1159).
233 Note that the article does not use the wording, appearing for instance in Article 12(2) (b) regarding exclusion from refugee status, 'prior to his or her admission *as a refugee* which means the time of issuing a residence permit based on the granting of refugee status', but only states 'prior to his or her admission to the Member State'. I believe this means the time of admission, not that of issue of a residence permit (as in the case of Article 12).

if related to the reasons for granting international protection, then Article 17(3) cannot apply.

As far as subsidiary protection is concerned, the Directive supplements the cessation and exclusion clauses with some provisions specifying the time when the assessment must (or can) take place. The differences with respect to the rules governing the equivalent protection applying to refugees are not many, but they are bizarre. The rule on obtaining protection through misrepresentation of facts is the same, as Article 19(3)(b) obligates States to revoke the protection if that misrepresentation constituted a 'decisive' factor. It mirrors the rule contained in Article 14(3)(b) allowing refugee status to end for additional reasons to those of Article 11 (Article 16 in the case of subsidiary protection). On the other hand, the rule postponing the reasons for exclusion to a time after the 'inclusion' procedure is not the same: Article 19(3)(a) refers to Article 17(1) and (2) imposing on States the *obligation* to revoke protection if, 'after having been granted subsidiary protection status', they discover that the person should have been excluded for one of the reasons contemplated. As we have seen, however, Article 17(1) contains two further reasons with respect to the equivalent provision concerning refugees (Article 12(2)), that is, those based on Article 33(2) of the Refugee Convention. In other words, while in the case of refugee status it is optional to equate the exceptions to the principle of *non-refoulement* set out in the Refugee Convention with the exclusion clauses, in the case of subsidiary protection it is obligatory (and not only: the standard is also less as Article 17(1)(d) does not require the person to have been found guilty of a particularly serious crime). This is highly contradictory, given that the exclusion clauses should not exist in this situation. Article 19(2) also provides for optional revocation of protection, but in a very different situation from that applying to refugees: its content is the same as that of Article 17(3), to which it makes reference, so that a person who committed a crime punishable by imprisonment before admission to the State – still on condition that he or she only left the country of origin to avoid sanctions – may be a reason to revoke protection even 'after having been granted subsidiary protection status'.

4.7 Preliminary remarks on the scope of the Procedures Directive *rationae materiae*

Articles 20 ff. of the new Qualification Directive contains rules on the content of international protection. These rules apply differently according to their beneficiaries and should be supplemented in the light of other secondary legislation detailing their content and adding further guarantees. The general framework is fairly complex but can be summarised as follows: by far the most important protection is that based on the principle of *non-refoulement*, described in the Procedures Directive,[234] although this should be interpreted also in the light of the rules on the

---

234 Like the old Qualification Directive, the Procedures Directive is subject to the same differentiated system of application in the Member States: Ireland and the UK decided

entry of third-country nationals (contained in the Schengen Borders Code[235]) and on repatriation (covered by Directive 2008/115/EU[236]). The remaining protection is covered not only by the Qualification Directive, but also by the rules on family reunification (Directive 2003/86/EC[237]), by Directive 2003/9/EC

to participate (see Recitals Nos 32 and 33), while the Directive does not apply to Denmark (Recital No. 34) and the States not belonging to the Schengen system are also excluded (Iceland, Liechtenstein, Norway and Switzerland). As pointed out earlier (see footnote 162, Chapter 3), the Directive will be replaced by the new Procedures Directive (Directive 2013/32/EU of the European Parliament and the Council of 26 June 2013 on common procedures for granting and withdrawing international protection, OJ L 180, 29 June 2013, p. 60 ff.), the deadline for its reception having been set at 20 July 2015, save for a few exceptions. Ireland and the UK have decided not to participate in the new Procedures Directive, in the same way as for the new Qualification Directive (see footnote 55): on this point see J. N. Stefanelli (2011: 1055 ff.).

235 Regulation (EC) No. 562/2006 of the European Parliament and of the Council of 15 March 2006 establishing a Community Code on the rules governing the movement of persons across borders (Schengen Borders Code), OJ L 105, 13 April 2006, p. 1 ff. For the first comments see S. Castellazzi (2006: 551 ff.) and G. Licastro (2006: 587 ff.). The Regulation was subsequently recast: see Regulation (EC) No. 296/2008 of the European Parliament and of the Council of 11 March 2008 amending Regulation (EC) No. 562/2006 establishing a Community Code on the rules governing the movement of persons across borders (Schengen Borders Code), as regards the implementing powers conferred on the Commission, OJ L 97, 9 April 2008, p. 60 f.; Regulation (EC) No. 81/2009 of the European Parliament and of the Council of 14 January 2009 amending Regulation (EC) No. 562/2006 as regards the use of the Visa Information System (VIS) under the Schengen Borders Code, OJ L 35, 4 February 2009, p. 56 ff.; Regulation (EU) No. 265/2010 of the European Parliament and of the Council of 25 March 2010 amending the Convention implementing the Schengen Agreement and Regulation (EC) No. 562/2006 as regards movements of persons with a long-stay visa, OJ L 85, 31 March 2010, p. 1 ff.; Regulation (EU) No. 610/2013 of the European Parliament and of the Council of 26 June 2013 amending Regulation (EC) No. 562/2006 establishing a Community Code on the rules governing the movement of persons across borders (Schengen Borders Code), the Convention implementing the Schengen Agreement, Regulations (EC) No. 1683/95 and (EC) No. 539/2001 of the Council and Regulations (EC) No. 767/2008 and (EC) No. 810/2009 of the European Parliament and of the Council, OJ L 182, 29 June 2013, p. 1 ff. The differentiated application of the Borders Code, which constitutes a development of the Schengen *acquis*, is very different from the system in force for acts relating to asylum: Ireland and the UK decided not to participate, coherently with their exclusion from the system to dismantle internal border controls, as did Denmark. Instead, associated members Iceland, Liechtenstein, Norway and Switzerland take part in the Code. Note that new Member States apply the Schengen rules gradually: for Bulgaria and Romania, see F. Cherubini (2010b: 111 ff.).

236 Directive 2008/115/EC of the European Parliament and of the Council of 16 December 2008 on common standards and procedures in Member States for returning illegally-staying third-country nationals, OJ L 348, 24 December 2008, p. 98 ff. The differentiated system is the same as that of Regulation (EC) No. 562/2006 (see footnote 235).

237 Directive 2003/86/EC of the Council of 22 September 2003 on the right to family reunification, OJ L 251, 3 October 2003, p. 12 ff. This is not a development of the

(the Reception Directive)[238] and by Directive 2003/109/EC[239] as amended by Directive 2011/51/EU[240] extending its scope to beneficiaries of international protection.

The overall purpose of the Procedures Directive is to implement the substance of the prohibition on *refoulement*, being the right to a proper assessment of an application for asylum in the course of which the intention of the *non-refoulement* principle must be guaranteed by allowing the applicant to remain (temporarily) in the host State. Thus, the prohibition applies to anyone wanting to submit an application for international protection.[241] However, some clarifications are necessary. To begin, Article 20(6) and (7) of the old Qualification Directive allowed States to reduce the benefits due to refugees and to beneficiaries of subsidiary protection where one or the other status 'has been obtained on the basis of activities engaged in for the sole or main purpose of creating the necessary conditions for being recognised'. I do not believe this option was available in respect of *non-refoulement*, as the references in the paragraphs to 'limits set out by the Geneva Convention' and to limits 'set out by international obligations of Member States' indicate. And in fact, in view of the ambiguous nature of the option, including in the light of the

Schengen *acquis* and therefore differentiated application only concerns Denmark, Ireland and the UK, none of which participate, the last two not having exercised their right to opt in.

238 Directive 2003/9/EC of the Council of 27 January 2003 laying down minimum standards for the reception of asylum-seekers in Member States, OJ L 31, 6 February 2003, p. 18 ff. The UK opted in but not Ireland (which did not exercise that right) or Denmark. Note that this Directive will be replaced by a new one (Directive 2013/33/EU of the European Parliament and of the Council of 26 June 2013 laying down standards for the reception of applicants for international protection, OJ L 180, 29 June 2013, p. 96 ff., on which see footnote 163, Chapter 3). Ireland and the UK decided not to opt in to this Directive: see also footnote 234.

239 Directive 2003/109/EC of the Council of 25 November 2003 concerning the status of third-country nationals who are long-term residents, OJ L 16, 23 January 2004, p. 44 ff. Ireland and the UK did not opt in, nor does the Directive apply to Denmark.

240 Directive 2011/51/EU of the European Parliament and of the Council of 11 May 2011 amending Directive 2003/109/EC of the Council to extend its scope to beneficiaries of international protection, OJ L 132, 19 May 2011, p. 1 ff.

241 At first sight, the Procedures Directive would seem to apply only to refugee status and not to subsidiary protection as well. Article 2, setting out the definitions needed to apply the Directive, contains no mention of it. However, according to Article 3(3), 'Where Member States employ or introduce a procedure in which asylum applications are examined both as applications on the basis of the Geneva Convention and as applications for other kinds of international protection given under the circumstances defined by Article 15 of Directive 2004/83/EC, they shall apply this Directive throughout their procedure'. The new Procedures Directive appropriately extends its scope specifically to all applications for international protection: 'This Directive shall apply to all applications for international protection made in the territory, including at the border, in the territorial waters or in the transit zones of the Member States, and to the withdrawal of international protection' (Article 3(1)).

non-discrimination rule,[242] the new Qualification Directive rightly eliminated paragraphs (6) and (7).

A second, more important issue is to identify which persons are protected by the prohibition on *refoulement*. Given that the beneficiaries must have made an application for protection, the question is whether that protection should extend to all non-nationals entitled to enter or remain in a Member State, assuming that they are within its jurisdiction. In other words, while an application for asylum opens the door to the procedure set out in Directive 2005/85/EC by virtue of the principle of *non-refoulement*, the question is whether the same or a similar procedure should apply where no application has been made. I believe the answer should be yes,[243] for a number of reasons. To begin, compliance with the prohibition on *refoulement* does not appear to depend on the presentation of an asylum application because it obliges States to gather all the information required to evaluate the potential risks in the country of destination with a view to removal there. In no part of the Refugee Convention or in any of the ECtHR case law is an exception to the prohibition granted on the basis of the potential beneficiaries' failure to apply. On the contrary, in the case of *Hirsi Jamaa* the ECtHR clearly held that the existence of an application was not relevant for the purpose of compliance with the prohibition on *refoulement*:

> Having regard to the circumstances of the case, the fact that the parties concerned had failed to expressly request asylum did not exempt Italy from fulfilling its obligations under Article 3.[244]

That said, EU legislation does not appear to uphold entirely the requirement to comply with the principle of *non-refoulement* regardless of the context in which the risk is assessed, whether by the procedure set out in Directive 2005/85/EC or by the procedure to evaluate the conditions for returning 'unlawfully-staying' third-country nationals. Certainly, EU legislation is designed to minimise the chance of a potential beneficiary of international protection being 'missed' by the system set up under the Procedures Directive. According to the Commission, an asylum application does not have to comply with specific formal requirements, it being sufficient for the person concerned to display fear.[245] Moreover, the Member States

---

242 On this point see G. Morgese (2012a: 269).
243 As does T. Spijkerboer (2010: 1267).
244 ECtHR, judgment of 23 February 2012, Application No. 27765/09, *Hirsi Jamaa et al. v. Italy*, available online at www.echr.coe.int, para. 133.
245 See the Commission Recommendation establishing a 'Practical Handbook for Border Guards (Schengen Handbook)' to be used by Member States' competent authorities when carrying out the border control of persons, 6 November 2006, C (2006) 5186 final, especially para. 10.1: 'The wish to apply for protection does not need to be expressed in any particular form. The word "asylum" does not need to be used expressly; the defining element is the expression of fear of what might happen upon return. In case of doubt on whether a certain declaration can be construed as a wish to apply for asylum or for another form of international protection, the border

have a disclosure obligation regarding the procedures to follow when making an asylum application.[246] However, in the general context of return procedures, even where no signs of fear have been shown by the person concerned, whom the authorities are obliged to inform of his or her right to make an application, States are not exempted from the obligation to respect the principle of *non-refoulement*. European Union legislation is not entirely satisfactory in this respect. Most of it is contained in the Returns Directive, which introduces 'a horizontal set of rules, applicable to all third-country nationals who do not or who no longer fulfil the conditions for entry, stay or residence in a Member State'.[247] Apart from the usual references contained in the recitals[248] and some procedural guarantees,[249] the most serious limit imposed by the Directive is that of Article 2(2)(a), according to which it does not apply to cases of people rejected at the border 'in accordance with Article 13 of the Schengen Borders Code' or to cases of people 'apprehended or intercepted by the competent authorities in connection with the *irregular* crossing

guards must consult the national authority(-ies) responsible for the examination of applications for international protection'.

246 Ibid., para. 10.2 ('All third country nationals who express the wish to apply for asylum/international protection at the border (including airport and seaport transit zones) must be given the opportunity to do so. To this end, border authorities must inform the applicants, in a language they may reasonably be expected to understand, of the procedure to be followed (how and where to make the application), as well as of their rights and obligations, including of the possible consequences of not complying with their obligations and not cooperating with the authorities'). Article 6(5) of the Procedures Directive provides as follows: 'Member States shall ensure that authorities likely to be addressed by someone who wishes to make an application for asylum are able to advise that person how and where he/she may make such an application and/or may require these authorities to forward the application to the competent authority'. There is no equivalent rule in Article 6 of the new Procedures Directive, although it has been 'moved' to Recital No. 26.

247 On the Returns Directive see A. Baldaccini (2010a: 114 ff.) and M. Schieffer (2010: 1505 ff.).

248 According to Recital No. 8, 'It is recognised that it is legitimate for Member States to return illegally staying third-country nationals, provided that fair and efficient asylum systems are in place which fully respect the principle of non-refoulement'. Recital No. 23 f. add that 'Application of this Directive is without prejudice to the obligations resulting from the Geneva Convention . . .' and that 'This Directive respects the fundamental rights and observes the principles recognised in particular by the Charter of Fundamental Rights of the European Union'.

249 Article 9 requires States to postpone the decision to remove a person when it might 'violate the principle of non-refoulement'. Article 12 simply requires that decisions be based on legal and factual arguments and include information on methods of appeal (moreover, 'The information on reasons in fact may be limited where national law allows for the right to information to be restricted, in particular in order to safeguard national security, defence, public security and for the prevention, investigation, detection and prosecution of criminal offences'). During the appeal it is not necessary to suspend the removal order, as according to Article 13 it is only optional. Finally, the right to assistance and legal representation is extended to the appeal process by a reference to the Procedures Directive, although the latter imposes very strict limits.

by land, sea or air of the external border of a Member State' (emphasis added). While the reference to Article 13 of the Schengen Borders Code does not exclude potential beneficiaries of international protection because it safeguards 'the application of special provisions concerning the right of asylum and to international protection . . .', the reference to persons irregularly staying in the country effectively incorporates everyone fleeing the danger of suffering serious violations of their human rights because it is unlikely that any of them will be able to show valid entry papers but will nonetheless try to set foot in a Member State. If they do make an application, the process takes its natural course, which is that of the Procedures Directive. Otherwise, whether for reasons attributable to the migrant or whether, more probably, because the border authorities do not inform the migrant of his or her rights, Article 4 of the Returns Directive offers even fewer guarantees than the rest of the provisions. Although these do include the prohibition on *refoulement*, the constant references to it, almost to the point of excess,[250] cannot by themselves ensure compliance without substantive and, above all, procedural guarantees such as those contained in Directive 2005/85/EC.[251] An identical argument applies to the references contained in the instruments that complete the Returns Directive – the re-admission agreements.[252] I think that provision should be made for specific guarantees not only where an application for asylum has been made, but more generally when a break in the relationship between the territory (or more correctly, the jurisdiction) of a Member State and a foreign national is involved:[253] if not all the guarantees offered by the Procedures Directive, then at least those derived from Article 4 of the new Qualification Directive, which specifies the elements on which a Member State must base its decision whether there is an actual risk of persecution in the country of origin.[254]

250 This is re-asserted in Article 5: 'When implementing this Directive, Member States shall take due account of: (a) the best interests of the child; (b) family life; (c) the state of health of the third-country national concerned, and respect the principle of non-refoulement'.

251 Although used in another context, the words of G. S. Goodwin-Gill (2011: 448) apply here as well: 'The problem, though, lies not in formal recognition of protection principles but, as ever, in operationalising the rules – in making protection a reality at the point of enforcement'.

252 See, for example, Article 18(1) of the Agreement between the European Community and the Russian Federation on readmission, OJ L 129, 17 May 2007, p. 40 ff., approved by Council Decision 2007/341/EC of 19 April 2007, according to which 'This Agreement shall be without prejudice to the rights, obligations and responsibilities of the Community, the Member States and the Russian Federation arising from International Law, and in particular from: (a) the Convention of 28 July 1951 and the Protocol of 31 January 1967 relating to the Status of Refugees; (b) the European Convention of 4 November 1950 for the Protection of Human Rights and Fundamental Freedoms . . .'. On the EU's readmission agreements in general see F. Graziani (2005: 243 ff.) and G. Cellamare (2010: 369 ff.).

253 See also UNHCR (2008c).

254 Of course, not all can be used when the person concerned does not indicate a wish to obtain international protection. However, the rules on return should at least obligate

4.8 Admission of asylum-seekers

There are no specific rules governing the admission of asylum-seekers as the system applicable to them must be deduced from the Procedures Directive and from the Schengen Borders Code. The latter contains several provisions safeguarding asylum-seekers:[255] Article 3(b), according to which

> This Regulation shall apply to any person crossing the internal or external borders of Member States, without prejudice to . . . (b) the rights of refugees and persons requesting international protection, in particular as regards non-refoulement;

Article 5(4)(c) setting out the exceptions to the requirements for a foreign national to enter the 'territory' of the EU, without prejudice to 'humanitarian grounds', 'national interest' and 'international obligations'; and Article 13(1) providing that the rejection of persons who do not meet the entry conditions must be without prejudice to the 'special provisions concerning the right of asylum and to international protection'. In addition, another safeguard is contained in Article 11 of the Returns Directive. On the one hand, this obligates Member States to 'accompany' the return decision with an entry ban while, on the other, adding at paragraph (5) that this is without prejudice to the right to international protection as defined by the Qualification Directive.

Thus, while the Schengen Borders Code acts as a sort of watershed for asylum-seekers, who are not subject to the entry requirements applying to other third-country nationals, the Procedures Directive, for its part, nowhere states explicitly that they have the right to enter the territory of a Member State simply because they have made or want to make an asylum application. Nonetheless, although the position of the EU rules is not clear, it emerges from several provisions that the applicant's right to remain in the host State is ensured while a decision as to whether he or she is entitled to international protection is being reached in accordance with the Procedures Directive. Article 3(1) of the Procedures Directive states that the right to remain refers 'to all applications for asylum made in the territory, including at the border or in the transit zones of the Member States'.[256] Furthermore, Article 7 authorises asylum-seekers 'to remain in the Member State, for the sole purpose of the procedure, until the determining authority has made a decision . . .'.[257] This should already be sufficient, in itself,

> States to take account of 'all relevant facts as they relate to the country of origin . . . including laws and regulations of the country of origin and the manner in which they are applied', and of the 'individual position and personal circumstances . . ., including factors such as background, gender and age, so as to assess whether, on the basis of the applicant's personal circumstances, the acts to which the applicant has been or could be exposed would amount to persecution or serious harm'.

255 See A. Epiney and A. Egbuna-Joss (2010: 106 f.).
256 Similarly, see Article 3(1) of the new Procedures Directive.
257 This is mirrored by Article 9 of the new Procedures Directive.

to demonstrate that while a formal right to entry is not clearly granted by the EU rules, in practice[258] the need to comply with Articles 3 and 7 is sufficient guarantee that the principle of *non-refoulement* will be respected. As mentioned earlier, the rationale for the prohibition indicates that States have an obligation to guarantee temporary (and conditional) residence to asylum-seekers, rather than that there exists a right of entry in the full sense. In other words, although it may appear captious, once again the principle of *non-refoulement* prevents removal – the danger of which to the applicant must be assessed by appropriate procedure – but it does not guarantee a right of entry. This is almost certainly confirmed by Recital No. 9 of the Returns Directive, according to which

> a third-country national who has applied for asylum in a Member State should not be regarded as staying illegally on the territory of that Member State until a negative decision on the application, or a decision ending his or her right of stay as asylum seeker has entered into force.

An EU practice designed to hamper or even prevent the movement of potential asylum-seekers largely confirms this. Because applicants are entitled to a procedure and to temporary residence once in the jurisdiction of a Member State, the EU has introduced measures to block flows at the point of departure, engaging in operations in the territory (and often with the cooperation) of third countries. These are termed non-arrival measures and consist mainly of rules applying to carriers and the coordination of border controls organised by Frontex (European Agency for the Management of Operational Cooperation at the External Borders of the Member States of the European Union).[259] The rules, some of which go back to the Convention Implementing the Schengen Agreement, require carriers (i.e. any physical or legal entity professionally transporting persons by air, sea or land) to make sure that the persons carried have the necessary documents for entry into a Member State.[260] The obligation is reinforced by additional elements, above

---

258　A. Epiney and A. Egbuna-Joss (2010: 108).

259　The Agency was established by Council Regulation (EC) No. 2007/2004 of 26 October 2004 establishing a European Agency for the Management of Operational Cooperation at the External Borders of the Member States of the European Union, OJ L 349, 25 November 2004, p. 1 ff., amended by Regulation (EC) No. 863/2007 of the European Parliament and of the Council of 11 July 2007, OJ L 199, 31 July 2007, p. 30 ff., and lastly by Regulation (EU) No. 1168/2011 of the European Parliament and of Council of 25 October 2011, OJ L 304, 22 November 2011, p. 1 ff. On the Agency's activities and their connection with the issue of security see A. W. Neal (2009: 333 ff.) and S. Léonard (2010: 231 ff.).

260　Article 26(1)(b) of the Convention Implementing the Schengen Agreement of 14 June 1985 between the Governments of the States of the Benelux Economic Union, the Federal Republic of Germany and the French Republic, on the Gradual Abolition of Checks at their Common Borders (Schengen Implementation Agreement), OJ L 239, 22 September 2000, p. 19 ff.: 'The carrier shall be obliged to take all the necessary measures to ensure that an alien carried by air or sea is in possession of

all an undertaking on the part of States to impose 'penalties on carriers which transport aliens who do not possess the necessary travel documents'.[261] It has rightly been pointed out that as it is wholly unlikely that an asylum-seeker will be able to meet the conditions (presently) set by Article 5(1) of the Schengen Borders Code,[262] the obligations in question 'considerably impede access to asylum processes and other forms of international protection in EU states, and in many cases render it impossible'.[263]

As to border controls, it is clear that activities taking place, with or without the coordination of Frontex, in a Member State's territorial waters or contiguous zone must be in observance of the principle of *non-refoulement*.[264] As explained, the

the travel documents required for entry into the territories of the Contracting Parties'.

261 Carriers are also required to file data on the persons transported (see Council Directive 2004/82/EC of 29 April 2004 on the obligation of carriers to communicate passenger data, OJ L 261, 6 August 2004, p. 24 ff.) and 'immediately to assume responsibility for' the foreign national transported by them who has been refused entry (Article 26(1)(a) of the Convention Implementing the Schengen Agreement as supplemented by Council Directive 2001/51/EC of 28 June 2001 supplementing the provisions of Article 26 of the Convention implementing the Schengen Agreement of 14 June, OJ L 187, 10 July 2001, p. 45 ff.).

262 'For intended stays on the territory of the Member States of a duration of no more than 90 days in any 180-day period, which entails considering the 180-day period preceding each day of stay, the entry conditions for third-country nationals shall be the following: (a) they are in possession of a valid travel document entitling the holder to cross the border satisfying the following criteria: (i) its validity shall extend at least three months after the intended date of departure from the territory of the Member States. In a justified case of emergency, this obligation may be waived; (ii) it shall have been issued within the previous 10 years; (b) they are in possession of a valid visa, if required pursuant to Council Regulation (EC) No 539/2001 of 15 March 2001 listing the third countries whose nationals must be in possession of visas when crossing the external borders and those whose nationals are exempt from that requirement, except where they hold a valid residence permit or a valid long-stay visa; (c) they justify the purpose and conditions of the intended stay, and they have sufficient means of subsistence, both for the duration of the intended stay and for the return to their country of origin or transit to a third country into which they are certain to be admitted, or are in a position to acquire such means lawfully; (d) they are not persons for whom an alert has been issued in the SIS for the purposes of refusing entry; (e) they are not considered to be a threat to public policy, internal security, public health or the international relations of any of the Member States, in particular where no alert has been issued in Member States' national data bases for the purposes of refusing entry on the same grounds'.

263 Also according to R. Weinzierl and U. Lisson (2007: 28). The rule on the responsibility of carriers transporting third-country nationals without the necessary entry documents has already been criticised in the past: on this point see H. Meijers (1990: 428 ff.).

264 Note that Council Decision 2010/252/EU of 26 April 2010 supplementing the Schengen Borders Code as regards the surveillance of the sea external borders in the context of operational cooperation coordinated by the European Agency for the Management of Operational Cooperation at the External Borders of the Member

principle applies irrespective of the place *from which* a person is removed, only the place *to which* he or she is sent having relevance, on condition of course that responsibility for the removal measure can be attributed to one or more Member States.[265] What concerns us here is the applicability of the principle in territorial waters or in a contiguous zone of a third country, such activities apparently having been undertaken as part of non-arrival measures above all by Spain, with the coordination of Frontex.[266] The version of the principle of *non-refoulement* in Article 33(1) of the Refugee Convention does not apply in such cases because, as with the UK's practice of screening potential asylum-seekers, when they are in the 'free' zone of the departure airport they are not 'outside their country of origin' as Article 1 of the Refugee Convention requires.[267] Apart from responsibility for violating the right of asylum-seekers to leave their country – in addition to that of the third country with which the operations are coordinated, assuming this to be the asylum-seekers' country of origin – it is clear, as emphasised earlier,[268] that because they are sent back to (*recte*: are not allowed to leave) a country where they are 'at risk' (possibly even of indirect *refoulement*), the relevant ECHR rules are violated, above all Article 3.[269] Of course, there is only violation if the persons

States of the European Union, OJ L 111, 4 May 2010, p. 20 ff., refers to the principle of *non-refoulement* (see paragraph (1.2) of the Annex on the rules for sea border operations coordinated by the Agency). Nevertheless, there are serious doubts that operations are always conducted in compliance with the prohibition: on this point see E. De Capitani (2009: 11 f.) and V. Moreno-Lax (2011: 174 ff.). On the compatibility of Frontex coordinated actions with the law of the sea, see instead V. Moreno-Lax (2010: 621 ff.). Decision 2010/252/EU was annulled by the ECJ (although it will remain in force until new legislation is adopted, a proposal for which has already been submitted: see proposal for a regulation of the European Parliament and of the Council establishing rules for the surveillance of the external sea borders in the context of operational cooperation coordinated by the European Agency for the Management of Operational Cooperation at the External Borders of the Member States of the European Union, COM/2013/0197 final) following an application of the European Parliament, which considered that the Council had thereby overstepped the powers of implementation provided in Article 12(5) of the Schengen Borders Code: see judgment of 5 September 2012, Case C-355/10, *European Parliament v. Council of Europe*, not yet published.

265 The responsibility of the EU is probably not involved as Frontex's role is simply to coordinate activities. However, although the Agency always tends to minimise its role in such operations, there are some doubts about this: see E. De Capitani (2009: 12) and G. S. Goodwin-Gill (2011: 451). Of course, if the coordinated operations are unlawful because of how the provisions of secondary legislation are formulated then the EU is potentially responsible, regardless of the role played by Frontex. In the event of an appeal on the basis of the ECHR (obviously when the EU has completed the joining process), the mechanism of co-respondent could also prove useful is such cases.

266 See E. Papastavridis (2010: 87 ff.). For a fuller discussion (and recent developments), see F. Cherubini (2014: 30 ff.).

267 E. Papastavridis (2010: 104 f.). On this point see also footnote 278, Chapter 1.

268 See § 2.4. On this point see also L. den Hertog (2013: 205 ff.).

269 See E. Papastavridis (2010: 105 ff.), G. S. Goodwin-Gill (2011: 450 f.) and L. den Hertog (2013: 205 ff.).

sent back are within the jurisdiction of an EU Member State. It is not a very convincing argument to maintain that the presence of a third-country official aboard the vehicles (particularly boats) of the Member State concerned can 'break' the link between the people intercepted and the area of State control to which they are subject.[270] In reality, the prevailing position is that *non-refoulement* applies to these cases as well, partly on the basis that treaties should be implemented in good faith, which frankly does not happen when such actions are justified on grounds that are at the very least 'misconceived'.[271] The immediate consequence of this is that once the asylum-seekers have been intercepted, the risk of persecution to each one in the country of destination must be assessed by appropriate procedure: the procedure set out in Directive 2005/85/EC where there is an application for international protection, or a procedure that complies with minimum standards where for whatever reason such an application has not been made.[272]

Article 7 of the Procedures Directive contains the rule that is the linchpin of the whole system regulating asylum: it obligates Member States to authorise asylum-seekers to stay in their territory until a decision on status has been reached. The provision is more generally part of the 'basic principles and guarantees' that the Directive states must be observed while processing applications. Article 7 allows some exceptions, however, which it is worth commenting on. These are set out in paragraph (2), under which States can refuse to authorise an applicant to stay in their territory if a subsequent application will not be further examined, or when the States intend to

> surrender or extradite, as appropriate, a person either to another Member State pursuant to obligations in accordance with a European arrest warrant or otherwise, or to a third country, or to international criminal courts or tribunals.

The first exception should be read in conjunction with Articles 32 and 34 of the Directive, to which Article 7(2) refers. Apart from defining what constitutes a subsequent application,[273] they require that before deciding whether to make

270 G. S. Goodwin-Gill (2011: 453).
271 Similarly, G. S. Goodwin-Gill (2011: 453) regarding the Agency's assertion: 'Frontex again suggests that "merely" advising the source country of the location of vessels to be intercepted falls short of any act that might generate international responsibility'.
272 As the Stockholm Programme suggests, asylum applications can still be examined following procedures conducted *in* the third country. Although this suggestion was put forward in the past by Germany and the UK, several apparently insuperable arguments weigh against it, as demonstrated by L. den Hertog (2013: 205 ff.). For more on this point see O. Lynskey (2006: 230 ff.).
273 The Directive considers four situations in which the subsequent application is made: after the previous one has been withdrawn, even implicitly (Article 32(2)(a)); after a decision (not necessarily a final one) has been issued (Article 32(2)(b)); after the person concerned has agreed to have his or her case be part of an application made

a further examination, States must in any case conduct a preliminary assessment to ascertain whether, in substance, any new elements have emerged with respect to the previous application.[274] Before such assessment, Article 7(1) applies and therefore the applicant has the right to stay in the State, at least until it is completed. Although a preliminary assessment must be made in compliance with the usual principles and guarantees applying to the 'principal' procedure, under Article 34(1) it is subject to the basic safeguards of Article 10.[275] Once it has been completed, the State can decide not to examine the application further, and the derogation provided in Article 7(2)[276] will apply, including if the applicant appeals against the negative decision resulting from the preliminary assessment.[277] On the other hand, if the preliminary assessment reveals 'new elements or findings . . . which significantly add to the likelihood of the applicant qualifying as a refugee or as deserving subsidiary protection', the main procedure re-opens.[278]

on his or her behalf (Article 32(7)); and after an applicant who has presented an application 'at a later date' fails, either intentionally or through gross negligence, to go to a reception centre or appear before the competent authorities at a specified time. The new Procedures Directive is less clear on the question of subsequent applications. It appears to retain the first two situations (Article 41(1)(a)–(b)) and adds to the third the case of third parties making an application in the name of a minor (Article 40(6)(b)); it eliminates the case of applications made 'at a later date'.

274 These must be elements used to prove new facts. Thus, according to the Belgian Council of State, new elements cannot consist in new evidence concerning known facts (see the decision of 21 October 2009, No. 187.209). The District Court of Haarlem held that new evidence cannot be admitted if the applicant could have presented it when the first application was examined (see the decisions of 3 March 2009, AWB 09/5250, AWB 09/5249, AWB 09/5529). In the case of a separate application, after the person concerned has agreed to have the case be part of the application made by the person of whom he or she is a dependent, it is not a matter of examining new facts but of assessing whether separate examination is justified (this is the same in the new Procedures Directive, including where the previous application was made in the name of a minor: see Article 40(6)). In the situation described in Article 33 (application 'at a later date') new elements must be considered, as according to T. Spijkerboer (2010: 1298) it is equivalent to an implicit withdrawal of the application.

275 See below, § 4.10. The new Procedures Directive states explicitly that derogations may be used 'only where the determining authority considers that a return decision will not lead to direct or indirect refoulement in violation of that Member State's international and Union obligations' (Article 41(1)).

276 In the situation described in Article 32(7), a negative decision at the end of the preliminary assessment means that the applicant's case is again examined as part of the application of the person of whom he or she is a dependent. In this specific case, the derogation will always be inapplicable.

277 Thus, States also have an obligation, under Article 34(3)(a), to inform the applicant 'in an appropriate manner of the outcome of the preliminary examination and, in case the application will not be further examined, of the reasons for this and the possibilities for seeking an appeal or review of the decision' (see also Article 42(3) of the new Procedures Directive).

278 If a subsequent application is made following the withdrawal, including implicit withdrawal, of a previous application or following a decision in regard, the main procedure must re-open 'as soon as possible' in accordance with Article 34(3)(b).

The other derogation, which does not appear in the Commission's proposal, is more problematic as, without providing additional guarantees, it allows States to avoid any assessment of the risk of persecution to the applicant in the country of destination as a result of his or her surrender or extradition. Specifically, the rule does not obligate States to verify the conditions that the applicant will face when surrendered or extradited to another Member State, or a third State, or an international court or tribunal, with the risk that such conditions might constitute a violation of the principle of *non-refoulement*. I do not think it is correct to make the irrefutable presumption, as the Directive appears to do, that the applicant is being entrusted to 'safe' hands. On the concept of 'safe' country (Member State or third State), its safety cannot be established once and for all as each Member State must examine all elements, including those relating to the individual applicant, before deciding whether the surrender or extradition violates the principle of *non-refoulement* in the case in question. This applies regardless of the country or entity to which the applicant is delivered or extradited, be it an EU Member State, a third State, or even an international court or tribunal. The possibility that the fate awaiting the applicant in one of these countries or entities may constitute a violation of the principle of *non-refoulement* is very relevant because neither the fact that a State is a member of the EU nor the international nature of the court or tribunal are absolute guarantees that human rights will be protected, as indeed has been demonstrated in practice. Without going into the vast ECtHR case law on respect of the right to a fair trial and the questions raised about the European arrest warrant's observance of basic rights[279] – regardless of the many references to it contained in Framework Decision 2002/584[280] – we need only consider some of the doubts raised by the working of international courts and tribunals, which are at least sufficient to forestall any irrefutable presumption such as that of Article 7(2) of the Directive. Some of these tribunals are not permanently established institutions,[281] and often the decision to undertake a criminal prosecution seems somewhat arbitrary,[282] without counting the number of unexplained deaths that occur during detention, notably those in the Dutch prison of Scheveningen, where the number is well above the national average.[283]

279 On this point see A. Chelo (2010: *passim*).
280 Council Framework Decision 2002/584/GAI of 13 June 2002 on the European arrest warrant and the surrender procedures between Member States, OJ L 190, 18 July 2002, p. 1 ff. On these references see A. Damato (2005: 225 ff.), who maintains that it is partly thanks to them that the Framework Decision respects basic rights.
281 For example the International Criminal Tribunal for the former Yugoslavia and the International Criminal Tribunal for Rwanda.
282 Consider what happened during the recent events involving Libya and the possibility of a less 'selective' involvement of the International Criminal Court: on this point see U. Villani (2011: 58).
283 For example, in Italy in 2011 there were 186 deaths in prison among a population of about 67,000 inmates; this gives an average, including deaths from natural causes, of less than 1%. During detention in Scheveningen, apart from the death of Slobodan Milošević from cardiac arrest, both Slavko Dokmanović (1998) and Milan Babić

Although in practice States appear to adopt a markedly more restrictive stance, as extradition usually follows the examination of an application,[284] automatic mechanisms continue to operate where an applicant is surrendered to another Member State or to an international court. The new Procedures Directive certainly contains explicit references to the obligation to allow applicants to stay in the country, which does not appear in the current version. Under Article 9(3) the derogation to the applicant's right to remain in the Member State to which the application is addressed can be used 'only where the competent authorities are satisfied that an extradition decision will not result in direct or indirect *refoulement* in violation of the international and Union obligations of that Member State'. This amendment, which in fact does not really add to what Member States already do insofar as it is not intended to affect surrender procedures (the European arrest warrant or request of an international court), only extradition to a third country, is not enough to bring the Directive into line with the principle of *non-refoulement*. It is likely that it will suffer the same fate as surrender under Dublin II, which similarly does not impose (or prohibit) an assessment of the risk of persecution or serious harm in the Member State of destination (see below, section 4.11).

4.9 Treatment of asylum-seekers under the Reception Directive

During the examination of asylum applications, Member States are required by EU law to comply with a set of obligations in addition to the chief ones related to the principle of *non-refoulement*. These are enshrined in Directive 2003/9/EC, known as the Reception Directive.[285] Like some of the acts forming part of the first asylum package (such as the old Procedures Directive), the Reception Directive only concerns people who have applied for recognition of refugee status and therefore does not include potential beneficiaries of subsidiary protection. According to the Commission, the reason for this is that 'at the time of its adoption,

---

(2006) committed suicide, the latter only a few days before the death of Milošević: this makes a total of three deaths in a population of 64 inmates, including those later transferred to other prisons, giving an average of well over 4%.

284 See the Report from the Commission to the European Parliament and the Council of 8 September 2010 on the application of Directive 2005/85/EC, COM (2010) 465 final, para. 5.1.2.

285 See footnote 238. Member States had great difficulty implementing the Directive and the Commission initiated infringement procedures for many of them (see the Report from the Commission to the European Parliament and the Council of 8 September 2010 on the application of Directive 2005/85/EC, COM (2010) 765 final, para. 2). Two of these procedures resulted in a guilty verdict for Austria and Greece: see ECJ, judgment of 26 October 2006, Case C-102/06, *Commission of the European Communities* v. *Republic of Austria, EC Reports*, 2006, p. I-111 f., and judgment of 19 April 2007, Case C-72/06, *Commission of the European Communities* v. *Hellenic Republic*, ibid., 2007, p. I-57 f.

such a concept was not yet part of the EU asylum *acquis*'.[286] However, the scope of the new Reception Directive has been extended to all applicants for international protection, including subsidiary protection.[287] A further exclusion is provided in Article 3(3), which states that the Directive does not apply in the event of mass influxes, which are instead governed by Directive 2001/55/EC,[288] as will be discussed later.

One of the most important provisions of the Reception Directive,[289] which links up with the corresponding provisions of the Refugee Convention (Article 31, on which see above, section 1.8) and the ECHR (Article 5, on which see above, section 2.3), is Article 7 on the freedom of movement of asylum-seekers.[290] It asserts that asylum-seekers have the right to freedom of movement in the host Member State or in that part of its territory assigned to them[291] before stating that 'when it proves necessary, for example for legal reasons or reasons of public order, Member States may confine an applicant to a particular place in accordance with their national law'. Clearly, there is virtually no limit on the State's margin for discretion except the indication 'necessary'. In practice, not only do all Member States detain

---

286 Report from the Commission COM (2007) 745 final, para. 3.1.

287 See Article 3 of Directive 2013/33/EU.

288 Council Directive 2001/55/EC of 20 July 2001 on minimum standards for giving temporary protection in the event of a mass influx of displaced persons and on measures promoting a balance of efforts between Member States in receiving such persons and bearing the consequences thereof, OJ L 212, 7 August 2001, p. 12 ff. Instead, the provisions of the Reception Directive apply after the Member State where the application was lodged has determined that another Member State is competent to examine it in accordance with Dublin II: see ECJ, judgment of 27 September 2012, Case C-179/11, *Cimade and Groupe d'information et de soutien des immigrés (GISTI)* v. *Ministre de l'Intérieur, de l'Outre-mer, des Collectivités territoriales et de l'Immigration*, not yet published.

289 Regarding the others, which often leave States a considerable margin of discretion, see M. Peek (2010: 871 ff.) and the bibliography therein.

290 Note that according to the ECJ (judgment of 30 May 2013, Case C-534/11, *Mehmet Arslan* v. *Policie ČR, Krajské ředitelství policie Ústeckého kraje, odbor cizinecké policie*, not yet published), the detention of a person applying for protection does not come under the Returns Directive when the nature of the treatment changes, that is, when a third-country national detained for the purpose of removal makes an application for protection: this was the case of a Turkish national detained to prevent him escaping before being removed as he had in the past, who in the meantime had made an application for protection. The ECJ allowed that the treatment could continue, pursuant to the Reception Directive (and partly to the Procedures Directive) if the purpose of the Returns Directive ('*not applicable* during the procedure in which an application for asylum is examined', emphasis added) could be defeated because it was impossible for a Member State 'to prevent ... the person concerned from automatically securing release by making an application for asylum' (ibid., para. 60).

291 '1. Asylum seekers may move freely within the territory of the host Member State or within an area assigned to them by that Member State. The assigned area shall not affect the unalienable sphere of private life and shall allow sufficient scope for guaranteeing access to all benefits under this Directive. 2. Member States may decide on the residence of the asylum seeker for reasons of public interest, public order or, when necessary, for the swift processing and effective monitoring of his or her application'.

asylum-seekers, but the conditions of their confinement are entirely arbitrary.[292] Some States impose detention merely because the applicant entered the country illegally, thus going beyond not only Article 7 of the Reception Directive regarding the need for the measure to be in proportion to its purpose, but also Article 18 of the Procedures Directive expressly prohibiting Member States from arresting a person 'for the sole reason that he/she is an applicant for asylum'.

A comparison between these provisions and the parameters established by international law gives two different outcomes. In appearance, the Reception Directive does not diverge greatly from the ECtHR's ruling regarding Article 5 ECHR, for States enjoy broad discretion in that case too, not even having to carry out a test of necessity, which the Reception Directive requires. However, the Directive cannot obligate States to comply with the standards of the Refugee Convention. Article 7 contains no mention of the criteria suggested by UNHCR in connection with Article 31(2) of the Refugee Convention prohibiting States from placing restrictions on the freedom of movement of refugees, applicants included, 'other than those which are necessary'.[293] In commenting the Directive, UNHCR itself affirmed that States should allow detention only in exceptional cases, when there is no other way to achieve the purposes of the Directive,[294] these being merely to identify the applicant, verify the contents of his or her application, punish fraud, and maintain national security and law and order.

The new Reception Directive pays greater attention to the recommendations of UNHCR. Article 8 is clearer about the 'last resort' nature of detention measures and details the situations in which they are justified. However, these include[295] one reason not mentioned in the UNHCR guidelines and which I believe could create a clearer conflict between the Directive and international law. Article 8(c) allows

---

292 Report from the Commission COM (2007) 745 final, para. 3.4.1.
293 Regarding these principles see UNHCR (1999).
294 UNHCR (2003a).
295 'An applicant may be detained only: (a) in order to determine or verify his or her identity or nationality; (b) in order to determine those elements on which the application for international protection is based which could not be obtained in the absence of detention, in particular when there is a risk of absconding of the applicant . . .; (d) when he or she is detained subject to a return procedure under Directive 2008/115/EC of the European Parliament and of the Council of 16 December 2008 on common standards and procedures in Member States for returning illegally staying third-country nationals, in order to prepare the return and/or carry out the removal process, and the Member State concerned can substantiate on the basis of objective criteria, including that he or she already had the opportunity to access the asylum procedure, that there are reasonable grounds to believe that he or she is making the application for international protection merely in order to delay or frustrate the enforcement of the return decision; (e) when protection of national security or public order so requires; (f) in accordance with Article 28 of Regulation (EU) No 604/2013 of the European Parliament and of the Council of 26 June 2013 establishing the criteria and mechanisms for determining the Member State responsible for examining an application for international protection lodged in one of the Member States by a third-country national or a stateless person'.

detention 'in order to decide, in the context of a procedure, on the applicant's right to enter the territory'. This provision evidently endorses the practice of States, which is to regard illegal entry itself as sufficient reason for detention. Adding to this the fact that asylum-seekers usually do not have the documents required for legal entry, it is obvious that such a provision (again) bypasses the requirements laid down in Article 18 of the Procedures Directive, and re-stated by the new Reception Directive,[296] that detention cannot be justified merely because the person is an asylum-seeker.

The provisions of the Reception Directive, then, do not apply in cases of mass influx, which are covered by Directive 2001/55/EC.[297] The distinction between the two Directives lies in the decision by which the Council, pursuant to Article 5(1) of the Directive on mass influx, establishes by a qualified majority and on a proposal from the Commission 'the existence of a mass influx of displaced persons'.[298] It follows that, failing such a decision but in a situation where a large number of asylum-seekers arrive at the border of a Member State, the general system will apply, including the Reception Directive. This is borne out by the Procedures Directive: at Article 35, concerning one of the special situations in which the procedure may derogate from the basic principles and guarantees (i.e. the border procedure), paragraph (5) allows States to apply the procedure 'at the border or in a transit zone' in the case of 'particular types of arrivals, or arrivals involving a large number of third country nationals or stateless persons'.[299]

The Council decision is based on the concept of displaced persons contained in Article 2(c), according to which they are third-country nationals or stateless persons who have fled their country voluntarily or otherwise

and are unable to return in safe and durable conditions because of the situation prevailing in that country, who may fall within the scope of Article 1A of the Geneva Convention or other international or national instruments giving international protection.

The same provision also lists specific situations in which displaced persons can be identified as persons 'who have fled areas of armed conflict or endemic violence' and persons 'at serious risk of, or who have been the victim of, systematic or generalised violations of their human rights'. This has several consequences.

---

296 See Article 8 of Directive 2013/33. Article 22 of the new Procedures Directive refers to the Reception Directive regarding the conditions of detention, remedying their omission in the present Article 18.

297 On this see N. Arenas (2005b: 435 ff.) and A. Skordas (2010: 818 ff.). Regarding the practice in the case of mass influx prior to Directive 2001/55/EC see K. Kerber (1997: 453 ff.).

298 The Directive has not been applied to date because the Council has never sought to exercise the powers conferred on it by Article 5.

299 See also Article 3(3) of the new Procedures Directive.

To begin, the list of specific situations is not absolute and the Council, which has some discretion whether or not to issue a decision pursuant to Article 5, could be of the opinion that other reasons make secure repatriation impossible. Although the *travaux préparatoires* point in the opposite direction,[300] I believe this opens up the possibility of extending temporary protection to so-called climate refugees,[301] people who have fled their country as a result of natural disasters, a reason not mentioned in Article 1A of the Refugee Convention. The provision also makes it clear that refugees in the true sense of the term, as defined in Article 1, may also figure among the displaced persons. Thus, beneficiaries of temporary protection and refugees are not the same, although it is likely that the former may also include the latter.[302]

The mechanism designed to differentiate the beneficiaries in one category from those in the other, according to the Directive, confirms this. In line with the general approach described above (section 1.7), temporary protection is a system designed to prevent the rejection of a mass influx of persons (which may well include refugees) provided States in the area (in the present case, the EU) share the burden of admitting them and, if appropriate, examining their situation in the light of the Refugee Convention. Article 3(1) of Directive 2001/55/EC states that 'temporary protection shall not prejudice recognition of refugee status under the Geneva Convention'. More important is the rule giving the beneficiary of temporary protection the possibility to apply for recognition of refugee status, as provided in Article 17.[303] Another key provision is Article 18, identifying the State responsible for examining an application as the one 'which has accepted his transfer onto its territory' on the basis of the cooperation that underpins (and conditions) the operation of the whole Directive.

As the refugees are 'separated' from the mass influx inside the Member States concerned and according to their reception capabilities, the rest of the people are left with a very weak form of protection that is destined to terminate when the deadline arrives (one year, with the possibility of extensions to be established by the Council) or as a result of a Council decision that repatriation is possible.

---

300 See A. Skordas (2010: 828).
301 On which see S. M. Christiansen (2010) and among Italian writers S. Ianovitz (2011: 141 ff.).
302 Like the Reception Directive, which followed it, the Directive on Temporary Protection does not take account of the position of beneficiaries of subsidiary protection, who cannot, therefore, be likened to refugees for the purpose of its application. Thus, they are not different from any other beneficiary of temporary protection and in fact the situations listed in Article 2(c) appear very similar to those envisaged by Article 15 of the new Qualification Directive regarding subsidiary protection.
303 According to Article 19(1), 'The Member States may provide that temporary protection may not be enjoyed concurrently with the status of asylum seeker while applications are under consideration'. I believe that this is confirmation that once the application has been made, and if there is no Council decision establishing the presence of an influx of displaced persons, the general mechanism set out in the Reception, Procedures and Qualification Directives should apply.

Apart from the right based on the principle of *non-refoulement*, the nature of the rights to which the beneficiaries of temporary protection are entitled is clear evidence of how little impact they have on the Member States undertaking to protect the displaced persons in accordance with the Directive. To give one example, Article 15 apparently grants a typical benefit to both asylum-seekers and existing beneficiaries of international protection, family reunification. In fact, the Directive on mass influx does not obligate States to guarantee that beneficiaries of temporary protection can be joined by family members, even if these enjoy or should enjoy the same protection. Article 15 creates an obligation (or possibility, depending on the relationship) to bring together in the same Member State all members of a family unit included in the category of displaced persons established by Council decision. Thus, Article 15 simply rationalises the identification of the Member State where displaced persons belonging to the same family will reside.

4.10 Assessment of applications for international protection: A) Principles and guarantees

The assessment procedure must observe additional principles and guarantees: the application must be examined 'individually, objectively and impartially', the authorities making the assessment must have specific expertise in the area and they must have access to sources of 'precise and up-to-date' information – Article 8(2)(b) mentions UNHCR[304] – on the situation in the country of origin as well as in the countries through which the applicant transited. The provision repeats briefly the contents of Article 4 of the new Qualification Directive regarding the examination of the facts and circumstances that must be taken into consideration when assessing an application. However, Article 4 is more detailed about the elements on which the examination is based. States are required to cooperate with the applicant but they can, as indeed is the practice,[305] require him or her 'to submit as soon as possible all the elements needed to substantiate the application for international protection'. According to some writers,[306] this constitutes a burden of proof for the applicant. The fact that States are required to cooperate with the applicant would indicate that this burden should not be interpreted too strictly. As we have seen,[307] UNHCR does not deny that the burden of proof lies with the applicant, but allows that the authorities examining the application have the right to verify the facts, particularly as the applicant's conditions are unlikely

---

304 The ECJ has confirmed that UNHCR's involvement is not compulsory during the part of the procedure in which the Member State responsible for examining the application is determined: see judgment of 30 May 2013, Case C-528/11, *Zuheyr Frayeh Halaf* v. *Darzhavna agentsia za bezhantsite pri Ministerskia savet*, not yet published.

305 See the Report from the Commission COM (2010) 314 final, para. 5.1.1.

306 K. Hailbronner and S. Alt (2010: 1027 f.).

307 Footnote 302, Chapter 1.

to allow him or her to provide sufficient evidence in support of an application. This interpretation of the provision has been upheld recently by a decision of the ECJ confirming that the obligation on States to cooperate

> means, in practical terms, that if, for any reason whatsoever, the elements provided by an applicant for international protection are not complete, up to date or relevant, it is necessary for the Member State concerned to cooperate actively with the applicant, at that stage of the procedure, so that all the elements needed to substantiate the application may be assembled.[308]

A 'flexible' interpretation of Article 4(1) of the new Qualification Directive is advocated in paragraph (5) which, in line with UNHCR, relieves the applicant of any duty of proof when he or she has generally been shown to be in good faith and credible.[309] The obligation to submit the necessary elements 'as soon as possible' must be treated in the light of the applicant's personal circumstances,[310] although this does not mean that very important effects (application evidently unfounded) cannot be attributed to the failure to comply with this obligation, as has indeed occurred.[311] The effect of setting a limit for submitting evidence is 'mitigated' by Article 8(1) of the Procedures Directive, according to which examination of an application cannot be refused only because it is presented at a later date. If the elements required are presented at the same time as a late application, they must be allowed because the application cannot be rejected only because it was not made as soon as possible.

One very important aspect of the principles and guarantees is the personal interview, the aim of which is to determine the elements that will decide the application. It is obligatory, in the sense that the applicant has the option to request it and the State must grant that possibility.[312] There are exceptions, however, of

---

308 ECJ, judgment of 22 November 2012, Case C-277/11, *M. M.* v. *Minister for Justice and Law Reform (M. M.)*, not yet published, para. 66. The Court added that 'a Member State may also be better placed than an applicant to gain access to certain types of documents'.

309 For example, because 'the applicant has made a genuine effort to substantiate his application' or 'the applicant's statements are found to be coherent and plausible and do not run counter to available specific and general information relevant to the applicant's case'.

310 For example, the competent authorities cannot refuse to admit documents which they know to exist and must allow the applicant a reasonable length of time to produce them: see District Court of Utrecht, decision of 12 April 2011, AWB 10/43531.

311 See the Report from the Commission COM (2010) 314 final, para. 5.1.1.

312 In the judgment in the case of *M. M.* the ECJ clarified that the requirement to conduct a personal interview derives directly from the Charter of Fundamental Rights of the European Union, particularly Article 41, which provides for the right to good administration, thus obligating internal courts to ensure that it is observed not only in the procedure for determining refugee status (in which case there is an express guarantee) but also in the procedure relating to subsidiary protection (for which the guarantee

which States take ample advantage.[313] The exceptions provided in the Procedures Directive leave States plenty of discretion in the matter. Article 12(2)(c) for example[314] allows the personal interview to be omitted in the cases envisaged in Article 23(4)(a), (c), (g), (h) and (j), to which it refers. These provisions, which add a further possibility by allowing priority or fast-track procedures,[315] albeit in observance of all the other principles and guarantees, list among the reasons for omission issues raised by the applicant that are not relevant, representations that are improbable, applications made only to delay or prevent the enforcement of a removal order (all derogations are used by four States, including the UK) and subsequent applications (used by nine States).[316] Point (c) in particular allows the interview to be omitted if the applicant comes from a safe third country. As this is a reason for the inadmissibility of an application, it may prevent elements concerning the individual person from emerging in the course of an assessment of the risk of persecution in the country of destination, possibly in the course of an accelerated procedure. Although the concept of safe third country appears in almost all national procedures, it is not often applied in practice. In fact just two Member States use it, and only in order to derogate from the obligation to hold a personal interview if requested by the applicant.

The principles and guarantees described must be applied in all procedures involving a preliminary assessment of the applicant's eligibility for protection. The Directive allows some derogation here as well, listing a few circumstances in which the principles and guarantees may not apply. It also establishes some conditions in which the application will not be examined or will be inadmissible. Regarding the derogations, Article 24 states that these are possible in the case of subsequent

does not exist, at least when the procedure is separate from that for refugee status: see footnote 241). Therefore, according to the Court, the applicant 'must be able to make known his views before the adoption of any decision that does not grant the protection requested . . ., the fact that the applicant has already been duly heard when his application for refugee status was examined' does not imply that this formality can be overlooked (para. 95).

313 See the Report from the Commission COM (2010) 314 final, para. 5.1.4.

314 The interview can also be omitted if '(a) the determining authority is able to take a positive decision on the basis of evidence available; or (b) the competent authority has already had a meeting with the applicant for the purpose of assisting him/her with completing his/her application and submitting the essential information regarding the application . . .'. The new Procedures Directive only retains the contents of point (a) and eliminates the case in point (b) and the broader possibility of point (c). It adds a new possibility, allowing the interview to be omitted if 'the determining authority is of the opinion that the applicant is unfit or unable to be interviewed owing to enduring circumstances beyond his or her control' (Article 14(2)).

315 According to the ECJ, in the judgment of 31 January 2013, Case C-175/11, *H. I. D., B. A. v. Refugee Applications Commissioner and others (H. I. D.)*, not yet published, the possibilities listed in Article 23 of the Procedures Directive are not absolute and Member States can resort to them in other cases (in the case in question the criteria used were the applicant's country of origin or of habitual residence).

316 See the Report from the Commission COM (2010) 314 final, para. 5.1.4.

applications, applications presented at the border or in transit zones and applications made by people who have entered or are about to enter a Member State
illegally from a safe European third country. The last has been held void by
the ECJ for the reasons described earlier,[317] while the second is discussed above.
Leaving these two derogations aside, the most important one relates to applications
made at the border or in transit zones. This will clearly apply in the majority of
cases, as asylum applications are made by people with no other right of entry
except by submitting an application. While these derogations can only apply if
States have decided to maintain existing procedures, as noted by several writers,[318]
they constitute a major deviation from the principles and guarantees normally
provided. In particular, there is no right to an individual, objective and impartial
assessment or to free legal assistance.[319]

4.11 B) Exclusion on the basis of Dublin III

It is more problematic when the Member State is not required to examine the
application or this can be considered inadmissible. The first case occurs when
another Member State is competent to examine the application according to
one of the criteria set out in the Dublin III Regulation.[320] The purpose of this,
as pointed out earlier, is to eliminate the problem of refugees 'in orbit' and prevent asylum shopping. It establishes the criteria by which a Member State where

317 ECJ, judgment of 6 May 2008, Case C-133/06, *European Parliament* v. *European Council,
     EC Reports*, 2008, p. I-3189 ff., which, for the same reasons given in footnote 400,
     Chapter 1, nullifies Article 36(3) of the Procedures Directive.
318 T. Spijkerboer (2010: 1301).
319 The new Procedures Directive greatly restricts the derogations from the principles and
     guarantees that must accompany the procedure for examining an application for
     international protection: see proposal for a directive of the European Parliament and
     of the Council on minimum standards on procedures in Member States for granting
     and withdrawing international protection (Recast), 21 October 2009, COM(2009)
     554 final, especially p. 6.
320 Regulation (EU) No 604/2013 of the European Parliament and of the Council of
     26 June 2013 establishing the criteria and mechanisms for determining the Member
     State responsible for examining an application for international protection lodged
     in one of the Member States by a third-country national or a stateless person, OJ L
     180, 29 June 2013, p. 31 ff. As mentioned earlier (see § 3.13), this replaces, as of
     1 January 2014, Council Regulation (EC) No. 343/2003 of 18 February 2003
     establishing the criteria and mechanisms for determining the Member State
     responsible for examining an application for asylum lodged in one of the Member
     States by a third-country national (Dublin II), OJ L 50, 25 February 2003, p. 1 ff. The
     two Regulations contain unequal (and complex) systems of differentiated application:
     only Dublin II has been joined by Iceland, Liechtenstein, Norway and Switzerland
     under specific agreements (see § 3.11). Of Denmark, Ireland and the UK, the first
     has joined only Dublin II under a specific agreement (see, again, § 3.11), while the
     others were subject to Dublin II and are now subject to Dublin III having decided
     to opt in.

a first asylum application has been lodged[321] must determine the Member State responsible, which is obliged to take charge of the applicant.[322] The criteria are laid down in Article 7 ff. (previously Article 5 ff. of Dublin II) and concern the protection of minors, the protection of family unity,[323] the applicant's greater

321 As for the old Procedures Directive still in force (see footnote 241), as well as for the old Reception Directive, also still in force (see § 4.9), Dublin II does not apply to applicants for subsidiary protection (see Article 2(c)). As the Commission has pointed out (see Report from the Commission to the European Parliament and the Council on the evaluation of the Dublin system, COM(2007) 299 final, 6 June 2007, para. 2.3), this has had repercussions mainly on the application of the criteria designed to preserve family unity (on this point see also footnote 323).

322 The determination procedure requires the applicant to be identified on the basis of Regulation (EU) No. 603/2013 of the European Parliament and of the Council of 26 June 2013 on the establishment of 'Eurodac' for the comparison of fingerprints for the effective application of Regulation (EU) No. 604/2013 establishing the criteria and mechanisms for determining the Member State responsible for examining an application for international protection lodged in one of the Member States by a third-country national or a stateless person and on requests for the comparison with Eurodac data by Member States' law enforcement authorities and Europol for law enforcement purposes, and amending Regulation (EU) No 1077/2011 establishing a European Agency for the operational management of large-scale systems in the area of freedom, security and justice, OJ L 180, 29 June 2013, p. 1 ff., which replaced Council Regulation (EC) No. 2725/2000 of 11 December 2000 concerning the establishment of 'Eurodac' for the comparison of fingerprints for the effective application of the Dublin Convention, OJ L 316, 15 December 2000, p. 1 ff. The procedure follows the methods set out in Commission Regulation (EC) No. 1560/2003 of 2 September 2003 laying down detailed rules for the application of Council Regulation (EC) No 343/2003 establishing the criteria and mechanisms for determining the Member State responsible for examining an asylum application lodged in one of the Member States by a third-country national, OJ L 222, 5 September 2003, p. 3 ff. On the first Eurodac Regulation see E. R. Brouwer (2002: 231 ff.), J. P. Aus (2006), S. Peers and N. Rogers (2006b: 259 ff.) and L. Schuster (2011: 401 ff.); on the procedure for taking charge of applicants, see A. Hurwitz (2009: 111 ff.).

323 In that Regulation, family unity and the interests of minors were protected by an additional rule, bypassing the criteria established, respectively, by Articles 7–8 and 6 of Dublin II. This was the humanitarian clause contained in Article 15 of the Regulation, according to which '1. Any Member State, even where it is not responsible under the criteria set out in this Regulation, may bring together family members, as well as other dependent relatives, on humanitarian grounds based in particular on family or cultural considerations. In this case that Member State shall, at the request of another Member State, examine the application for asylum of the person concerned. The persons concerned must consent. 2. In cases in which the person concerned is dependent on the assistance of the other on account of pregnancy or a new born child, serious illness, severe handicap or old age, Member States shall normally keep or bring together the asylum seeker with another relative present in the territory of one of the Member States, provided that family ties existed in the country of origin. 3. If the asylum seeker is an unaccompanied minor who has a relative or relatives in another Member State who can take care of him or her, Member States shall if possible unite the minor with his or her relative or relatives, unless this is not in the best interests of the minor'. Regarding Article 15(2), the ECJ held, adopting a broad

'attachment' to another Member State because he or she possesses a permit to stay, a visa, or has simply transited there, even if in violation of the rules on entry, or in the 'international' areas of an airport.

The new system introduced with Dublin III makes significant changes to the previous rules, particularly in the light of the judicial cases they have given rise to. By exonerating the State where the first application was lodged from the duty to examine it, Dublin II established a presumption regarding the safety of the Member State of destination, which instead, according to the Refugee Convention and to case law regarding the ECHR, should be assessed independently and individually. That is to say that by handing over the applicant to the Member State responsible according to the criteria, the State doing so was not required to check whether it observed the principle of *non-refoulement*. And yet the Member State to which the applicant was delivered might well be a place 'of risk', and the applicant might be in danger of torture, persecution, or of being in turn sent on to a third country where he or she would be at risk (indirect *refoulement*). This circumstance should have been the object of an assessment, but this was not contemplated by Dublin II.

Both the ECJ and, to some extent, the ECtHR were called to give an opinion on this point, although the outcomes were as expected and virtually identical. Both cited the sovereignty clause, then enshrined in Article 3(2) of Dublin II, whereby the Member State in which the application was lodged was entitled to examine it in derogation of the criteria established by Article 5 ff. Both Courts correctly deduced from this that the Member States have discretionary power to determine the State responsible for examining the application. Neither of the Courts considered that the Regulation might not be in accordance with basic rights (under the ECHR or more generally those recognised by EU legal system), only that its implementation by the Member States might violate those rights. The Regulation did not impose an absolute obligation to deliver the applicant to the Member State determined according to the criteria of Article 5 ff., allowing the option of exercising the sovereignty clause which, while it 'safeguarded' the Dublin II system, also enabled Member States to implement it in accordance with basic rights, including those enshrined in the ECHR.

Examining the actions of Belgium, which, following the criteria mentioned, had sent an asylum applicant to Greece, the ECtHR ruled out the relevance of the Regulation – which, in any case, would not be 'direct', but via and within the

concept of beneficiaries of the rule in question, that 'a Member State may derogate from that obligation to keep the persons concerned together only if such a derogation is justified because an exceptional situation has arisen' (judgment of 6 November 2012, Case C-245/11, *K* v. *Bundesasylant*, not yet published, para. 46), thereby making family reunification virtually compulsory. The new Regulation, Dublin III, has not only extended its scope to applicants for subsidiary protection (see footnote 321), but has also made reunification effectively obligatory, even though it has been narrowed to a smaller circle of family members than prescribed by Dublin II according to the ECJ (ibid., para. 33 ff.).

limits of equivalent protection, according to the judgment in the well-known *Bosphorus* case.[324] Its reason for doing so was that

> under the Regulation, the Belgian authorities could have refrained from transferring the applicant if they had considered that the receiving country, namely Greece, was not fulfilling its obligations under the Convention. Consequently, the Court considers that the impugned measure taken by the Belgian authorities did not strictly fall within Belgium's international legal obligations.[325]

Similarly, in a later case the ECJ held that the Regulation did not contain an irrefutable presumption about the safety of the country (of destination) responsible for examining the application. After asserting that an EU Member State may not be safe,[326] the Court imposed on Member States the obligation to

> not transfer an asylum seeker to the 'Member State responsible' within the meaning of Regulation No 343/2003 where they cannot be unaware that systemic deficiencies in the asylum procedure and in the reception conditions of asylum seekers in that Member State amount to substantial grounds for believing that the asylum seeker would face a real risk of being subjected to inhuman or degrading treatment within the meaning of Article 4 of the Charter.[327]

However, the ECJ was clearer about the link between this obligation and the sovereignty clause; the ECtHR could not be expected to go as far as this once the relevance of Dublin II had been excluded. According to the ECJ, therefore, the obligation did not stem from an immediate need to apply the clause because the Regulation established a hierarchy of other criteria for determining a (different) State responsible. If the first criterion produced a result that was not compatible with the principle of *non-refoulement*, the Member State where the

324 ECtHR, judgment of 30 June 2005, Application No. 45036/98, *Bosphorus* v. *Ireland*, available online at www.echr.coe.int, on which see, including for the extensive references in the literature and for critical comments, N. Napoletano (2010: 40 ff.).

325 ECtHR (Grand Chamber), judgment of 21 January 2011, Application No. 30696/09, *M. S. S.* v. *Belgium and Greece (M. S. S.)*, available online at www.echr.coe.int, para. 340. On this see L. Magi (2011: 824 ff.) and P. Mallia (2011: 107 ff.).

326 ECJ, judgment of 21 December 2011, Joined Cases C-411/10 and C-493/10, *N. S.* v. *Secretary of State for the Home Department* and *M. E. and others* v. *Refugee Applications Commissioner and Minister for Justice, Equality and Law Reform (N. S.)*, not yet published, para. 81, on which see G. Cellamare (2012a: 95 ff.) and G. Morgese (2012b: 147 ff.). The fact that the presumption is not irrefutable can also be deduced from internal case law, on which see again G. Cellamare (2009: 5 f.).

327 *N. S.*, para. 94.

first application was lodged could (but did not have to[328]) apply the other criteria and if they produced a different result could begin the process for taking charge of the applicant.[329]

The way the Dublin III Regulation is formulated reflects this, particularly the sovereignty clause, which appears to reprise the words of the ECJ. According to the new Article 3,

> Where it is impossible to transfer an applicant to the Member State primarily designated as responsible because there are substantial grounds for believing that there are systemic flaws in the asylum procedure and in the reception conditions for applicants in that Member State, resulting in a risk of inhuman or degrading treatment within the meaning of Article 4 of the Charter of Fundamental Rights of the European Union, the determining Member State shall continue to examine the criteria set out in Chapter III in order to establish whether another Member State can be designated as responsible.

Once the State applying Dublin III has been designated responsible, the next step is to verify, according to the usual rules based on the application of the Refugee Convention and the ECHR, if the applicant's transfer violates the principle of *non-refoulement* as enshrined in the two acts. In the case in point, the ECtHR had little difficulty deciding that Greece was a country 'of risk', there being insufficient guarantees either of access to asylum procedures or that the applicant would not be transferred to a third country where he or she would be at risk of persecution (indirect *refoulement*); similarly, detention conditions there did not comply with Article 3 ECHR.[330] The same concept had been asserted in several documents, notably by UNHCR.[331] Consequently, Belgium could not reasonably ignore that the situation in Greece was such that the transfer of the applicant there would be contrary to the principle of *non-refoulement*. Similar concepts have been expressed by the ECJ, although perhaps because it is keener to safeguard the interests of the EU it clarified that violations which an applicant might suffer in the Member State of destination (the one responsible for examining the application under

---

328 It goes without saying that the Member State in question does not have the reverse obligation either, that is to use the sovereignty clause as the only alternative to the first criterion (when this has proved fruitless because of conditions in the first State identified): see ECJ, judgment of 14 November 2013, Case C-4/11, *Bundesrepublik Deutschland v. Kaveh Puid*, not yet published.

329 *N. S.*, para. 5 f. The Court ruled that the criteria could be used progressively on condition that 'The Member State in which the asylum seeker is present must, however, ensure that it does not worsen a situation where the fundamental rights of that applicant have been infringed by using a procedure for determining the Member State responsible which takes an unreasonable length of time. If necessary, that Member State must itself examine the application in accordance with the procedure laid down in Article 3(2) of Regulation No 343/2003' (ibid., para. 98).

330 *M. S. S.*, para. 344 ff.

331 See UNHCR (2008a).

Dublin II, now Dublin III) do not concern *every* rule of the common European asylum system, only where 'there are substantial grounds for believing that there are systemic flaws in the asylum procedure and reception conditions for asylum applicants in the Member State responsible, resulting in inhuman or degrading treatment'.[332]

Perhaps the most interesting aspect to emerge from the ECtHR ruling is that one of the arguments Belgium used in its defence was the failure to exhaust all possible internal remedies.[333] The Court held in this regard that these remedies were not efficient and effective and thus absolved the applicant from the obligation to exhaust them before bringing the case, and further recognised that there had been a violation of Article 13 ECHR taken in conjunction with Article 3 ECHR.[334] This is an extremely important ruling because it is linked to the fact that the Procedures Directive does not place any obligation on Member States to guarantee effective means of challenging the decision to transfer the applicant to the country determined according to the criteria of Dublin II. Article 39 of the Procedures Directive does lay down the right to an effective remedy, but only against a decision that the application is unfounded or inadmissible, leaving out the case where it is not examined in compliance with Dublin II.[335] Dublin III introduces a new article, Article 27, obligating States to recognise the applicant's right 'to an effective remedy, in the form of an appeal or a review, in fact and in law, against a transfer decision, before a court or tribunal'.

4.12 C) Inadmissible application and safe third country

Dublin III makes it clear that a Member State always has the option of sending an applicant to a third country 'subject to the rules and safeguards laid down in Directive 2013/32/EU' (Article 3(3)).[336] Article 25 of the Procedures Directive confirms that an asylum application need not be examined by the Member State in which it is lodged, as the applicant can be sent to a third country, and lists a number of situations in which the application may be deemed inadmissible.[337] Leaving aside the situations in which an applicant already has refugee status in another Member State or enjoys a similar form of protection in a third country,[338]

---

332 *N. S.*, para. 86.
333 *M. S. S.*, para. 335.
334 Ibid., para. 385 ff.
335 Similarly, see Article 46 of the new Procedures Directive.
336 But see footnote 399, Chapter 1.
337 As does Article 33 of the new Procedures Directive.
338 The first case raises no problem, and anyway existing case law indicates that the State where the inadmissible application is lodged must ascertain that no further or subsequent risks exist in the EU Member State where the applicant has refugee status: see High Court of Ireland, decision of 23 November 2010, *AQS and KIS* v. *Refugee Applications Commissioner, The Minister for Justice, Equality and Law Reform*. The case of the

which raise few problems, there are some comments worth making on point (c), according to which an application may be deemed inadmissible if 'a country which is not a Member State is considered as a safe third country for the applicant, pursuant to Article 27'.

The safe third country concept is not, as we have seen (above, section 1.6), itself incompatible with the Refugee Convention, nor are there any elements for arriving at a different conclusion from that of the case law relating to the ECHR. However, UNHCR has specified the conditions for applying the concept: it cannot bypass an individual examination of the application; it must be based on specific elements designed to verify whether the country in question is safe; and, lastly, the safe country must have a link with the applicant, must admit him or her, and must be willing to examine the application for protection. The Procedures Directive contains some discrepancies regarding each of these elements, which legal theorists have not failed to note.[339] In reality, it does not deviate overmuch from the recommendations of UNHCR as regards the first two conditions. Individual examination in accordance with the Procedures Directive is envisaged in almost all the countries that use – rarely, in fact – the safe third country concept (they do not include five Member States, among them Italy). Then, it is rare for the elements used to evaluate the safety of that country not to be among those indicated in the Directive.[340] Indeed, the Commission has found that only two Member States fail to take proper account of whether the third country observes the principle of *non-refoulement*.[341]

country of first asylum poses a few more problems. According to M. Spatti (2007: 234) it includes countries where the applicant may enjoy sufficient protection *in the future*, but that possibility must be verified in the same way as for the safe third country. In my opinion, shared by S. H. Legomsky (2003: 591), the concept of first asylum country is instead limited to territories in which the applicant already has refugee status or similar protection. This would appear to be confirmed in practice, on which see the Report from the Commission COM (2010) 465 final, para. 5.2.3.

339 See G. Bartolini (2008: 177 ff.).

340 Article 27(1), cited at point (c), lists the criteria to be used to establish whether a third country is safe: '(a) life and liberty are not threatened on account of race, religion, nationality, membership of a particular social group or political opinion; (b) the principle of non-refoulement in accordance with the Geneva Convention is respected; (c) the prohibition of removal, in violation of the right to freedom from torture and cruel, inhuman or degrading treatment as laid down in international law, is respected; and (d) the possibility exists to request refugee status and, if found to be a refugee, to receive protection in accordance with the Geneva Convention'. Article 38 of the new Procedures Directive is almost identical, merely specifying that a country is not safe if there is a risk of serious harm pursuant to Article 15 of the new Qualification Directive.

341 See Report from the Commission COM (2010) 465 final, para. 5.2.4. Just because internal regulations do not include, among the criteria for evaluating the safety of the third country, observance of the principle of *non-refoulement*, this does not prevent the court from taking it into account following ECtHR case law: see, regarding the UK (one of the two Member States 'incriminated'), the Upper Tribunal (Immigration and Asylum Chamber), decision of 13 November 2010, *The Secretary of State for the Home Department* v. *RR*.

The other conditions are more difficult. Article 27(2) of the Procedures Directive only makes use of the safe third country concept subject to, among others, the 'rules requiring a connection between the person seeking asylum and the third country concerned on the basis of which it would be reasonable for that person to go to that country'. States implementing this provision often consider a very weak, if not virtually inexistent, connection, to the extent that for some of them transit alone is sufficient. In other cases, internal rules establish broad criteria that are often extremely vague.[342] However, possibly the most sensitive issue is that of the conditions for the applicant's access to procedures guaranteeing that his or her asylum application will be properly examined in the third country of destination. As some writers have pointed out,[343] the risk here is that access will only be virtual as under some of the third country's internal rules examination of applications may be refused if they were not made at the time of first entry. Given that applicants must have at least transited through the third country and that in most cases they do not arrive directly from the countries where they are at risk of persecution, the general framework of procedures for obtaining the examination of an asylum application in safe third countries should be thoroughly assessed by the internal authorities. Instead, the general manner in which the safe third country concept is used seems to disregard this requirement. The fact that the Procedures Directive includes such situations among those eligible for fast-track procedures and considers that the individual interview may be omitted and that the asylum application may be deemed inadmissible indicates that the safe third country concept is implemented in a very summary fashion, unlikely to take all the factors into account, particularly the question of access to the procedure, which the Directive itself mentions.

4.13 Recognition of refugee status: right of residence and right to family unity

Once the authorities have accepted the application they must examine its merits. If the outcome is positive, the beneficiary of international protection will be granted some rights, most of which are enshrined in the new Qualification Directive. If the outcome is negative, the applicant may appeal the decision,[344] in

---

342 See the Report from the Commission COM (2010) 465 final, para. 5.2.4: 'National measures . . . merely refer to a person who "was present" (SI), "has transited and had an opportunity at the border or within the territory to contact the authorities" (RO and the UK), "has remained or transited and there is a connection which may, in principle, allow the person to address that country" (PT), "has stayed" (CZ), or "has resided" (BG, EL and MT) in a third country. No relevant rules are laid down in AT, FI, LT and SK. In EE, ES, LU, CY, national rules require the authorities to establish a connection without specifying the applicable criteria'.

343 G. Bartolini (2008: 187).

344 Article 39 of the Procedures Directive mentions an 'effective remedy before a court or tribunal', an expression on which the ECJ has recently ruled. In the case of *H. I. D.*,

accordance with the rules set out in Article 39 ff. of the Procedures Directive.[345] One case in which an application will be considered unfounded is that of a safe country of origin. This can only be designated by the States, the ECJ having declared void the part of the Procedures Directive that provided for its designation by EU institutions. Many States resort to the concept, which is basically used to deny, in general and preventively, that any person coming from one of the countries on the list drawn up by each Member State may be a refugee or a person eligible for subsidiary protection. This much is clear even from the elements connecting the applicant to the country, which Article 31 of the Directive defines as citizenship or habitual residence (in the case of stateless persons). This leads to the problem of the criteria for determining the safety of the country of origin, described in full in Annex II of the Procedures Directive,[346] and the need to guarantee the applicant that the presumption regarding the 'safety' of his or her country of origin can be rebutted. According to the Commission, Member States resorting to the concept usually comply with the requirements of Annex II and with the obligation to conduct an individual examination that will reveal any elements rebutting the presumption of safety.[347]

The rights of beneficiaries of international protection differ according to whether the person is a refugee or a beneficiary of subsidiary protection. Both have rights that mirror some of those enshrined in the Refugee Convention, with the difference that they are often broader in the case of refugees. For example, the right to remain in the country, to which both categories are entitled, is for a duration of three years (renewable) in the case of refugees and one year (also

citing its own case law on the notion of 'jurisdiction', the Court held that the Irish Refugee Appeals Tribunal met the criteria necessary to qualify as such.

345 It can be deduced from Article 39(3) of the Procedures Directive that the applicant does not have a right to remain in the host Member State: States are accorded the option, although they must allow 'the possibility of legal remedy or protective measures'.

346 'A country is considered as a safe country of origin where, on the basis of the legal situation, the application of the law within a democratic system and the general political circumstances, it can be shown that there is generally and consistently no persecution as defined in Article 9 of Directive 2004/83/EC, no torture or inhuman or degrading treatment or punishment and no threat by reason of indiscriminate violence in situations of international or internal armed conflict. In making this assessment, account shall be taken, inter alia, of the extent to which protection is provided against persecution or mistreatment by: (a) the relevant laws and regulations of the country and the manner in which they are applied; (b) observance of the rights and freedoms laid down in the European Convention for the Protection of Human Rights and Fundamental Freedoms and/or the International Covenant for Civil and Political Rights and/or the Convention against Torture, in particular the rights from which derogation cannot be made under Article 15(2) of the said European Convention; (c) respect of the non-refoulement principle according to the Geneva Convention; (d) provision for a system of effective remedies against violations of these rights and freedoms'.

347 See the Report from the Commission COM (2010) 465 final, para. 5.2.5.

renewable) for beneficiaries of subsidiary protection. Some inequality of treatment still exists in respect of some rights, including one very important right if only because it entails further consequences: this is the right to family reunification accorded by human rights treaties, notably Article 8 ECHR. It is not wholly enshrined in the new Qualification Directive, but it does appear in Directive 2003/86/EC.[348] The scope of the latter is not quite the same as that of the new Qualification Directive, however, and therefore the system of family reunification is the result of a complex and ill-coordinated set of rules based on the two Directives.

According to scholarly writers,[349] the system can usually be constructed by 'picking' the most favourable elements from the two Directives. However, it can only function for the situations envisaged, as neither of the Directives is more generous than the other. For instance, regarding potential beneficiaries, the system in Directive 2003/86 does not apply to subsidiary protection beneficiaries, who are only covered by the limited provisions of the new Qualification Directive.[350] On the other hand, the Qualification Directive is based on a concept of family member that is occasionally broader than that of Directive 2003/86.[351] Moreover, while Directive 2003/86 contains a very vague rule on the rights of family members (such as residence permit, work permit, and so on), the new Qualification Directive is much more precise on this point.[352] There are two major discrepancies with respect to the parameter established by Article 8 ECHR, as interpreted by the ECtHR. First, the system applying to beneficiaries of subsidiary protection appears unable to guarantee full rights to reunification

---

348 On which see F. Scatzu (2008: 244 ff.) and K. Hailbronner and C. Carlitz (2010: 160 ff.), including the bibliography. On the implementation of the Directive in Italy see M. B. Deli (2008: 247 ff.).

349 K. Hailbronner and C. Carlitz (2010: 252).

350 Following the Stockholm Programme, the Commission has considered extending the scope of the Directive on reunification to include beneficiaries of subsidiary protection: see Green Paper on the Right to Family Reunification of third-country nationals living in the European Union (Directive 2003/86/EC), COM (2011) 735 final, para. 4.1.

351 The effects of the new Qualification Directive, which is limited to family units already formed in the country of origin, extend to the unmarried partner of a person with the following status: 'in a stable relationship, where the law or practice of the Member State concerned treats unmarried couples in a way comparable to married couples under its law relating to third-country nationals', a case that Directive 2003/86 leaves to the decision of Member States. However, Directive 2003/86 does not require, for the purpose of reunification, unmarried underage children of the couple (one of which has refugee status) to be dependent, unlike Article 2(h) of the new Qualification Directive.

352 Directive 2003/86 only provides for a right to housing, work and training in Article 14, while according to Article 23(2) of the new Qualification Directive, using the same ambiguous wording as in paragraph (1) ('Member States shall ensure that'), family members enjoy the same benefits envisaged in Articles 24–34 containing rules on the issue of residence permits, travel documents, access to employment and even access to integration measures.

because Article 23(1) of the new Qualification Directive – the only one applicable to them – does not offer adequate guarantees. It merely states that 'Member States shall ensure that family unity can be maintained'. Article 4 of Directive 2003/86 concerning only refugees, instead, asserts very clearly that 'the Member States shall authorise the entry and residence . . . of the . . . family members'. Second, as several writers have noted,[353] the notion of family members, be it the one based on the new Qualification Directive, or the other contained in the Directive on family reunification, is far more limited than the notion established by the ECtHR.

Other rights are more convergent and no difference exists between the position of a refugee and a beneficiary of subsidiary protection. The most important rights are those to which a beneficiary of international protection is entitled in respect of a procedure to revoke one or other status; they are contained in some of the rules regarding assessment thanks to the reference to them contained in Article 38 of the Procedures Directive. While the substantive requirements for revocation in the case of refugees, on the one hand, and beneficiaries of subsidiary protection, on the other, differ, the guarantees that the procedure must observe are identical and include the right to a personal interview, the right to appeal the revocation order and the right to legal assistance for that appeal. More recently a major amendment was made to the Directive concerning the status of third-country nationals who are long-term residents, extending its provisions to beneficiaries of international protection. Thus, given the five years of continuous residence usually required by the Directive, even a beneficiary of international protection can obtain a more permanent residence permit, with broader rights than those accompanying international protection status.

---

353 F. Seatzu (2008: 273 ff.).

Conclusions

The foregoing analysis suggests several final considerations. It is clear that the rules enshrined in the Refugee Convention are applied inconsistently and that national courts often arrive at completely contrasting solutions to the issues those rules fail to resolve. As I have tried to show, even in key areas such as assessment procedures the Convention allows States enormous freedom of manoeuvre, with the result that they often take an opposite line to the one recommended by UNHCR. Because that agency does not have the power to bind States and thus provide the main source of interpretation of the rules of the Convention, a door has been opened, allowing a series of elements to influence the way States construe the Convention. First, their geographical position makes some States an easier 'target' for immigrants, including asylum-seekers, potentially leading to the adoption of 'defensive' practices. Contingent events can often raise States' defences (for instance, 11 September) or generate sudden mass influxes (such as war). And the richest countries, traditionally places of refuge, may appear attractive to the rest of the world. All these factors, and others too, can alter the way the Refugee Convention is applied. That instrument is neither sufficiently exhaustive and detailed nor equipped with suitable control mechanisms to limit the scope for States to act independently; in other words, mechanisms to confine them within narrower and more closely monitored boundaries. This is not surprising. As is usual in international law, States themselves erect the boundaries within which they have power to act, in this case in relation to the right of asylum. We should not forget that the Refugee Convention was drafted at a time in history when the principles related to human rights had not yet been asserted. This weakness was surely aggravated by the Convention's universal scope, which did not come about as a result of greater 'homogeneity' among the States taking part in the negotiations, as instead happens in a regional context.

The 1951 Refugee Convention joins the 1950 Rome Convention for the Protection of Human Rights and Fundamental Freedoms. The latter contains no rules governing the right of asylum, ranking it possibly even lower than the Refugee Convention in terms of providing a system to regulate this matter. The reason for the importance of the ECHR lies in its strength: the ECtHR. It is thanks to the Court that a prohibition on *refoulement* broader in some respects than the principle enshrined in Article 33 of the Refugee Convention was imposed as a result of the protection *par ricochet* implicit in the ECHR regulations, notably Article 3.

The second instrument, not originally designed to safeguard asylum-seekers, thus has a more profound impact than the first, which instead was drafted solely and expressly to protect refugees. This is confirmed by the very significant fact that in the EU, subsidiary protection, which should be the offshoot of case law relating to the ECHR, has a far greater application than the institution of refuge derived from the Refugee Convention. In other words, in the EU the number of beneficiaries of subsidiary protection is far greater than the number of refugees. This speaks volumes not only (and not so much) about the relationship between the ECHR and the Refugee Convention – particularly about their ability/inability to expand in scope, mainly owing to their different control mechanisms – but also about the approach taken by the Qualification Directive (both old and new versions), in which the figure of the refugee continues to occupy a central role. In sum, EU legislation does not appear to keep pace with reality, given that what clearly emerges as the 'principal' protection is subsidiary to that of the Refugee Convention. The latter shows signs of becoming obsolete, at least within the context of a system, like that of Europe, with an instrument, the ECHR, that brings with it the mechanism governed by the ECtHR.

There is an even more interesting aspect from this point of view that is worth mentioning. It should not be forgotten that the main reason why the EU stepped in to implement the rules on asylum, whether those of the Refugee Convention or of the ECHR, as interpreted by the ECtHR, was the need to regulate asylum in a uniform manner. This was a necessary step towards establishing a common juridical space in which, among other things, the freedom of movement of European citizens is assured as this would be hindered by the presence of internal border controls. The origin of the Schengen Agreements illustrates very clearly the link between the desire to create that space and the harmonisation of legislation on asylum and immigration in general. What is of interest is the fact that the statistics on successful applications for international protection vary greatly from one EU State to another. This means that the sought-after uniformity is far from having been achieved, considering the enormous variation in the percentage of applications (definitively) accepted. In 2008 that percentage ranged from 84 per cent in Finland, to 51 per cent in the Netherlands, and to 2 per cent in Spain. In 2009 the United Kingdom granted 40 per cent of applications, while Ireland and Greece accepted only 3 per cent and 1 per cent respectively. And so on up to 2013, with 78 per cent for Italy against 16 per cent for Germany and 14 per cent for France. This is evidence of the collapse of the Dublin II system, which was based specifically on the fact that an application made in one Member State should in principle have the same chance of success as in any other State adopting the system. Clearly, this is not so. Reception conditions, which should be similar, have added a nail to the coffin of Dublin II: the ECtHR's judgment against Belgium and Greece (*M. S. S.*) has made some cautious European States wary of the reception system in place in other countries (such as Italy).

In reality, I believe that a partial solution has already been adopted. I do not refer to the instruments soon to replace the whole system of asylum in the EU, as their potential contribution to overcoming the problems described appears, at least at first sight, inadequate. The real turning point is the 'freeing up' of the ECJ's power to issue preliminary rulings. Accordingly, in the EU at least, a set of rules that, on the one hand, are quite detailed but lacking in guidelines (the Refugee Convention) and, on the other, contain only a nod to the right of asylum but have the backing of the powerful mechanism based on the ECtHR, will have a single source of interpretation. There is nothing new here: the ECJ has always been a driving force of European integration. Once the 'incoming tide', to use Lord Denning's expression, gets under way (if it does), it is difficult to know where it will lead. Certainly, as requests for referral from national courts find their way to Luxembourg, a single judgment (for virtually all the Member States) will be pronounced on the doubts of interpretation and omissions that still plague both international instruments, but particularly the Refugee Convention, as well as on the major discrepancies between them and EU legislation. Whether or not that single judgment will also be a definitive one will depend on the outcome of the EU's prospective accession to the ECHR, now awaiting the opinion of the ECJ pursuant to Article 218(11) TFEU. If that accession goes ahead, then it will be the ECtHR that will have ultimate responsibility for the entire system.

This policy is a reflection of the phase in which the process of European integration now finds itself: unable to offer solutions to today's most pressing problems because competence is dispersed between the EU and Member States. Although I am confident that the involvement of Europe's courts will overcome this hurdle (which is nothing new in the process of European integration), I do not believe it is enough on its own. Asylum and immigration policy need to be put back into one hand only, be it that of the EU (which would take on the role for the first time) or, as some politicians harking back to 'the old days' have suggested, that of the individual Member States. And there is more. Going further in this direction, possibly into the realms of fantasy, if the EU were to be given exclusive competence in this field, then even the bureaucracy in charge of applying the rules on asylum and immigration would need to be 'Europeanised'. This would probably entail a strengthening of Frontex that would bring it out of the shadows where it has operated so far; controls might be stepped up over activities that for the time being *de facto* escape censure even by the ECJ.

Despite the gigantic step forward that will be made when the two courts of Europe take on a more incisive role, regulation of the right of asylum in the EU is beset by an underlying conflict, as indeed are other 'delicate' matters (economic policy, to name but one): the need to serve two masters, the EU on one side and Member States on the other. This makes it ineffective, not so much in terms of content as with respect to the way the individual rules are formed. To repeat the colourful metaphor used by the first President of the Executive Committee instituted by the Convention Implementing the Schengen Agreement (see footnote 22, Chapter 3), moving controls from the door of the apartment to the door of the building may not be easy in an apartment block with an immensely complicated decision-making process. Today's asylum policy is a build-up of successive layers that have made it highly disjointed. Although by nature it should be the product of a unitary vision uniformly implemented, it has become full of pitfalls, an amalgam of national interests, internal political feuding and facile demagoguery. There are no winners, only losers – from the asylum-seekers to those operating in the field, whether activists or law enforcement officers, dealing with a dramatic reality that is a million miles away from the seats of power that should provide the solution.

Bibliography

Adepoju, A., F. van Noorloos and A. Zoomers (2009) 'Europe's Migration Agreements with Migrant-Sending Countries in the Global South: A Critical Review', *International Migration*, p. 42 ff.

Adinolfi, A. (1993) 'Quali procedure e garanzie per la cessazione dello status di rifugiato?', *Rivista di diritto internazionale*, p. 1106 ff.

Adinolfi, A. (1998) 'La circolazione dei cittadini di Stati terzi: obblighi comunitari e normativa nazionale', in B. Nascimbene (a cura di), *La libera circolazione dei lavoratori*, Milano, p. 123 ff.

Adinolfi, A. (2001) 'Commento agli artt. 66–69', in F. Pocar (a cura di), *Commentario breve ai Trattati della Comunità e dell'Unione europea*, Padova, p. 315 ff.

Adinolfi, A. (2005a) 'Free movement and access to work of citizens of the new Member States: the transitional measures', *Common Market Law Review*, p. 469 ff.

Adinolfi, A. (2005b) 'La libertà di circolazione delle persone', in G. Strozzi (a cura di), *Diritto dell'Unione europea Parte speciale*, II ed., Torino, p. 69 ff.

Adinolfi, A. (2009) 'Riconoscimento dello status di rifugiato e della protezione sussidiaria: verso un sistema comune europeo?', *Rivista di diritto internazionale*, p. 669 ff.

Adjin-Tettey, E. (1997–1998) 'Reconsidering the Criteria for Assessing Well-Founded Fear in Refugee Law', *Manitoba Law Journal*, p. 127 ff.

Albert, M. (2010) 'Governance and *Prima Facie* Refugee Status Determination: Clarifying the Boundaries of Temporary Protection, Group Determination, and Mass Influx', *Refugee Survey Quarterly*, p. 61 ff.

Albors-Llorens, A. (1998) 'Changes in the Jurisdiction of the European Court of Justice under the Treaty of Amsterdam', *Common Market Law Review*, p. 1273 ff.

Alborzi, M. R. (2006) *Evaluating the Effectiveness of International Refugee Law: The Protection of Iraqi Refugees*, Leiden, Boston.

Alcindor, L. (1929) 'Asile (droit d')', in *Répertoire de droit international*, tome 2, Paris, p. 32 ff.

Andrade, P. G. (2010) 'Extraterritorial Strategies to Tackle Irregular Immigration by Sea: A Spanish Perspective', in B. Ryan, V. Mitsilegas (eds), *Extraterritorial Immigration Control. Legal Challenges*, Leiden, Boston, p. 311 ff.

Andrijasevic, R. (2010) 'DEPORTED: The Right to Asylum at EU's External Border of Italy and Libya', *International Migration*, p. 148 ff.

Antoniu, G. (1978) 'Immunité, extraterritorialité et droit d'asile en droit pénal international', *Revue internationale de droit pénal*, p. 573 ff.

Anzilotti, D. (1923) *Corso di diritto internazionale (Introduzione – I soggetti – Gli organi). Lezioni tenute nell'Università di Roma nell'anno scolastico 1922–1923*, Roma.

Arai-Takahashi, Y. (2002) '"Uneven, But in the Direction of Enhanced Effectiveness" – A Critical Analysis of "Anticipatory Ill-treatment" under Article 3 ECHR', *Netherlands Quarterly of Human Rights*, p. 5 ff.

Arcari, M. (2007) 'L'attribuzione allo Stato di atti di genocidio nella sentenza della Corte internazionale di giustizia nel caso *Bosnia-Erzegovina c. Serbia*', *Diritti umani e diritto internazionale*, p. 565 ff.

Arenas, N. (2005a) 'Combatants and armed elements as refugees. The interplay between international humanitarian law and international refugee law', in P. A. Fernández-Sánchez (ed.), *The New Challenges of Humanitarian Law in Armed Conflicts: In Honour of Professor Juan Antonio Carrillo-Salcedo*, Leiden, Boston, p. 227 ff.

Arenas, N. (2005b) 'The Concept of "Mass Influx of Displaced Persons" in the European Directive Establishing the Temporary Protection System', *European Journal of Migration and Law*, p. 435 ff.

Arias Fernández, G. (2011) 'Frontex and the Illegal Immigration in the European Union', in J. M. Sobrino Heredia (sous la direction de), *Sûreté maritime et violence en mer*, Bruxelles, p. 29 ff.

Attinà, F. (2004) 'The Euro-Mediterranean project of security partnership in comparative perspective', *Jean Monnet Working Paper in Comparative and International Politics*, September, available online at aei.pitt.edu

Aus, J. P. (2006) 'Eurodac: A Solution Looking for a Problem?', *European Integration online Papers*, available at eior.or.at.

Bahramy, A. (1938) *Le droit d'asile*, Paris.

Bailliet, C. M. (2003) 'The *Tampa* Case and its Impact on Burden Sharing at Sea', *Human Rights Quarterly*, p. 741 ff.

Bailliet, C. M. (2007) 'Examining Sexual Violence in the Military Within the Context of Eritrean Asylum Claims Presented in Norway', *International Journal of Refugee Law*, p. 471 ff.

Baldaccini, A. (2010a) 'The EU Directive on Return: Principles and Protests', *Refugee Survey Quarterly*, p. 114 ff.

Baldaccini, A. (2010b) 'Extraterritorial Borders Control in the EU: the Role of Frontex in Operations at Sea', in B. Ryan, V. Mitsilegas (eds), *Extraterritorial Immigration Control. Legal Challenges*, Leiden, Boston, p. 229 ff.

Balladore Pallieri, G. (1938) *Diritto internazionale pubblico*, Milano.

Bank, R. (1999) 'The Emergent EU Policy on Asylum and Refugees', *Nordic Journal of International Law*, p. 1 ff.

Barnes, R. (2004) 'Refugee Law at Sea', *International and Comparative Law Quarterly*, p. 47 ff.

Barontini, G. (1992) 'Sulla competenza per l'esame delle domande di asilo secondo le Convenzioni di Schengen e di Dublino', *Rivista di diritto internazionale*, p. 335 ff.

Bartolini, G. (2008) 'Osservazioni in margine alla "direttiva procedure"' 2005/85/CE', in P. Benvenuti (a cura di), *Flussi migratori e fruizione dei diritti fondamentali*, Ripa di Fagnano Alto, p. 177 ff.

Barutciski, M. and A. Suhrke (2001) 'Lessons from the Kosovo Refugee Crisis: Innovations in Protection and Burden-sharing', *Journal of Refugee Studies*, p. 95 ff.

Battjes, H. (2006) *European Asylum Law and International Law*, Leiden, Boston.

Battjes, H. (2009) 'In Search of a Fair Balance: The Absolute Character of the Prohibition of *Refoulement* under Article 3 ECHR Reassessed', *Leiden Journal of International Law*, p. 583 ff.

Bayefsky, A. F. (ed.) (2006) *Human rights and refugees, internally displaced persons, and migrant workers: essays in memory of Joan Fitzpatrick and Arthur Helton*, Leiden, Boston.

Beghè Loreti, A. (1990) *Rifugiati e richiedenti asilo nell'area della Comunità europea*, Padova.

Bellucci, S. (2002) *Schengen nel nuovo millennio*, IV ed., Roma.

Benedetti, E. (2010) *Il diritto di asilo e la protezione dei rifugiati nell'ordinamento comunitario dopo l'entrata in vigore del Trattato di Lisbona*, Padova.

Bernardi, E. (1987) 'Asilo politico', in *Digesto delle discipline pubblicistiche*, vol. I, Torino, p. 421 ff.

Bertini, S. (2003) 'La politica europea in materia di immigrazione, asilo e libera circolazione delle persone. I rapporti con i Paesi terzi', in G. Bonvicini, G. L. Tosato (a cura di), *Le relazioni internazionali dell'Unione europea dopo i Trattati di Amsterdam e Nizza*, Torino, p. 183 ff.

Bettati, M (1985) *L'asile politique en question*, Paris.

Bettis, R. (2010) 'The Iraqi Refugee Crisis: Whose Problem Is It? Existing Obligations Under International Law, Proposal to Create a New Protocol to the 1967 Refugee Convention, & U.S. Foreign Policy Recommendations to the Obama Administration', *Transnational Law & Contemporary Problems*, p. 261 ff.

Betts, A. and J. Milner (2006) 'The Externalisation of EU Asylum Policy: The Position of African States', *Centre on Migration, Policy and Society Working Paper No. 36*, available online at www.compas.ox.ac.uk.

Bevilacqua, M. (1999) 'Richiedenti asilo e rifugiati politici nel sistema di Schengen', *Nuova rassegna di legislazione, dottrina e giurisprudenza*, p. 1214 ff.

Bhabha, J. (1994–1995) 'European Harmonisation of Asylum Policy: A Flawed Process', *Virginia Journal of International Law*, p. 101 ff.

Biavati, P. (1998) 'Prime note sulla giurisdizione comunitaria dopo il Trattato di Amsterdam', *Rivista trimestrale di diritto e procedura civile*, p. 805 ff.

Bilgin, P., E. Soler i Lecha and A. Bilgiç (2011) 'European Security Practices vis-à-vis the Mediterranean Implications in Value Terms', *DIIS Working Paper*, available online at www.academia.edu

Billet, C. (2010) 'EC Readmission Agreements: A Prime Instrument of the External Dimension of the EU's Fight against Irregular Immigration. An Assessment after Ten Years of Practice', *European Journal of Migration and Law*, p. 45 ff.

Blake, N. and R. Husain (2003) *Immigration, asylum and human rights*, Oxford.

Bliss, M. (2000) '"Serious Reasons for Considering": Minimum Standards of Procedural Fairness in the Application of the Article 1F Exclusion Clauses', *International Journal of Refugee Law*, p. 92 ff.

Boccardi, I. (2002) *Europe and refugees: towards an EU asylum policy*, The Hague.

Boeles, P. and A. Terlouw (1997) 'Minimum Guarantees for Asylum Procedures', *International Journal of Refugee Law*, p. 472 ff.

Bohmer, C. and A. Shuman (2008) *Rejecting refugees: Political asylum in the 21st century*, London, New York.

Bolesta-Koziebrodzki, L. (1962) *Le droit d'asile*, Leyde.

Bonafé, B. (2010) 'La nozione di persecuzione nel diritto dell'Unione europea in materia di rifugiati e la responsabilità internazionale dello Stato', in A. Caligiuri, G. Cataldi, N. Napoletano (a cura di), *La tutela dei diritti umani in Europa*, Padova, p. 277 ff.

Bonetti, P. (2008) 'Il diritto d'asilo in Italia dopo l'attuazione della direttiva comunitaria sulle qualifiche e sugli status di rifugiato e di protezione sussidiaria', *Diritto, immigrazione e cittadinanza*, p. 13 ff.

Bonetti, P. (2011) 'Il diritto di asilo nella Costituzione italiana', in C. Favilli (a cura di), *Procedure e garanzie del diritto d'asilo*, Padova, p. 35 ff.

Borelli, S. (2006) 'Allontanamento dello straniero dal territorio e norme internazionali per la tutela dei diritti umani', in L. Zagato (a cura di), *Verso una disciplina comune europea del diritto d'asilo*, Padova, p. 99 ff.

Bostock, C. M.-J. (2002) 'The International Legal Obligations owed to the Asylum Seekers on the *MV Tampa*', *International Journal of Refugee Law*, p. 279 ff.

Boumghar, M. (2011) 'La licéité internationale des opérations menées par Frontex', in J. M. Sobrino Heredia (sous la direction de), *Sûreté maritime et violence en mer*, Bruxelles, p. 103 ff.

Boutillon, S. (2003–2004) 'The Interpretation of Article I of the 1951 Convention Relating to the Status of Refugees by the European Union: Toward Harmonization', *Georgia Immigration Law Journal*, p. 111 ff.

Brandl, U. (2004) 'Distribution of asylum seekers in Europe? Dublin II regulation determining the responsibility for examining an asylum application', in C. Dias Urbano de Sousa (under the supervision of), *The Emergence of a European Asylum Policy*, Bruxelles, p. 33 ff.

Breitenmoser, S. and G. E. Wilms (1989–1990) 'Human Rights v. Extradition: The Soering Case', *Michigan Journal of International Law*, p. 845 ff.

Brochmann, G. and S. Lavenex (2002) 'Neither In or Out: The Impact of EU Asylum and Immigration policies on Norway and Switzerland', in S. Lavenex, M. Uçarer (eds), *Migration and the Externalities of European Integration*, Lanham, Boulder, New York, Oxford, p. 55 ff.

Brouwer, E. R. (2002) 'Eurodac: Its Limitations and Temptations', *European Journal of Migration and Law*, p. 231 ff.

Bruin, R. and K. Wouters (2003) 'Terrorism and the Non-Derogability of Non-Refoulement', *International Journal of Refugee Law*, p. 5 ff.

Byrne, R., G. Noll and J. Vedsted-Hansen (eds) (2002) *New Asylum Countries? Migration Control and Refugee Protection in an Enlarged European Union*, The Hague, London, New York.

Cabral de Moncada, H. (1945) 'O asilo interno em Direito internacional público', *Boletim da Faculdade de Direito*, p. 55 ff. and p. 469 ff.

Caggiano, G. (1990) 'Asilo, ingresso, soggiorno ed espulsione dello straniero nella nuova legge sull'immigrazione', *La Comunità Internazionale*, p. 31 ff.

Caggiano, G. (2008) 'Le nuove politiche dei controlli alle frontiere, dell'asilo e dell'immigrazione nello Spazio unificato di libertà, sicurezza e giustizia', in P. Benvenuti (a cura di), *Flussi migratori e fruizione dei diritti fondamentali*, Ripa di Fagnano Alto, p. 101 ff.

Calamia, A. M. (1980) *Ammissione ed allontanamento degli stranieri*, Milano.

Cannizzaro, E. (2001) 'L'armonizzazione delle politiche di asilo in sede comunitaria e la Convenzione di Ginevra sui rifugiati del 1951', *Rivista di diritto internazionale*, p. 440 ff.

Carasco, E. (2003) 'Canada-United States "Safe Third Country Agreement": To What Purpose?', *Annuaire canadien de Droit international*, p. 305 ff.

Carbone, A. (2001) 'La protezione temporanea: l'evoluzione dell'istituto nell'ordinamento italiano e l'applicazione nell'emergenza Kossovo', *Gli Stranieri*, n. 2, p. 85 ff.

Carella, G. (1992) 'Esodi di massa e diritto internazionale', *Rivista di diritto internazionale*, p. 903 ff.

Carella, G. (2005) 'Lotta al terrorismo e protezione dei rifugiati', in U. Leanza (a cura di), *Le migrazioni. Una sfida per il diritto internazionale, comunitario e interno*, Napoli, p. 177 ff.

Carlier, J.-Y. (1999) 'The Geneva Refugee Definition and the "Theory of Three Scales"', in F. Nicholson, P. Twomey (eds), *Refugee Rights and Realities: Evolving International Concepts and Regimes*, Cambridge, New York, p. 37 ff.

Carlier, J.-Y., D. Vanheule, K. Hullmann and C. Peña (eds) (1997) *Who Is a Refugee?*, The Hague, London, Boston.

Caron, P. G. (1968) 'Asilo. Diritto canonico e diritto pubblico statuale, medioevale e moderno', in *Novissimo digesto italiano*, vol. I, parte 2, p. 1036 ff.

Carrera, S. (2007) 'The EU Border Management Strategy: Frontex and the Challenges of Irregular Immigration in the Canary Islands', *CEPS Working Document No. 261/March*, available online at www.ceps.eu

Carrera, S., L. den Hertog, and J. Parkin (2012) 'EU Migration Policy in the wake of the Arab Spring: What prospects for EU-Southern Mediterranean Relations?', *MEDPRO Technical Report No. 15*, August, available online at www.ceps.be

Cassarino, J.-P. (2010a) 'Dealing with Unbalanced Reciprocities: Cooperation on Readmission and Implications', in J.-P. Cassarino (ed.), *Unbalanced Reciprocities: Cooperation on Readmission in the Euro-Mediterranean Area*, Washington, p. 1 ff.

Cassarino, J.-P. (2010b) *Readmission Policy in the European Union*, available online at www.cadmus.eui.eu

Cassese, A. (2006) 'The Multifaceted Criminal Notion of Terrorism in International Law', *Journal of International Criminal Justice*, p. 933 ff.

Castellaneta, M. (2011) 'Ritardi nel processo di adesione dell'Unione europea alla CEDU', *Notizie e commenti sul diritto internazionale e dell'Unione europea*, available at www.marinacastellaneta.it

Castellaneta, M. (2012) 'Sull'immigrazione patto "segreto" Italia Libia', *Notizie e commenti sul diritto internazionale e dell'Unione europea*, available at www.marinacastellaneta.it

Castellano, D. (a cura di) (2008) *Il diritto di asilo in Europa: problemi e prospettive*, Napoli.

Castellazzi, S. (2006) 'Nuove regole comunitarie in tema di attraversamento delle frontiere', *Il diritto dell'economia*, p. 551 ff.

Castrogiovanni, I. (1994) 'Sul *refoulement* dei profughi haitiani intercettati in acque internazionali', *Rivista di diritto internazionale*, p. 474 ff.

Cavasino, E. (2010) 'Il diritto d'asilo nell'ordinamento italiano: struttura, garanzie, effettività', in A. Caligiuri, G. Cataldi, N. Napoletano (a cura di), *La tutela dei diritti umani in Europa*, Padova, p. 297 ff.

Cellamare, G. (2006) *La disciplina dell'immigrazione nell'Unione europea*, Torino.

Cellamare, G. (2009) 'In tema di limiti di carattere umanitario all'operare del regolamento Dublino II', *Sud in Europa*, aprile, p. 5 ff.

Cellamare, G. (2010) 'Gli accordi di riammissione dell'Unione europea', *Studi sull'integrazione europea*, p. 369 ff.

Cellamare, G. (2012a) 'Asilo politico: considerata relativa e non assoluta la presunzione di rispetto dei diritti fondamentali', *Guida al diritto*, fasc. 6, p. 95 ff.

Cellamare, G. (2012b) 'Brevi note sulla sentenza della Corte europea dei diritti dell'uomo nell'affare *Hirsi Jamaa e altri c. Italia*', *Studi sull'integrazione europea*, p. 491 ff.

Chelo, A. (2010) *Il mandato di arresto europeo*, Padova.

Cherubini, F. (2010a) 'The European Union between the Implementation of the UN Measures against International Terrorism and the Respect for Human Rights', in A. M. Gallore (ed.), *Terrorism: Motivation, Threats and Prevention*, New York, p. 25 ff.

Cherubini, F. (2010b) 'The Treaty of accession of Bulgaria and Romania to the EU and the free movement of persons', in L. P. Harrison (ed.), *Social Policy: Challenges, Developments and Implications*, New York, p. 111 ff.

Cherubini, F. (2011) 'Terrorismo (diritto internazionale)', in *Enciclopedia del diritto. Annali (V)*, p. 1213 ff.

Cherubini, F. (2014) 'La cooperazione fra Unione europea e paesi del Nordafrica nella lotta all'immigrazione irregolare', in F. Anghelone, A. Ungari (a cura di), *Atlante Geopolitico del Mediterraneo 2014*, Roma, p. 15 ff.

Chimni, B. S. (ed.) (2000) *International Refugee Law: A Reader*, New Delhi.

Choupilov, V. P. (1978) 'L'immunité, l'extraterritorialité et le droit d'asile en droit pénal international', *Revue internationale de droit pénal*, p. 611 ff.

Christiansen, S. M. (2010) *Environmental Refugees: A Legal Perspective*, Nijmegen.

Chueca Sancho, Á. G. (2009) 'La política de inmigración de la UE en el Mediterráneo o el síndrome de las tres "R"', in Á. G. Chueca Sancho, V. L. Gutiérrez Castillo, I. Blázquez Rodríguez (coordinadores), *Las migraciones internacionales en el Mediterráneo y Unión Europea*, Barcelona, p. 23 ff.

Cieslak, M. and W. Michalski (1978) 'Immunité, extraterritorialité e droit d'asile', *Revue internationale de droit pénal*, p. 565 ff.

Ciprotti, P. (1958) 'Asilo (diritto di). b) Diritto canonico ed ecclesiastico', in *Enciclopedia del diritto*, vol. II, Milano, p. 203 s.

Ciucǎ, A. (2011) 'On the Charter of Fundamental Rights of the European Union and the EU accession to the European Convention on Human Rights', *Eastern Journal of European Studies*, p. 57 ff.

Cohen-Jonathan, G. (1989) *La Convention européenne des droits de l'homme*, Aix-en-Provence, Paris.

Coleman, N. (2003) '*Non-Refoulement* Revised. Renewed Review of the Status of *Non-Refoulement* as Customary International Law', *European Journal of Migration and Law*, p. 23 ff.

Coleman, N. (2009) *European Readmission Policy: Third Country Interests and Refugee Rights*, Leiden, Boston.

Coles, G. J. L. (1978–1980) 'Temporary Refuge and the Large Scale Influx of Refugees', *Australian Yearbook of International Law*, p. 189 ff.

Concolino, B. (2008) 'Divieto di tortura e sicurezza nazionale: l'espulsione di presunti terroristi', *Diritti umani e diritto internazionale*, p. 627 ff.

Condinanzi, M. (2005) 'La nozione di "giudice avverso le cui decisioni non può proporsi ricorso di diritto interno" nel Titolo IV del Trattato CE. Osservazioni in margine al caso *Dem'yanenko*', in U. Leanza (a cura di), *Le migrazioni. Una sfida per il diritto internazionale, comunitario e interno*, Napoli, p. 435 ff.

Condinanzi, M., A. Lang and B. Nascimbene (2006) *Cittadinanza dell'Unione e libera circolazione delle persone*, II ed., Milano.

Conetti, G. (1967) 'Il V Colloquio internazionale sul diritto d'asilo', *Rassegna di diritto pubblico*, p. 798 ff.

Conroy, M. A. (2009) 'Refugees Themselves: The Asylum Case for Parents of Children at Risk of Female Genital Mutilation', *Harvard Human Rights Journal*, p. 109 ff.

Consoli, D. (2011) 'Il riconoscimento in via giurisdizionale del diritto di asilo', in C. Favilli (a cura di), *Procedure e garanzie del diritto d'asilo*, Padova, p. 209 ff.

Corkery, A. (2006) 'The Contribution of the UNHCR Executive Committee to the Development of International Refugee Law', *Australian International Law Journal*, p. 97 ff.

Cortese, B. (2006) 'L'esternalizzazione delle procedure di riconoscimento dello status di rifugiato: l'approccio dell'Unione europea, tra prassi degli Stati membri e competenze comunitarie', in L. Zagato (a cura di), *Verso una disciplina comune europea del diritto d'asilo*, Padova, p. 199 ff.

Craig, S. and M. Fletcher (2005) 'Deflecting Refugees: A Critique of the EC Asylum Procedures Directive', in P. Shah (ed.), *The Challenge of Asylum to Legal Systems*, London, Sydney, Portland, p. 53 ff.

Crawford, J. (2010) *The International Law of Responsibility*, Oxford.

Crépeau, F. and J. Y. Carlier (1999) 'Intégration régionale et politique migratoire. Le "modèle" européen entre coopération et communautarisation', *Journal de droit international*, p. 953 ff.

Crifò, G. (1958) 'Asilo (diritto di). a) Premessa storica. 1) Diritti antichi', in *Enciclopedia del diritto*, vol. II, Milano, p. 191 ff.

Crifò, G. (1966) 'Esilio. Parte storica', in *Enciclopedia del diritto*, vol. XV, Milano, p. 712 ff.

Cruz, A. (1999) 'Achievements in the Fields of Immigration and Asylum since January 1998', *European Journal of Migration and Law*, p. 243 ff.

Curti Gialdino, C. (1998) 'Schengen e il terzo pilastro: il controllo giurisdizionale secondo il Trattato di Amsterdam', in *L'Italia e Schengen. Lo spazio di libertà, sicurezza e giustizia tra problemi applicativi e prospettive: atti del Convegno organizzato dal Comitato di controllo sull'attuazione e il funzionamento della Convenzione di Schengen*, Roma, p. 41 ff.

Cutler, C. D. (2004–2005) 'The U.S.-Canada Safe Third Country Agreement: Slamming the Door on Refugees', *ILSA Journal of International and Comparative Law*, p. 121 ff.

Da Lomba, S. (2004) *The Right to Seek Refugee Status in the European Union*, Antwerp, Oxford, New York.

Da Lomba, S. (2011) 'The EU Qualification Directive and Refugee *Sur Place*', in F. A. N. J. Goudappel, H. S. Raulus (eds.), *The Future of Asylum in the European Union*, The Hague, p. 61 ff.

Damato, A. (1991) 'Estradizione e divieto di trattamenti inumani o degradanti nella Convenzione europea dei diritti dell'uomo', *Rivista internazionale dei diritti dell'uomo*, p. 648 ff.

Damato, A. (2005) 'Il mandato d'arresto europeo e la sua attuazione nel diritto italiano (II)', in *Il diritto dell'Unione europea*, p. 203 ff.

Daniele, L. (2004) 'Commento all'art. 68', in A. Tizzano (a cura di), *Trattati dell'Unione europea e della Comunità europea*, Milano, p. 460 ff.

Davy, U. (2011) 'Article 32', in A. Zimmermann (ed.), *The 1951 Convention Relating to the Status of Refugees and its 1967 Protocol: A Commentary*, Oxford, p. 1277 ff.

De Bonis, A. (2011) 'La procedura amministrativa per il riconoscimento della protezione internazionale in Italia', in C. Favilli (a cura di), *Procedure e garanzie del diritto d'asilo*, Padova, p. 187 ff.

De Capitani, E. (2009) *A Chronicle of a European Freedom Security and Justice Space*, available at www.europeanrights.eu

de Jong, C. D. (1999) 'Is There a Need for a European Asylum Policy?', in F. Nicholson, P. Twomey (eds), *Refugee Rights and Realities: Evolving International Concepts and Regimes*, Cambridge, New York, p. 357 ff.

De Sena, P. (2002) *La nozione di giurisdizione statale nei trattati sui diritti dell'uomo*, Torino.

Del Guercio, A. (2008) 'Il principio di non-refoulement tra dottrina dei diritti umani e sistema internazionale di protezione dei rifugiati', in L. Cimmino, N. Ramazzo (a cura di), *Diritti umani nell'era della globalizzazione e dei conflitti*, Napoli, p. 19 ff.

Del Guercio, A. (2010) 'Il diritto dei migranti all'unità familiare nella giurisprudenza della Corte europea dei diritti umani e nell'ordinamento dell'Unione europea', in A. Caligiuri, G. Cataldi, N. Napoletano (a cura di), *La tutela dei diritti umani in Europa*, Padova, p. 387 ff.

Del Vecchio, A. (1973) 'Comunità europee e GATT', *Il diritto degli scambi internazionali*, p. 274 ff.

Deli, M. B. (2008) 'Il ricongiungimento familiare nell'attuazione in Italia della direttiva 2003/86', in P. Benvenuti (a cura di), *Flussi migratori e fruizione dei diritti fondamentali*, Ripa di Fagnano Alto, p. 247 ff.

Delicato, V. (2011) 'La cooperazione fra Italia e Libia per il contrasto dell'immigrazione irregolare', in C. Favilli (a cura di), *Procedure e garanzie del diritto d'asilo*, Padova, p. 279 ff.

den Boer, M. (2002) 'To What Extent Can There Be Flexibility in the Application of Schengen in the New Member States', in M. Anderson, J. Apap (eds), *Police and Justice Cooperation and the New Borders*, The Hague, London, New York, p. 139 ff.

den Heijer, M. (2013) 'Reflections on *Refoulement* and Collective Expulsion in the *Hirsi* Case', *International Journal of Refugee Law*, p. 265 ff.

den Hertog, L. (2013) 'Fundamental Rights and the Extra-Territorialisation of EU Border Policy: a Contradiction in Terms?', in D. Bigo, S. Carrera, E. Guild (eds), *Foreigners, Refugees or Minorities? Rethinking People in the Context of Border Controls and Visas*, Farnham, p. 205 ff.

Desimio, G. (2008) 'Il futuro regime comune europeo in materia di asilo: prime risposte al Libro verde della Commissione delle Comunità europee', *Cassazione penale*, p. 2144 ff.

Di Pascale, A. (2010) 'Migration Control at Sea: The Italian case', in B. Ryan, V. Mitsilegas (eds), *Extraterritorial Immigration Control. Legal Challenges*, Leiden, Boston, p. 281 ff.

Dominioni, O. (1978) 'Immunity, Extraterritoriality and the Right of Asylum in International Criminal Law', *Revue internationale de droit pénal*, p. 539 ff.

Doublet, J. (1957) 'Problèmes de Sécurité Sociale et Communauté Européenne du Charbon et de l'Acier', *Annuaire français de droit international*, p. 574 ff.

Duffy, A. (2008) 'Expulsion To Face Torture? Non-Refoulement in International Law', *International Journal of Refugee Law*, p. 373 ff.

Durante, F. (1984) 'La tutela internazionale dei rifugiati e diritti dell'uomo', in *Studi in onore di G. Sperduti*, Milano, p. 558 ff.

Durieux, J.-F. and J. McAdam (2004) 'Non-Refoulement Through Time: The Case for a Derogation Clause to the Refugee Convention in Mass Influx Emergencies', *International Journal of Refugee Law*, p. 4 ff.

Duxbury, A. (2008) 'Excluding the Undesirable: Interpreting Article 1F (a) of the Refugee Convention in Australia', in D. A. Blumenthal, T. L. H. McCormack (eds), *The Legacy of Nuremberg: Civilising Influence or Institutionalised Vengeance?*, Leiden, Boston, p. 259 ff.

Edwards, A. (2003) 'Tampering with Refugee Protection: The Case of Australia', *International Journal of Refugee Law*, p. 192 ff.

Edwards, A. (2011a) 'Article 17', in A. Zimmermann (ed.), *The 1951 Convention Relating to the Status of Refugees and its 1967 Protocol: A Commentary*, Oxford, p. 951 ff.

Edwards, A. (2011b) 'Article 18', in A. Zimmermann (ed.), *The 1951 Convention Relating to the Status of Refugees and its 1967 Protocol: A Commentary*, Oxford, p. 973 ff.

Edwards, A. (2011c) 'Article 19', in A. Zimmermann (ed.), *The 1951 Convention Relating to the Status of Refugees and its 1967 Protocol: A Commentary*, Oxford, p. 983 ff.

Eeckhout, P. (2000) 'The European Court of Justice and the "Area of Freedom, Security and Justice": Challenges and Problems', in D. O'Keeffe (ed.), *Judicial Review in European Union Law*, The Hague, London, Boston, p. 153 ff.

Eggli, A. V. (2002) *Mass Refugee Influx and the Limits of Public International Law*, The Hague, London, New York.

El-Enany, N. (2008) 'Who Is the New European Refugee?', *European Law Review*, p. 313 ff.

Elberling, B. (2011) 'Article 16', in A. Zimmermann (ed.), *The 1951 Convention Relating to the Status of Refugees and its 1967 Protocol: A Commentary*, Oxford, p. 931 ff.

Epiney, A. and A. Egbuna-Joss (2010) 'Regulation (EC) No 562/2006 of the European Parliament and of the Council of 15 March 2006 establishing a Community Code on the rules governing the movement of persons across borders (Schengen Borders Code)', in K. Hailbronner (ed.), *EU Immigration and Asylum Law. Commentary on EU Regulations and Directives*, München, p. 103 ff.

Errera, R. (2011) 'The CJEU and Subsidiary Protection: Reflections on Elgafaji – and After', *International Journal of Refugee Law*, p. 93 ff.

Esposito, C. (1958) 'Asilo (diritto di). d) diritto costituzionale', in *Enciclopedia del diritto*, vol. II, Milano, p. 222 ff.

Evola, M. (2010) 'La riunificazione familiare dello straniero nei trattati sui diritti umani', *Diritti umani e diritto internazionale*, p. 279 ff.

Favilli, C. (2011) 'La protezione internazionale nell'ordinamento dell'Unione Europea', in C. Favilli (a cura di), *Procedure e garanzie del diritto d'asilo*, Padova, p. 121 ff.

Feller, E., V. Türk, and F. Nicholson (eds) (2003) *Refugee Protection in International Law: UNHCR's Global Consultations on International Protection*, Cambridge.

Fennelly, N. (1998) 'Preserving the Legal Coherence within the New Treaty: The European Court of Justice after the Treaty of Amsterdam', *Maastricht Journal of European and Comparative Law*, p. 185 ff.

Ferrari, G. (2004) 'La Convenzione sullo status dei rifugiati. Aspetti storici', talk given at the Università degli Studi di Roma 'La Sapienza', 16 January 2004, as part of the 12th multidisciplinary course 'Asilo: dalla Convenzione di Ginevra alla Costituzione europea', available at www.unhcr.it

Fink, M. (2012) 'Frontex Working Arrangements: Legitimacy and Human Rights Concerns Regarding "Technical Relationships"', *Merkourios: Utrecht Journal of International and European Law*, p. 20 ff.

Fioravanti, C. (2009) 'Scatole cinesi. Quale controllo democratico sulla cooperazione "italo-libica-europea" in materia d'immigrazione?', in G. Brunelli, A. Pugiotto, P. Veronesi (a cura di), *Scritti in onore di Lorenza Carlassare*, vol. II, Napoli, p. 539 ff.

Fischer-Lescano, A., T. Löhr and T. Tohidipur (2009) 'Border Controls at Sea: Requirements Under International Human Rights and Refugee Law', *International Journal of Refugee Law*, p. 256 ff.

Fitzpatrick, J. (2000) 'Temporary Protection of Refugees: Elements of a Formalized Regime', *The American Journal of International Law*, p. 279 ff.

Fitzpatrick, J. and R. Bonoan (2003) 'Cessation of Refugee Protection', in E. Feller, V. Türk, F. Nicholson (eds), *Refugee Protection in International Law. UNHCR's Global Consultations on International Protection*, Cambridge, p. 491 ff.

Flinterman, C. (2006) 'Expulsion of Aliens (Article 1 of Protocol No. 7)', in P. van Dijk, F. van Hoof, A. van Rijn, L. Zwaak (eds), *Theory and Practice of the European Convention on Human Rights*, IV ed., Oxford, p. 965 ff.

Fonteyne, J.-P. L. (1978–1980) 'Burden-Sharing: An Analysis of the Nature and Function of International Solidarity in Cases of Mass Influx of Refugees', *Australian Yearbook of International Law*, p. 162 ff.

Fornari, M. (2002) 'Soccorso di profughi in mare e diritto di asilo: questioni di diritto internazionale sollevate dalla vicenda della nave Tampa', *La Comunità Internazionale*, p. 61 ff.

Fornari, M. (2006) 'La Convenzione europea per la prevenzione della tortura e delle pene o trattamenti inumani o degradanti', in L. Pineschi (a cura di), *La tutela internazionale dei diritti umani. Norme, garanzie, prassi*, Milano, p. 571 ff.

Foster, M. (2001–2002) 'Causation in Context: The Nexus Clause in the Refugee Convention', *Michigan Journal of International Law*, p. 265 ff.

Foster, M. and J. Pobjoy (2011) 'A Failed Case of Legal Exceptionalism? Refugee Status Determination in Australia's "Excised" Territory', *International Journal of Refugee Law*, p. 583 ff.

Franchini, C. (2011) 'Lo *status* di rifugiato nella Convenzione di Ginevra del 1951', in C. Favilli (a cura di), *Procedure e garanzie del diritto d'asilo*, Padova, p. 73 ff.

Fridegotto, M. (1992) *L'Accordo di Schengen: riflessi internazionali ed interni per l'Italia*, Milano.

Frulli, M. (2007) 'Un passo avanti e due indietro: responsabilità individuale e responsabilità statale nella sentenza della Corte internazionale di giustizia nel caso *Bosnia-Erzegovina c. Serbia*', *Diritti umani e diritto internazionale*, p. 579 ff.

Gammeltoft-Hansen, T. (2011) *Access to Asylum: International Refugee Law and the Globalisation of Migration Control*, Cambridge.

Garbagnati, M. G. (1996) 'La cooperazione in materia di immigrazione ed asilo', in N. Parisi, D. Rinoldi (a cura di), *Giustizia e affari interni nell'Unione europea*, Torino, p. 59 ff.

Garlick, M. (2006) 'The EU Discussions on Extraterritorial Processing: Solution or Conundrum?', *International Journal of Refugee Law*, p. 601 ff.

Garofalo, L. (2000) 'Sulla competenza a titolo pregiudiziale della Corte di giustizia secondo l'art. 68 del Trattato CE', *Il diritto dell'Unione europea*, p. 805 ff.

Gavouneli, M. (2006) 'Shamayev & 12 Others v. Georgia & Russia. App. No. 36378/02. European Court of Human Rights, April 12, 2005', *American Journal of International Law*, p. 674 ff.

Gestri, M. (2011) 'La politica europea dell'immigrazione: solidarietà tra Stati membri e misure nazionali di regolarizzazione', in A. Ligustro, G. Sacerdoti (a cura di), *Problemi e tendenze del diritto internazionale dell'economia: liber amicorum in onore di Paolo Picone*, Napoli, p. 895 ff.

Gianelli, A. (2008a) 'Il carattere assoluto dell'obbligo di *non-refoulement*: la sentenza Saadi della Corte europea dei diritti dell'uomo', *Rivista di diritto internazionale*, p. 449 ff.

Gianelli, A. (2008b) 'Obbligo di "non-refoulement" ed assicurazioni diplomatiche', in *Studi in onore di Vincenzo Starace*, Napoli, p. 363 ff.

Gianelli, A. (2009) 'L'adesione dell'Unione europea alla CEDU secondo il Trattato di Lisbona', *Il diritto dell'Unione europea*, p. 678 ff.

Giardina, A. (1973) 'La Corte europea ed i rapporti fra diritto comunitario e diritto internazionale', *Rivista di diritto internazionale privato e processuale*, p. 582 ff.

Gil-Bazo, M.-T. (2008) 'The Charter of Fundamental Rights of the European Union and the Right to Be Granted Asylum in the Union's Law', *Refugee Survey Quarterly*, p. 33 ff.

Gil-Bazo, M.-T (2011) 'Article 40', in A. Zimmermann (ed.), *The 1951 Convention Relating to the Status of Refugees and its 1967 Protocol: A Commentary*, Oxford, p. 1567 ff.

Gilbert, G. (2003) 'Current Issues in the Application of the Exclusion Clauses', in E. Feller, V. Türk, F. Nicholson (eds), *Refugee Protection in International Law. UNHCR's Global Consultations on International Protection*, Cambridge, p. 425 ff.

Gilbert, G. (2004) 'Is Europe Living Up to Its Obligations to Refugees', *The European Journal of International Law*, p. 963 ff.

Gilbert, G. (2005) 'Exclusion and Evidentiary Assessment', in G. Noll (ed.), *Proof, Evidentiary Assessment and Credibility in Asylum Procedures*, Leiden, Boston, p. 161 ff.

Gilbert, G. S. (1983) 'Right of Asylum: A Change of Direction', *The International and Comparative Law Quarterly*, p. 633 ff.

Ginzberg, L. (1902) 'Asylum – in Rabbinical Literature', in *The Jewish Encyclopedia*, vol. II, New York, p. 257 ff.

Gioia, A. (2004) 'Terrorismo internazionale, crimini di guerra e crimini contro l'umanità', *Rivista di diritto internazionale*, p. 38 ff.

Girerd, P. (1999) 'L'article 68: un renvoi préjudiciel d'interprétation et d'application incertaines', *Revue Trimestrielle de Droit Européen*, p. 239 ff.

Giriodi, M. (1896) 'Asilo (Diritto di) – (Storia del Diritto)', in *Digesto italiano*, vol. IV, parte I, Torino, p. 777 ff.

Giuliano, M. (1958) 'Asilo (diritto di). c) diritto internazionale', in *Enciclopedia del diritto*, vol. II, Milano, p. 204 ff.

Glen, S. J. (2007–2008) 'Is the United States *Really* a not "Safe Third Country": A Contextual Critique of the Federal Court of Canada's Decision in *Canadian Council for Refugees, et al. v. Her Majesty the Queen*', *Georgetown Immigration Law Journal*, p. 587 ff.

Goodwin-Gill, G. S. (1978) *International Law and the Movement of Persons Between States*, Oxford.

Goodwin-Gill, G. S. (1986) '*Non-Refoulement* and the New Asylum Seekers', *Virginia Journal of International Law*, p. 897 ff.

Goodwin-Gill, G. S. (2011) 'The Right to Seek Asylum: Interception at Sea and the Principle of Non Refoulement', *International Journal of Refugee Law*, p. 443 ff.

Goodwin-Gill, G. S. and H. Lambert (eds) (2010) *The Limits of Transnational Law: Refugee Law, Policy Harmonization and Judicial Dialogue in the EU*, Cambridge.

Goodwin-Gill, G. S. and J. McAdam (2007) *The Refugee in International Law*, III ed., Oxford, New York.

Gortázar, C. (2004) 'Asylum Procedures', in C. Dias Urbano de Sousa (under the supervision of), *The Emergence of a European Asylum Policy*, Bruxelles, p. 87 ff.

Gottwald, M. (2006) 'Asylum Claims and Drug Offences: the Seriousness Threshold of Article 1F (b) of the 1951 Geneva Convention Relating to the Status of Refugees and the UN Drug Conventions', *International Journal of Refugee Law*, p. 81 ff.

Goudappel, F. A. N. J. and H. S. Raulus (eds) (2011) *The Future of Asylum in the European Union*, The Hague.

Gowlland-Debbas, V. (ed.) (1996) *The problem of refugees in the light of contemporary international law issues: papers presented at the colloquium organized by the Graduate Institute of International Studies in collaboration with the Office of the United Nations High Commissioner for Refugees, Geneva 26 and 27 May, 1994*, The Hague, Boston, London.

Grahl-Madsen, A. (1966–1972) *The Status of Refugees in International Law*, 2 volumes, Leiden.

Grahl-Madsen, A. (1980) *Territorial Asylum*, Stockholm.

Grahl-Madsen, A. (1983) 'Identifying the World's Refugees', in G. D. Loescher, A. Scanlan (eds), *The Global Refugee Problem: U.S. and World Respond*, Beverly Hills, London, New Delhi, p. 11 ff.

Grahl-Madsen, A. (1997) *Commentary of the Refugee Convention 1951 (Articles 2–11, 13–37)*, available at www.unhcr.org

Grassano, P. (1998) 'Della condizione giuridica dell'asilante e del rifugiato politico nel nostro ordinamento', *Lo Stato Civile Italiano*, p. 813 ff.

Graziani, F. (2005) 'Gli accordi di riammissione', in U. Leanza (a cura di), *Le migrazioni. Una sfida per il diritto internazionale, comunitario e interno*, Napoli, p. 243 ff.

Guarneri, G. (2004) 'Il caso "Soering" davanti la Corte europea dei diritti dell'uomo', in C. Zanghì, L. Panella (a cura di), *Cooperazione giudiziaria in materia penale e diritti dell'uomo*, Torino, p. 93 ff.

Guidi, M. (2010) 'Sulle condizioni per il riconoscimento dello status di rifugiato a un apolide palestinese si pronuncia la Corte di giustizia', *Gli Stranieri*, n. 3, p. 155 ff.

Guidi, M. (2011) 'La Corte europea dei diritti dell'uomo afferma, ancora una volta, la violazione degli articoli 3 e 34 della CEDU da parte dell'Italia', *Gli Stranieri*, n. 1, p. 109 ff.

Guild, E. (1999) 'The Impetus to Harmonise: Asylum Policy in the European Union', in F. Nicholson, P. Twomey (eds), *Refugee Rights and Realities: Evolving International Concepts and Regimes*, Cambridge, New York, p. 313 ff.

Guild, E. (2004) 'Seeking Asylum: Storm Clouds Between International Commitments and EU Legislative Measures', *European Law Review*, p. 198 ff.

Guild, E. (2006) 'The Europeanisation of Europe's Asylum Policy', *International Journal of Refugee Law*, p. 630 ff.

Gunn, T. J. (2003) 'The Complexity of Religion and the Definition of "Religion" in International Law', *Harvard Human Rights Journal*, p. 189 ff.

Hadaway, H. (2005) 'Safe Third Countries in Australian Refugee Law: *NAGV v Minister for Immigration and Multicultural Affairs*', *Sydney Law Review*, p. 727 ff.

Hailbronner, K. (1992) 'Perspectives of Harmonisation of the Law of Asylum after the Maastricht Summit', *Common Market Law Review*, p. 917 ff.

Hailbronner, K. (1997a) 'The New Title on Free Movement of Persons, Asylum and Immigration in the TEC', in M. den Boer (ed.), *Schengen, Judicial Cooperation and Policy Coordination*, Maastricht, p. 201 ff.

Hailbronner, K. (1997b) 'Readmission Agreements and the Obligation on States under Public International Law to Readmit their Own and Foreign Nationals', *Zeitschrift für ausländisches öffentliches Recht und Völkerrecht*, p. 1 ff.

Hailbronner, K. (1998) 'European Immigration and Asylum Law Under the Amsterdam Treaty', *Common Market Law Review*, p. 1047 ff.

Hailbronner, K. (1999) 'The Treaty of Amsterdam and Migration Law', *European Journal of Migration and Law*, p. 9 ff.

Hailbronner, K. (2000) *Immigration and Asylum Law and Policy of the European Union*, The Hague, London, Boston.

Hailbronner, K. (2005) 'The Directive on Minimum Standards on Procedures for Granting and Withdrawing Refugee Status', in F. Julien-Laferrière, H. Labayle, Ö. Edström (eds), *The European Immigration and Asylum Policy: Critical Assessments Five Years after Amsterdam Treaty*, Bruxelles, p. 279 ff.

Hailbronner, K. and S. Alt (2010) 'Council Directive 2004/83/EC of 29 April 2004 on minimum standards for the qualification and status of third country nationals or stateless persons as refugees or as persons who otherwise need international protection and the content of the protection granted, Articles 1–10', in K. Hailbronner (ed.), *EU Immigration and Asylum Law. Commentary on EU Regulations and Directives*, München, p. 1006 ff.

Hailbronner, K. and C. Carlitz (2010) 'Council Directive 2003/86/EC of 22 September 2003 on the right to family reunification', in K. Hailbronner (ed.), *EU Immigration and Asylum Law. Commentary on EU Regulations and Directives*, München, p. 160 ff.

Hailbronner, K. and C. Thiery (1997) 'Schengen II and Dublin: Responsibility for Asylum Applications in Europe', *Common Market Law Review*, p. 957 ff.

Haines, R. (2003) 'Gender-related Persecution', in E. Feller, V. Türk, F. Nicholson (eds), *Refugee Protection in International Law. UNHCR's Global Consultations on International Protection*, Cambridge, p. 319 ff.

Hamood, S. (2008) 'EU-Libya Cooperation on Migration: A Raw Deal for Refugees and Migrants?', *Journal of Refugee Studies*, p. 19 ff.

Harris, D., M. O'Boyle and C. Warbrick (2009) *Law of the European Convention on Human Rights*, II ed., Oxford.

Harvey, C. J. (1998) 'The European Regulation of Asylum: Constructing a Model of Regional Solidarity', *European Public Law*, p. 561 ff.

Hathaway, J. C. (1991) *The Law of Refugee Status*, Markham.

Hathaway, J. C. (1993) 'Harmonizing for Whom? The Devaluation of Refugee Protection in the Era of European Economic Integration', *Cornell International Law Journal*, p. 719 ff.

Hathaway, J. C. (2005) *The Rights of Refugees under International Law*, Cambridge.

Hathaway, J. C. and M. Foster (2003) 'The Causal Connection ("Nexus") to a Convention Ground Discussion Paper No. 3 Advanced Refugee Law Workshop International

Association of Refugee Law Judges Auckland, New Zealand, October 2002', *International Journal of Refugee Law*, p. 461 ff.

Hathaway, J. C. and C. J. Harvey (2001) 'Framing Refugee Protection in the New World Disorder', *Cornell International Law Journal*, p. 257 ff.

Hathaway, J. C. and W. S. Hicks (2004–2005) 'Is There a Subjective Element in the Refugee Convention's Requirement of "Well Founded Fear"?', *Michigan Journal of International Law*, p. 505 ff.

Haun, E. (2007) *The Externalisation of Asylum Procedures : An Adequate EU Refugee Burden Sharing System?*, Frankfurt am Main.

Heckman, G. P. (2008) 'Canada's Refugee Status Determination System and the International Norm of Independence', *Refuge*, n. 2, p. 79 ff.

Hellmann, G. (ed.) (2006) *Germany's EU Policy on Asylum and Defence: De-Europeanization by Default?*, Basingstoke.

Helton, A. C. (1983–1984) 'Persecution on Account of Membership in a Social Group As a Basis for Refugee Status', *Columbia Human Rights Law Review*, p. 39 ff.

Helton, A. C. and J. Münker (1999) 'Religion and Persecution: Should the United States Provide Refuge to German Scientologists?', *International Journal of Refugee Law*, p. 310 ff.

Heringa, A. W. and L. Zwaak (2006) 'Right to Respect for Privacy (Article 8)', in P. van Dijk, F. van Hoof, A. van Rijn, L. Zwaak (eds), *Theory and Practice of the European Convention on Human Rights*, IV ed., Oxford, p. 663 ff.

Hreblay, V. (1998) *Les accords de Schengen. Origine, fonctionnement, avenir*, Bruxelles.

Hughes, J. and F. Liebaut (eds) (1998) *Detention of Asylum Seekers in Europe: Analysis and Perspectives*, The Hague.

Hurwitz, A. (1999) 'The 1990 Dublin Convention: A Comprehensive Assessment', *International Journal of Refugee Law*, p. 646 ff.

Hurwitz, A. (2004) 'Commentaires sur la détermination de l'État membre responsable de l'examen d'une demande d'asile et la répartition des charges entre États membres', in C. Dias Urbano de Sousa (under the supervision of), *The Emergence of a European Asylum Policy*, Bruxelles, p. 71 ff.

Hurwitz, A. (2009) *The Collective Responsibility of States to Protect Refugees*, New York.

Ianovitz, S. (2011) 'I "rifugiati climatici": una questione aperta', *Diritti umani e diritto internazionale*, p. 141 ff.

Ivaldi, P. (2002) 'Il rinvio pregiudiziale: linee evolutive', *Comunicazioni e Studi dell'Istituto di Diritto Internazionale e Straniero dell'Università di Milano*, p. 273 ff.

Jackson, I. C. (1999) *The Refugee Concept in Group Situations*, The Hague.

Jacobs, F. G., R. C. A. White and C. Ovey (2010) *The European Convention on Human Rights*, V ed., Oxford.

Jacqué, J. P. (2011) 'The Accession of the European Union to the European Convention on Human Rights and Fundamental Freedoms', *Common Market Law Review*, p. 995 ff.

Janis, M. W., R. S. Kay and A. W. Bradley (2008) *European Human Rights Law. Text and Materials*, III ed., Oxford.

Joly, D. (1989) 'Le Droit d'Asile dans la Communauté Européenne', *International Journal of Refugee Law*, p. 365 ff.

Joly, D. (1994) 'The Porous Dam: European Harmonization Policy in the Nineties', *International Journal of Refugee Law*, p. 159 ff.

Joly, D. (1999) 'A New Asylum Regime in Europe', in F. Nicholson, P. Twomey (eds), *Refugee Rights and Realities: Evolving International Concepts and Regimes*, Cambridge, New York, p. 336 ff.

Jubilut, L. L. (2006) 'Refugee Law and Protection in Brazil: a Model in South America?', *Journal of Refugee Studies*, p. 22 ff.

Julien-Laferrière, F. (2004) 'Le Statut des personnes protégées', in C. Dias Urbano de Sousa (under the supervision of), *The Emergence of a European Asylum Policy*, Bruxelles, p. 195 ff.

Juma, M. K. (2000) 'Asylum and the Politics of Humanitarian Assistance in East Africa', *American Society of International Law Proceedings*, p. 136 s.

Kälin, W. (2000–2001) 'Non-State Agents of Persecution and the Inability of the State to Protect', *Georgetown Immigration Law Journal*, p. 415 ff.

Kälin, W. (2003) 'Supervising the 1951 Convention Relating to the Status of Refugees: Article 35 and Beyond', in E. Feller, V. Türk, F. Nicholson (eds), *Refugee Protection in International Law. UNHCR's Global Consultations on International Protection*, Cambridge, p. 613 ff.

Kälin, W., M. Caroni and L. Heim (2011) 'Article 33, para. 1', in A. Zimmermann (ed.), *The 1951 Convention Relating to the Status of Refugees and its 1967 Protocol: A Commentary*, Oxford, p. 1327 ff.

Kälin, W. and J. Künzli (2000) 'Article 1F (b): Freedom Fighters, Terrorists, and the Notion of Serious Non-Political Crimes', *International Journal of Refugee Law*, p. 47 ff.

Keller, S., U. Lunacek, B. Lochbihler and H. Flautre (2011) *Frontex Agency: Which Guarantees for Human Rights?*, available online at www.migreurop.org

Kerber, K. (1997) 'Temporary Protection: An Assessment of the Harmonisation Policies of European Union Member States', *International Journal of Refugee Law*, p. 453 ff.

Kidd, J. (1994) 'Extradition and Expulsion Orders and the European Convention on Human Rights: The Soering Decision and Beyond', *Bracton Law Journal*, p. 67 ff.

Kirchheimer, O. (1959) 'Asylum', *The American Political Science Review*, p. 985 ff.

Kirişci, K. (2002) 'Immigration and Asylum Issues in EU-Turkish Relations: Assessing EU's Impact on Turkish Policy and Practice', in S. Lavenex, M. Uçarer (eds), *Migration and the Externalities of European Integration*, Lanham, Boulder, New York, Oxford, p. 125 ff.

Kjærum, M. (2002) 'Refugee Protection Between State Interests and Human Rights: Where Is Europe Heading?', *Human Rights Quarterly*, p. 513 ff.

Klepp, S. (2010a) 'A Contested Asylum System: The European Union between Refugee Protection and Border Control in the Mediterranean Sea', *European Journal of Migration and law*, p. 1 ff.

Klepp, S. (2010b) 'Italy and its Libyan Cooperation Program: Pioneer of the European Union's Refugee Policy', in J.-P. Cassarino (ed.), *Unbalanced Reciprocities: Cooperation on Readmission in the Euro-Mediterranean Area*, Washington, p. 77 ff.

Kneebone, S. (2006) 'The Pacific Plan: The Provision of "Effective Protection"?', *International Journal of Refugee Law*, p. 696 ff.

Kneebone, S. (ed.) (2009) *Refugees, Asylum Seekers and the Rule of Law: Comparative Perspectives*, Cambridge.

Kneebone, S. and M. O'Sullivan (2011) 'Article 1 C', in A. Zimmermann (ed.), *The 1951 Convention Relating to the Status of Refugees and its 1967 Protocol: A Commentary*, Oxford, p. 481 ff.

Koh, H. H. (1994) 'Reflections on *Refoulement* and *Haitian Centers Council*', *Harvard International Law Journal*, p. 1 ff.

Kojanec, G. (1977) 'Asilo territoriale: problematica nell'ambito delle Nazioni Unite', *La Comunità Internazionale*, p. 618 ff.

Kortenberg, H. (1998) 'Closer Cooperation in the Treaty of Amsterdam', *Common Market Law Review*, p. 833 ff.

Kuijper, P. J. (2000) 'Some Legal Problems Associated with the Communitarization of Policy Visas, Asylum and Immigration under the Amsterdam Treaty and Incorporation of the Schengen Acquis', *Common Market Law Review*, p. 345 ff.

Kwakwa, V. E. (2000) 'Article 1F (c): Acts Contrary to the Purposes and Principles of the United Nations', *International Journal of Refugee Law*, p. 79 ff.

Labayle, H. (1997) 'Un espace de liberté, de sécurité et de justice', *Revue Trimestrielle de Droit Européen*, p. 813 ff.

Lambert, H. (2006a) 'The EU Asylum Qualification Directive, Its Impact on the Jurisprudence of the United Kingdom and International Law', *International and Comparative Law Quarterly*, p. 161 ff.

Lambert, H. (2006b) *The Position of Aliens in Relation to the European Convention on Human Rights*, Strasbourg.

Lambert, H. (ed.) (2010) *International Refugee Law*, Aldershot.

Lauterpacht, E. and D. Bethlehem (2003) 'The Scope and Content of the Principle of *Non-Refoulement*: Opinion', in E. Feller, V. Türk, F. Nicholson (eds), *Refugee Protection in International Law. UNHCR's Global Consultations on International Protection*, Cambridge, p. 87 ff.

Lavenex, S. (2001) *The Europeanisation of Refugee Policies: Between Human Rights and Internal Security*, Aldershot.

Leckie, S. and E. Simperingham (2011a) 'Article 13', in A. Zimmermann (ed.), *The 1951 Convention Relating to the Status of Refugees and its 1967 Protocol: A Commentary*, Oxford, p. 883 ff.

Leckie, S. and E. Simperingham (2011b) 'Article 21', in A. Zimmermann (ed.), *The 1951 Convention Relating to the Status of Refugees and its 1967 Protocol: A Commentary*, Oxford, p. 1003 ff.

Leduc, F. (1977) 'L'asile territorial et Conférence des Nations Unies de Genève janvier 1977', *Annuaire français du droit international*, p. 221 ff.

Legomsky, S. H. (2003) 'Secondary Refugee Movements and the Return of Asylum Seekers to Third Countries: The Meaning of Effective Protection', *International Journal of Refugee Law*, p. 567 ff.

Legomsky, S. H. (2006) 'The USA and the Caribbean Interdiction Program', *International Journal of Refugee Law*, p. 677 ff.

Leich, M. N. (1982) 'Contemporary Practice of the United States Relating to International Law', *American Journal of International Law*, p. 374 ff.

Leimsidor, B. (2006) 'The Concept of "Safe Third Country" in Asylum Legislation, Regulation and Practice: Political, Humanitarian and Practical Considerations', in L. Zagato (a cura di), *Verso una disciplina comune europea del diritto d'asilo*, Padova, p. 39 ff.

Lenzerini, F. (2009) *Asilo e diritti umani*, Milano.

Lenzerini, F. (2012) 'Il principio del *non-refoulement* dopo la sentenza *Hirsi* della Corte europea dei diritti dell'uomo', *Rivista di diritto internazionale*, p. 721 ff.

Léonard, S. (2009) 'The Creation of FRONTEX and the Politics of Institutionalisation in the EU External Borders Policy', *Journal of Contemporary European Research*, p. 371 ff.

Léonard, S. (2010) 'EU Border Security and Migration into the European Union: FRONTEX and Securitisation through Practices', *European Security*, p. 231 ff.

Lerner, N. (1980) *The U.N. Convention on the Elimination of all Forms of Racial Discrimination*, Alphen aan den Rijn.

Lester, E. (2011a) 'Article 23', in A. Zimmermann (ed.), *The 1951 Convention Relating to the Status of Refugees and its 1967 Protocol: A Commentary*, Oxford, p. 1041 ff.

Lester, E. (2011b) 'Article 24', in A. Zimmermann (ed.), *The 1951 Convention Relating to the Status of Refugees and its 1967 Protocol: A Commentary*, Oxford, p. 1057 ff.

Lester, E. (2011c) 'Article 25', in A. Zimmermann (ed.), *The 1951 Convention Relating to the Status of Refugees and its 1967 Protocol: A Commentary*, Oxford, p. 1127 ff.

Licastro, G. (2006) 'Il "Codice frontiere Schengen"', *Diritto comunitario e degli scambi internazionali*, p. 587 ff.

Liguori, A. (2000) 'L'immigrazione e l'Unione europea', *Diritto comunitario e degli scambi internazionali*, p. 427 ff.

Liguori, A. (2012) 'La Corte europea dei diritti dell'uomo condanna l'Italia per i respingimenti verso la Libia del 2009: il caso *Hirsi*', *Rivista di diritto internazionale*, p. 415 ff.

Liguori, A. and N. Ricciuti (2012) 'Frontex ed il rispetto dei diritti umani nelle operazioni congiunte alle frontiere esterne dell'Unione europea', *Diritti umani e diritto internazionale*, p. 539 ff.

Lillich, R. B. (1991) 'The *Soering* Case', *The American Journal of International Law*, p. 128 ff.

Lock, T. (2010) 'EU Accession to the ECHR: Implications for the Judicial Review in Strasbourg', *European Law Review*, p. 777 ff.

Lock, T. (2011) 'Walking on a Tightrope: The Draft ECHR Accession Agreement and the Autonomy of the EU Legal Order', *Common Market Law Review*, p. 1025 ff.

Loescher, G., A. Betts and J. Milner (2008) *The United Nations High Commissioner for Refugees (UNHCR): the Politics and Practice of Refugee Protection into the Twenty-First Century*, London, New York.

Loper, K. (2006) 'Hong Kong's International Legal Obligations toward Refugees and Asylum Seekers', for Consideration at the Joint Meeting of the Legislative Council Panels on Welfare Services and Security on the situation of asylum seekers, refugees and claimants against torture in Hong Kong, available at www.hku.ak

Lorenzen, P. (2000) 'Rifugiati, richiedenti asilo e profughi', *Rivista internazionale dei diritti dell'uomo*, p. 643 ff.

Lynskey, O. (2006) 'Complementing and Completing the Common European Asylum System: A Legal Analysis of the Emerging Extraterritorial Elements of EU Refugee Protection Policy', *European Law Review*, p. 230 ff.

Mafrolla, E. M. (2001) 'L'evoluzione del regime internazionale in materia di asilo: tra sovranità territoriale e dovere umanitario', *Rivista internazionale dei diritti dell'uomo*, p. 532 ff.

Mafrolla, E. M. (2002) 'L'impatto del regime comune europeo in materia di asilo nei paesi dell'Europa centrale', *Rivista internazionale dei diritti dell'uomo*, p. 68 ff.

Magi, L. (2011) 'Protezione dei richiedenti asilo "par ricochet" o protezione "par moitié"? La Grande Camera ripartisce fra gli Stati contraenti le responsabilità per violazione della Convenzione europea conseguenti al trasferimento di un richiedente asilo in attuazione del regolamento "Dublino II"', *Rivista di diritto internazionale*, p. 824 ff.

Magner, T. (2004) 'A Less than "Pacific" Solution for Asylum Seekers in Australia', *International Journal of Refugee Law*, p. 53 ff.

Malintoppi, A. (studi e documenti raccolti da) (1983) *L'asilo politico territoriale*, Roma.

Mallia, P. (2011) 'Case of M.S.S. v. Belgium and Greece: A Catalyst in the Re-thinking of the Dublin II Regulation', *Refugee Survey Quarterly*, p. 107 ff.

Manca, L. (2003) *L'immigrazione nel diritto dell'Unione europea*, Milano.

Mancini, F. (1989) 'Politica comunitaria e nazionale delle migrazioni nella prospettiva dell'Europa sociale', *Rivista di diritto europeo*, p. 309 ff.

Manganaro, F. (2009) 'Diritto d'asilo e Convenzione europea dei diritti dell'uomo', in F. Astone, F. Manganaro (a cura di), *Cittadinanza inclusiva e flussi migratori*, Soveria Mannelli, p. 219 ff.

Marchesi, A. (2008) 'Diritto di asilo e procedure di riconoscimento del diritto all'asilo. Brevi considerazioni', in P. Benvenuti (a cura di), *Flussi migratori e fruizione dei diritti fondamentali*, Ripa di Fagnano Alto, p. 167 ff.

Marchisio, S. (2005) 'Rifugiati, profughi e altre esigenze di protezione nel diritto comunitario', in U. Leanza (a cura di), *Le migrazioni. Una sfida per il diritto internazionale, comunitario e interno*, Napoli, p. 327 ff.

Martín Arribas, J. J. and P. Dembour van Overbergh (2001) 'La cuestión prejudicial a la luz del artículo 68 del Tratado de la Comunidad europea', *Revista de Derecho Comunitario Europeo*, p. 231 ff.

Marx, R. (2001) 'Adjusting the Dublin Convention: New Approaches to Member States Responsibility for Asylum Applications', *European Journal of Migration and Law*, p. 7 ff.

Marx, R. (2011) 'Article 1 E', in A. Zimmermann (ed.), *The 1951 Convention Relating to the Status of Refugees and its 1967 Protocol: A Commentary*, Oxford, p. 571 ff.

Marx, R. and W. Staff (2011) 'Article 3', in A. Zimmermann (ed.), *The 1951 Convention Relating to the Status of Refugees and its 1967 Protocol: A Commentary*, Oxford, p. 643 ff.

McAdam, J. (2005) 'The European Union Qualification Directive: The Creation of a Subsidiary Protection Regime', *International Journal of Refugee Law*, p. 461 ff.

McAdam, J. (2007) *Complementary Protection in International Refugee Law*, Oxford, New York.

McBride, J. (2009) *Access to Justice for Migrants and Asylum Seekers in Europe*, Strasbourg.

McDougall, C. (2013) *The Crime of Aggression under the Rome Statute of the International Criminal Court*, Cambridge.

Meijers, H. (1990) 'Refugees in Western Europe. "Schengen" affects the Entire Refugee Law', *International Journal of Refugee Law*, p. 428 ff.

Metzger, A. (2011) 'Article 14', in A. Zimmermann (ed.), *The 1951 Convention Relating to the Status of Refugees and its 1967 Protocol: A Commentary*, Oxford, p. 895 ff.

Miele, M. (1968) 'La protezione internazionale diretta del diritto di asilo politico dell'individuo', *Revista española de derecho internacional*, p. 514 ff.

Migliazza, A. (1968) 'Asilo. Diritto internazionale', in *Novissimo digesto italiano*, vol. I, parte 2, Torino, p. 1039 ff.

Migliazza, A. (1980) 'Asilo (Diritto internazionale)', in *Novissimo digesto italiano. Appendice*, vol. I, Torino, p. 433 ff.

Mignolli, A. (2012) 'Il progetto di accordo di adesione dell'Unione europea alla CEDU: alcuni spunti di riflessione', *Studi sull'integrazione europea*, p. 541 ff.

Mikhaïlov, D. (1978) 'Immunité, extraterritorialité et droit d'asile en droit pénal de la République populaire de Bulgarie', *Revue internationale de droit pénal*, p. 451 ff.

Miltner, B. (2006–2007) 'Irregular maritime migration: refugee protection issues in rescue and interception', *Fordham International Law Journal*, p. 75 ff.

Missorici, M. and C. Romano (1998) 'Libertà di circolazione e soggiorno: i cittadini degli Stati terzi tra cittadinanza europea e politica delle migrazioni', *Rivista internazionale dei diritti dell'uomo*, p. 44 ff.

Mole, N. and C. Meredith (2010) *Asylum and the European Convention on Human Rights*, Strasbourg.

Moore, A. F. (2007) 'Unsafe in America: A Review of the U.S.-Canada Safe Third Country Agreement', *Santa Clara Law Review*, p. 201 ff.

Moreno-Lax, V. (2010) 'The EU Regime on Interdiction, Search and Rescue, and Disembarkation: The Frontex Guidelines for Intervention at Sea', *The International Journal of Marine and Coastal Law*, p. 621 ff.

Moreno-Lax, V. (2011) 'Seeking Asylum in the Mediterranean: Against a Fragmentary Reading of EU Member States' Obligations Accruing at Sea', *International Journal of Refugee Law*, p. 174 ff.

Moreno-Lax, V. (2012) '*Hirsi Jamaa and Others v Italy* or the Strasbourg Court versus Extraterritorial Migration Control?', *Human Rights Law Review*, p. 574 ff.

Moreno Quintana, L. M. (1952) *Derecho de asilo*, Buenos Aires.

Morgenstern, F. (1949) 'The Right of Asylum', *The British Year Book of International Law*, p. 327 ff.

Morgese, G. (2011a) 'La Corte si pronuncia sul rapporto tra terrorismo e rifugiati', *Sud in Europa*, maggio, p. 15 s.

Morgese, G. (2011b) 'Gli sviluppi della politica dell'Unione europea in materia di asilo in base al Programma di Stoccolma', *Gli Stranieri*, p. 155 ff.

Morgese, G. (2012a) 'La direttiva 2011/95/UE sull'attribuzione e il contenuto della protezione internazionale', *La Comunità Internazionale*, p. 255 ff.

Morgese, G. (2012b) 'Regolamento Dublino II e applicazione del principio di mutua fiducia tra Stati membri: la pronunzia della Corte di giustizia nel caso *N.S. e altri*', *Studi sull'integrazione europea*, p. 147 ff.

Morning, A. (2008) 'Reconstructing Race in Science and Society: Biology Textbooks, 1952–2002', *American Journal of Sociology*, p. S106 ff.

Morozzo della Rocca, P. (a cura di) (2008) *Immigrazione e cittadinanza. Profili normativi e orientamenti giurisprudenziali*, Torino.

Musalo, K. (2002) 'Claims for Protection Based on Religion or Belief: Analysis and Proposed Conclusions', *UNHCR Legal and Protection Policy Research Series*, PPLA/2002/01, December, available at www.unhcr.org

Musalo, K., J. Moore and R. A. Boswell (2011) *Refugee Law and Policy: A Comparative and International Approach*, Durham.

Nagy, B. (2011a) 'Article 29', in A. Zimmermann (ed.), *The 1951 Convention Relating to the Status of Refugees and its 1967 Protocol: A Commentary*, Oxford, p. 1215 ff.

Nagy, B. (2011b) 'Article 30', in A. Zimmermann (ed.), *The 1951 Convention Relating to the Status of Refugees and its 1967 Protocol: A Commentary*, Oxford, p. 1227 ff.

Napoletano, N. (2010) 'L'evoluzione della tutela dei diritti fondamentali nell'Unione europea', in A. Caligiuri, G. Cataldi, N. Napoletano (a cura di), *La tutela dei diritti umani in Europa*, Padova, p. 33 ff.

Napoletano, N. (2012) 'La condanna dei "respingimenti" operati dall'Italia verso la Libia da parte della Corte europea dei diritti umani: molte luci e qualche ombra', *Diritti umani e diritto internazionale*, p. 436 ff.

Nascimbene, B. (1995) 'Il diritto di asilo e lo *status* di rifugiato. Profili di diritto interno e comunitario', in *Studi in ricordo di Antonio Filippo Panzera*, vol. II, Bari, p. 519 ff.

Nascimbene, B. (1999a) 'L'incorporazione degli Accordi di Schengen nel quadro dell'Unione europea e il futuro ruolo del Comitato parlamentare di controllo', *Rivista italiana di diritto pubblico comunitario*, p. 731 ff.

Nascimbene, B. (1999b) 'L'Unione europea e i diritti dei cittadini dei Paesi terzi', in *Il trattato di Amsterdam*, Milano, p. 257 ff.

Nascimbene, B. (2011a) 'Il diritto d'asilo. Gli standard di tutela dell'Unione europea e il confronto con gli standard internazionali', in L. S. Rossi (a cura di), *La protezione dei diritti fondamentali. Carta dei diritti UE e standards internazionali*, Napoli, p. 25 ff.

Nascimbene, B. (2011b) 'Il diritto di asilo nel Trattato sul funzionamento dell'Unione Europea', in C. Favilli (a cura di), *Procedure e garanzie del diritto d'asilo*, Padova, p. 105 ff.

Neal, A. W. (2009) 'Securitization and Risk at the EU Border: The Origins of FRONTEX', *Journal of Common Market Studies*, p. 333 ff.

Nicholson, F. (2006) 'Challenges to Forging a Common European Asylum System in Line with International Obligations', in S. Peers, N. Rogers (eds), *EU Immigration and Asylum Law: Text and Commentary*, Leiden, Boston, p. 505 ff.

Niessen, J. (1996) 'The European Union's Migration and Asylum Policies', in E. Guild (Compilation and Commentary), *The Developing Immigration and Asylum Policies of the European Union*, The Hague, London, Boston, p. 3 ff.

Niessen, J. (2009) *Legal Framework for the Integration of Third Country Nationals*, Leiden.

Noll, G. (2001) 'Formalism v. Empiricism: Some Reflections on the Dublin Convention on the Occasion of Recent European Case Law', *Nordic Journal of International Law*, p. 161 ff.

Noll, G. (2004) 'International Protection Obligations and the Definition of Subsidiary Protection in the EU Qualification Directive', in C. Dias Urbano de Sousa (under the supervision of), *The Emergence of a European Asylum Policy*, Bruxelles, p. 183 ff.

Noll, G. (2005a) 'Evidentiary Assessment Under the Refugee Convention: Risk, Pain and the Intersubjectivity of Fear', in G. Noll (ed.), *Proof, Evidentiary Assessment and Credibility in Asylum Procedures*, Leiden, Boston, p. 141 ff.

Noll, G. (2005b) 'Introduction: Re-Mapping Evidentiary Assessment in Asylum Procedures', in G. Noll (ed.), *Proof, Evidentiary Assessment and Credibility in Asylum Procedures*, Leiden, Boston, p. 1 ff.

Noll, G. (2005c) 'Salvation by the Grace of State? Explaining Credibility Assessment in the Asylum Procedure', in G. Noll (ed.), *Proof, Evidentiary Assessment and Credibility in Asylum Procedures*, Leiden, Boston, p. 197 ff.

Noll, G. (2005d) 'Seeking Asylum at Embassies: A Right to Entry under International Law?', *International Journal of Refugee Law*, p. 542 ff.

Noll, G. (2011) 'Article 31', in A. Zimmermann (ed.), *The 1951 Convention Relating to the Status of Refugees and its 1967 Protocol: A Commentary*, Oxford, p. 1243 ff.

Nuvolone, P. (1970) 'Delitto politico e diritto d'asilo', *L'Indice Penale*, p. 169 ff.

O'Keeffe, D. (1991) 'The Schengen Convention: A Suitable Model for European Integration?', *Yearbook of European Law*, p. 185 ff.

O'Sullivan, M. (2008) 'Withdrawing Protection under Article 1C(5) of the 1951 Convention: Lessons from Australia', *International Journal of Refugee Law*, p. 586 ff.

Ocello, E. (2009) 'La detenzione dei richiedenti asilo nel diritto comunitario alla luce della giurisprudenza della Corte di Strasburgo: il caso *Saadi c. Regno Unito*', *Il diritto dell'Unione europea*, p. 87 ff.

Ocello, E. (2011) 'Il trattenimento dei richiedenti asilo secondo le norme dell'Unione Europea e la giurisprudenza della Corte europea dei diritti umani', in C. Favilli (a cura di), *Procedure e garanzie del diritto d'asilo*, Padova, p. 219 ff.

Onorato, P. (1988) 'Diritto d'asilo ed estradizione per reati politici nello Stato contemporaneo', *Questione giustizia*, p. 447 ff.

Opie, R. A. (2006) 'Human Rights Violations by Peacekeepers: Finding a Framework for Attribution of International Responsibility', *New Zealand Law Review*, p. 1 ff.

Palermo, P. (2009) 'Il diritto di asilo in equilibrio tra Convenzione di Ginevra, diritto comunitario e giurisprudenza delle Corti europee', *Famiglia e diritto*, p. 957 ff.

Panizzon, M. (2012) 'Readmission Agreements of EU Member States: A Case for EU Subsidiary or Dualism?', *Refugee Survey Quarterly*, p. 101 ff.

Panzera, A. F. (1978) *Attività terroristiche e diritto internazionale*, Napoli.

Paoletti, E. (2010) 'Relations among Unequals? Readmission between Italy and Libya', in J.-P. Cassarino (ed.), *Unbalanced Reciprocities: Cooperation on Readmission in the Euro-Mediterranean Area*, Washington, p. 54 ff.

Paoli, U. E. (1968) 'Asilo. Diritto greco e romano', in *Novissimo digesto italiano*, vol. I, parte 2, Torino, p. 1035 s.

Papadimitriou, P. N. and I. F. Papageorgiou (2005) 'The New "Dubliners": Implementation of European Council Regulation 343/2003 (Dublin-II) by the Greek Authorities', *Journal of Refugee Studies*, p. 299 ff.

Papagianni, G. (2001–2002) 'Free Movement of Persons in the Light of the New Title IV TEC: From Intergovernalism towards a Community Policy', *Yearbook of European Law*, p. 107 ff.

Papastavridis, E. (2010) '"Fortress Europe" and FRONTEX: Within or Without International Law?', *Nordic Journal of International Law*, p. 75 ff.

Parisi, N. (1996) 'Il "terzo pilastro" dell'Unione europea: il terzo pilastro del Trattato di Maastricht', in N. Parisi, D. Rinoldi (a cura di), *Giustizia e affari interni nell'Unione europea*, Torino, p. 33 ff.

Pedrazzi, M. (2006) 'Il diritto d'asilo nell'ordinamento internazionale agli albori del terzo millennio', in L. Zagato (a cura di), *Verso una disciplina comune europea del diritto d'asilo*, Padova, p. 13 ff.

Peek, M. (2010) 'Council Directive 2003/9/EC of 27 January 2003 laying down minimum standards for the reception of asylum seekers', in K. Hailbronner (ed.), *EU Immigration and Asylum Law. Commentary on EU Regulations and Directives*, München, p. 871 ff.

Peers, S. (1996) 'Towards equality: Actual and Potential Rights of Third Country Nationals in the European Union', *Common Market Law Review*, p. 9 ff.

Peers, S. (1998) 'Who's Judging the Watchmen? The Judicial System of the "Area of Freedom Security and Justice"', *Yearbook of European Law*, p. 337 ff.

Peers, S. (2005) 'EC Law on Family Members of Persons Seeking or Receiving International Protection', in P. Shah (ed.), *The Challenge of Asylum to Legal Systems*, London, Sydney, Portland, p. 83 ff.

Peers, S. (2006) 'Human Rights in the EU Legal Order: Practical Relevance for EC Immigration and Asylum Law', in S. Peers, N. Rogers (eds), *EU Immigration and Asylum Law: Text and Commentary*, Leiden, Boston, p. 115 ff.

Peers, S. (2011) *EU Justice and Home Affairs*, III ed., Oxford.

Peers, S. and N. Rogers (2006a) 'Asylum Procedures', in S. Peers, N. Rogers (eds), *EU Immigration and Asylum Law: Text and Commentary*, Leiden, p. 367 ff.

Peers, S. and N. Rogers (2006b) 'Eurodac', in S. Peers, N. Rogers (eds), *EU Immigration and Asylum Law: Text and Commentary*, Leiden, p. 259 ff.

Peers, S. and N. Rogers (2006c) 'Minimum Standards for Reception', in S. Peers, N. Rogers (eds), *EU Immigration and Asylum Law: Text and Commentary*, Leiden, p. 297 ff.

Peers, S. and N. Rogers (2006d) 'Refugee Definition and Subsidiary Protection', in S. Peers, N. Rogers (eds), *EU Immigration and Asylum Law: Text and Commentary*, Leiden, p. 323 ff.

Peers, S. and N. Rogers (2006e) 'Responsibility for Applications for Asylum', in S. Peers, N. Rogers (eds), *EU Immigration and Asylum Law: Text and Commentary*, Leiden, p. 221 ff.

Peers, S. and N. Rogers (2006f) 'Temporary Protection', in S. Peers, N. Rogers (eds), *EU Immigration and Asylum Law: Text and Commentary*, Leiden, p. 453 ff.

Peláez-Marón, J. M. (2005) 'The Refugees: From the International Humanitarian Law to the European Constitution. Good Intentions but Less than It Looks', in P. A.

Fernández-Sánchez (ed.), *The New Challenges of Humanitarian Law in Armed Conflicts: In Honour of Professor Juan Antonio Carrillo-Salcedo*, Leiden, Boston, p. 227 ff.

Pendo Berkowitz, N. (2006) 'Gender and EU Asylum Law', in S. Peers, N. Rogers (eds), *EU Immigration and Asylum Law: Text and Commentary*, Leiden, p. 539 ff.

Perassi, T. (1950) (présentés au nom de la cinquième Commission en 1950 par), 'L'asile en droit international public (à l'exclusion de l'asile neutre). 2. Rapport supplémentaire et projet définitif de Résolutions', *Annuaire de l'Institut de Droit International*, p. 162 ff.

Pérez Sola, N. (1997) 'La politica di asilo e di rifugio in Spagna', *Politica del diritto*, p. 333 ff.

Pérez Sola, N. (2009) 'La protección internacional en el nuevo proyecto de ley de asilo y refugio', in Á. G. Chueca Sancho, V. L. Gutiérrez Castillo, I. Blázquez Rodríguez (coordinadores), *Las migraciones internacionales en el Mediterráneo y Unión Europea*, Barcelona, p. 211 ff.

Perkowski, N. (2012) 'A Normative Assessment of the Aims and Practices of the European Border Management Agency Frontex', *Refugee Studies Centre Working Paper*, April, available online at www.rsc.ox.ac.uk

Perris, C. (1937) 'Asilo (Diritto di)', in *Nuovo digesto italiano*, vol. I, Torino, p. 767 s.

Phuong, C. (2005) 'Protecting Refugees in the Context of Immigration Controls', in P. Shah (ed.), *The Challenge of Asylum to Legal Systems*, London, Sydney, Portland, p. 33 ff.

Pirrone, P. (2008) 'Esternalizzazione della procedura di accertamento dello *status* di rifugiato e tutela dei diritti dell'uomo', in P. Benvenuti (a cura di), *Flussi migratori e fruizione dei diritti fondamentali*, Ripa di Fagnano Alto, p. 215 ff.

Pisani, M. (1970) 'Delitto politico, estradizione, diritto d'asilo', *Diritto internazionale*, p. 213 ff.

Plastina, N. (2009) 'Lotta al terrorismo: la Corte di Strasburgo conferma la natura assoluta dell'obbligo di "non refoulement" in relazione all'art. 3 CEDU', *Cassazione Penale*, p. 3205 ff.

Plender, R. and N. Mole (1999) 'Beyond the Geneva Convention: Constructing a *de facto* Right of Asylum from International Human Rights Instruments', in F. Nicholson, P. Twomey (eds), *Refugee Rights and Realities. Evolving International Concepts and Regimes*, Cambridge, New York, p. 81 ff.

Pollak, J. and P. Slominski (2009) 'Experimentalist but not Accountable Governance? The Role of Frontex in Managing the EU's External Borders', *West European Politics*, p. 904 ff.

Pollet, K. (2000) 'The Amsterdam Treaty and Immigration and Asylum Policies: A Legal Analysis', *Revue des Affaires Européennes*, p. 57 ff.

Popovic, A. (2005) 'Evidentiary Assessment and *Non-Refoulement*: Insights From Criminal Procedure', in G. Noll (ed.), *Proof, Evidentiary Assessment and Credibility in Asylum Procedures*, Leiden, Boston, p. 27 ff.

Pustorino, P. (2012) 'Art. 3: Proibizione della tortura', in S. Bartole, P. De Sena, G. Zagrebelsky (a cura di), *Commentario breve alla Convenzione europea dei diritti dell'uomo*, Padova, p. 63 ff.

Qafisheh, M. M. and V. Azarov (2011) 'Article 1 D', in A. Zimmermann (ed.), *The 1951 Convention Relating to the Status of Refugees and its 1967 Protocol: a Commentary*, Oxford, p. 537 ff.

Quintano Ripollés, A. (1951) 'Asilo', in *Nueva enciclopedia jurídica*, tomo 3, Barcelona, p. 49 ff.

Raestad, A. (1950) (présenté au nom de l'ancienne septième Commission en 1939 par), 'L'asile en droit international public (à l'exclusion de l'asile neutre). 1. Rapport', *Annuaire de l'Institut de Droit International*, p. 133 ff.

Rasiah, N. (2006) '*A v Secretary of State for the Home Department (No 2)*: Occupying the Moral High Ground?', *The Modern Law Review*, p. 995 ff.

Reale, E. (1938) 'Le droit d'asile', in *Recueil de Cours de l'Académie de Droit international*, p. 473 ff.

Ricci, M. (1982) 'Asilo, estradizione e terrorismo. Per una Convenzione europea sull'asilo territoriale', *Affari Sociali Internazionali*, p. 69 ff.

Riccio, L. (1991) 'Sulla provenienza da uno Stato contraente della Convenzione di Ginevra come motivo di denegato ingresso del richiedente asilo', *Rivista di diritto internazionale privato e processuale*, p. 397 ff.

Rijpma, J. J. and M. Cremona (2007) 'The Extra-Territorialisation of EU Migration Policies and the Rule of Law', *European University Institute Working Papers*, Law 01, available online at cadmus.eui.eu

Rikhof, J. (2009) 'War Criminals Not Welcome. How Common Law Countries Approach the Phenomenon of International Crimes in the Immigration and Refugee Context', *International Journal of Refugee Law*, p. 453 ff.

Roberts, A. (2004) 'Righting Wrongs or Wronging Rights? The United States and Human Rights Post-September 11', *European Journal of International Law*, p. 721 ff.

Robinson, N. (1953) *Convention Relating to the Status of Refugees. Its History, Contents and Interpretation*, New York.

Roig, A. (2007) 'EC Readmission Agreements: A Re-evaluation of the Political Impasse', *European Journal of Migration and Law*, p. 363 ff.

Ronzitti, N. (1987) 'L'Italia e il diritto d'asilo territoriale: aspetti giuridici e umanitari', *Politica internazionale*, n. 4, p. 11 ff.

Ronzitti, N. (2009a) 'Il Trattato Italia-Libia di amicizia, partenariato e cooperazione', *Dossier XVI legislatura, Contributi di Istituti di ricerca specializzati*, n. 108, gennaio, available at www.iai.it

Ronzitti, N. (2009b) 'The Treaty on Friendship, Partnership and Cooperation between Italy and Libya: New Prospects for Cooperation in the Mediterranean?', *Bulletin of Italian Politics*, p. 125 ff.

Rossano, R. (2004) 'Il regolamento comunitario sulla determinazione dello Stato membro competente ad esaminare la domanda di asilo', *Diritto comunitario e degli scambi internazionali*, p. 371 ff.

Ruotolo, G. M. (2008) 'Diritto d'asilo e *status* di rifugiato in Italia alla luce del diritto internazionale e della prassi interna recente', *Diritto pubblico comparato ed europeo*, p. 1818 ff.

Rycroft, R. (2005) 'Communicative Barriers in the Asylum Account', in P. Shah (ed.), *The Challenge of Asylum to Legal Systems*, London, Sydney, Portland, p. 223 ff.

Saccucci, A. (2011) 'Diritto di asilo e Convenzione europea dei diritti umani', in C. Favilli (a cura di), *Procedure e garanzie del diritto d'asilo*, Padova, p. 147 ff.

Sadat-Akhavi, S. A. (2003) *Methods of Resolving Conflicts Between Treaties*, Leiden, Boston.

Salerno, F. (2011) 'L'obbligo internazionale di *non-refoulement* dei richiedenti asilo', in C. Favilli (a cura di), *Procedure e garanzie del diritto d'asilo*, Padova, p. 3 ff.

Saulle, M. R. (2006) 'Migrazione e asilo nella Comunità e nell'Unione europea', in M. R. Saulle, L. Manca (a cura di), *L'integrazione dei cittadini di paesi terzi nell'Europa allargata*, Napoli, p. 9 ff.

Schieffer, M. (2010) 'Directive 2008/115/EC of the European Parliament and of the Council of 16 December 2008 on common standards and procedures in Member States for returning illegally staying third-country nationals', in K. Hailbronner (ed.), *EU Immigration and Asylum Law. Commentary on EU Regulations and Directives*, München, p. 1505 ff.

Schmahl, S. (2011a) 'Article 1 A, para. 1', in A. Zimmermann (ed.), *The 1951 Convention Relating to the Status of Refugees and its 1967 Protocol: A Commentary*, Oxford, 2011, p. 247 ff.

Schmahl, S. (2011b) 'Article 1 B', in A. Zimmermann (ed.), *The 1951 Convention Relating to the Status of Refugees and its 1967 Protocol: A Commentary*, Oxford, 2011, p. 467 ff.

Schmahl, S. (2011c) 'Article I Protocol Relating to the Status of Refugees', in A. Zimmermann (ed.), *The 1951 Convention Relating to the Status of Refugees and its 1967 Protocol: A Commentary*, Oxford, 2011, p. 611 ff.

Schokkenbroek, J. (2006) 'Prohibition of Collective Expulsion of Aliens (Article 4 of Protocol No. 4)', in P. van Dijk, F. van Hoof, A. van Rijn, L. Zwaak (eds), *Theory and Practice of the European Convention on Human Rights*, IV ed., Oxford, p. 953 ff.

Schuster, L. (2011) 'Dublin II and Eurodac: Examining the (Un)intended(?) Consequences', *Gender, Place and Culture*, p. 401 ff.

Schutte, J. J. E. (1991) 'Schengen: Its Meaning for the Free Movement of Persons in Europe', *Common Market Law Review*, p. 549 ff.

Sciso, E. (1986) *Gli accordi internazionali confliggenti*, Bari.

Seatzu, F. (2008) 'Il diritto al ricongiungimento familiare nel diritto dell'Unione europea', in P. De Cesari (a cura di), *Persona e famiglia*, Torino, p. 244 ff.

Sera, J. M. (1996) 'The Case for Accession by the European Union to the European Convention for the Protection of Human Rights', *Boston University International Law Journal*, p. 151 ff.

Shea, M. P. (1992) 'Expanding Judicial Scrutiny of Human Rights in Extradition Cases After *Soering*', *Yale Journal of International Law*, p. 85 ff.

Shraga, D. (1999) 'La qualité de membre non représenté: le cas du siège vacant', *Annuaire français de droit international*, p. 649 ff.

Simeon, J. C. (2009) 'Exclusion Under Article 1F (A) of the 1951 Convention in Canada', *International Journal of Refugee Law*, p. 193 ff.

Simeon, J. C. (ed.) (2010) *Critical Issues in International Refugee Law: Strategies Toward Interpretative Harmony*, Cambridge, New York.

Simmonds, K. R. (1988) 'The Concertation of Community Migration Policy', *Common Market Law Review*, p. 177 ff.

Skordas, A. (2010) 'Council Directive 2001/55/EC of 20 July 2001 on minimum standards for giving temporary protection in the event of a mass influx of displaced persons and on measures promoting a balance of efforts between Member States in receiving such persons and bearing the consequences thereof', in K. Hailbronner (ed.), *EU Immigration and Asylum Law. Commentary on EU Regulations and Directives*, München, p. 818 ff.

Smith, A. T. H. (2006) 'Disavowing Torture in the House of Lords', *The Cambridge Law Journal*, p. 251 ff.

Smrkolj, M. (2010) 'International Institutions and Individualized Decision-Making: An Example of UNHCR's Refugee Status Determination', in A. von Bogdandy (ed.), *The Exercise of Public Authority by International Institutions: Advancing International Institutional Law*, Heidelberg, p. 165 ff.

Spatti, M. (2007) 'La disciplina comunitaria relativa all'allontanamento dei richiedenti asilo verso "Paesi sicuri"', *Diritto pubblico comparato ed europeo*, p. 217 ff.

Spijkerboer, T. (2004) 'Full Circle? The Personal Scope of the International Protection in the Geneva Convention and the Draft Directive on Qualification', in C. Dias Urbano de Sousa (under the supervision of), *The Emergence of a European Asylum Policy*, Bruxelles, p. 167 ff.

Spijkerboer, T. (2009) 'Subsidiarity and "Arguability": the European Court of Human Rights' Case Law on Judicial Review in Asylum Cases', *International Journal of Refugee Law*, p. 48 ff.

Spijkerboer, T. (2010) 'Council Directive 2005/85/EC of 1 December 2005 on minimum standards on procedures in Member States for granting and withdrawing refugee status', in K. Hailbronner (ed.), *EU Immigration and Asylum Law. Commentary on EU Regulations and Directives*, München, p. 1257 ff.

Staffans, I. (2012) *Evidence in European Asylum Procedures*, Leiden, Boston.

Staples, H. (1999) *The Legal Status of Third Country Nationals Resident in the European Union*, The Hague, London, Boston.

Steenbergen, J. D. M. (1999) 'All the King's Horses . . . Probabilities and Possibilities for the Implementation of the New Title IV EC Treaty', *European Journal of Migration and Law*, p. 29 ff.

Stefanelli, J. N. (2011) 'Whose Rule of Law? An Analysis of the UK's Decision Not to Opt-in to the EU Asylum Procedures and Reception Conditions Directives', *International and Comparative Law Quarterly*, p. 1055 ff.

Stéfanini, P. and F. Doublet (1991) 'Le droit d'asile en Europe: la Convention relative à la détermination de l'État responsable de l'examen d'une demande d'asile présentée auprès d'un État membre des Communautés européennes', *Revue du Marché Commun*, p. 391 ff.

Steinbock, D. J. (1999) 'The Refugee Definition as Law: Issues of Interpretation', in F. Nicholson, P. Twomey (eds), *Refugee Rights and Realities: Evolving International Concepts and Regimes*, Cambridge, New York, p. 13 ff.

Steinorth, C. (2008) '*Üner v The Netherlands*: Expulsion of Long-term Immigrants and the Right to Respect for Private and Family Life', in *Human Rights Law Review*, p. 185 ff.

Stenberg, G. (1990) *Non-expulsion and Non-refoulement: the Prohibition against Removal of Refugees with Special Reference to Articles 32 and 33 of the 1951 Convention Relating to the Status of Refugees*, Uppsala.

Stevens, D. (2005) 'Asylum Seekers in the New Europe: Time For A Rethink', in P. Shah (ed.), *The Challenge of Asylum to Legal Systems*, London, Sydney, Portland, p. 13 ff.

Storey, H. (2008) 'EU Refugee Qualification Directive: A Brave New World?', *International Journal of Refugee Law*, p. 1 ff.

Strozzi, G. (1981) 'Rifugiati e asilo territoriale', in E. Vitta, V. Grementieri (a cura di), *Codice degli atti internazionali sui diritti dell'uomo*, Milano, p. 351 ff.

Strozzi, G. (1990) 'Rifugiati e asilo politico nella legge n. 39 del 1990', *Rivista di diritto internazionale*, p. 93 ff.

Strozzi, G. (1991) 'Profughi albanesi e diritto d'asilo', *Rivista di diritto internazionale*, p. 97 ff.

Strozzi, G. (2011) 'Il sistema integrato di tutela dei diritti fondamentali dopo Lisbona: attualità e prospettive', *Il diritto dell'Unione europea*, p. 837 ff.

Sweeney, J. A. (2009) 'Credibility, Proof and Refugee Law', *International Journal of Refugee Law*, p. 700 ff.

Sztucki, J. (1999) 'Who is a Refugee? The Convention Definition: Universal or Obsolete?', in F. Nicholson, P. Twomey (eds), *Refugee Rights and Realities: Evolving International Concepts and Regimes*, Cambridge, New York, p. 55 ff.

Tancredi, A. (2010) 'Assicurazioni diplomatiche e divieto "assoluto" di *refoulement* alla luce di alcune recenti pronunzie della Corte europea dei diritti umani', *Diritti umani e diritto internazionale*, p. 41 ff.

Taylor, S. (1996) 'Australia's "Safe Third Country" Provisions Their Impact on Australia's Fulfilment of Its Non-Refoulement Obligations', *University of Tasmania Law Review*, p. 198 ff.

Taylor, S. (2006) 'Protection Elsewhere/Nowhere', *International Journal of Refugee Law*, p. 283 ff.

Teichmann, M. (2011) 'Article 15', in A. Zimmermann (ed.), *The 1951 Convention Relating to the Status of Refugees and its 1967 Protocol: A Commentary*, Oxford, p. 909 ff.

Teitgen-Colly, C. (2006) 'The European Union and Asylum: An Illusion of Protection', *Common Market Law Review*, p. 1503 ff.

Tessenyi, G. (2006) 'Massive Refugee Flows and Europe's Temporary Protection', in S. Peers, N. Rogers (eds), *EU Immigration and Asylum Law: Text and Commentary*, Leiden, p. 487 ff.

Thym, D. (2008) 'Respect for Private and Family Life Under Article 8 ECHR in Immigration Cases: A Human Right to Regularize Illegal Stay?', *International and Comparative Law Quarterly*, p. 87 ff.

Tizzano, A. (1999) 'A proposito dell'inserzione dell'acquis di Schengen nei Trattati comunitari: l'accordo "del Consiglio" con Islanda e Norvegia', *Il diritto dell'Unione europea*, p. 521 ff.

Tizzano, A. (2011) 'Les Cours européennes et l'adhésion de l'Union à la CEDH', *Il diritto dell'Unione europea*, p. 29 ff.

Tomuschat, C. (1996) 'State Responsibility and the Country of Origin', in V. Gowlland-Debbas (ed.), *The Problem of Refugees in The Light of Contemporary International Law Issues*, The Hague, London, Boston, p. 59 ff.

Tondini, M. (2010) '*Fishers of Men?* The Interception of Migrants in the Mediterranean Sea and Their Forced Return to Libya', *INEX Paper*, October, available online at www.papers.ssrn.com

Toth, A. G. (1998) 'The Legal Effects of the Protocols Relating to the United Kingdom, Ireland and Denmark', in T. Heukels, N. Blokker, M. Brus (eds), *The European Union after Amsterdam*, The Hague, London, Boston, p. 227 ff.

Toy, C. H. (1902) 'Asylum – Biblical Data', in *The Jewish Encyclopedia*, vol. II, New York, p. 256 s.

Trahan, J. (2011) 'The Rome Statute's Amendment on the Crime of Aggression: Negotiations at the Kampala Review Conference', *International Criminal Law Review*, p. 49 ff.

Traversa, E. (1988) 'Il coordinamento delle politiche migratorie nazionali nei confronti degli stranieri extracomunitari', *Rivista di diritto europeo*, p. 5 ff.

Trevisanut, S. (2008a) 'L'Europa e l'immigrazione clandestina via mare: FRONTEX e diritto internazionale', *Il diritto dell'Unione europea*, p. 367 ff.

Trevisanut, S. (2008b) 'The Principle of *Non-Refoulement* At Sea and the Effectiveness of Asylum Protection', *Max Planck Yearbook of United Nations Law*, p. 205 ff.

Trevisanut, S. (2011) 'Diritto di asilo e contrasto all'immigrazione irregolare via mare', in C. Favilli (a cura di), *Procedure e garanzie del diritto d'asilo*, Padova, p. 241 ff.

Tryfon, K. (2012) 'The Contribution of EUROPOL and FRONTEX in Combating the Phenomenon of Illegal Immigration in Hellas', *Review of European Studies*, p. 188 ff.

Türk, V. (2003) 'UNHCR's Supervisory Responsibility', *New Issues in Refugee Research*, Working Paper No. 67, available at www.unhcr.org.

Udina, M. (1967) 'L'asilo politico territoriale nel diritto internazionale e secondo la Costituzione italiana', *Diritto internazionale*, p. 258 ff.

Udina, M. (1968) 'La Dichiarazione delle Nazioni Unite sull'asilo territoriale', *La Comunità Internazionale*, p. 293 ff.

Udina, M. (1972) 'Asilo politico territoriale e diritti dell'uomo', in *Studi in onore di Francesco Santoro-Passarelli*, vol. VI, *Diritto Pubblico, Storia, Teoria generale*, Napoli, p. 948 ff.

Udina, M. (1974) 'L'asilo territoriale nell'ambito delle Comunità europee', *Rivista di diritto europeo*, p. 5 ff.

UNHCR (1992a) *Handbook on Procedures and Criteria for Determining Refugee Status under the 1951 Convention and the 1967 Protocol relating to the Status of Refugees*, available at www.refworld.org.

UNHCR (1992b) *UNHCR Position Relating to the Resolution on Safe Countries of Origin*, London, 30 November – 1 December, available at www.refworld.org.

UNHCR (1993) *Note on International Protection*, A/AC.96/815, 31 August, available at www.refworld.org

UNHCR (1994) *Refugee Children: Guidelines on Protection and Care*, available at www.refworld.org

UNHCR (1996) *Considerations on the 'Safe Third Country' Concept*, July, available at www.refworld.org

UNHCR (1997a) *Guidelines on Policies and Procedures in Dealing with Unaccompanied Children Seeking Asylum*, February, available at www.refworld.org

UNHCR (1997b) *Note on Cessation Clauses*, 30 May, available at www.refworld.org

UNHCR (1997c) *UNHCR Note on the Principle of Non-Refoulement*, November, available at www.refworld.org

UNHCR (1998) *Implementation of the Dublin Convention: Some UNHCR Observations*, 1 May, available at www.refworld.org

UNHCR (1999) *UNHCR's Revised Guidelines on Applicable Criteria and Standards relating to the Detention of Asylum-Seekers*, 26 February, available at www.refworld.org

UNHCR (2001a) *Revisiting the Dublin Convention: Some Reflections by UNHCR in Response to the Commission Staff Working Paper*, 19 January, available at www.refworld.org

UNHCR (2001b) *Global Consultations on International Protection/Third Track: Asylum Processes (Fair and Efficient Asylum Procedures)*, 31 May, available at www.refworld.org

UNHCR (2001c) *UNHCR's Observations on the European Commission's Proposal for a Council Directive on Minimum Standards for the Qualification and Status of Third Country Nationals and Stateless Persons as Refugees or as Persons Who Otherwise Need International Protection*, 1 November, available at www.refworld.org

UNHCR (2001d) *Addressing Security Concerns Without Undermining Refugee Protection – UNHCR's Perspective*, 29 November, available at www.refworld.org

UNHCR (2002a) *Guidelines on International Protection No. 1: Gender-Related Persecution Within the Context of Article 1A(2) of the 1951 Convention and/or its 1967 Protocol Relating to the Status of Refugees*, 7 May, available at www.refworld.org

UNHCR (2002b) *Guidelines on International Protection No. 2: 'Membership of a Particular Social Group' Within the Context of Article 1A(2) of the 1951 Convention and/or its 1967 Protocol Relating to the Status of Refugees*, 7 May, available at www.refworld.org

UNHCR (2002c) *UNHCR Comments on the Draft Agreement between Canada and the United States of America for 'Cooperation in the Examination of Refugee Status Claims from Nationals of Third Countries'*, 26 July, available at www.refworld.org

UNHCR (2002d) *Declaration of Cessation – Timor Leste*, 22 December, available at www.refworld.org

UNHCR (2003a) *UNHCR Annotated Comments on Council Directive 2003/9/EC of 27 January 2003 Laying Down Minimum Standards for the Reception of Asylum Seekers*, July, available at www.refworld.org

UNHCR (2003b) *UNHCR's Concerns with the Designation of Bosnia and Herzegovina as a Safe Country of Origin*, July, available at www.refworld.org

UNHCR (2003c) *Guidelines on International Protection No. 4: 'Internal Flight or Relocation Alternative' Within the Context of Article 1A(2) of the 1951 Convention and/or 1967 Protocol Relating to the Status of Refugees*, 23 July, available at www.refworld.org

UNHCR (2003d) *Guidelines on International Protection No. 5: Application of the Exclusion Clauses: Article 1F of the 1951 Convention relating to the Status of Refugees*, 4 September, available at www.refworld.org

UNHCR (2003e) *Agenda for Protection*, October, Third edition, available at www.refworld.org

UNHCR (2004a) *Guidelines on International Protection No. 6: Religion-Based Refugee Claims under Article 1A(2) of the 1951 Convention and/or the 1967 Protocol relating to the Status of Refugees*, 28 April, available at www.refworld.org

UNHCR (2004b) *UNHCR Comments on the The Nationality, Immigration and Asylum Act 2002 (Specification of Particularly Serious Crimes) Order 2004*, November, available at www.refworld.org

UNHCR (2005) *UNHCR Annotated Comments on the EC Council Directive 2004/83/EC of 29 April 2004 on Minimum Standards for the Qualification and Status of Third Country Nationals or Stateless Persons as Refugees or as Persons Who Otherwise Need International Protection and the Content of the Protection Granted*, 28 January, available at www.refworld.org

UNHCR (2006) *Advisory Opinion on the Scope of the National Security Exception Under Article 33(2) of the 1951 Convention Relating to the Status of Refugees*, 6 January, available at www.refworld.org

UNHCR (2007a) *Advisory Opinion on the Extraterritorial Application of Non-Refoulement Obligations under the 1951 Convention relating to the Status of Refugees and its 1967 Protocol*, 26 January, available at www.refworld.org

UNHCR (2007b) *Asylum in the European Union. A Study of the Implementation of the Qualification Directive*, November, available at www.refworld.org

UNHCR (2008a) *UNHCR Position on the Return of Asylum-Seekers to Greece under the 'Dublin Regulation'*, 15 April, available at www.refworld.org

UNHCR (2008b) *Applicability of Ceased Circumstances Cessation Clauses to Refugees from Sierra Leone*, 2 June, available at www.refworld.org

UNHCR (2008c) *UNHCR Position on the Proposal for a Directive on Common Standards and Procedures in Member States for Returning Illegally Staying Third-Country Nationals*, 16 June, available at www.refworld.org

UNHCR (2008d) *Guidance Note on Refugee Claims Relating to Sexual Orientation and Gender Identity*, 21 November, available at www.refworld.org

UNHCR (2010) *UNHCR comments on the European Commission's proposal for a Directive of the European Parliament and of the Council on minimum standards for the qualification and status of third country nationals or stateless persons as beneficiaries of international protection and the content of the protection granted*, 29 July, available at www.refworld.org

UNHCR (2012) *Guidelines on International Protection No. 9: Claims to Refugee Status Based on Sexual Orientation and/or Gender Identity within the Context of Article 1A(2) of the 1951 Convention and/or its 1967 Protocol Relating to the Status of Refugees*, 23 October, available at www.refworld.org

UNHCR (2013) *International Protection Considerations with regard to people fleeing the Syrian Arab Republic, Update II*, 22 October, available at www.refworld.org

UNHCR (2014) *UNHCR Position on Returns to Mali – Update I*, January, available at www.refworld.org

van de Mark, G. (1995–1996) 'Administrative Law: One Strike and You're Out Al-Salehi v. Immigration & Naturalization Serv., 47 F.3d 390 (10th Cir. 1995)', *Washburn Law Journal*, p. 212 ff.

van der Klaauw, J. (2002) 'European Asylum Policy and the Global Protection Regime: Challenges for UNHCR', in S. Lavenex, M. Uçarer (eds), *Migration and the Externalities of European Integration*, Lanham, Boulder, New York, Oxford, p. 33 ff.

van Krieken, P. J. (ed.) (1999) *Refugee Law in Context: The Exclusion Clause*, The Hague.

van Selm-Thorburn, J. (1998) *Refugee Protection in Europe: Lessons of the Yugoslav Crisis*, The Hague.

Vedsted-Hansen, J. (2011a) 'Article 27', in A. Zimmermann (ed.), *The 1951 Convention Relating to the Status of Refugees and its 1967 Protocol: A Commentary*, Oxford, p. 1163 ff.

Vedsted-Hansen, J. (2011b) 'Article 28', in A. Zimmermann (ed.), *The 1951 Convention Relating to the Status of Refugees and its 1967 Protocol: A Commentary*, Oxford, p. 1177 ff.

Vermeulen, B., T. Spijkerboer, K. Zwaan and R. Fernhout (1998) *Persecution by Third Parties*, Nijmegen, May, available at cmr.jur.ru.nl

Vibeke Eggli, A. (2002) *Mass Refugee Influx and the Limits of Public International Law*, The Hague, London, New York.

Villani, U. (2004) 'I diritti fondamentali tra Carta di Nizza, Convenzione europea dei diritti dell'uomo e progetto di Costituzione europea', *Il diritto dell'Unione europea*, p. 73 ff., now in U. Villani, *Studi su La protezione internazionale dei diritti umani*, Roma, 2005, p. 129 ff.

Villani, U. (2011) 'L'intervento militare in Libia: *responsibility to protect* o . . . responsabilità per aggressione?', *I diritti dell'uomo. Cronache e battaglie*, n. 2, p. 109 ff.

Villani, U. (2012) 'Osservazioni sulla sentenza della Corte europea nell'affare *Hirsi Jamaa* e sui problemi relativi alla sua esecuzione', *I diritti dell'uomo. Cronache e battaglie*, n. 1, p. 9 ff.

Villani, U. (2013) *Istituzioni di diritto dell'Unione europea*, III ed., Bari.

Vismara, G. (1958) 'Asilo (diritto di). a) Premessa storica. 2) Diritto intermedio', in *Enciclopedia del diritto*, vol. II, Milano, p. 198 ff.

von Mises, L. (1949) *Human Action: A treatise on economics*, New Haven.

von Sternberg, M. R. (2002) *The Grounds of Refugee Protection in the Context of International Human Rights and Humanitarian Law: Canadian and United States Case Law Compared*, The Hague, London, New York.

Wagner, E. (1998) 'The Integration of Schengen into the Framework of the European Union', *Legal Issues of European Integration*, n. 2, p. 1 ff.

Wallace, R. (1996) *Refugees and Asylum: A Community Perspective*, London, Dublin, Edinburgh.

Walter, C. (2011) 'Article 5', in A. Zimmermann (ed.), *The 1951 Convention Relating to the Status of Refugees and its 1967 Protocol: A Commentary*, Oxford, p. 657 ff.

Warbrick, C. (1989–1990) 'Coherence and the European Court of Human Rights: The Adjudicative Background to the Soering Case', *Michigan Journal of International Law*, p. 1073 ff.

Weber, A. (1998) 'Possibilità e limiti dell'armonizzazione europea del diritto d'asilo prima e dopo Amsterdam', *Rivista italiana di diritto pubblico comunitario*, p. 1003 ff.

Weinzierl, R. and U. Lisson (2007) *Border Management and Human Rights. A Study of EU Law and the Law of the Sea*, Berlin.

Weis, P. (1960) 'The Concept of the Refugee in International Law', *Journal du droit international*, p. 928 ff.

Weis, P. (1966) 'Territorial Asylum', *Indian Journal of International Law*, p. 181 s.

Weis, P. (1979) 'The Draft United Nations Convention on Territorial Asylum', *The British Year Book of International Law*, p. 151 ff.

Weis, P. (1995) *The Refugee Convention, 1951. The Travaux Préparatoires Analysed*, Cambridge.

Weiss, T. G. and D. A. Korn (2006) *Internal Displacement: Conceptualization and Its Consequences*, London.

Wiebringhaus, H. (1967) 'Le droit d'asile en Europe', *Annuaire français de droit international*, p. 566 ff.

Willheim, E. (2003) 'MV *Tampa*: The Australian Response', *International Journal of Refugee Law*, p. 160 ff.

Wilsher, D. (2003) 'Non-State Actors and the Definition of a Refugee in the United Kingdom: Protection, Accountability or Culpability?', *International Journal of Refugee Law*, p. 68 ff.

Wilsher, D. (2005) 'Detention of Asylum Seekers and Refugees and International Human Rights Law', in P. Shah (ed.), *The Challenge of Asylum to Legal Systems*, London, Sydney, Portland, p. 145 ff.

Wouters, C. W. (2009) *International legal standards for the protection from refoulement: a legal analysis of the prohibitions on refoulement contained in the refugee convention, the European convention on human rights, the international covenant on civil and political rights and the convention against torture*, Antwerp, Oxford, Portland.

Xenos, D. (2011) *The Positive Obligations of the State Under the European Convention of Human Rights*, London.

Yamagami, S. (1995) 'Determination of Refugee Status in Japan', *International Journal of Refugee Law*, p. 60 ff.

Zábalo Escudero, M. E. (2009) 'La familia como medio de integración del extranjero en la sociedad receptora', in Á. G. Chueca Sancho, V. L. Gutiérrez Castillo, I. Blázquez Rodríguez (coordinadores), *Las migraciones internacionales en el Mediterráneo y Unión Europea*, Barcelona, p. 265 ff.

Zaniboni, E. (2005) 'Verso l'erosione dell'elemento territoriale dell'istituto dell'asilo nel diritto internazionale?', in U. Leanza (a cura di), *Le migrazioni. Una sfida per il diritto internazionale, comunitario e interno*, Napoli, p. 291 ff.

Zard, M. (2002) 'Exclusion, terrorism and the Refugee Convention', *Forced Migration Review*, n. 13, p. 32 ff.

Zimmermann, A. and J. Dörschner (2011) 'Article 22', in A. Zimmermann (ed.), *The 1951 Convention Relating to the Status of Refugees and its 1967 Protocol: a Commentary*, Oxford, p. 1019 ff.

Zimmermann, A. and C. Mahler (2011) 'Article 1 A, para. 2', in A. Zimmermann (ed.), *The 1951 Convention Relating to the Status of Refugees and its 1967 Protocol: A Commentary*, Oxford, p. 281 ff.

Zimmermann, A. and P. Wennholz (2011a) 'Article 1 F', in A. Zimmermann (ed.), *The 1951 Convention Relating to the Status of Refugees and its 1967 Protocol: A Commentary*, Oxford, p. 579 ff.

Zimmermann, A. and P. Wennholz (2011b) 'Article 33, para. 2', in A. Zimmermann (ed.), *The 1951 Convention Relating to the Status of Refugees and its 1967 Protocol: A Commentary*, Oxford, p. 1397 ff.

Zink, K. F. (1962) *Das Asylrecht in der Bundesrepublik Deutschland nach dem Abkommen vom 28. Juli 1951 über die Rechtsstellung der Flüchtlinge, unter besonderer Berücksichtigung der Rechtsprechung der Verwaltungsgerichte*, Nürnberg.

Ziotti, P. (1988a) 'La difficile tutela del diritto d'asilo', in L. Carlassare (a cura di), *Le garanzie giurisdizionali dei diritti fondamentali*, Padova, p. 99 ff.

Ziotti, P. (1988b) *Il diritto d'asilo nell'ordinamento italiano*, Padova.

Zorzi Giustiniani, F. (2008) 'La tutela internazionale degli sfollati: protezione e assistenza', in P. Benvenuti (a cura di), *Flussi migratori e fruizione dei diritti fondamentali*, Ripa di Fagnano Alto, p. 387 ff.

Index

Lightning Source UK Ltd.
Milton Keynes UK
UKOW06n1019130315

247784UK00001B/46/P